ZECHARIAH

WISDOM COMMENTARY

Volume 40

Zechariah

Leslie J. Hoppe, OFM

Lauress Wilkins Lawrence
Volume Editor

Barbara E. Reid, OP
General Editor

A Michael Glazier Book

LITURGICAL PRESS

Collegeville, Minnesota

litpress.org

1   2   3   4   5   6   7   8   9

Library of Congress Cataloging-in-Publication Data

Names: Hoppe, Leslie J., author. | Lawrence, Lauress Wilkins, editor. | Reid, Barbara E., editor.

Title: Zechariah / Leslie J. Hoppe, OFM.

Description: Collegeville, Minnesota : Liturgical Press, [2024] | Series: Wisdom commentary ; volume 40 | "Lauress Wilkins Lawrence, Volume Editor, Barbara E. Reid, OP, General Editor". | Includes bibliographical references and index. | Summary: "This commentary on Zechariah provides a feminist interpretation of Scripture in serious, scholarly engagement with the whole text, not only those texts that explicitly mention women. It addresses not only issues of gender but also those of power, authority, ethnicity, racism, and classism"— Provided by publisher.

Identifiers: LCCN 2023048838 (print) | LCCN 2023048839 (ebook) | ISBN 9780814681640 (hardcover) | ISBN 9780814681893 (epub) | ISBN 9780814669808 (pdf)

Subjects: LCSH: Bible. Zechariah—Commentaries. | Bible. Zechariah—Feminist criticism. | BISAC: RELIGION / Biblical Commentary / Old Testament / Prophets | RELIGION / Biblical Studies / Exegesis & Hermeneutics

Classification: LCC BS1665.53 .H67 2024 (print) | LCC BS1665.53 (ebook) | DDC 224/.9807—dc23/eng/20231222

LC record available at https://lccn.loc.gov/2023048838

LC ebook record available at https://lccn.loc.gov/2023048839

Contents

Abbreviations

BibInt	Biblical Interpretation Series
BJS	Brown Judaic Studies
BK	*Bibel und Kirche*
BLS	Bible and Literature Series
BRLA	Brill Reference Library of Judaism
BW	Bible and Women
BZ	*Biblische Zeitschrift*
BZABR	Beihefte zur Zeitschrift für altorientalische und biblische Rechtsgeschichte
BZAW	Beihefte zur Zeitschrift für die alttestamentliche Wissenschaft
CBA	Catholic Biblical Association
CBQ	*Catholic Biblical Quarterly*
CBQMS	*Catholic Biblical Quarterly* Monograph Series
FCB	Feminist Companion to the Bible
FRLANT	Forschungen zur Religion und Literatur des Alten und Neuen Testaments
GBS	Guides to Biblical Scholarship
HAR	*Hebrew Annual Review*
HCOT	Historical Commentary on the Old Testament
HeyJ	*Heythrop Journal*
HSM	Harvard Semitic Monographs
HTR	*Harvard Theological Review*
ICC	International Critical Commentary
IFT	Introductions in Feminist Theology
ISBL	Indiana Studies in Biblical Literature
ITC	International Theological Commentary
JAAR	*Journal of the American Academy of Religion*
JANER	*Journal of Ancient Near Eastern Religions*
JBL	*Journal of Biblical Literature*
JFA	*Journal of Field Archaeology*
JFSR	*Journal of Feminist Studies in Religion*
JHebS	*Journal of Hebrew Scriptures*

JNSL	*Journal of Northwest Semitic Languages*
JPS	Jewish Publication Society
JSNT	*Journal for the Study of the New Testament*
JSNTSup	Journal for the Study of the New Testament Supplement series
JSOT	*Journal for the Study of the Old Testament*
JSOTSup	Journal for the Study of the Old Testament Supplement series
JSP	*Journal for the Study of the Pseudepigrapha*
KAT	Kommentar zum Alten Testament
LHBOTS	Library of the Hebrew Bible/Old Testament Studies
LXX	The Septuagint
MT	Masoretic Text
NABRE	New American Bible Revised Edition
NCBC	New Century Bible Commentary
NIB	*New Interpreters Bible*
NICOT	New International Commentary on the Old Testament
NJPS	New Jewish Publication Society of America Tanakh
NRSVue	New Revised Standard Version Updated Edition
OBT	Overtures to Biblical Theology
OTE	*Old Testament Essays*
OTL	Old Testament Library
OTM	Old Testament Message
OtSt	Oudtestamentische Studiën
PL	Patrologia Latina
RelS	*Religious Studies*
RHR	*Revue de l'histoire des religions*
SAT	Schriften des Alten Testaments
SBL	Society of Biblical Literature
SBLSS	Society of Biblical Literature Symposium Series
SBS	Stuttgarter Bibelstudien
SemeiaSt	Semeia Studies

SJOT	*Scandinavian Journal of the Old Testament*
STDJ	Studies on the Texts of the Desert of Judah
SymS	Symposium Series
TDOT	*Theological Dictionary of the Old Testament*. Edited by G. Johannes Botterweck and Helmer Ringgren. Translated by John T. Willis et al. 17 vols. Grand Rapids: Eerdmans, 1974–2021.
TOTC	Tyndale Old Testament Commentaries
TS	*Theological Studies*
VT	*Vetus Testamentum*
VTSup	Supplements to Vetus Testamentum
WCS	Wisdom Commentary Series
WMANT	Wissenschaftliche Monographien zum Alten und Neuen Testament
ZAW	*Zeitschrift für die Alttestamentliche Wissenschaft*
ZThK	*Zeitschrift für Theologie und Kirche*

Contributors

Dr. Ulrike Sals, born in 1971, worked at several universities in Germany (Würzburg, Greifswald, Hamburg, Rostock) and in Bern, Switzerland. She published a monograph about Babylon texts in the Bible (*Die Biographie der "Hure Babylon,"* 2004) as well as several papers. Her second book (forthcoming) treats the Book of Numbers.

Rabbi David Fox Sandmel, PhD, is a consultant and educator specializing in interreligious/interfaith relations. He is a consultant to the Executive Board of the International Council of Christians and Jews (iccj.org) and Scholar in Residence at the Maine Jewish Museum. He is a past chair of the International Jewish Committee for Interreligious Consultations (ijcic.net). From 2014 to 2022 he was director of Interreligious Engagement at ADL (Anti-Defamation League). He held the Crown-Ryan Chair of Jewish Studies at the Catholic Theological Union in Chicago (2002–2014) and was Jewish Scholar at the Institute for Christian & Jewish Studies in Baltimore (1998–2001) where he directed the publication of *"Dabru Emet: A Jewish Statement on Christians and Christianity."* He was a visiting professor at the Pontifical Gregorian University in Rome in spring 2024.

Lena-Sofia Tiemeyer is professor in Old Testament exegesis, ALT School of Theology, Sweden, and research associate at the Department of Old Testament and Hebrew Scripture, University of Pretoria, South Africa. She has published several monographs and edited volumes on Isaiah and Zechariah. More recently, she has written a reception-historical commentary on Jonah, *Jonah through the Centuries* (2022), as well as a monograph devoted to Jonathan, *In Search of Jonathan* (2023).

Maxbetter Vizelberg, a native of New Orleans, Louisiana, has been cultivating his interest in veterinary medicine since a young age. From being read Russian children's stories about "Doctor Aybolit" by his grandmother to interning at the Israeli Wildlife Hospital to working at numerous small animal hospitals, he has thoroughly enjoyed learning about and sharing his joy of animals with others over the years. He studied biology at Harvard before pursuing veterinary studies at Tufts. He prides himself on educating others to help give their animals the best possible lives and strives to provide the best medical care to his patients. Outside the clinic, he can be found rapping at open mics, playing soccer and basketball, biking around New York City, and going on hikes with family and friends.

Foreword

"Tell It on the Mountain"— or, "And You Shall Tell Your Daughter [as Well]"

Athalya Brenner-Idan

Universiteit van Amsterdam/Tel Aviv University

What can Wisdom Commentary do to help, and for whom?
The commentary genre has always been privileged in biblical studies. Traditionally acclaimed commentary series, such as the International Critical Commentary, Old Testament and New Testament Library, Hermeneia, Anchor Bible, Eerdmans, and Word—to name but several— enjoy nearly automatic prestige, and the number of women authors who participate in those is relatively small by comparison to their growing number in the scholarly guild. There certainly are some volumes written by women in them, especially in recent decades. At this time, however, this does not reflect the situation on the ground. Further, size matters. In that sense, the sheer size of the Wisdom Commentary is essential. This also represents a considerable investment and the possibility of reaching a wider audience than those already "converted."

Expecting women scholars to deal especially or only with what are considered strictly "female" matters seems unwarranted. According to Audre Lorde, "The master's tools will never dismantle the master's house."[1] But this maxim is not relevant to our case. The point of this commentary is not to destroy but to attain greater participation in the interpretive dialogue about biblical texts. Women scholars may bring additional questions to the readerly agenda as well as fresh angles to existing issues. To assume that their questions are designed only to topple a certain male hegemony is not convincing.

At first I did ask myself: is this commentary series an addition to calm raw nerves, an embellishment to make upholding the old hierarchy palatable? Or is it indeed about becoming the Master? On second and third thoughts, however, I understood that becoming the Master is not what this is about. Knowledge is power. Since Foucault at the very least, this cannot be in dispute. Writing commentaries for biblical texts by feminist women and men for women and for men, of confessional as well as non-confessional convictions, will sabotage (hopefully) the established hierarchy but will not topple it. This is about an attempt to integrate more fully, to introduce another viewpoint, to become. What excites me about the Wisdom Commentary is that it is not offered as just an alternative supplanting or substituting for the dominant discourse.

These commentaries on biblical books will retain nonauthoritative, pluralistic viewpoints. And yes, once again, the weight of a dedicated series, to distinguish from collections of stand-alone volumes, will prove weightier.

That such an approach is especially important in the case of the Hebrew Bible/Old Testament is beyond doubt. Women of Judaism, Christianity, and also Islam have struggled to make it their own for centuries, even more than they have fought for the New Testament and the Qur'an. Every Hebrew Bible/Old Testament volume in this project is evidence that the day has arrived: it is now possible to read *all* the Jewish canonical books as a collection, for a collection they are, with guidance conceived of with the needs of women readers (not only men) as an integral inspiration and part thereof.

In my Jewish tradition, the main motivation for reciting the Haggadah, the ritual text recited yearly on Passover, the festival of liberation from

---

1. Audre Lorde, "The Master's Tools Will Never Dismantle the Master's House," in *Sister Outsider: Essays and Speeches* (Berkeley, CA: Crossing Press, 1984, 2007), 110–14. First delivered in the Second Sex Conference in New York, 1979.

bondage, is given as "And you shall tell your son" (from Exod 13:8). The knowledge and experience of past generations is thus transferred to the next, for constructing the present and the future. The ancient maxim is, literally, limited to a male audience. This series remolds the maxim into a new inclusive shape, which is of the utmost consequence: "And you shall tell your son" is extended to "And you shall tell your daughter [as well as your son]." Or, if you want, "Tell it on the mountain," for all to hear.

This is what it's all about.

Editor's Introduction to Wisdom Commentary

"She Is a Breath of the Power of God" (Wis 7:25)

Barbara E. Reid, OP
General Editor

Wisdom Commentary is the first series to offer detailed feminist interpretation of every book of the Bible. The fruit of collaborative work by an ecumenical and interreligious team of scholars, the volumes provide serious, scholarly engagement with the whole biblical text, not only those texts that explicitly mention women. The series is intended for clergy, teachers, ministers, and all serious students of the Bible. Designed to be both accessible and informed by the various approaches of biblical scholarship, it pays particular attention to the world in front of the text, that is, how the text is heard and appropriated. At the same time, this series aims to be faithful to the ancient text and its earliest audiences; thus the volumes also explicate the worlds behind the text and within it. While issues of gender are primary in this project, the volumes also address the intersecting issues of power, authority, ethnicity, race, class, and religious belief and practice. The fifty-eight volumes include the books regarded as canonical by Jews (i.e., the Tanakh); Protestants (the "Hebrew Bible" and the New Testament); and Roman Catholic, Anglican, and Eastern

Orthodox Communions (i.e., Tobit, Judith, 1 and 2 Maccabees, Wisdom of Solomon, Sirach/Ecclesiasticus, Baruch, including the Letter of Jeremiah, the additions to Esther, and Susanna and Bel and the Dragon in Daniel).

A Symphony of Diverse Voices

Included in the Wisdom Commentary series are voices from scholars of many different religious traditions, of diverse ages, differing sexual identities, and varying cultural, racial, ethnic, and social contexts. Some have been pioneers in feminist biblical interpretation; others are newer contributors from a younger generation. A further distinctive feature of this series is that each volume incorporates voices other than that of the lead author(s). These voices appear alongside the commentary of the lead author(s), in the grayscale inserts. At times, a contributor may offer an alternative interpretation or a critique of the position taken by the lead author(s). At other times, they may offer a complementary interpretation from a different cultural context or subject position. Occasionally, portions of previously published material bring in other views. The diverse voices are not intended to be contestants in a debate or a cacophony of discordant notes. The multiple voices reflect that there is no single definitive feminist interpretation of a text. In addition, they show the importance of subject position in the process of interpretation. In this regard, the Wisdom Commentary series takes inspiration from the Talmud and from *The Torah: A Women's Commentary* (ed. Tamara Cohn Eskenazi and Andrea L. Weiss; New York: URJ Press and Women of Reform Judaism, The Federation of Temple Sisterhoods, 2008), in which many voices, even conflicting ones, are included and not harmonized.

Contributors include biblical scholars, theologians, and readers of Scripture from outside the scholarly and religious guilds. At times, their comments pertain to a particular text. In some instances they address a theme or topic that arises from the text.

Another feature that highlights the collaborative nature of feminist biblical interpretation is that a number of the volumes have two lead authors who have worked in tandem from the inception of the project and whose voices interweave throughout the commentary.

Woman Wisdom

The title, Wisdom Commentary, reflects both the importance to feminists of the figure of Woman Wisdom in the Scriptures and the distinct wisdom that feminist women and men bring to the interpretive process. In the Scriptures, Woman Wisdom appears as "a breath of the power of God, and a pure emanation of the glory of the Almighty" (Wis 7:25), who was present and active in fashioning all that exists (Prov 8:22-31; Wis 8:6). She is a spirit who pervades and penetrates all things (Wis 7:22-23), and she provides guidance and nourishment at her all-inclusive table (Prov 9:1-5). In both postexilic biblical and nonbiblical Jewish sources, Woman Wisdom is often equated with Torah, e.g., Sirach 24:23-34; Baruch 3:9–4:4; 2 Baruch 38:2; 46:4-5; 48:33, 36; 4 Ezra 5:9-10; 13:55; 14:40; 1 Enoch 42.

The New Testament frequently portrays Jesus as Wisdom incarnate. He invites his followers, "take my yoke upon you, and learn from me" (Matt 11:29), just as Ben Sira advises, "put your neck under her [Wisdom's] yoke, and let your souls receive instruction" (Sir 51:26). Just as Wisdom experiences rejection (Prov 1:23-25; Sir 15:7-8; Wis 10:3; Bar 3:12), so too does Jesus (Mark 8:31; John 1:10-11). Only some accept his invitation to his all-inclusive banquet (Matt 22:1-14; Luke 14:15-24; compare Prov 1:20-21; 9:3-5). Yet, "wisdom is vindicated by her deeds" (Matt 11:19, speaking of Jesus and John the Baptist; in the Lukan parallel at 7:35 they are called "her [wisdom's] children"). There are numerous parallels between what is said of Wisdom and of the *Logos* in the Prologue of the Fourth Gospel (John 1:1-18). These are only a few of many examples. This female embodiment of divine presence and power is an apt image to guide the work of this series.

Feminism

There are many different understandings of the term "feminism." The various meanings, aims, and methods have developed exponentially in recent decades. Feminism is a perspective and a movement that springs from a recognition of inequities toward women, and it advocates for changes in whatever structures prevent full flourishing of human beings and all creation. Three waves of feminism in the United States are commonly recognized. The first, arising in the mid-nineteenth century and lasting into the early twentieth, was sparked by women's efforts to be involved in the public sphere and to win the right to vote. In the 1960s and 1970s, the second wave focused on civil rights and equality for women. With the third wave, from the 1980s forward, came global feminism and the emphasis on the contextual nature of interpretation. Now a fourth wave is emerging, with a stronger emphasis on the intersectionality of women's concerns with those of other marginalized groups and the increased use of the internet as a platform for discussion and activism.[1] As feminism has matured, it has recognized that inequities based on gender are interwoven with power imbalances based on race, class, ethnicity, religion, sexual identity, physical ability, and a host of other social markers.

Feminist Women and Men

Men as well as nonbinary people who choose to identify with and partner with feminist women in the work of deconstructing systems of domination and building structures of equality are rightly regarded as feminists. Some men readily identify with experiences of women who are discriminated against on the basis of sex/gender, having themselves had comparable experiences; others who may not have faced direct discrimination or stereotyping recognize that inequity and problematic characterization still occur, and they seek correction. This series is pleased to include feminist men and nonbinary persons both as lead authors and as contributing voices.

Feminist Biblical Interpretation

Women interpreting the Bible from the lenses of their own experience is nothing new. Throughout the ages women have recounted the biblical stories, teaching them to their children and others, all the while interpreting them afresh for their time and circumstances.[2] Following is a very brief sketch of select foremothers who laid the groundwork for contemporary feminist biblical interpretation.

One of the earliest known Christian women who challenged patriarchal interpretations of Scripture was a consecrated virgin named Helie, who lived in the second century CE. When she refused to marry, her

---

1. See Martha Rampton, "Four Waves of Feminism" (October 25, 2015), at https://www.pacificu.edu/magazine/four-waves-feminism; and Ealasaid Munro, "Feminism: A Fourth Wave?," *Political Insight* (September 2013), https://journals.sagepub.com/doi/pdf/10.1111/2041-9066.12021.

2. For fuller treatments of this history, see chap. 7, "One Thousand Years of Feminist Bible Criticism," in Gerda Lerner, *Creation of Feminist Consciousness: From the Middle Ages to Eighteen-Seventy* (New York: Oxford University Press, 1993), 138–66; Susanne Scholz, "From the 'Woman's Bible' to the 'Women's Bible,' The History of Feminist Approaches to the Hebrew Bible," in *Introducing the Women's Hebrew Bible*, IFT 13 (New York: T&T Clark, 2007), 12–32; Marion Ann Taylor and Agnes Choi, eds., *Handbook of Women Biblical Interpreters: A Historical and Biographical Guide* (Grand Rapids: Baker Academic, 2012).

parents brought her before a judge, who quoted to her Paul's admonition, "It is better to marry than to be aflame with passion" (1 Cor 7:9). In response, Helie first acknowledges that this is what Scripture says, but then she retorts, "but not for everyone, that is, not for holy virgins."[3] She is one of the first to question the notion that a text has one meaning that is applicable in all situations.

A Jewish woman who also lived in the second century CE, Beruriah, is said to have had "profound knowledge of biblical exegesis and outstanding intelligence."[4] One story preserved in the Talmud (b. Ber. 10a) tells of how she challenged her husband, Rabbi Meir, when he prayed for the destruction of a sinner. Proffering an alternate interpretation, she argued that Psalm 104:35 advocated praying for the destruction of sin, not the sinner.

In medieval times the first written commentaries on Scripture from a critical feminist point of view emerge. While others may have been produced and passed on orally, they are for the most part lost to us now. Among the earliest preserved feminist writings are those of Hildegard of Bingen (1098–1179), German writer, mystic, and abbess of a Benedictine monastery. She reinterpreted the Genesis narratives in a way that presented women and men as complementary and interdependent. She frequently wrote about the Divine as feminine.[5] Along with other women mystics of the time, such as Julian of Norwich (1342–ca. 1416), she spoke authoritatively from her personal experiences of God's revelation in prayer.

In this era, women were also among the scribes who copied biblical manuscripts. Notable among them is Paula Dei Mansi of Verona, from a distinguished family of Jewish scribes. In 1288, she translated from Hebrew into Italian a collection of Bible commentaries written by her father and added her own explanations.[6]

Another pioneer, Christine de Pizan (1365–ca. 1430), was a French court writer and prolific poet. She used allegory and common sense

---

3. Madrid, Escorial MS, a II 9, f. 90 v., as cited in Lerner, *Feminist Consciousness*, 140.

4. See Judith R. Baskin, "Women and Post-Biblical Commentary," in *The Torah: A Women's Commentary*, ed. Tamara Cohn Eskenazi and Andrea L. Weiss (New York: URJ Press and Women of Reform Judaism, The Federation of Temple Sisterhoods, 2008), xlix–lv, at lii.

5. Hildegard of Bingen, *De Operatione Dei*, 1.4.100; PL 197:885bc, as cited in Lerner, *Feminist Consciousness*, 142–43. See also Barbara Newman, *Sister of Wisdom: St. Hildegard's Theology of the Feminine* (Berkeley: University of California Press, 1987).

6. Emily Taitz, Sondra Henry, and Cheryl Tallan, *The JPS Guide to Jewish Women 600 B.C.E.–1900 C.E.* (Philadelphia: JPS, 2003), 110–11.

to subvert misogynist readings of Scripture and celebrated the accomplishments of female biblical figures to argue for women's active roles in building society.[7]

By the seventeenth century, there were women who asserted that the biblical text needs to be understood and interpreted in its historical context. For example, Rachel Speght (1597–ca. 1630), a Calvinist English poet, elaborates on the historical situation in first-century Corinth that prompted Paul to say, "It is good for a man not to touch a woman" (1 Cor 7:1). Her aim was to show that the biblical texts should not be applied in a literal fashion to all times and circumstances. Similarly, Margaret Fell (1614–1702), one of the founders of the Religious Society of Friends (Quakers) in Britain, addressed the Pauline prohibitions against women speaking in church by insisting that they do not have universal validity. Rather, they need to be understood in their historical context, as addressed to a local church in particular time-bound circumstances.[8]

Along with analyzing the historical context of the biblical writings, women in the eighteenth and nineteenth centuries began to attend to misogynistic interpretations based on faulty translations. One of the first to do so was British feminist Mary Astell (1666–1731).[9] In the United States, the Grimké sisters, Sarah (1792–1873) and Angelina (1805–1879), Quaker women from a slaveholding family in South Carolina, learned biblical Greek and Hebrew so that they could interpret the Bible for themselves. They were prompted to do so after men sought to silence them from speaking out against slavery and for women's rights by claiming that the Bible (e.g., 1 Cor 14:34) prevented women from speaking in public.[10] Another prominent abolitionist, Isabella Baumfree, was a former slave who adopted the name Sojourner Truth (ca. 1797–1883); she quoted the Bible liberally in her speeches[11] and in so doing challenged cultural assumptions and biblical interpretations that undergird gender inequities.

---

7. See further Taylor and Choi, *Handbook of Women Biblical Interpreters*, 127–32.

8. Her major work, *Women's Speaking Justified, Proved and Allowed by the Scriptures*, published in London in 1666, gave a systematic feminist reading of all biblical texts pertaining to women.

9. Mary Astell, *Some Reflections upon Marriage* (New York: Source Book Press, 1970, reprint of the 1730 edition; earliest edition of this work is 1700), 103–4.

10. See further Sarah Grimké, *Letters on the Equality of the Sexes and the Condition of Woman* (Boston: Isaac Knapp, 1838).

11. See, for example, her most famous speech, "Ain't I a Woman?," delivered in 1851 at the Ohio Women's Rights Convention in Akron; Modern History Sourcebook, https://sourcebooks.fordham.edu/mod/sojtruth-woman.asp.

Another monumental work that emerged in nineteenth-century England was that of Jewish theologian Grace Aguilar (1816–1847), *The Women of Israel*,[12] published in 1845. Aguilar's approach was to make connections between the biblical women and contemporary Jewish women's concerns. She aimed to counter the widespread antisemitic notion that women were degraded in Jewish law and that only in Christianity were women's dignity and value upheld. Her intent was to help Jewish women find strength and encouragement by seeing the evidence of God's compassionate love in the history of every woman in the Bible. While not a full commentary on the Bible, Aguilar's work stands out for its comprehensive treatment of every female biblical character, including even the most obscure references.[13]

The first person to produce a full-blown feminist commentary on the Bible was Elizabeth Cady Stanton (1815–1902). A leading proponent in the United States for women's right to vote, she found that whenever women tried to make inroads into politics, education, or the work world, the Bible was quoted against them. Along with a team of like-minded women, she produced her own commentary on every text of the Bible that concerned women. Her pioneering two-volume project, *The Woman's Bible*, published in 1895 and 1898, urges women to recognize that texts that degrade women come from the men who wrote the texts, not from God, and to use their common sense to rethink what has been presented to them as sacred.[14]

Nearly a century later, *The Women's Bible Commentary*, edited by Carol A. Newsom and Sharon H. Ringe (Louisville: Westminster John Knox, 1992), appeared. This one-volume commentary features North American feminist scholarship on each book of the Protestant canon. Like Cady Stanton's commentary, it does not contain comments on every section of the biblical text but only on those passages deemed relevant to women. It was revised and expanded in 1998 to include the Apocrypha/ Deuterocanonical books, and the contributors to this new volume reflect the global face of contemporary feminist scholarship. The revisions made in the third edition, which appeared in 2012, represent the profound

---

12. The full title is *The Women of Israel or Characters and Sketches from the Holy Scriptures and Jewish History: Illustrative of the Past History, Present Duties, and Future Destiny of the Hebrew Females, as Based on the Word of God.*

13. See further Eskenazi and Weiss, *The Torah: A Women's Commentary*, xxxviii; Taylor and Choi, *Handbook of Women Biblical Interpreters*, 31–37.

14. While Cady Stanton's work was groundbreaking in its feminist approach, it nonetheless reflected racist and antisemitic attitudes she and the like-minded white Christian women who worked with her held.

advances in feminist biblical scholarship and include newer voices (with Jacqueline E. Lapsley as an additional editor). In both the second and third editions, *The* has been dropped from the title.

Also appearing at the centennial of Cady Stanton's *The Woman's Bible* were two volumes edited by Elisabeth Schüssler Fiorenza with the assistance of Shelly Matthews. The first, *Searching the Scriptures: A Feminist Introduction* (New York: Crossroad, 1993), charts a comprehensive approach to feminist interpretation from ecumenical, interreligious, and multicultural perspectives. The second volume, published in 1994, provides critical feminist commentary on each book of the New Testament as well as on three books of Jewish Pseudepigrapha and eleven other early Christian writings.

In Europe, similar endeavors have been undertaken, such as the one-volume *Kompendium Feministische Bibelauslegung*, edited by Luise Schottroff and Marie-Theres Wacker (Gütersloh: Gütersloher Verlagshaus, 2007), featuring German feminist biblical interpretation of each book of the Bible, along with Deuterocanonical apocryphal books, and several extrabiblical writings. This work, now in its third edition, was translated into English.[15] A multivolume project, The Bible and Women: An Encyclopaedia of Exegesis and Cultural History, edited by Mary Ann Beavis, Irmtraud Fischer, Mercedes Navarro Puerto, and Adriana Valerio, is currently in production. This project presents a history of the reception of the Bible as embedded in Western cultural history and focuses particularly on gender-relevant biblical themes, biblical female characters, and women recipients of the Bible. The volumes are published in English, Spanish, Italian, and German.[16]

---

15. *Feminist Biblical Interpretation: A Compendium of Critical Commentary on the Books of the Bible and Related Literature*, trans. Lisa E. Dahill, Everett R. Kalin, Nancy Lukens, Linda M. Maloney, Barbara Rumscheidt, Martin Rumscheidt, and Tina Steiner (Grand Rapids: Eerdmans, 2012). Another notable collection is the three volumes edited by Susanne Scholz, *Feminist Interpretation of the Hebrew Bible in Retrospect*, Recent Research in Biblical Studies 5, 8, 9 (Sheffield: Sheffield Phoenix, 2013, 2014, 2016).

16. The first volume, on the Torah, appeared in Spanish in 2009, in German and Italian in 2010, and in English in 2011 (Atlanta: SBL). The other available volumes are as follows: *Feminist Biblical Studies in the Twentieth Century*, ed. Elisabeth Schüssler Fiorenza (2014); *The Writings and Later Wisdom Books*, ed. Christl M. Maier and Nuria Calduch-Benages (2014); *Gospels: Narrative and History*, ed. Mercedes Navarro Puerto and Marinella Perroni; Amy-Jill Levine, English ed. (2015); *The High Middle Ages*, ed. Kari Elisabeth Børresen and Adriana Valerio (2015); *Early Jewish Writings*, ed. Eileen Schuller and Marie-Theres Wacker (2017); *Faith and Feminism in Nineteenth-Century Religious Communities*, ed. Michaela Sohn-Kronthaler and Ruth Albrecht (2019); *The*

Another groundbreaking work is the collection The Feminist Companion to the Bible Series, edited by Athalya Brenner (Sheffield: Sheffield Academic, 1993–2015), which comprises twenty volumes of commentaries on the Old Testament. The parallel series, Feminist Companion to the New Testament and Early Christian Writings, edited by Amy-Jill Levine with Marianne Blickenstaff and Maria Mayo Robbins (Sheffield: Sheffield Academic, 2001–2010), contains thirteen volumes. These two series are not full commentaries on the biblical books but comprise collected essays on discrete biblical texts.

Works by individual feminist biblical scholars in all parts of the world abound, and they are now too numerous to list in this introduction. Feminist biblical interpretation has reached a level of maturity that now makes possible a commentary series on every book of the Bible. In recent decades, women have had greater access to formal theological education, have been able to learn critical analytical tools, have put their own interpretations into writing, and have developed new methods of biblical interpretation. Until recent decades the work of feminist biblical interpreters was largely unknown, both to other women and to their brothers in the synagogue, church, and academy. Feminists now have taken their place in the professional world of biblical scholars, where they build on the work of their foremothers and connect with one another across the globe in ways not previously possible. In a few short decades, feminist biblical criticism has become an integral part of the academy.

Methodologies

Feminist biblical scholars use a variety of methods and often employ a number of them together.[17] In the Wisdom Commentary series, the authors will explain their understanding of feminism and the feminist reading strategies used in their commentary. Each volume treats the biblical text in blocks of material, not an analysis verse by verse. The entire text

---

Early Middle Ages, ed. Franca Ela Consolino and Judith Herrin (2020); *Prophecy and Gender in the Hebrew Bible*, ed. L. Juliana Claassens and Irmtraud Fischer (2021); *Rabbinic Literature*, ed. Tal Ilan, Lorena Miralles-Maciá, and Ronit Nikolsky (2022); *Ancient Christian Apocrypha*, ed. Outi Lehtipuu and Silke Petersen (2022); and *The Jewish Middle Ages*, ed. Carol Bakhos and Gerhard Langer (2023). For further information, see https://www.bibleandwomen.org.

17. See the seventeen essays in Caroline Vander Stichele and Todd Penner, eds., *Her Master's Tools? Feminist and Postcolonial Engagements of Historical-Critical Discourse* (Atlanta: SBL, 2005), which show the complementarity of various approaches.

is considered, not only those passages that feature female characters or that speak specifically about women. When women are not apparent in the narrative, feminist lenses are used to analyze the dynamics in the text between male characters, the models of power, binary ways of thinking, and the dynamics of imperialism. Attention is given to how the whole text functions and how it was and is heard, both in its original context and today. Issues of particular concern to women—e.g., poverty, food, health, the environment, water—come to the fore.

One of the approaches used by early feminists and still popular today is to lift up the overlooked and forgotten stories of women in the Bible. Studies of women in each of the Testaments have been done, and there are also studies on women in particular biblical books.[18] Feminists recognize that the examples of biblical characters can be both empowering and problematic. The point of the feminist enterprise is not to serve as an apologetic for women; it is rather, in part, to recover women's history and literary roles in all their complexity and to learn from that recovery.

Retrieving the submerged history of biblical women is a crucial step for constructing the story of the past so as to lead to liberative possibilities for the present and future. There are, however, some pitfalls to this approach. Sometimes depictions of biblical women have been naïve and romantic. Some commentators exalt the virtues of both biblical and contemporary women and paint women as superior to men. Such reverse discrimination inhibits movement toward equality for all. In addition, some feminists challenge the idea that one can "pluck positive images out of an admittedly androcentric text, separating literary characterizations from the androcentric interests they were created to serve."[19] Still other feminists find these images to have enormous value.

18. See, e.g., Alice Bach, ed., *Women in the Hebrew Bible: A Reader* (New York: Routledge, 1999); Tikva Frymer-Kensky, *Reading the Women of the Bible* (New York: Schocken Books, 2002); Carol Meyers, Toni Craven, and Ross S. Kraemer, eds., *Women in Scripture* (Grand Rapids: Eerdmans, 2001); Irene Nowell, *Women in the Old Testament* (Collegeville, MN: Liturgical Press, 1997); Katharine Doob Sakenfeld, *Just Wives? Stories of Power and Survival in the Old Testament and Today* (Louisville: Westminster John Knox, 2003); Mary Ann Getty-Sullivan, *Women in the New Testament* (Collegeville, MN: Liturgical Press, 2001); Bonnie Thurston, *Women in the New Testament: Questions and Commentary*, Companions to the New Testament (New York: Crossroad, 1998).

19. J. Cheryl Exum, "Second Thoughts about Secondary Characters: Women in Exodus 1.8–2.10," in *A Feminist Companion to Exodus to Deuteronomy*, FCB 6, ed. Athalya Brenner (Sheffield: Sheffield Academic, 1994), 75–87, at 76.

One other danger with seeking the submerged history of women is the tendency for Christian feminists to paint Jesus and even Paul as libera-tors of women in a way that demonizes Judaism.[20] Wisdom Commentary aims to enhance understanding of Jesus as well as Paul as Jews of their day and to forge solidarity among Jewish and Christian feminists.

Feminist scholars who use historical-critical methods analyze the world behind the text; they seek to understand the historical context from which the text emerged and the circumstances of the communities to whom it was addressed. In bringing feminist lenses to this approach, the aim is not to impose modern expectations on ancient cultures but to unmask the ways that ideologically problematic mind-sets that produced the ancient texts are still promulgated through the text. Feminist biblical scholars aim not only to deconstruct but also to reclaim and reconstruct biblical history as women's history, in which women were central and active agents in creating religious heritage.[21] A further step is to construct meaning for contemporary women and men in a liberative movement toward transformation of social, political, economic, and religious struc-tures.[22] In recent years, some feminists have embraced new historicism, which accents the creative role of the interpreter in any construction of history and exposes the power struggles to which the text witnesses.[23]

20. See Judith Plaskow, "Anti-Judaism in Feminist Christian Interpretation," in *Searching the Scriptures: A Feminist Introduction*, vol. 1, ed. Elisabeth Schüssler Fiorenza with Shelly Matthews (New York: Crossroad, 1993), 117–29; Amy-Jill Levine, "The New Testament and Anti-Judaism," in *The Misunderstood Jew: The Church and the Scandal of the Jewish Jesus* (San Francisco: HarperSanFrancisco, 2006), 87–117.

21. See, for example, Phyllis A. Bird, *Missing Persons and Mistaken Identities: Women and Gender in Ancient Israel* (Minneapolis: Fortress, 1997); Elisabeth Schüssler Fiorenza, *In Memory of Her: A Feminist Theological Reconstruction of Christian Origins* (New York: Crossroad, 1994); Ross Shepard Kraemer and Mary Rose D'Angelo, eds., *Women and Christian Origins* (New York: Oxford University Press, 1999).

22. See, e.g., Sandra M. Schneiders, *The Revelatory Text: Interpreting the New Testament as Sacred Scripture*, rev. ed. (Collegeville, MN: Liturgical Press, 1999), whose aim is to engage in biblical interpretation not only for intellectual enlightenment but, even more important, for personal and communal transformation. Elisabeth Schüssler Fiorenza (*Wisdom Ways: Introducing Feminist Biblical Interpretation* [Maryknoll, NY: Orbis Books, 2001]) envisions the work of feminist biblical interpretation as a dance of Wisdom that consists of seven steps that interweave in spiral movements toward liberation, the final one being transformative action for change.

23. See Gina Hens-Piazza, *The New Historicism*, GBS, Old Testament Series (Min-neapolis: Fortress, 2002).

Literary critics analyze the world of the text: its form, language patterns, and rhetorical function.[24] They do not attempt to separate layers of tradition and redaction but focus on the text holistically, as it is in its present form. They examine how meaning is created in the interaction between the text and its reader in multiple contexts. Within the arena of literary approaches are reader-oriented approaches, narrative, rhetorical, structuralist, post-structuralist, deconstructive, ideological, autobiographical, and performance criticism.[25] Narrative critics study the interrelation among author, text, and audience through investigation of settings, both spatial and temporal; characters; plot; and narrative techniques (e.g., irony, parody, intertextual allusions). Reader-response critics attend to the impact that the text has on the reader or hearer. They recognize that when a text is detrimental toward women there is the choice either to affirm the text or to read against the grain toward a liberative end. Rhetorical criticism analyzes the style of argumentation and attends to how the author is attempting to shape the thinking or actions of the hearer. Structuralist critics analyze the complex patterns of binary oppositions in the text to derive its meaning.[26] Post-structuralist approaches challenge the notion that there are fixed meanings to any biblical text or that there is one universal truth. They engage in close readings of the text and often engage in intertextual analysis.[27] Within

24. Phyllis Trible was among the first to employ this method with texts from Genesis and Ruth in her groundbreaking book *God and the Rhetoric of Sexuality*, OBT (Philadelphia: Fortress, 1978). Another pioneer in feminist literary criticism is Mieke Bal (*Lethal Love: Feminist Literary Readings of Biblical Love Stories* [Bloomington: Indiana University Press, 1987]). For surveys of recent developments in literary methods, see Terry Eagleton, *Literary Theory: An Introduction*, 3rd ed. (Minneapolis: University of Minnesota Press, 2008); Janice Capel Anderson and Stephen D. Moore, eds., *Mark and Method: New Approaches in Biblical Studies*, 2nd ed. (Minneapolis: Fortress, 2008); Michal Beth Dinkler, *Literary Theory and the New Testament*, AYBRL (New Haven: Yale University Press, 2019).

25. See, e.g., J. Cheryl Exum and David J. A. Clines, eds., *The New Literary Criticism and the Hebrew Bible* (Valley Forge, PA: Trinity Press International, 1993); Elizabeth Struthers Malbon and Edgar V. McKnight, eds., *The New Literary Criticism and the New Testament* (Valley Forge, PA: Trinity Press International, 1994).

26. See, e.g., David Jobling, *The Sense of Biblical Narrative: Three Structural Analyses in the Old Testament*, JSOTSup 7 (Sheffield: University of Sheffield Press, 1978).

27. See, e.g., Stephen D. Moore, *Poststructuralism and the New Testament: Derrida and Foucault at the Foot of the Cross* (Minneapolis: Fortress, 1994); *The Bible in Theory: Critical and Postcritical Essays* (Atlanta: SBL, 2010); Yvonne Sherwood, *A Biblical Text and Its Afterlives: The Survival of Jonah in Western Culture* (Cambridge: Cambridge University Press, 2000).

this approach is deconstructionist criticism, which views the text as a site of conflict, with competing narratives. The interpreter aims to expose the fault lines and overturn and reconfigure binaries by elevating the underling of a pair and foregrounding it.[28] Feminists also use other postmodern approaches, such as ideological and autobiographical criticism. The former analyzes the system of ideas that underlies the power and values concealed in the text as well as that of the interpreter.[29] The latter involves deliberate self-disclosure while reading the text as a critical exegete.[30] Performance criticism attends to how the text was passed on orally, usually in communal settings, and to the verbal and nonverbal interactions between the performer and the audience.[31]

From the beginning, feminists have understood that interpreting the Bible is an act of power. In recent decades, feminist biblical scholars have developed hermeneutical theories of the ethics and politics of biblical interpretation to challenge the claims to value neutrality of most academic biblical scholarship. Feminist biblical scholars have also turned their attention to how some biblical writings were shaped by the power of empire and how this still shapes readers' self-understandings today. They have developed hermeneutical approaches that reveal, critique, and evaluate the interactions depicted in the text against the context of empire, and they consider implications for contemporary contexts.[32] Feminists also analyze

28. David Penchansky, "Deconstruction," in *The Oxford Encyclopedia of Biblical Interpretation*, ed. Steven McKenzie (New York: Oxford University Press, 2013), 196–205. See, for example, Danna Nolan Fewell and David M. Gunn, *Gender, Power, and Promise: The Subject of the Bible's First Story* (Nashville: Abingdon, 1993); David Rutledge, *Reading Marginally: Feminism, Deconstruction and the Bible*, BibInt 21 (Leiden: Brill, 1996).

29. See David Jobling and Tina Pippin, eds., *Ideological Criticism of Biblical Texts*, SemeiaSt 59 (Atlanta: Scholars Press, 1992); Terry Eagleton, *Ideology: An Introduction* (London: Verso, 2007).

30. See, e.g., Ingrid Rosa Kitzberger, ed., *Autobiographical Biblical Criticism: Between Text and Self* (Leiden: Deo, 2002); P. J. W. Schutte, "When *They*, *We*, and the *Passive* Become *I*—Introducing Autobiographical Biblical Criticism," *HTS Teologiese Studies / Theological Studies* 61 (2005): 401–16.

31. See, e.g., Holly E. Hearon and Philip Ruge-Jones, eds., *The Bible in Ancient and Modern Media: Story and Performance* (Eugene, OR: Cascade Books, 2009).

32. E.g., Gale Yee, ed., *Judges and Method: New Approaches in Biblical Studies* (Minneapolis: Fortress, 1995); Warren Carter, "Matthaean Christology in Roman Imperial Key: Matthew 1.1," in *The Gospel of Matthew in Its Roman Imperial Context*, ed. John Riches and David C. Sim (London: T&T Clark, 2005); Warren Carter, *The Roman Empire and the New Testament: An Essential Guide* (Nashville: Abingdon, 2006); Elisabeth Schüssler Fiorenza, *The Power of the Word: Scripture and the Rhetoric of Empire* (Minneapolis:

the dynamics of colonization and the mentalities of colonized peoples in the exercise of biblical interpretation. As Kwok Pui-lan explains, "A postcolonial feminist interpretation of the Bible needs to investigate the deployment of gender in the narration of identity, the negotiation of power differentials between the colonizers and the colonized, and the reinforcement of patriarchal control over spheres where these elites could exercise control."[33] Methods and models from sociology and cultural anthropology are used by feminists to investigate women's everyday lives, their experiences of marriage, childrearing, labor, money, illness, etc.[34]

As feminists have examined the construction of gender from varying cultural perspectives, they have become ever more cognizant that the way gender roles are defined within differing cultures varies radically. As Mary Ann Tolbert observes, "Attempts to isolate some universal role that cross-culturally defines 'woman' have run into contradictory evidence at every turn."[35] Some women have coined new terms to highlight the particularities of their socio-cultural context. Many African American feminists, for example, call themselves *womanists* to draw attention to the double oppression of racism and sexism they experience.[36] Similarly, many US Hispanic feminists speak of themselves as *mujeristas* (*mujer* is

---

Fortress, 2007); Judith E. McKinlay, *Reframing Her: Biblical Women in Postcolonial Focus* (Sheffield: Sheffield Phoenix, 2004).

33. Kwok Pui-lan, *Postcolonial Imagination and Feminist Theology* (Louisville: Westminster John Knox, 2005), 9. See also Musa W. Dube, ed., *Postcolonial Feminist Interpretation of the Bible* (St. Louis: Chalice, 2000); Christl M. Maier and Carolyn J. Sharp, eds., *Prophecy and Power: Jeremiah in Feminist and Postcolonial Perspective*, LHBOTS 577 (London: Bloomsbury T&T Clark, 2013); L. Juliana Claassens and Carolyn J. Sharp, eds., *Feminist Frameworks and the Bible: Power, Ambiguity, and Intersectionality*, LHBOTS 630 (London: Bloomsbury T&T Clark, 2017).

34. See, for example, Carol Meyers, *Rediscovering Eve: Ancient Israelite Women in Context* (New York: Oxford University Press, 2013); Luise Schottroff, *Lydia's Impatient Sisters: A Feminist Social History of Early Christianity*, trans. Barbara and Martin Rumscheidt (Louisville: Westminster John Knox, 1995); Susan Niditch, *"My Brother Esau Is a Hairy Man": Hair and Identity in Ancient Israel* (New York: Oxford University Press, 2008).

35. Mary Ann Tolbert, "Social, Sociological, and Anthropological Methods," in *Searching the Scriptures*, 1:255–71, at 265.

36. Alice Walker coined the term (*In Search of Our Mothers' Gardens: Womanist Prose* [New York: Harcourt Brace Jovanovich, 1967, 1983]). See also Katie Geneva Cannon, "The Emergence of Black Feminist Consciousness," in *Feminist Interpretation of the Bible*, ed. Letty M. Russell (Philadelphia: Westminster, 1985), 30–40; Renita J. Weems, *Just a Sister Away: A Womanist Vision of Women's Relationships in the Bible* (San Diego: Lura Media, 1988); Nyasha Junior, *An Introduction to Womanist Biblical Interpretation* (Louisville: Westminster John Knox, 2015).

Spanish for "woman").[37] Others prefer to be called "Latina feminists."[38] As a gender-neutral or nonbinary alternative, many today use Latinx or Latine. *Mujeristas*, Latina and Latine feminists emphasize that the context for their theologizing is *mestizaje* and *mulatez* (racial and cultural mixture), done *en conjunto* (in community), with *lo cotidiano* (everyday lived experience) of Latina women as starting points for theological reflection and the encounter with the divine. Intercultural analysis has become an indispensable tool for working toward justice for women at the global level.[39]

Some feminists are among those who have developed interpretations from the perspectives of lesbian, gay, bisexual, transgender, queer and/ or questioning, intersex, asexual, and other ways people choose to identify (LGBTQIA+). These approaches focus on issues of sexual identity and use various reading strategies. Some point out the ways in which categories that emerged in recent centuries are applied anachronistically to biblical texts to make modern-day judgments. Others show how the Bible is silent on contemporary issues about sexual identity. Still others examine same-sex relationships in the Bible by figures such as Ruth and Naomi or David and Jonathan. In recent years, queer theory has emerged; it emphasizes the blurriness of boundaries not just of sexual identity but also of gender roles. Queer critics often focus on texts in which figures transgress what is traditionally considered proper gender behavior.[40]

37. Ada María Isasi-Díaz (*Mujerista Theology: A Theology for the Twenty-First Century* [Maryknoll, NY: Orbis Books, 1996]) is credited with coining the term.

38. E.g., María Pilar Aquino, Daisy L. Machado, and Jeanette Rodríguez, eds., *A Reader in Latina Feminist Theology* (Austin: University of Texas Press, 2002).

39. See, e.g., María Pilar Aquino and María José Rosado-Nunes, eds., *Feminist Intercultural Theology: Latina Explorations for a Just World*, Studies in Latino/a Catholicism (Maryknoll, NY: Orbis Books, 2007). See also Michelle A. Gonzalez, "Latina Feminist Theology: Past, Present, and Future," *JFSR* 25 (2009): 150–55. See also Elisabeth Schüssler Fiorenza, ed., *Feminist Biblical Studies in the Twentieth Century: Scholarship and Movement*, BW 9.1 (Atlanta: SBL Press, 2014), who charts feminist studies around the globe as well as emerging feminist methodologies.

40. See, e.g., Bernadette J. Brooten, *Love Between Women: Early Christian Responses to Female Homoeroticism* (Chicago: University of Chicago Press, 1996); Mary Rose D'Angelo, "Women Partners in the New Testament," *JFSR* 6 (1990): 65–86; Deirdre J. Good, "Reading Strategies for Biblical Passages on Same-Sex Relations," *Theology and Sexuality* 7 (1997): 70–82; Deryn Guest, *When Deborah Met Jael: Lesbian Biblical Hermeneutics* (London: SCM, 2005); Teresa J. Hornsby and Ken Stone, eds., *Bible Trouble: Queer Reading at the Boundaries of Biblical Scholarship*, SemeiaSt 67 (Atlanta: SBL, 2011); Joseph A. Marchal, "Queer Studies and Critical Masculinity Studies in Feminist Biblical Studies," in *Feminist Biblical Studies in the Twentieth Century*, ed. Schüssler Fiorenza, 261–80.

Feminists have also been engaged in studying the reception history of the text[41] and have engaged in studies in the emerging fields of disability theory and of children in the Bible.

Feminists also recognize that the struggle for women's equality and dignity is intimately connected with the struggle for respect for Earth and for the whole of the cosmos. Ecofeminists interpret Scripture in ways that highlight the link between human domination of nature and male subjugation of women. They show how anthropocentric ways of interpreting the Bible have overlooked or dismissed Earth and Earth community. They invite readers to identify not only with human characters in the biblical narrative but also with other Earth creatures and domains of nature, especially those that are the object of injustice. Some use creative imagination to retrieve the interests of Earth implicit in the narrative and enable Earth to speak.[42]

Biblical Authority

By the late nineteenth century, some feminists, such as Elizabeth Cady Stanton, began to question openly whether the Bible could continue to be regarded as authoritative for women. They viewed the Bible itself as the source of women's oppression, and some rejected its sacred origin and saving claims. Some decided that the Bible and the religious traditions that enshrine it are too thoroughly saturated with androcentrism and patriarchy to be redeemable.[43]

In the Wisdom Commentary series, questions such as these may be raised, but the aim of this series is not to lead readers to reject the authority of the biblical text. Rather, the aim is to promote better understanding of the contexts from which the text arose and of the rhetorical effects it has on people in contemporary contexts. Such understanding can lead to a deepening of faith, with the Bible serving as an aid to bring flourishing of life.

41. See Sharon H. Ringe, "When Women Interpret the Bible," in *Women's Bible Commentary*, ed. Carol A. Newsom, Sharon H. Ringe, and Jacqueline E. Lapsley, 3rd ed. (Louisville: Westminster John Knox, 2012), 5; Taylor and Choi, *Handbook of Women Biblical Interpreters*; Yvonne Sherwood, "Introduction," in *The Bible and Feminism: Remapping the Field*, ed. Yvonne Sherwood with Anna Fisk (New York: Oxford University Press, 2017).

42. E.g., Norman C. Habel and Peter Trudinger, *Exploring Ecological Hermeneutics*, SymS 46 (Atlanta: SBL, 2008); Mary Judith Ress, *Ecofeminism in Latin America*, Women from the Margins (Maryknoll, NY: Orbis Books, 2006).

43. E.g., Mary Daly, *Beyond God the Father: A Philosophy of Women's Liberation* (Boston: Beacon, 1985).

Language for God

Because of the ways in which the term "God" has been used to symbol-ize the divine in predominantly male, patriarchal, and monarchical modes, feminists have designed new ways of speaking of the divine. Some have called attention to the inadequacy of the term *God* by trying to visually destabilize our ways of thinking and speaking of the divine. Rosemary Radford Ruether proposed *God/ess*, as an unpronounceable term pointing to the unnameable understanding of the divine that transcends patriarchal limitations.[44] Some have followed traditional Jewish practice, writing *G-d*. Elisabeth Schüssler Fiorenza has adopted *G*d*.[45] Others draw on the biblical tradition to mine female and non-gender-specific metaphors and symbols.[46] In Wisdom Commentary, there is not one standard way of ex-pressing the divine; each author will use her or his preferred ways. The one exception is that when the tetragrammaton, YHWH, the name revealed to Moses in Exodus 3:14, is used, it will be without vowels, respecting the Jewish custom of avoiding pronouncing the divine name out of reverence.

Nomenclature for the Two Testaments

In recent decades, some biblical scholars have begun to call the two Testaments of the Bible by names other than the traditional nomen-clature: Old and New Testament. Some regard "Old" as derogatory, implying that it is no longer relevant or that it has been superseded. Consequently, terms like Hebrew Bible, First Testament, and Jewish Scriptures and, correspondingly, Christian Scriptures or Second Testa-ment have come into use. There are a number of difficulties with these designations. The term "Hebrew Bible" does not take into account that parts of the Old Testament are written not in Hebrew but in Aramaic.[47] Moreover, for Roman Catholics and Eastern Orthodox believers, the Old

---

44. Rosemary Radford Ruether, *Sexism and God-Talk: Toward a Feminist Theology* (Boston: Beacon, 1993).

45. Elisabeth Schüssler Fiorenza, *Jesus: Miriam's Child, Sophia's Prophet; Critical Issues in Feminist Christology* (New York: Continuum, 1994), 191n3.

46. E.g., Sallie McFague, *Models of God: Theology for an Ecological, Nuclear Age* (Phil-adelphia: Fortress, 1987); Catherine Mowry LaCugna, *God for Us: The Trinity and Christian Life* (San Francisco: HarperCollins, 1991); Elizabeth A. Johnson, *She Who Is: The Mystery of God in Feminist Theological Discourse* (New York: Crossroad, 1992). See further Elizabeth A. Johnson, "God," in *Dictionary of Feminist Theologies*, ed. Letty M. Russell and J. Shannon Clarkson (Louisville: Westminster John Knox, 1996), 128–30.

47. Gen 31:47; Jer 10:11; Ezra 4:7–6:18; 7:12-26; Dan 2:4–7:28.

Testament includes books written in Greek—the Deuterocanonical books, considered Apocrypha by Protestants.[48] The term "Jewish Scriptures" is inadequate because these books are also sacred to Christians. Conversely, "Christian Scriptures" is not an accurate designation for the New Testament, since the Old Testament is also part of the Christian Scriptures. Using "First and Second Testament" also has difficulties, in that it can imply a hierarchy and a value judgment.[49] Jews generally use the term Tanakh, an acronym for Torah (Pentateuch), Nevi'im (Prophets), and Ketuvim (Writings).

In Wisdom Commentary, if authors choose to use a designation other than Tanakh, Old Testament, and New Testament, they will explain how they mean the term.

Translation

Modern feminist scholars recognize the complexities connected with biblical translation, as they have delved into questions about philosophy of language, how meanings are produced, and how they are culturally situated. Today it is evident that simply translating into gender-neutral formulations cannot address all the challenges presented by androcentric texts. Efforts at feminist translation must also deal with issues around authority and canonicity.[50]

Because of these complexities, the editors of the Wisdom Commentary series have chosen to use an existing translation, the New Revised Standard Version Updated Edition (NRSVue),[51] which is provided for easy reference at the top of each page of commentary. The NRSVue was produced by a team of ecumenical and interreligious scholars, is a fairly literal translation, and uses inclusive language for human beings. Brief discussions about problematic translations appear in the inserts labeled "Translation Matters." When more detailed discussions are available, these will be indicated in footnotes. In the commentary, wherever Hebrew

---

48. Representing the *via media* between Catholic and reformed, Anglicans generally consider the Apocrypha to be profitable, if not canonical, and utilize select Wisdom texts liturgically.

49. See Levine, *The Misunderstood Jew*, 193–99.

50. Elizabeth Castelli, "*Les Belles Infidèles*/Fidelity or Feminism? The Meanings of Feminist Biblical Translation," in *Searching the Scriptures*, 1:189–204, here 190.

51. The volumes of Wisdom Commentary produced through 2023 use the edition of NRSV published in 1989; subsequent volumes use the updated edition, NRSVue, released in 2021.

or Greek words are used, English translation is provided. In cases where a wordplay is involved, transliteration is provided to enable understanding.

Art and Poetry

Artistic expression in poetry, music, sculpture, painting, and various other modes is very important to feminist interpretation. Where possible, art and poetry are included in the print volumes of the series. In a number of instances, these are original works created for this project. Regrettably, copyright and production costs prohibit the inclusion of color photographs and other artistic work.

Glossary

Because there are a number of excellent readily available resources that provide definitions and concise explanations of terms used in feminist theological and biblical studies, this series will not include a glossary. We refer you to works such as *Dictionary of Feminist Theologies*, edited by Letty M. Russell and J. Shannon Clarkson, and volume 1 of *Searching the Scriptures*, edited by Elisabeth Schüssler Fiorenza with the assistance of Shelly Matthews. Individual authors in the Wisdom Commentary series will define the way they are using terms that may be unfamiliar.

A Concluding Word

In just a few short decades, feminist biblical studies has grown exponentially, both in the methods that have been developed and in the number of scholars who have embraced it. We realize that this series is limited and will soon need to be revised and updated. It is our hope that Wisdom Commentary, by making the best of current feminist biblical scholarship available in an accessible format to ministers, preachers, rabbis, teachers, scholars, and students, will aid all readers in their advancement toward God's vision of dignity, equality, and justice for all.

Acknowledgments

There are a great many people who have made this series possible: first, Peter Dwyer, retired director of Liturgical Press, and Hans Christoffersen, editorial director of Liturgical Press, who have believed in this project and have shepherded it since it was conceived in 2008. I am grateful to Therese L. Ratliff, the Press's director and CEO, who is now championing this project.

Editorial consultants Athalya Brenner-Idan and Elisabeth Schüssler Fiorenza have not only been an inspiration with their pioneering work but have encouraged us all along the way with their personal involvement. Volume editors Mary Ann Beavis, Carol J. Dempsey, Amy-Jill Levine, Linda M. Maloney, Song-Mi Suzie Park, Ahida Pilarski, Sarah Tanzer, and Lauress Wilkins Lawrence have lent their extraordinary wisdom to the shaping of the series, have used their extensive networks of relationships to secure authors and contributors, and have worked tirelessly to guide their work to completion. Others who have contributed greatly to the shaping of the project are Linda M. Day, Gina Hens-Piazza, Mignon Jacobs, Seung Ai Yang, and Barbara E. Bowe of blessed memory (d. 2010). Editorial and research assistant Susan M. Hickman provided invaluable support with administrative details and arrangements at the outset of the project. I am grateful to Brian Eisenschenk and Christine Henderson who assisted Susan Hickman with the Wiki. I am especially thankful to Lauren L. Murphy and Justin Howell for their work in copyediting; and to the staff at Liturgical Press, especially Colleen Stiller, retired production manager; Angie Steffens, production manager; Elizabeth Elin, production coordinator; Stephanie Lancour, production editor; Julie Surma, desktop publisher; and Tara Durheim, marketing director.

Author's Introduction

Visions of a New Day

The book of Zechariah is not an easy read. It has confounded Jewish and Christian interpreters for centuries. When it comes to understanding the words of Zechariah, the twelfth-century Jewish commentator Abraham Ibn Ezra remarked that readers are "like blind people without a wall upon which to lean."[1] The Protestant reformer Martin Luther admitted that, when it came to the closing chapter of Zechariah, he was compelled to "give up."[2] Ibn Ezra and Luther were men of faith. They were educated and familiar with the Scriptures, yet the book of Zechariah puzzled them both. Modern interpreters have found Zechariah a challenge as well. For example, Julia M. O'Brien describes the book as "filled with puzzling images, and its parts do not easily fit together."[3]

---

1. Ezra Frazer, *Abraham Ibn Ezra to Haggai, Zechariah, and Malachi: A Critical Edition, Translation, and Supercommentary with an Analytic Introduction* (PhD diss., Yeshiva University, 2018), 250.

2. "Here, in this chapter, I give up. For I am not sure what the prophet is talking about." See Albert Wolters, "Zechariah 14: A Dialogue with the History of Interpretation," *Mid-America Journal of Theology* 13 (2002): 56; Richard Dinda, ed., *Luther's Works*, vol. 20: *Lectures on the Minor Prophets III* (St. Louis: Concordia, 1973), 337.

3. Julia M. O'Brien, *Nahum, Habakkuk, Zephaniah, Haggai, Zechariah, Malachi*, AOTC (Nashville: Abingdon, 2004), 158.

Only the foolhardy regard the meaning of any biblical text as immediately self-evident. Finding meaning involves a sustained conversation between the text and its readers. This commentary can serve as an interlocutor in that conversation. Though much of the book of Zechariah may appear to be obscure and opaque, this commentary attempts to take another look at Zechariah from a distinctly contemporary hermeneutical perspective—that of feminist biblical interpretation. It offers the perspectives of feminism as guides in the interplay between text and reader. The work of women interpreters of Zechariah will be a helpful guide in this effort. As the Pontifical Biblical Commission has recognized, biblical interpretation from a feminist perspective "helps to unmask and correct certain commonly accepted interpretations which were tendentious and sought to justify the male domination of women" and "ensures that new questions are put to the biblical text, which in turn occasions new discoveries."[4]

Of course, women were among those who first heard the prophet's words, though much of what appears in the book does not specifically focus on women's concerns. Still, we can ask how Jewish women in the late sixth century BCE would have heard the prophet's words. Did the prophet's words reflect women's experience and shed light on that experience? How would the prophet's words impact women's lives? Did women find the prophet's words to be supportive, irrelevant, or harmful? Also, would women, children, the elderly, slaves, and gentiles have read the prophet's call to speak truth and practice justice as applicable to them as the *subject*, meaning the prophet was speaking directly to them, or as *object*, meaning that the prophet was speaking about them as benefitting from the justice that was to characterize the postexilic Jewish community? Similarly, do the affirmations, negations, and emphases in Zechariah shed light on women's concerns today? Can women of faith, both Jewish and Christian, find in this book nourishment, guidance, and challenge in their life of faith or will they find the book one more obstacle to living authentically as believers and as women?

Answering these questions will not be easy since the book of Zechariah has a narrow focus. Its principal concerns are the restoration of the Jewish community in its ancestral homeland and the survival of that community in the face of economic, political, and religious challenges. Zechariah does

---

4. Pontifical Biblical Commission, "The Interpretation of the Bible in the Church," *Origins* 23 (January 6, 1994), E.2.

not explicitly deal with women's lives and experience. It will be the task of this commentary to call attention to all those affected by the text but not specifically addressed in the text—especially the women of Yehud.[5] By paying attention to the women and others on the margins of the Jewish community, a more complete picture of the Jewish community in the Persian period will emerge. By giving voice to those "in the shadows" of the Jewish community we will learn what they might have heard in the prophet's words. In addition, this commentary will identify how Zechariah resonates with the concerns of feminist readers today. Among these are the language and imagery used to speak of God, war and violence, social justice, the environment, the economy, the community's leadership, and the relationship among different ethnic groups. A significant guide in a feminist reading of Zechariah is the secondary literature on this book by women scholars. They have demonstrated exegetical and hermeneutical insight into Zechariah that has made invaluable contributions to both the academy and the synagogue and church.

As is the case with any hermeneutical method, patterns of feminist interpretation are evolving as is feminism, the ideological foundation of this approach to appropriating the biblical text for believers today. The approach taken here as a part of the Wisdom Commentary is to offer a commentary of the *textus receptus* of the book of Zechariah. This approach, of course, is not the only way to provide a feminist reading of Zechariah. The advantage of a commentary is that it demands that the interpreter deal with the entire book as it is without ignoring problematic passages and without creating a hypothetical text. The disadvantage of a commentary is that it requires more attention to the historical and ideological context from which the text emerged. Feminist interpretation, like any advocacy hermeneutic, focuses more on the value of the text as shedding its light on contemporary existence. To give each pattern of interpretation its due, this commentary attempts to describe what impact the text had on the women of Persian period Yehud and the text's potential in speaking to the lives of women today.

---

5. Yehud (יהוד) is the Aramaic equivalent of the Hebrew word יהודה ("Judah"). Yehud was a province of the Persian satrapy "Beyond the River [Euphrates]." Aramaic was the *lingua franca* in the Persian Empire. The word "Yehud" never appears in the book of Zechariah, which uses the Hebrew "Judah" twenty-two times and "Jerusalem" forty-two times in speaking of the homeland of the Jewish community. This commentary uses Yehud as a geographical term to speak of that part of the southern Levant where Jews lived during the Persian period (sixth to fourth centuries BCE).

Contexts

A first step in any attempt to understand and appreciate biblical texts is to identify the context in which those texts emerged. Similarly, since biblical interpretation is a dialogical enterprise, it is necessary that the interpreters' context be clear as well.

Like most books of the Hebrew Bible, Zechariah is a composite work. Chapters 1–8 have become known as "Proto-Zechariah." Three dates appear in these chapters (1:1, 7; 7:1) that suggest that the prophet Zechariah was active in the two-year period between 520 and 518 BCE. At that time, the Jewish community was in the process of reconstituting itself in its ancestral homeland following the decree of Cyrus the Great (2 Chr 36:22-23; Ezra 1:1-4). Cyrus encouraged the Jews living in Babylonia to relocate to Jerusalem and rebuild the temple that had been destroyed by the Babylonians in 587 BCE. Reestablishing a viable Jewish community in Yehud was not a simple matter. Only a fraction of the territory of the former kingdom of Judah was reconstituted as the Persian province of Yehud. There were tensions between the Jews who arrived from Babylon and the descendants of those Judeans who were not forced to migrate. Economic and political obstacles complicated the rebuilding of the temple. The community had to develop a new pattern of civil and religious leadership since the Judean state and monarchy no longer existed and the priesthood was in disarray. There was no clear vision of what the future of the Jewish community was to be. Zechariah 1–8 speaks to this situation as it calls for the completion of the temple's reconstruction and as it offers support to the patterns of leadership that developed in the postexilic Jewish community of Yehud. Amid this uncertainty, the one source of stability was the family. Women created the atmosphere in which the family could provide the stability essential for the early postexilic community in Yehud.

Zechariah 9–14, known as Deutero-Zechariah, comes from a later time—probably the time that the book of the Twelve took the shape it now has among the Latter Prophets of the Hebrew Bible. Those chapters contain no dates to help determine the precise time of their composition. Also, it is likely that the collections that make up these chapters do not all come from the same period. There is a reference to Greece in 9:13, suggesting that some portions of Deutero-Zechariah may be as late as the fourth century BCE, following the victory of Alexander the Great over the Persians at the battle of Issus in 333 BCE. Some commentators suggest that chapters 9–14 are made of two separate components based on the recurrence of the titles in 9:1 and 12:1. They speak of chapters 12–14 as Trito-Zechariah.[6]

Although the book of Zechariah contains diverse components, its organization is uncomplicated. The book's prologue (1:1-6) calls for repentance. Next comes accounts of several visions accompanied by interpreting oracles (1:7–6:15). Following the vision accounts, there is a report concerning an inquiry about days of fasting (7:1–8:23). The book concludes with two collections of prophetic pronouncements (9–11 and 12–14). The book is a composition under a single person's name, suggesting that there is an integrity to the book. The first six chapters of the book focus on the Judean restoration. The final chapter's eschatological perspective looks forward to a cosmic restoration. The book then begins with Judah and Jerusalem and ends with a universalist vision. Its structure serves to broaden its readers' horizons as it describes the universality of YHWH's[7] sovereignty that will manifest itself "on that day."

Historical Context

The book of Zechariah reflects the unsettled times of the early postexilic period. The Jewish community of Yehud was a small part of the Persian Empire. Though the Persians were not as harsh as were the Assyrians and Babylonians, the Jews of Yehud remained a subject people whose ability to chart their own destiny was limited. The Persians, however, did recognize the Torah as the local law in Yehud. There were tensions between the people of Yehud and their immediate neighbors—especially with the province of Samaria. There were tensions within the Jewish community—between the people of means and the poor and between the Jews relocating from Babylonia and the families of those who remained in the land following the fall of Jerusalem in 587 BCE. The development of leadership, civil and religious, was a particular challenge. The Persians

---

6. E.g., Albert Wolters suggests that the book of Zechariah is divided into three parts: chapters 1–8, 9–11, and 12–14. See his *Zechariah*, HCOT (Leuven: Peeters, 2014), 22. This division is not based on the historical context of each division since Wolters maintains that the entire book was composed by the prophet Zechariah in the sixth century. This departure from the scholarly consensus is due, in part, to Wolters's evangelical background. Both chapter 9–11 and 12–14 have a distinct eschatological perspective, which distinguished them from chapters 1–8.

7. This commentary will use YHWH as the divine name when יהוה or one of its abbreviated forms appears in the MT. The NRSVue, the NABRE, and the JPS normally render יהוה as Lord.

installed Zerubbabel, whom the Chronicler claimed was a member of the former royal family of Judah, as governor (פחה) of Yehud.[8] It is likely that some Jews did expect a restoration of the Judean state and the Davidic dynasty, but in the end, nothing came of those expectations. The temple remained in ruins and its priests scattered, though the Persian authorities encouraged and supported the rebuilding of the Jerusalem temple. In these circumstances, the prophet spoke of a future of peace and prosperity for Judah and Jerusalem.

The book of Zechariah comes from a time of transition in the religious life of the Jewish people. The temple-based and priestly led religion of the monarchic period was undergoing a fundamental change. Unfortunately, the precise contours of the beginnings of that change are still a subject of speculation. It appears that some Jews began gathering in small groups for prayer and the reading of sacred texts. While the temple was still in ruins such gatherings were a way to nourish people's religious life. Even after the temple was rebuilt, such gatherings probably continued, especially among people who did not live in proximity to the temple. These gatherings were the beginning of what became the "synagogue."[9] What came to be regarded as the Scriptures came to have growing influence in the Jewish community. Those skilled in the interpretation of the Scriptures rose to prominence in the community. These and other developments in the Jewish community eventually gave rise to the Judaism of the rabbis. The book of Zechariah took shape at the beginning of this process of transformation. Chapters 1–8 look for the restoration of worship in the temple presided over by the high priest while chapter 14 speaks of a transformation of holiness that was one of the ideas that brought Judaism into being.

---

8. First Chronicles 3:16-19 provides Zerubbabel with a Davidic genealogy, though it is unlikely that the Persians would have taken the risk of inflaming hopes for the restoration of the house of David by appointing a member of the former royal family of Judah as governor. See J. Maxwell Miller and John H. Hayes, *A History of Ancient Israel and Judah* (Philadelphia: Westminster, 1986), 456, and Jon L. Berquist, *Judaism in Persia's Shadow: A Social and Historical Approach* (Minneapolis: Fortress, 1995), 63.

9. For the origins of the synagogue, see Anders Runesson, Donald Binder, and Birger Olsson, eds., *The Ancient Synagogue from Its Origins to 200 CE: A Source Book*, Ancient Judaism and Early Christianity 72 (Leiden: Brill, 2007). It is important to distinguish between "synagogue" as a Jewish religious assembly and "synagogue" as a single-purpose building devoted to worship and study. Such buildings first appear in the second century CE although there are several first-century buildings that have been identified as synagogues. There is some dispute about such identifications.

The Contemporary Context

The context out of which this commentary comes is the contemporary struggle of women in both church and society for the recognition of their rights, their autonomy, and their dignity as *women*. Since the late nineteenth century, this struggle has been about a variety of issues in the United States: the right to vote, equal pay for equal work, maternity leave, the right of privacy and autonomy concerning health care issues, the "glass ceiling" in the corporate world and the world of higher education and public service, affordable childcare, and more. In addition to these concerns, women want their voices to be heard on issues such as health care, climate change, war and peace, gun control, immigration—all the issues that confront society today. Women of faith want to have the opportunity to contribute to their respective communities of faith in a measure equal to men—to be partners in worship, service, and administration. Communities of faith are usually examples of "traditional societies" in which change can and does happen but often at an agonizingly slow pace. One goal of the series of which this commentary is a part is to help hasten the day when people in church and society will recognize the dignity and rights of women, freeing them to realize their full potential for the transformation of the world into a place where justice, peace, and love triumph.

Author's Context

This commentary is the product of an effort to discover whether and to what extent the women of the early postexilic Jewish community found the book of Zechariah to be a source of light in a dark period of their community's life. At the same time, this commentary hopes to suggest how women today may engage a male prophet who lived two and a half millennia ago. Will women today resonate with the prophet's affirmations, negations, and emphases? Will they find them enlightening, challenging, affirming, disappointing, infuriating, irrelevant?

The book of Zechariah is a product of another time and culture. It has a narrow focus: the Judean restoration following the decree of Cyrus the Great calling for the Judeans in Babylon to leave their homes and lives there to make their way to Jerusalem where they are to build a temple for their ancestral deity. The women who made this journey faced a formidable task. They had to travel to a place that most had never seen to help restore Jewish life in circumstances they had never faced. They had to care for their families. They had to feed and clothe them, care for the very young and the very old. They joined in the efforts to construct a temple to take the place of the one destroyed by the Babylonians. The book of Zechariah ignores their contribution to the Judean restoration as its primary concerns are the completion of the temple-building project, the leadership of the Jewish community, and the morale of that community in the early years of the restoration, taking for granted the irreplaceable contribution women make to their families and communities. This narrow focus of the book is disappointing but not entirely unexpected. One purpose of this commentary is to bring the women of sixth-century BCE Yehud out from the shadows. Especially helpful in achieving this goal is the work of women biblical scholars, who have made significant contributions to the study of the book of Zechariah. This commentary is indebted to their work as the notes and bibliography show.

This is not a full-scale, critical commentary. There are two such commentaries available in English: the two-volume commentary by Carol and Eric Meyers in the Anchor Bible series (*Haggai, Zechariah 1–8: A New Translation with Introduction and Commentary*; *Zechariah 9–14: A New Translation with Introduction and Commentary*) and the commentary by Mark J. Boda in the New International Commentary on the Old Testament series (*The Book of Zechariah*). This commentary is indebted to both of these two magisterial works. They have given the book of Zechariah the attention that it has not always received from the community of biblical scholars. No serious work on Zechariah can proceed without consulting the work of these scholars.

This commentary attempts to look at the book of Zechariah with feminist eyes. This is easier said than done. The relationship between biblical interpretation and feminism has developed over the years because feminism as an intellectual, social, and political movement continues to develop. Feminism is no longer dominated by the concerns of white intellectuals from the West. Postcolonial feminism focuses on the experiences and concerns of women from Central and South America, Africa, and Asia. Ecofeminism brings environmental issues to the forefront. Feminism must find its place in the postmodern world of changing identities, borders, and boundaries. Feminism has become a complex philosophical, social, political, and cultural phenomenon; it is not the case that "one size fits all." A feminist from South Africa will see matters differently from a feminist from the United States. A feminist in the world of politics will have an agenda that differs from a feminist whose world is in social services. A Unitarian feminist will have issues that differ from those of a Roman Catholic feminist. The principal goal of some feminists is to bring about the equality of men and women within the established social structure. Other feminists see that patriarchy is fundamentally oppressive so they aim to change all oppressive social institutions while still other feminists see women's struggles as one aspect of a larger class struggle caused by the inherently oppressive capitalist economic system.

The feminist lens with which this commentary will examine the book of Zechariah will necessarily be narrow since it will focus on a work that does not directly deal with gender issues. The authors and editors who produced the book of Zechariah were almost certainly male. They worked out of an ancient Near Eastern context that delineated clear lines between men and women, between the obligations that men and women had to their families, and between societal expectations of male and female behavior. Zechariah's views about the role and status of women in society were typical of the thinking of his time. As Tikva Frymer-Kensky has pointed out, the biblical writers have little to say about women as such. While biblical writers presume a social structure in which women are subordinate, there are no overall statements about women, and in fact, the Bible is gender neutral for the most part:

> Contrary to all assumptions—my own included—the Hebrew Bible, unlike other ancient literature, does not present any ideas about women as the "Other." The role of woman is clearly subordinate, but the Hebrew Bible does not "explain" or justify this subordination by portraying women as different or inferior. . . . There are no personality traits or psychological characteristics that are unique to women, and the familiar Western notions of "feminine wiles," the "battle between the sexes," "sisterly solidarity," and "sex as weapon" are all absent. . . . The only misogynist statement in the Bible comes very late in biblical development . . . and shows the introduction of the classical Greek denigration of women into Israel.[10]

Although the Bible makes no generalizations about women as being inherently inferior to men, Frymer-Kensky points out that it does presume a reality in which women are socially subordinate to men:

> The Bible's view of gender sets up a dramatic clash between theory and reality. On the one hand, women occupied a socially subordinate position. On the other hand, the Bible did not label them as inferior. This gap between ideology and social structure has a major disadvantage: it

---

10. Tikva Frymer-Kensky, *Reading the Women of the Bible: A New Interpretation of Their Stories* (New York: Schocken Books, 2002), xv–xvi.

did not explain people's lives, did not give people a way to understand why women had no access to public decision making. Such dissonance could not last forever: one of the two had to give, and the Bible's vision of a gender-neutral humanity ultimately gave way in the face of ongoing patriarchy. At the same time, the biblical vision had the enormous advantage of not adding prejudice to powerlessness.[11]

In other words, Frymer-Kensky believes that while the Bible acknowledges and accepts a system in which normative societal expectations place women at a disadvantage, the Bible also presumes that there is no difference between men and women in their thinking and behavior. With this in mind, we recognize that Zechariah presumes a social structure that had long placed women as socially inferior to men, but that did not presume that women's characters are inferior to men's characters or that their participation in the covenantal community is less meaningful.

Zechariah features almost no women characters in the vision accounts of chapters 1–6. Still, gendered imagery does appear in significant ways in the book. At first, this imagery may appear to be stereotypical. Julia O'Brien observes that in Zechariah "men are individuated and strong, while women are generic and vulnerable." O'Brien is also correct that these assignments are at times unstable, since the prophet depicts men who lack authority, and powerful women who possess a potency that "refuses to be contained."[12] In this sense, the book exaggerates expected roles "to the point of parody," providing a means by which to critique what readers consider "normal" behavior.

Frymer-Kensky makes another point that is relevant to a feminist commentary on Zechariah: biblical attitudes toward women, and other marginalized people of Yehud, mirror the experience of Israel vis-à-vis the foreign nations. Israel, the small, the marginalized, the forgotten, sees itself not as a man but as a woman. Similarly, Jerusalem is בת ציון ("daughter Zion"), the woman who has every right to claim a relationship with God and yet too often suffers at the hands of foreign nations who want to take advantage of her vulnerability. Frymer-Kensky's arguments about the biblical writers' attitudes toward women and toward Israel's role in relation to the nations correspond with our reading of the book of Zechariah. While Zechariah presumes a particular social hierarchy in which men

---

11. Frymer-Kensky, *Reading the Women of the Bible*, xvii.

12. Julia M. O'Brien, "Zechariah," in *Women's Bible Commentary*, ed. Carol A. Newsom, Sharon H. Ringe, and Jacqueline E. Lapsley, 3rd ed. (Louisville: Westminster John Knox, 2012), 346.

are political and religious leaders, it also includes women in its vision of the final restoration and makes no ideological claims that distinguish the qualitative role of women in this restoration from the role of men. When it comes to Zechariah's descriptions of Israel, the book's gendered language regarding both Jerusalem and Israel reflects the view that Israel is subordinate in various ways to the foreign nations and yet qualitatively equal, and more than that, Zechariah presumes Israel's election.

Finally, the feminist lens with which this commentary reads the book of Zechariah brings into sharp focus issues and concerns that arise from women's experiences of inequality and oppression. The predominance of martial imagery in Zechariah is disconcerting. That the book consistently speaks of God as יהוה צבאות ("YHWH of armies") is troublesome. It has had the effect of sacralizing war and portraying a life of religious commitment as "warfare." While the martial imagery in Zechariah reflects the historical and political circumstances of the early postexilic period, a feminist hermeneutic finds this usage to be a serious obstacle in appropriating the book today. Second, the book pays almost no attention to women and their place in the Jewish community. No woman is mentioned by name in the book except for the enigmatic woman in chapter 5, and she is named "Wickedness." Any conclusions about the role and status of women in postexilic society based on the book of Zechariah must come by way of inference. Third, the references to Yehud's neighbors in the southern Levant as enemies who must be neutralized may reflect the rivalries in the region. Still, there does not appear to be any desire for reconciliation and positive relations with the nations except in the indeterminate future of the eschaton. Finally, Zechariah limits its treatment of the community's leaders to two males: Joshua, the high priest, and Zerubbabel, the governor. This leaves the women of the postexilic Jewish community in the shadows and thereby legitimates the patriarchal and hierarchical pattern of leadership, leaving contemporary readers to ask about the contributions of women to the Judean restoration.

Fortunately, feminists can resonate with some affirmations that the book of Zechariah makes. Although some see the phrase identifying Jerusalem as בת ציון ("daughter Zion") as based on a daughter's dependence on and subordination to her father and thereby reinforcing and legitimating a patriarchal social order, such usage may also reflect the affective dimension of YHWH with Judah. This metaphor may point to the permanence of the bond that binds YHWH to Judah—that judgment is not God's last word to the people of Judah. Second, Zechariah identifies just intersocietal relations as a key to the Judean restoration, which cannot be successful unless honesty and integrity are features of the community's life. Finally, the book ends with an eschatological vision that is universal in scope. The people whom Yehud counted among its enemies will join in the worship of YHWH. This vision counterbalances the martial coloring of the visions in the book.

Another feature of the author's context is methodology. The historical-critical method guides the exegetical analysis of the book of Zechariah. A careful and disciplined use of this method enables today's reader to become contemporaneous with the people who first heard or read the book of Zechariah by uncovering the experiences of the people and prophet revealed by this book. The object of this study is the *textus receptus* of the book, which has its compositional history, which will be attended to in the commentary itself without the creation of hypothetical texts and the raising of issues that are not central to the goal of the Wisdom Commentary series. There are, of course, limits to what the historical-critical method can accomplish. Still, it is an approach to the Bible that has proven its worth over more than one hundred years. Generations of biblical scholars have employed this method to minimize the possibility of eisegesis and to prepare the ground for the hermeneutical enterprise, which aims to make the biblical text contemporaneous with the reader. As described above, feminist biblical interpretation will guide this commentary's attempt to find meaning for readers today.

Interaction with the biblical text is understandably shaped in part by the interpreter's experience so let me conclude by describing my own "context" as a student of the book of Zechariah. I am a Franciscan friar and a Roman Catholic priest. Most of my academic formation for the ordained ministry took place in an exclusively Catholic and all-male setting. It was not until my last year of preparation for ordination that I had the benefit of studying in an ecumenical and inclusive setting. My graduate education in Old Testament studies took place in a secular, private university where I had the benefit of studying with professors and peers from a variety of religious and nonreligious backgrounds. It was at this time that I came in contact with feminism. All but two years of a thirty-nine-year teaching career took place in schools of theology that were inclusive, ecumenical, and interfaith in orientation with students from a variety of cultural backgrounds. I am in sympathy with the goal of respecting all women's experiences, identities, knowledge, and strengths, and I support efforts to empower women to enjoy their rights as independent human beings. Working on this commentary has been an education not only with regard to the book of Zechariah but also with regard to the efforts of women to achieve the goals that feminism has identified and promotes.

Dramatis Personae

There are several important characters in the book of Zechariah that call for some attention at this point. Although a fuller treatment of each will appear in the commentary proper, what follows highlights some of the central characters in the book.

The Prophet Zechariah

The name Zechariah is a common one in the Bible, borne by thirty-two individuals. The name means "YHWH remembers." It was particularly popular in the postexilic period since it reflects the hope that God will remember the covenant and restore the people's fortunes following the fall of the kingdom of Judah and the Davidic dynasty, the destruction of the Jerusalem temple, and the forced migration of Judah's elite to Babylon. It is the name of the principal character in the book of Zechariah, the eleventh and largest book in the collection of the Twelve (also known as the "Minor Prophets"). The book asserts that it is a collection of messages from God that came to the prophet Zechariah: 1:1, 7 and 7:1, 8. These third-person introductory formulas suggest that they are a product of an editing process.

Almost nothing is known about the historical Zechariah. His father and grandfather are named, but no female relatives or children are mentioned (1:1). According to Nehemiah 12:16, Zechariah was a priest. Ezra 5:1 and 6:14 identify Zechariah as a prophet and a contemporary of the prophet Haggai. Though the dates given in 1:1, 7 lend a veneer of historicity to the accounts of the visions and oracles found in the book of Zechariah, it is important to remember that in the book, Zechariah is a *literary* character rather than a historical figure. When this commentary mentions "Zechariah" or "the prophet," it refers to this literary character.

YHWH

The name of the deity appearing in the book of Zechariah is almost exclusively יהוה, occurring nearly 140 times—fifty-three times as part of the formula יהוה צבאות.[13] The JPS, NRSVue, and NABRE render the former as LORD and the latter as LORD of hosts. Some readers object to this way of rendering the Tetragrammaton since the word "Lord" carries with it sexist and hierarchical connotations in English. Another concern is that the expression "LORD of hosts" is a title that imagines the deity to be commanding heavenly

---

13. In 4:14 and 6:5 the deity is called אדון כל הארץ ("The Lord of all the earth").

and earthly armies. By the time Zechariah was composed, יהוה צבאות was a traditional formula whose martial connections were not necessarily in the forefront of people's consciousness, though unrest caused by armies passing near Yehud could have prompted the use of this traditional title. Still, the rendering of the Tetragrammaton as "Lord" and the use of "Lord of hosts" as a title for the deity perpetuates a male, martial, and hierarchical image of God that is best left to antiquity. This commentary will render יהוה YHWH. This rendering without vowels respects Jewish tradition, which avoids pronouncing the proper name of God.

The book of Zechariah paints contrasting pictures of God. From the outset the book portrays YHWH as a compassionate God desirous of a relationship with the people of Yehud (1:16-17). At the same time, this relationship will be set on a firm footing only through repentance (1:4) and after testing and purification of the people (13:9). Zechariah affirms that judgment was not the last word for Judah. The book reflects the conviction that the social, political, and military upheavals of the period were the harbingers of a new age for the people of Yehud. It provided its first readers with the opportunity to look to the future with confidence and assurance. The people and their leadership, the temple and its priesthood can look forward to a new day since God "will again choose Jerusalem" (2:12). The book presents the nations as obstacles to the restoration of Jerusalem and its people (chapters 9–14) though, in the end, the nations, too, can join in the worship of God in Jerusalem if they do not oppose God's plans for Judah (14:16-19).

The book reflects the unsettled times during which it was produced. Yehud's geographical setting ensured that its people witnessed armies passing back and forth as the Persians sought to extend and consolidate their control of the ancient Near East, its peoples and resources. It is not surprising that God be described as a powerful military leader who subdues those who have been agents of Yehud's misery and who continue to threaten its well-being. God wishes to put an end to the military threats to Yehud (9:8-10). This martial imagery, reassuring to the people of Yehud in the late sixth century BCE, should be appropriated today only with the greatest of circumspection because such imagery can normalize—if not sacralize—violence.

Jerusalem/Zion

Zechariah mentions Jerusalem/Zion almost as many times as it mentions God. Although the book supports and encourages the reconstruction of the temple, it makes few references to the temple (1:16; 4:6-10;

6:9-15; 8:9). This contrasts with the forty-three times Jerusalem and the nine times Zion appear in the book. In virtually every instance, Jerusalem is cast in a positive light. It is the object of God's care. God promises to restore the city, protect it from its enemies, and ensure its peace and prosperity. It is safe to hold that the book of Zechariah is about Jerusalem and its future.

The book of Zechariah personifies Jerusalem/Zion as בת ציון ("daughter Zion," 2:10; 9:9) and as בת ירושלם ("daughter Jerusalem," 9:9).[14] Some interpreters see this personification as reflecting the social and familial system in ancient Israel. Gina Hens-Piazza defines a daughter as "a female lacking jurisdiction over herself."[15] This metaphor, then, supports the social standing of women as subordinate to and dependent on their fathers until their marriage, when they become dependent on their husbands. The characterization of Jerusalem as עיר־האמת ("faithful city," 8:3) may lend some support to this perspective since the characterization suggests that Jerusalem has fulfilled her responsibilities to God. Still, there is an affective dimension to the בת ציון metaphor. God's concern for Jerusalem is like that of a father for the daughter God loves and protects (1:14). Ignoring the affective dimension of the "daughter Jerusalem/Zion" metaphor unnecessarily diminishes its scope. Feminist discourse that focuses largely on issues of power, hierarchically ordered social identity and relationships, runs the risk of failing to appreciate the broader extent of the "daughter Zion/Jerusalem" metaphor.

Community Leaders

A significant challenge for the Jewish community of Yehud was leadership. The Babylonians brought an end to the Judean national state and its ruling dynasty (2 Kgs 25). It was clear that the Persians were not going to restore these either. The primary concern of Yehud's Persian masters was to maximize benefits to the empire by the exploitation of Yehud's economy through taxation. Governors appointed by the Persians and supported by the Persian military ensured Yehud's stability and the efficient collection of taxes. The Jewish community was allowed to shape its own internal affairs freely if it continued to pay the tribute that the Persians required of it. This kept the Persians in firm control

14. In Hebrew, cities have a feminine grammatical gender. In the ancient Near East, it was common to speak of cities as daughters of their patron deity.

15. Gina Hens-Piazza, "Zion's Destiny as Theological Disclosure: Mapping of a Metaphor across Isaiah," *CBQ* 84 (2022): 5.

of Yehud's economic resources.[16] The limited autonomy enjoyed by the Jewish community allowed it to develop its own patterns of leadership. The book of Zechariah is a witness to the community's attempts at providing leadership for itself. Although women did have roles in both official and charismatic leadership in Judah before the exile,[17] the book of Zechariah does not give any woman a role in Yehud's leadership.

With the fall of the Judahite state and the Davidic dynasty, the monarchy was no longer available as a force to unify the community. Still, it is not surprising that the Jewish community looked to Zerubbabel, the Persian-appointed governor of Yehud. The book of Zechariah mentions Zerubbabel by name just four times (4:6-7, 9-10). Although one of these highlights the role he will have in the reconstruction of the temple, this does not imply that Zechariah wishes to portray him as a royal figure. Temple building was a royal prerogative in the ancient Near East. Zerubbabel's association with the building of the temple suggests that he is the enigmatic person identified in the book as "Branch" (3:8; 6:12-13). Despite what some Jews may have hoped, nothing came of Zerubbabel's service as governor after the work on the temple was completed. He goes without any further mention in the biblical record except in the genealogies of Jesus in the New Testament (Matt 1:12-13; Luke 3:27).

The book of Zechariah associates Joshua, the high priest, with Zerubbabel —although not explicitly. It is assumed that the "two anointed ones" of 4:14 were Zerubbabel and Joshua. Without the monarchy, the Jewish community of Yehud came to define itself in terms of the temple and its worship that the priests oversaw. This pattern of self-definition effectively pushed women to the periphery since the priesthood was an exclusively male profession. Although women participated in the worship that took place in the temple, they had no explicit role in the development of temple cult. Yehud's religion as it developed during the two hundred years of Persian rule had a profound and lasting effect on the role and status of women in the Jewish and Christian sects that were the heirs of the Judaism of the postexilic period. Both contemporary

---

16. Berquist, *Judaism in Persia's Shadow*, 134.

17. E.g., the mother of the reigning king of Judah was known as the גבירה (e.g., 2 Kgs 10:13; Jer 13:18), which was a position that carried with it influence and power. Athaliah, the mother of King Ahaziah, was able to assume the throne of Judah and rule as queen for nearly seven years (2 Kgs 11:1-3). The prophet Huldah was asked to authenticate the lawbook found in the temple even though Jeremiah was active at the time (2 Kgs 22:14). Of course, Jeremiah was not held in high esteem by the royal court while Huldah was daughter-in-law of a court official.

Judaism and Christianity are still struggling with issues of the inclusion of women in religious thought and observance. Of course, women have made significant contributions to both Jewish and Christian life. Still, the task of locating women at the center from the periphery is a task that remains to be completed by both communities of faith.

Zechariah does see the renewal of the priesthood in the person of the high priest Joshua as an essential component of Jewish life in Yehud. Still, the book is not an uncritical champion of priestly authority.[18] Chapters 3, 4, and 6 mention Joshua by name, describing his positive contributions in both the religious and civil spheres, but he goes unmentioned after chapter 6. In chapter 7 the book speaks only of priests, who are faulted because of their failures in matters of social justice (vv. 9-10). Priests play no part in chapters 9–14 at all, and the book ends by envisioning the abandonment of the categories of holiness that were central to the privileged position enjoyed by the temple and its priests (14:20-21). Far from promoting priestly privilege, the book shows some concern over priestly hierocracy in Yehud during the early part of the Persian period. Acknowledging this concern is the first step in dealing with the reality of male domination in areas of religious leadership.

The phenomenon of prophecy undergoes a similar development in Zechariah. The book begins by illustrating the significance of the prophetic voice in the Jewish community. The prophet is the recipient of revelation that describes how the renewal of Jewish life is to proceed in Yehud following the return from exile in Babylon. The prophet/visionary assists both Zerubbabel and Joshua as the renewal begins. In chapters 9–14, prophets come under criticism that reaches its highpoint in 13:2-6. The way prophecy is depicted in chapter 13 is the very opposite of its portrayal in chapters 1–6.

The concluding chapter of the book of Zechariah appears to see the future of the Jewish community in Yehud as involving the restoration of the monarchy (9:9-10).[19] Calls for the renewal of the house of David appear in 12:10, 12; 13:1, though chapter 14 speaks of only YHWH as king without any mention of a king from the house of David (vv. 9, 16-17).

---

18. See Mark J. Boda, "Perspectives on Priests in Haggai–Malachi," in *Prayer and Poetry in the Dead Sea Scrolls and Related Literature: Essays in Honor of Eileen Schuller on the Occasion of Her 65th Birthday*, ed. Jeremy S. Penner, Ken M. Penner, and Cecilia Wassen, STJD 98 (Leiden: Brill, 2012), 13–33.

19. Matthew, the most Jewish of the Gospels, cites Zechariah 9:9-10 as fulfilled by the triumphal entry of Jesus into Jerusalem (Matt 21:4). John 12:14-15 also cites Zechariah 9.

The book then offers a realistic assessment on the potential of the Davidic dynasty as facilitating the renewal of Jewish life in Yehud.

Effective leadership was an essential component in the renewal of Jewish life at the beginning of the Persian period in Yehud. While Zerubbabel, Joshua, and the prophet/visionary of the book had their contributions to make, the book of Zechariah does not absolutize any one pattern of leadership. In the end, only YHWH could lead the Jews of Yehud into the future. There is no warrant in Zechariah for making any pattern of leadership in the Jewish or Christian community normative. Control, power, and domination are not goals of religious leadership. Inclusion, solidarity, and community call for bringing people from the periphery into the center. Authentic religious leadership needs to bring people in rather than keep people out.

Feminist Possibilities in Zechariah

A surface reading of the book of Zechariah leaves the impression that there is little in the book that resonates with hopes of women and men who demand that society recognize the dignity, autonomy, and rights of women. The book has a different focus. It aims to provide its readers/ hearers with a view of the Judean restoration that transcends the reconstruction of the Jerusalem temple, development of the community's leadership, or the restoration of the kingdom of Judah and the Davidic dynasty. The book begins with a call for repentance and ends with God's determination to transform not only the Jewish community of Yehud but the nations as well. The inclusive aspect of the book's final vision of the future is the key to its compatibility with a feminist vision of humanity's future: a future that is free of injustice, domination, and prejudice fueled by sexist and stereotypical thinking, a future in which all people can develop their potential in freedom and respect. The prophet spoke to people who were hoping for a better future. The prophet's goal was to fuel that hope. The prophet does not say all that ought to be said. The prophet could have been clearer and less dependent on the phantasmagorical. Still, the rabbis found enough in the book to include it among the Scriptures of the Jewish community. Although the prophet's vision of the Judean restoration was myopic to the extent that it failed to be more concrete and explicit about the role of women in the restoration, there is enough in the book that feminists can embrace. We just need to look a bit harder. The goal of this commentary is to do just that.

Zechariah 1:1-21

Visions of New Possibilities

Zechariah begins with what is likely the work of the editor who was responsible for the inclusion of the book into the book of the Twelve (Minor Prophets). The opening verse of the chapter speaks of the prophet in the third person and is set in a specific moment in the life of the Jewish community of Yehud. The word given to the prophet has a distinct Deuteronomic coloring to it. Again, this is likely the work of the editor who was influenced by the growing importance of the Deuteronomic and Deuteronomistic traditions in the postexilic Jewish community. The prophecy of Zechariah properly begins with the first two visions that the prophet narrates in verses 7-21. The prophet gets to the heart of the matter as he quotes God as saying, "My house shall be built in [Jerusalem]" (v. 16). The theological rationale for the rebuilding of the temple is God's "zeal" for Judah and Jerusalem (Zech 1:14).[1]

The Past Is No Model (1:1-6)

The book of Zechariah begins with an unusually specific date for the beginning of the prophet's activity: October/November 520 BCE.[2] This

1. Erin Villareal, *Jealousy in Context: The Social Implications of Emotions in the Hebrew Bible* (University Park, PA: Eisenbrauns, 2022), 126.
2. Unlike dates given in Zech 1:7 and 7:1, no day is provided. The Syriac version does supply the day ("the first day of the eighth month"). Joyce Baldwin, however,

Zech 1:1-6

¹In the eighth month, in the second year of Darius, the word of the LORD came to the prophet Zechariah son of Berechiah son of Iddo, saying: ²"The LORD was very angry with your ancestors. ³Therefore say to them: Thus says the LORD of hosts: Return to me, says the LORD of hosts, and I will return to you, says the LORD of hosts. ⁴Do not be like your ancestors, to whom the former prophets proclaimed, 'Thus says the LORD of hosts: Return from your evil ways and from your evil deeds.' But they did not hear or heed me, says the LORD. ⁵Your ancestors, where are they? And the prophets, do they live forever? ⁶But my words and my statutes, which I commanded my servants the prophets, did they not overtake your ancestors? So they repented and said, 'The LORD of hosts has dealt with us according to our ways and deeds, just as he planned to do.'"

means that the prophet began to preach two months after Haggai had made his appearance (see Hag 1:1). The biographical data in most other prophetic books provide a more general chronological setting for the prophets' ministries, by naming the kings during whose reign a particular prophet spoke. (For example, see Isa 1:1 and Jer 1:2-3.) The books of Haggai and Zechariah, however, specify the time when these two prophets first spoke to the Jewish community of Yehud. One reason for this specificity may be that editors of these two books wanted to set the activity of both prophets in the time just before the end of the seventy years of divine judgment on Judah, as predicted by Jeremiah (see Zech 1:12; Jer 25:11; and 29:10).

"The word of YHWH came to Zechariah"³ at a time of nationalistic stirrings in Yehud, which was a backwater province of the Persian Empire. The empire was racked by unrest caused by conflicts over succession to the throne following the death of Cambyses in 522 BCE. With the support of the Persian army, Darius I asserted his claim but faced opposition in Babylon and elsewhere. These upheavals led some people to suspect

maintains that the MT reflects the original. The style of the date in the Syriac does not conform to the style of dates given in Haggai and Zechariah. Also, the Syriac often engages in harmonization. See her *Haggai, Zechariah, Malachi: An Introduction and Commentary*, TOTC (Downers Grove, IL: InterVarsity Press, 1972), 87.

3. This phrase points to the hand of the editor who refers to Zechariah in the third person. Elsewhere in the book, the prophet speaks in the first person ("the word of YHWH came to me," 6:9; 7:4; 8:1, 18).

that the Persian sun was setting. Among these were some Jews in Yehud, who were certain that the hour of God's triumph was imminent. That triumph would bring with it the restoration of the Judean state and the Davidic dynasty. As Haggai and Zechariah made their appearance, however, Darius succeeded in consolidating his power. He managed to put down the revolts in the empire (except for Media, which held out until 519 BCE), extinguishing any hope for restoring the former kingdom of Judah.[4] Yehud would remain a small part of the Persian Empire, subject to Persian kings. Hope for the restoration of the kingdom of Judah appeared to be forlorn. It seemed as if God had forgotten Israel (Ps 77:9; Isa 49:14). The book of Zechariah, however, affirms that God had not forgotten but remembered, as the prophet's name asserts.

The name Zechariah ("YHWH has remembered") was apparently a popular one in ancient Israel and Judah. The Hebrew Bible mentions no fewer than thirty individuals with that name.[5] It is a particularly appropriate name for a prophet who tried to persuade the people of Yehud that the serious trouble faced by Darius was a sign of a new move by God that will benefit their community. God will indeed remember the promises made to their ancestors. Believing that political unrest gripping the Persian Empire was the harbinger of God's imminent victory, the prophet urged the Jews still in Babylon to return to Jerusalem (Zech 2:6-7) and to see the rebuilding of the temple to its completion (Zech 6:15).

As is the case with most of the books of the Latter Prophets, the book of Zechariah introduces the prophet with a patronymic. Zechariah is identified by naming his two immediate male ancestors (Zech 1:1).[6] The text does not supply the names of the prophet's female ancestors. Although the book of Genesis identified the mothers of the eponymous ancestors of the Israelite tribes, as a rule the Old Testament does not name the mothers of most important characters in the story of ancient Israel.[7] The books of Kings, however, mention the names of the mothers of most

---

4. Jon L. Berquist, *Judaism in Persia's Shadow: A Social and Historical Approach* (Minneapolis: Fortress, 1995), 53.

5. For a list of individuals named Zechariah, see Stephen R. Miller, "Zechariah," in *Eerdmans Dictionary of the Bible*, ed. David Noel Freedman, Allen C. Myers, and Astrid B. Beck (Grand Rapids: Eerdmans, 2000), 1411–12.

6. Zech 1:1. See Ezra 5:1 and 6:14. These texts do not mention Berechiah but name Iddo as Zechariah's father. Nothing is known about Berechiah, but Neh 12:4 notes that Iddo was the head of a priestly clan among the returnees.

7. For example, David's mother is not named in the Bible though the Talmud identifies her as Nitzevet (B. Bat. 91a).

of Judah's kings, with Ahaz being a notable exception. Some of these women bore the title גְבִירָה[8] and apparently enjoyed a level of influence in the royal court that could not be ignored. Still, except for Athaliah (see 2 Kgs 11), the mothers of reigning kings served the interests of a male-dominated political system. Though Zechariah 1:1 mentions only the prophet's male forebears, this does not imply that prophecy in ancient Israel was confined to men.[9] Still, the Old Testament mentions only five women prophets: Miriam (Exod 15:20), Deborah (Judg 4:4), Huldah (2 Kgs 22:14), Noadiah (Neh 6:14), and Isaiah's wife (Isa 8:3). In none of these instances does the text suggest that women prophets were out of the ordinary. It is likely that as prophetism became professionalized, it became dominated by males as the literary record suggests.[10] Though Zechariah belonged to a priestly family (Neh 12:4, 16) and is one of the prophets who arose from a priestly background, neither the prophet himself nor the editor of the book mentions this explicitly.[11] This suggests that Zechariah's authority derived, not from his priestly lineage, but from his mission to call for repentance.[12] The statement that "the

8. The NRSVue translates this title as "queen mother," though this is inaccurate. Neither Kings nor Chronicles refers to either the wife or mother of any Israelite or Judahite king as "queen." Also, the semantic field of the word גבירה does not include motherhood. Ralph Klein suggests "great lady" as a preferable alternative. See his *2 Chronicles*, Hermeneia (Minneapolis: Fortress, 2012), 231. The role of these women has been the subject of recent study. See Susan Ackerman, "The Queen Mother and the Cult in Ancient Israel," *JBL* 112 (1993): 385–401; Niels-Erik A. Andreasen, "The Role of the Queen Mother in Israelite Society," *CBQ* 45 (1983): 179–94; Zafrira Ben-Barak, "The Status and Right of the *GĚBÎRÂ*," *JBL* 110 (1991): 23–34; Nancy R. Bowen, "The Quest for the Historical *Gĕbîrâ*," *CBQ* 63 (2001): 597–618; Marcin Sosik, "*GEBIRA* at the Judaean Court," *Scripta Judaica Cracoviensia* 7 (2009): 7–13. For a monograph on this topic, see Ginny Brewer-Boydston, *Good Queen Mothers, Bad Queen Mothers: The Theological Presentation of the Queen Mother in 1 and 2 Kings*, CBQMS 54 (Washington, DC: CBA, 2016).

9. See Wilda C. Gafney, *Daughters of Miriam: Women Prophets in Ancient Israel* (Minneapolis: Fortress, 2008).

10. Jonathan Stökl and Corrine L. Carvalho, eds., "Introduction," in *Prophets Male and Female: Gender and Prophecy in the Hebrew Bible, the Eastern Mediterranean, and the Ancient Near East*, AIL 15 (Atlanta: SBL, 2013), 7–8.

11. Other prophets from a priestly family include Moses (Deut 34:10-12), Samuel (1 Sam 1–3), Jeremiah (Jer 1:1), Ezekiel (1:3), and Zechariah, son of Jehoiada (2 Chr 24:20).

12. From a purely syntactical point of view, הנביא ("the prophet," v. 1) can stand in apposition to either Zechariah or Iddo. Given the context, it is more likely that הנביא is in apposition to Zechariah. The Chronicler does mention a prophet named Iddo and credits him with writing histories of Jeroboam and Abijah (2 Chr 9:29; 13:2), but the Iddo mentioned in Chronicles was not Zechariah's grandfather.

word of YHWH came to the prophet" (v. 1) and the messenger formula, "thus says YHWH of armies"[13] (v. 3), underscore the divine origin that Zechariah claims for the message he conveys to the people of Yehud.

Three phrases dominate the unit that begins Zechariah's prophecy. The first is the ancient title of Israel's God, יהוה צבאות ("YHWH of armies"). This title appears in four of the nine references to God in the book's opening lines (vv. 3a, 3b, 3c, 4). It also appears an astonishing fifty-three times in the book (forty-four times in chapters 1–8; nine times in chapters 9–14). This expression acts as a type of refrain serving to authenticate the prophet's words from the start. Also, use of this title connects Zechariah with other prophetic books, such as Isaiah 1–39, where the title appears fifty-six times; Jeremiah, who uses it eighty-two times; and Haggai, who uses it fourteen times. Although the title was first understood in military terms, e.g., 1 Samuel 15:2, it came to be associated with the Zion tradition, which portrays יהוה צבאות as the great king (Isa 6:3, 5) who dwells on Mount Zion (Isa 8:18). It is this latter association that is most relevant to the use of this title in Zechariah 1:1-6, where the prophet recounts visions of the restoration of Jerusalem and encourages the people of Yehud to have confidence in that restoration. It is ironic that Zechariah was using this title, with its martial and royal connotations, when Yehud was militarily and politically impotent.

Like all metaphors, יהוה צבאות is closely bound to its cultural and historical context, which makes the use of that metaphor problematic today. The martial imagery of this title is incompatible with a vision of reconciliation, inclusion, and peace. Imagining God at the head of cosmic and earthly military forces has led to a type of militant theism that is particularly dangerous today. That is the reason Paul VI cried out, "No more war! War never again!" in a speech to the United Nations General Assembly on October 4, 1965. October 4 is the feast day of St. Francis of Assisi, who brought an end to the wars between the Italian city-states by forbidding members of the Franciscan Third Order from bearing arms. The women's movement in the United States has been intertwined with the peace movement. Jane Addams and Dorothy Day exemplify the strategy of melding social reform and women's rights with the peace

---

13. The NRSVue and the NABRE translate יהוה צבאות as "LORD of hosts," which is the common English rendering of this title. Unfortunately, the word "hosts" can obscure the meaning of צבאות for most English speakers today. Carol L. Meyers and Eric M. Meyers use the literal "armies" for צבאות. See their *Haggai, Zechariah 1–8: A New Translation with Introduction and Commentary*, AB 25B (Garden City, NY: Doubleday, 1987), 90. The word "armies" makes clear the martial connotation of this title.

movement. By the 1970s, women became a principal constituency of the peace movement in the United States.

The image of God leading armies that will destroy God's enemies may be distasteful to some modern readers, but to the people of ancient Israel יהוה צבאות was a familiar title for God. The prophet, no doubt, used it to arouse hope for Yehud's future in view of Persian hegemony. In 519 BCE, Darius initiated steps to reintegrate Egypt into the Persian Empire. The Persian army—then the largest in the world—likely passed near Yehud on its way to Egypt. Undoubtedly this aroused great fear among the Jews.[14] Jerusalem was particularly vulnerable since its walls had not yet been re-built following their dismantling by the Babylonians in 587. The prophet's use of the ancient title was designed to allay anxiety as it affirmed that God was sovereign over the world and would protect Jerusalem and its people. At the same time, its use could hardly foment rebellion by the Jews of Yehud against imperial rule, given Yehud's military impotence; rather, the use of this title served to assure the Jews that they had a future as a people.

Though the title יהוה צבאות does not explicitly portray God as male, the strong implication is there. Imagining the deity with masculine meta-phors has led to the erroneous and unfortunate conclusion that men reflect the divine image more closely than women despite the affirma-tion in Genesis 1:27 that both male and female are made in the image of God. Still, ignoring this metaphor and its implications is unrealistic—it is ubiquitous in the Hebrew Bible. Teachers and preachers should be careful to set it in its cultural and historical context.

The second phrase is the messenger formula, כה אמר יהוה צבאות ("thus says YHWH of hosts," in 1:3, 4), found only in Jeremiah and the last three books in the collection of the Twelve (Haggai, Zechariah, and Malachi). In Zechariah, the phrase occurs seventeen times (1:3, 4, 14, 17; 2:12; 3:7; 6:12; 7:9; 8:2, 4, 6, 7, 9, 14, 19, 20, 23); only in Jeremiah does it occur more frequently. Mark Boda asserts that this phrase is the result of editorial work that attempted to associate Haggai, Zechariah, and Malachi with the earlier prophecy of Jeremiah.[15] The book of the Twelve presents Haggai, Zechariah, and Malachi as prophets who had a role in their day comparable to that of Jeremiah in his. Jeremiah announced a seventy-year exile as God's judgment on unfaithful Judah (Jer 25:11-12; 29:10). Haggai, Zechariah, and Malachi spoke as the seventy-year period of

---

14. Berquist, *Judaism in Persia's Shadow*, 61–62.

15. Mark J. Boda, *The Book of Zechariah*, NICOT (Grand Rapids: Eerdmans, 2016), 75.

judgment was ending. These prophets announced the restoration of Judah and Jerusalem.

The third significant phrase that appears four times in Zechariah 1:1-6 is "your ancestors" (אבותיכם [literally "your fathers"], in vv. 2, 4, 5, 6). The prophet states that forebears of the people to whom he spoke ignored "the former prophets," who had called them to repent from their "evil ways . . . and deeds" (v. 4). The result of their failure was the destruction of Judah's towns including Jerusalem with its temple, the end of the state and dynasty, and the forced migration of its elite classes to Babylon. Faced with that divine judgment, the ancestors finally repented (v. 6). Zechariah urges the Jewish community of Yehud to avoid repeating the failure of previous generations. Thus, in Zechariah 1:2-6, אבותיכם asserts that former generations of Judeans incurred God's anger and judgment because they failed to heed prophetic warnings. Although the prophet may have used אבותיכם to indict the male religious and political leadership of Judah, it should not be seen solely in exclusivist terms. As the NRSVue's gender-inclusive rendering "your ancestors" suggests, both the men and women of Yehud probably came under the prophet's criticism. While Judah's male leadership bore heavy responsibility for the fall of the national state, the entire community, women included, were expected to repent. Zechariah calls the men *and* women of his generation to distance themselves from the mistakes of their forebears that led to the fall of Judah and Jerusalem.

In speaking of the response of Yehud's forbears to earlier prophets, Zechariah uses the phrase הנביאים הראשנים ("the former prophets," v. 4), an expression that appears in no other book of the Hebrew Bible. The prophet regards those whose activity preceded his as having conveyed a message from God like his own. Indeed, some earlier prophets explicitly include both men *and* women in their oracles of judgment. For example, Jeremiah 2:20-37 weaves together indictments of women and men in a covenant lawsuit; Jeremiah 7:18 portrays idolatrous practices in Judah as a family affair:

> The children gather wood, the fathers kindle fire, and the women knead dough, to make cakes for the queen of heaven, and they pour out drink offerings to other gods, to provoke me to anger.

Similarly, in one of Ezekiel's visions, the prophet sees idolatry perpetrated by both men and women in the temple (Ezek 8:7-18). In fact, Ezekiel 13:17-23 singles out women who practiced divination for harsh judgment.

Verbs derived from שוב ("repent") appear in verses 3, 4, and 6. The prophet reminds the people of Yehud that "the former prophets" called their ancestors to repent, but they failed to respond. As a consequence, they experience judgment for disobeying the "words and . . . statutes" that God had commanded through the prophets (v. 6; see also 2 Kgs 17:13). Verse 6 asserts that Yehud's forebears (likely those in exile) finally did recognize their failures and did repent. The Deuteronomic themes of repentance and obedience in Zechariah's opening verses suggest that those who preserved and handed on the prophet's words were convinced that obedience to the commands in the Torah was the key to Yehud's future. Still, the obedience that the prophet calls for does not *lead* to God's return to Zion, for God already has returned; rather, repentance and obedience are appropriate *responses* to God's return to Zion.[16] This notion of God's return to Jerusalem frames chapters 1–8:

שבתי לירושלם   I have returned to Jerusalem (1:16)

שבתי אל ציון   I will return to Zion (8:3)

The active presence of God in the midst of Jerusalem ensures that the rebuilding project will be successful. God's presence among the people will give success to their efforts.

While Haggai advises the people of Yehud that their prosperity was linked to the rebuilding of the temple and restoration of sacrificial worship there (Hag 1:5-11), Zechariah focuses his attention on a more fundamental issue: the foundation of the people's life with God. For this prophet, obedience to God's "words and . . . statutes" (v. 6) is the key to an authentic relationship with God.[17] For Zechariah, then, the people's future was in the hands of the people themselves (v. 3), not in the hands of the priests who controlled the symbols of religion, and certainly not in the hands of either Persian or Jewish civil authorities. All the people of Yehud—including those without access to religious, political, and economic power—were morally responsible for Yehud's fate through their observance of the Torah.

16. This motif is probably derived from Ezekiel, which speaks of the departure of God's glory from the temple (10:1-22 and 11:22-25). That glory was to return to the restored temple (43:2-5; 44:4). In Zechariah 1:16 and 8:3 God announces that return.

17. The term "words and statutes" in v. 6 may refer to a collection of texts that eventually became codified in the Torah. Such codification was encouraged by the Persian authorities at the time Zechariah was active.

Zechariah presents a "democratization"—not of political and religious leadership, but of collective moral responsibility. When Zechariah calls attention to God's displeasure with Judah's forbears, he considers not only the failures of Judah's political leadership, which was in the hands of men, but also the failure of the entire community as a whole. Although effective leadership is a practical necessity, the prophet viewed the people's compliance with God's "words and . . . statutes" (v. 6) as much more decisive in shaping Yehud's future. It was God's return to Jerusalem (Zech 1:16 and 8:3) that gave the prophet confidence that Yehud's future could be different from its past because that future, in the end, was based on God's benevolence rather than on human potential. God's return to Zion called for a fundamental reorientation on the part of the people of Yehud, and the prophet admonished the people of Yehud to return to their God.

Conclusion

Zechariah spoke when events in the Persian Empire suggested the possibility of a positive shift in Yehud's political fortunes. The book begins with the prophet calling the people of Yehud to repent—a call that transcends class and gender. Speaking in God's name, the prophet calls all the people of Yehud—women and men—to return to God. This is the surest path to restoration (v. 3). Zechariah does not challenge Yehud's social order; the leadership of the community will remain in the hands of men. Still, all the people of Yehud are called to repentance, called to respond to prophetic preaching in a way that fundamentally differs from the response of their forbears. The prophet assures the people of Yehud that repentance and obedience will end an era of alienation from God, political repression, and economic challenges.

The Vision Accounts in Zechariah 1:7–6:15: An Overview

In Zechariah 1:7–6:15 the prophet recounts visions that he believed were divine communications that were to encourage the people of Yehud to have hope for the future because YHWH has "returned to Jerusalem with compassion" (1:16). What can readers today expect from these vision reports, and what strategies can help readers understand these perplexing texts? Are these reports autobiographical accounts of actual experiences in the prophet's life? Or are they highly stylized literary compositions that serve a theological or political purpose? Are the experiences of women in Persian-period Yehud reflected in these texts or are their experiences ignored? Do those visions signal an expectation of the end of the age or perspectives on life in this age? This overview offers context for readers today to explore these perplexing phantasmagorical biblical texts.

The Hebrew Scriptures reflect the belief that visions and dreams were authentic means of divine/human communication. For example, in Jacob's dream at Bethel, God stood beside him, repeating the promise of the land that his descendants were to inherit (Gen 28:12). Joseph's dreams were portents of his future status (Gen 37:5-8). Isaiah 6:1-13 and Ezekiel 1:4–3:17 portray visions as transformative, mystical experiences that take place as these prophets begin their activity. While prophets' visions often legitimate their words and actions, Deuteronomy 13:1-4 is wary of visionaries and dreamers and regards them as potential threats to the loyalty that Israel owes to God. Jeremiah 23:28 suggests that true revelation comes only from hearing God's word. Still, accounts of visionary experiences are cast mostly in a positive light throughout the Scriptures, e.g., Exodus 24:9-11; 1 Kings 22:19-23; Amos 7:1-3; and Daniel 7–8.

Accounts of dreams and visions are also common in early Jewish literature, especially in apocalyptic texts such as the book of Enoch.[18] Accounts of visions and dreams also appear in the New Testament. The gospels contain several accounts of revelatory dreams and visions, e.g., Luke 1:20; 2:13; John 1:12; Matthew 27:19; Luke 24:23, though most vision accounts in the New Testament are found in Acts and Revelation.[19] Visions of angels and other heavenly beings are also common in Talmudic and Midrashic literature.[20] In the West's medieval period, women visionaries such as Saint Catherine of Siena and Julian of Norwich played a significant role in ecclesiastical life. Similarly, any history of the Reformation needs to attend to the role of women visionaries in the development of Protestantism.[21] Spectral evidence was used to convict several women

---

18. For example, see Enoch 83–90.

19. Acts 9:10, 12; 10:3, 17, 19; 11:5; 12:9; 16:9-10; 18:9; 26:19. The book of Revelation characterizes itself as a vision that John saw, the meaning of which was explained to him by an angel (Rev 1:1).

20. Michael D. Swartz, "Jewish Visionary Tradition in Rabbinic Literature," in *The Cambridge Companion to the Talmud and Rabbinic Literature*, ed. Charlotte Elisheva Fonrobert and Martin S. Jaffee, Cambridge Companions to Religion (Cambridge: Cambridge University Press, 2007), 198–221.

21. Kirsi Stjerna, *Women and the Reformation* (Malden, MA: Blackwell, 2009), 2.

of witchcraft during the seventeenth-century Salem witch trials.[22] Such evidence was allowed by male judges, but the witnesses giving such evidence were most often women. Accounts of women visionaries have had a profound influence on popular piety in the Catholic Church. The prevalence of women as visionaries, especially in the medieval and modern periods, suggests that relating visionary experience provided opportunities for women to speak and be heard at times when religious authority in Catholicism was otherwise firmly in the hands of a male hierarchy. That some of these women have been declared saints is an indication of the significant influence these women visionaries have had in shaping Catholicism on a popular level. At the same time, the required approbation of women's visionary experiences by male clergy has been the hierarchy's way of controlling women visionaries' influence on the spiritual lives of Catholics.

Although dreams and visions have played a significant role in accounts of religious experience throughout the history of Judaism and Christianity, still the tendency of scholars in assessing dream/vision accounts in the Bible has been to regard them merely as literary creations or hallucinations. Using altered/alternate states of consciousness studies, John Pilch argues that scholars who regard dream/vision accounts in the Bible as literary fictions are imposing modern Western cultural assumptions on texts from the ancient Mediterranean world.[23] Pilch's work is a reminder that it is a serious mistake to divorce a biblical text from its historical and cultural contexts. Still, Pilch can only say that people from cultures in which dreams and visions are a normal form of divine-human communication *believed* that their dreams and visions were messages from God. It is quite another matter to hold that the deity was responsible for inducing the dreams of the dreamer or the visions of

---

22. Spectral evidence refers to a witness testimony that the accused person's spirit or spectral shape appeared to him or her in a dream at the time the accused person's physical body was at another location. Such evidence was accepted in the courts during the Salem witch trials on the basis that the devil and his minions were powerful enough to send their spirits, or specters, to pure, religious people to lead them into sin (https://definitions.uslegal.com/s/spectral-evidence). For a discussion of spectral evidence and its use during the Salem witch trials, see Sarah Kreutter, "The Devil's Specter: Spectral Evidence and the Salem Witchcraft Crisis," *The Spectrum: A Scholars Day Journal* 2 (2012): 1–26. Available at https://digitalcommons.brockport.edu/spectrum/vol2/iss1/8.

23. John J. Pilch, *Flights of the Soul: Visions, Heavenly Journeys, and Peak Experiences in the Biblical World* (Grand Rapids: Eerdmans, 2011).

the visionary. It should not be surprising that people from cultures that regard dreams and visions as normal vehicles for divine communication have such experiences.

It is unlikely, then, that the dream/vision accounts in Zechariah 1:7–6:15 were just literary creations created to make a theological point. The prophet believed that his experiences were messages from God about the imminent restoration of the fortunes of the Jewish people after a difficult period in the life of their community. The accounts of the prophet's visions have all the earmarks of the type of confused, incoherent, and puzzling dreams that reflect the common human experience of dreaming. The precise significance of the vision accounts remains obscure to readers today though their theological tendency is clear—at least in a general way.

One can assume that the visions in Zechariah were not considered extraordinary in their cultural and religious contexts, though they are among the most puzzling, enigmatic texts in the Bible. Still, at their core, these visions affirm Zechariah's belief that God had once again chosen to dwell in Jerusalem. The events of 587 BCE—the destruction of the temple, the scattering of its priesthood, the end of the kingdom of Judah and its ruling dynasty, and the forced migration of some of its citizenry—had left the people of Judah asking questions such as, "Have you not rejected us, O God?" (Ps 60:10). Then the fall of Babylon to Cyrus the Great in 539 BCE opened new possibilities for the Jewish people since the Persian king encouraged the Judeans in Babylon to return to Jerusalem and build a new temple for their God (2 Chr 36:22-23; Ezra 1:2-4).

Zechariah, of course, was not the only voice who spoke about these new possibilities. The unnamed prophet whose words are found in Isaiah 40–55 envisioned a grand restoration of Judah and Jerusalem that would lead the nations to join Israel in serving God. The book of Ezekiel ends with a vision of Israel reconstituted as a worshiping community. Like Isaiah 40–55, the horizon of Zechariah's visions is not limited to Yehud but encompasses "all the earth." The phrase כל־הארץ ("all the earth") occurs in six of Zechariah's eight visions (1:11; 4:10, 14; 5:3, 6; 6:5). In contrast to Ezekiel 43:1-12, Zechariah's expansive conception of divine activity and presence is not limited to the temple but rather extends from Jerusalem to "the whole earth" (Zech 6:5; cf. 2:10-11).

Although Zechariah's visions do not support a specific program of restoration, they do assume that the control of Yehud's political and religious institutions will remain in the hands of men. Zechariah does not challenge the assumption of male leadership for Yehud; therefore, many women today may see the visions in Zechariah 3–4 as providing another brick in the wall that excludes women from leadership opportunities in communities of faith and in broader society. Joshua, the high priest (Zech 3:1), is the subject of Zechariah's fourth vision, and Zerubbabel, whom Haggai identifies as "governor of Judah" (Hag 1:1), is the subject of the fifth (Zech 4:6). The prophet has visions authorizing those two men—symbolized as "two olive trees," "the two golden pipes," and "the two anointed ones" (Zech 4:3, 12, 14)—to oversee reconstruction of Jerusalem, resumption of worship in its temple, and restoration of Yehud as a just society.

Several scholars have claimed that the vision accounts as a literary unit have a concentric design or chiastic structure.[24] Such an analysis usually locates chapter 4 at the center of the vision reports. This chapter's central position in the purported chiasm supposedly highlights Zechariah's views regarding leadership of the Jewish community. Chiastic structures are often "in the eyes of the beholder." Not too much should be made of the place of chapter 4 in the accounts of the prophet's visions since the prophet does not dwell on Zerubbabel or Joshua beyond chapters 3 and 4 except for a single reference to Joshua in 6:11.[25] The remaining visions focus on other aspects of God's actions that will lead to a reversal of fortune for the people of Yehud. The issue of the leadership of the community is a secondary and limited concern. The principal affirmation of the vision accounts is that YHWH is returning to Jerusalem to effect the restoration of the Jewish community in its homeland.

In contrast to visions in which the two primary male leaders are positively portrayed, the depiction of female figures in Zechariah's visions is equivocal. For example, Zechariah 2:10 speaks of Zion as God's daughter. Such familial imagery indicates an affective dimension in the relationship between the people of Jerusalem and their God. At the same time, the prophet's repeated use of יהוה צבאות as a title for God evokes a martial image of the deity that diminishes the familial sense expressed by בת ציון

---

24. David A. Dorsey, *The Literary Structure of the Old Testament: A Commentary on Genesis–Malachi* (Grand Rapids: Baker, 1999), 318–19; Baruch Halpern, "The Ritual Background of Zechariah's Temple Song," *CBQ* 40 (1978): 167–90; Meyers and Meyers, *Haggai, Zechariah 1–8*, xliv–lv; Susan Niditch, *The Symbolic Vision in Biblical Tradition*, HSM 30 (Chico, CA: Scholars Press, 1983), 160, though Niditch sees only the first (1:1-7), middle (Zech 4), and final (6:1-8) visions comprising the concentric formation.

25. Zechariah 6:12 mentions "Branch" who is responsible for building the temple. This may be a veiled reference to Zerubbabel.

("daughter Zion").[26] The most striking female character in Zechariah's visions is a woman named "Wickedness," who appears in the prophet's seventh vision (Zech 5:5-11). Reading these vision accounts with a feminist lens can result in theological whiplash as one shifts from positive to negative images of women.

What do the accounts of Zechariah's visions offer to a feminist reader today? Ingrid E. Lilly asserts that the prophet's visions for Judahite society are predominantly male in their orientation. At the same time, she sees the book of Zechariah as primarily about "post-conflict rebuilding." Lilly argues that "reconciliation rather than male leadership is at the heart of the prophet's vision for a restored Jewish community."[27] Lilly suggests that Zechariah offers insight into how different groups of people experience and recover from conflict, particularly when inequality mars the process. With the experience of postapartheid South Africa in mind, she insists that the role of leadership in this process is to create a place where reconciliation and peacebuilding in the community can begin. Lilly notes that the notion of leadership found in Zechariah's vision makes that possible for the people of Yehud. Thus, the visions are more about rebuilding the Jewish community than about male leadership. The visions provide theological support for the rebuilding of Jewish society into a community of justice and equity.

The vision accounts, then, speak to a community that is attempting to reconstitute itself and its religious world, which were profoundly affected by the fall of the two Israelite kingdoms. The enigmatic character of these visions allows the prophet to affirm the resumption of God's interaction with the people of Yehud without having to offer a step-by-step program for the restoration. To begin the process of restoration the vision accounts assert that God used gentile nations to confront Israel and Judah with the consequences of their infidelity, though the nations went too far (Zech 1:15). The prophet's focus on the nations served to broaden the religious horizons of the Jewish community, affirming that God controlled the

26. Michael H. Floyd, "Welcome Back, Daughter Zion!," *CBQ* 70 (2008): 484–504; and the essays in *Daughter Zion: Her Portrait, Her Response*, ed. Mark J. Boda, Carol J. Dempsey, and LeAnn Snow Flesher, AIL 13 (Atlanta: SBL, 2012).

27. Ingrid E. Lilly, "Zechariah's Gendered Visions: A Feminist Biblical Theology of Reconciliation," in *After Exegesis: Feminist Biblical Theology; Essays in Honor of Carol A. Newsom*, ed. Patricia K. Tull and Jacqueline E. Lapsley (Waco, TX: Baylor University Press, 2015), 201.

destiny of all nations, and that the presence of God is not limited to the temple. The covenantal relationship between the people of Yehud and their God is not dependent on the existence of an independent, national state with a national cult overseen by a king and priests. Zechariah's visions reveal the restoration of the Jewish community as a community of justice and equity, a community committed to serving the God of Israel alone. The community's leaders are to facilitate this restoration. They are to be servants of the community, ensuring its welfare.

What, then, did the accounts of Zechariah's visions offer to those who first heard or read these vision accounts? First, they offered assurance of God's commitment to the future of the Jewish people. In concrete terms, the visions affirmed that God will protect the people of Yehud and Jerusalem from threats by foreign oppressors. Second, they promised the reconstitution of the political and religious life of the Jewish community. They asserted that God would ensure that the people and the land would be purged of idolatry. The response that the book called for from the people was repentance and commitment to God. The visions were vague about the precise contours of Yehud's religious and political life, to be sure. Still, they provided some measure of encouragement to the Jewish community still reeling from the effects of the fall of the kingdom of Judah, the destruction of the temple, and the forced migration of the kingdom's elite class. The prophet's visions assured the people of Yehud that they had a future. The horizon of the prophet's visions was not some far-off, distant time but the immediate future; the visions were about what God was doing to restore the fortunes of God's people and how they were called to respond.

The prophet's vision accounts are replete with fantastic imagery and striking symbolism. In the prophetic literature of the Hebrew Bible, visions are surprisingly rare, but they became a staple in apocalypses, leading some to characterize the book of Zechariah as an apocalypse or as "protoapocalyptic."[28] The vision reports of Zechariah 1:7–6:15, however, do not reflect an apocalyptic worldview, nor are they expressions

---

28. Some interpreters understand the visions of 1:7–6:15 as apocalyptic in form and ideology. Two of the more important of these are Hartmut Gese, "Anfang und Ende der Apokalyptik, dargestellt am Sacharjabuch," *ZThK* 70 (1973): 20–49, and Stephen L. Cook, *Prophecy & Apocalypticism: The Postexilic Social Setting* (Minneapolis: Fortress, 1995). A strong dissent has been made by Mark J. Boda, *The Book of Zechariah*, 100–102. Boda even cautions against using the term "protoapocalyptic" to describe the vision accounts since that term suggests an eschatological horizon for the visions.

of the apocalyptic genre, though they share some of the characteristics of this genre with genuine apocalyptic texts, such as Daniel 7–12 and the book of Revelation.[29] One such element is a heavenly figure guiding the visionary through an otherworldly kind of experience. Still, an apocalyptic worldview sets the destruction of evil and the triumph of good in the world to come or in an indeterminate future. In contrast, the horizon of Zechariah 1–8 differs markedly from that of apocalyptic; the prophet asserts that the transformation of Yehud's political and religious destiny will take place in the present age.

The goal of Zechariah's vision reports was to convince the people of Yehud that God was active for their good. The prophet was addressing people at a time when Yehud had been going nowhere. Its economy was stagnant, constrained by the taxes that the Persians imposed. Its political and military power was nonexistent. Work on the temple had stopped. The prophet was certain that with the exiles returning from Babylon, worship in the temple of Jerusalem would resume and, to some degree, priestly institutions would be reconstituted. The prophet's visions, then, describe *movement*—of horses and chariots, of a flying scroll and flying basket. The emphasis on movement in Zechariah's visions aimed to engage the people in a process of change and restoration that would reinvigorate the Jewish community to take charge of its future. Fantastic images excite people, and that is precisely what the people of Yehud needed. Certainly, the prophet's reports about what he had seen led people to wonder what these visions could mean and to think about their community's future. The prophet's visions stimulated hope for the Jewish community.

Conclusion

Fantasy has become a staple of popular American culture. The *Harry Potter* books, the *Star Wars* films, the *Game of Thrones* television series, and numerous electronic games have not slaked people's thirst for fantasy. It may be that Zechariah's vision reports resonate with a wider audience today. These visions are expressions of the prophet's claim that God is active for the good of God's people in the present world—that one does not have to wait patiently for the triumph of justice in some indeterminate future. The prophet encourages those who read and hear his words

---

29. For a definition of the apocalyptic genre, see John J. Collins, ed., *Apocalypse: The Morphology of a Genre*, SemeiaSt 14 (Missoula, MT: Scholars Press, 1979), 9.

to discern the presence and power of God in the present. He insists that divine judgment is not God's last word to God's people and that reconciliation and restoration are real and have already begun. God's people should respond with repentance and obedience.

The varied and sometimes enigmatic images in Zechariah's vision accounts engage the reader, puzzle the reader, infuriate the reader, challenge the reader, console the reader—both in ancient times and today. What they reveal is a God and a prophet committed to transforming the lives and fortunes of the people of Judah and Jerusalem in the late sixth century BCE. Both Jewish and Christian communities of faith find in these accounts a vision of God who is committed to the lives and fortunes of believers today living in a world of great complexity.

Visons 1 and 2: Patrolling Horses and Scattering Horns (1:7-21)

Zechariah's first vision (1:7-17) provides a theological foundation for the rest of the book. Riders on horseback announce that Jerusalem's long hard winter is about to end. God is returning to Jerusalem and the temple will be rebuilt. The political and economic situation of Yehud may not be reversed, but the prophet provides assurance that judgment is not God's last word to Judah and Jerusalem. In Zechariah 1:18-21 [2:1-4][30] the prophet envisions the destruction of the four nations, symbolized as bull's horns, as God's punishment for their "scattering" of the people of Israel and Judah. An interpreting angel plays an important role in both visions, explaining the images and instructing the prophet about God's message to the people of Yehud.

The First Vision: Patrolling Horses (1:7-17)

Verse 7 provides a specific date for the first of the prophet's visions: February 15, 519 BCE. The space between this date and the one given in 7:1 (December 7, 518 BCE) suggests that the visions did not all take place in one night but over almost a two-year period. Zechariah was the first biblical writer to use the Babylonian proper name for the month (in this case, שבט, "Shebat") rather than simply an ordinal number to designate the

---

30. When the versification in the NRSVue differs from that in the BHS, the NRSVue citation will be followed by the BHS citation in brackets.

Zech 1:7-17

⁷On the twenty-fourth day of the eleventh month, the month of Shebat, in the second year of Darius, the word of the LORD came to the prophet Zechariah son of Berechiah son of Iddo: ⁸In the night I saw a man mounted on a red horse! He was standing among the myrtle trees in the shadows, and behind him were red, sorrel, and white horses. ⁹Then I said, "What are these, my lord?" The angel who spoke with me said to me, "I will show you what they are." ¹⁰So the man who was standing among the myrtle trees answered, "They are those whom the LORD has sent to patrol the earth." ¹¹Then they spoke to the angel of the LORD who was standing among the myrtle trees, "We have patrolled the earth, and the whole earth remains at peace." ¹²Then the angel of the LORD said, "O LORD of hosts, how long will you withhold mercy from Jerusalem and the cities of Judah, with which you have been angry these seventy years?" ¹³Then the LORD replied with gracious and comforting

month in question.[31] Whereas the opening lines of some earlier prophetic books situated the prophets historically with reference to Judahite kings (e.g., Isa 1:1 and Jer 1:2), Zechariah marks the beginning of the prophet's activity with a reference to the Persian king Darius. Even "the word of YHWH" is announced in relation to Persian hegemony (v. 7), a subtle but clear reminder of Yehud's political standing as subject to Persian rule.

Shebat (January/February) lies in the middle of the rainy season, when the weather in Jerusalem is usually cold, wet, and unpleasant. The political and economic climate in Jerusalem in Shebat 519 BCE was no better than the weather. Yehud had been reduced to only a fraction of the territory of the former kingdom of Judah.[32] Yehud was not even a vassal state but simply a small portion of a Persian satrapy. Lacking political power, Yehud could not control its own economy and was burdened by taxes imposed by the Persians. From a political and economic perspective, Yehud was in the middle of a long, hard winter, and, for the people of Yehud, Shebat 519 BCE meant more than bad weather.

31. David L. Petersen, *Haggai and Zechariah 1–8: A Commentary*, OTL (Philadelphia: Westminster, 1984), 138.

32. In the eighth century BCE, the kingdom of Judah controlled an area that extended from Geba in the north to Beersheba in the south (about seventy-five miles), and from the Dead Sea in the east to the Shephelah in the west (about thirty-four miles). Yehud's territory went only from Bethel in the north to Hebron in the south—only thirty-five miles. Its east-west territory also ran from the Dead Sea to the Shephelah.

words to the angel who spoke with me. [14]So the angel who spoke with me said to me, "Proclaim this message: Thus says the LORD of hosts: I am very zealous for Jerusalem and for Zion, [15]and I am extremely angry with the nations that are at ease, for while I was only a little angry, they made the disaster worse. [16]Therefore, thus says the LORD: I have returned to Jerusalem with compassion; my house shall be built in it, says the LORD of hosts, and a measuring line shall be stretched out over Jerusalem. [17]Proclaim further: Thus says the LORD of hosts: My cities shall again overflow with prosperity; the LORD will again comfort Zion and again choose Jerusalem."

Taxation in Yehud

Speaking in the name of God, the prophet promised that the cities of Yehud would enjoy a time of prosperity upon God's return to Jerusalem. One obstacle to the promised prosperity was the burdensome taxes imposed by the imperial Persian government. The Persians respected the religious and social customs of the Jewish people, but they expected taxes to be paid. Among the reasons for the imperial encouragement and support for the rebuilding of the temple was that the temple was to be the agency for the collection of taxes. To fulfill this agency the temple itself and its personnel had to be stable economically. There were problems with ensuring that the temple would be properly funded (see, e.g., Mal 3:8-12; Neh 10; 13:10-13).

Unlike temples in Mesopotamia and Egypt, the Jerusalem temple did not hold land from which to derive an income.[33] The temple and its personnel were funded by the first fruits of the land, the firstlings of herd and flock, and the tithes owed to God, the owner of the land (Lev 25:23; Zech 1:17). These contributions were used to provide food for the priests, Levites, and their families. Any surplus was sold or traded for goods needed by the priests. These contributions made by the people of Yehud for the support of the temple were a "religious tax" that ensured a regular income for the temple. The priests of the temple had no political authority to impose

---

33. Peter R. Bedford, "The Economic Role of the Jerusalem Temple in Achaemenid Judah: Comparative Perspectives," in *Shai le-Sara Japhet: Studies in the Bible, Its Exegesis and Its Language*, ed. Mosheh Bar-Asher et al. (Jerusalem: Bialik Institute, 2007), 6.

this "religious tax." They had to exhort their fellow Jews to obey the prescriptions of the Torah that called for contributions to the temple and its personnel. A Persian royal commissioner was a member of the temple administration. It was his responsibility to ensure that a portion of the temple's income was given to the king.

In addition to the "religious tax" for the support of the temple, there were imperial taxes that were imposed by the Persian government and paid by the people of Yehud. Ezra 4:20 mentions three separate imperial taxes. The first is מדה (NRSVue: "tribute"). This tax went directly to the king. This tax was collected and stored in the temple. It could be paid in silver or in kind. It was from the proceeds of this tax that the Persian kings financed the building of the second temple (Ezra 6:8). The second imperial tax was the בלו (NRSVue: "custom"). This was a tax imposed on those who were able to work. The third was the הלך (NRSVue: "toll"). This was tax on property. It is likely that the king received most of what was raised by the בלו and the הלך although other individuals and institutions likely benefitted from the monies raised.[34]

The temple served as the collection point for both the religious and imperial taxes. It was a significant instrument of Persian imperial fiscal administration and the center of economic life in Yehud. The temple's administration connected the Jewish taxpayers of Yehud with the Persian government. The priests and Levites benefitted from their collaboration with the imperial authorities. The Persian policy that granted Yehud a type of limited autonomy may appear to be a form of religious tolerance, but it was a political and economic strategy that ensured a steady flow of taxes from Yehud into Persian coffers.[35]

These three imperial taxes in addition to the religious tax offered for the support of the temple required the peasant farmers of Yehud to set aside a substantial portion of their harvest just to cover taxes that they were obliged to pay. This placed a heavy burden on the subsistence farmers of Yehud. Some farmers went into debt to feed their families (Neh 5:2-3). Women, who were primarily responsible for the preparation of food for the family, had to make do with what was left of the harvest after the temple and imperial taxes were paid.

34. Joachim Schaper, "The Jerusalem Temple as an Instrument of the Achaemenid Fiscal Administration," *VT* 45 (1955): 538.

35. Schaper, "The Jerusalem Temple," 535.

There were circumstances in which women saw their children sold as slaves to repay the family's debt incurred because of oppressive taxation. At times, the family lost their land because of their indebtedness (Neh 5:4-5).

To appreciate the life situation of the Jewish community in the Persian period it is necessary to attend to the burden of taxation that the imperial authorities placed on the people of Yehud. This burden prevented the community from achieving the type of economic recovery that makes political power possible. In this light, the task of the prophet was a most difficult one. He had to persuade the people of Yehud that they had a future despite the bleak prospects of their present.

The time of day during which the prophet experienced the first vision also reflects the difficult situation of the Jews of Yehud. The vision takes place at night, and its setting is outdoors in a glen among myrtle trees.[36] The darkness of night conjures a sense of foreboding.[37] Being outdoors at night increases one's feeling of vulnerability since one cannot always see approaching danger. It is a time when predators, human and animal, have the advantage. In a striking reversal of imagery, the prophet's night vision offers hope and reassurance for the people of Yehud in troubling times.

The vision begins with the prophet seeing a male rider on a chestnut-colored horse standing in front of an indefinite number of horses of different colors.[38] The horses in the prophet's vision have normal coloration and there is nothing in the text to suggest that there is a special significance for any of these colors. Resisting the impulse to find allegorical

36. מצלה (NRSVue "glen") is a *hapax*. The LXX renders מצלה as τῶν κατασκίων ("a shaded area"). Meyers and Meyers (*Haggai, Zechariah 1–8*, 110–11) suggest that מצלה is derived from צל or צלל ("to grow dark") and translate במצלה as "in the shadows," as does the NABRE.

37. Boda observes that the Old Testament sees night as a time of "heightened spiritual activity." See his *The Book of Zechariah*, 118. It is true that the Old Testament does not "demonize" nighttime. After all, the Passover takes place at night. Still, there are texts that characterize the night as a dangerous time, e.g., Mic 3:6; Ps 91:5; Job 24:13-15.

38. For a discussion of the different colors of horses in 1:8, see Petersen, *Haggai and Zechariah 1–8*, 143; and Max Rogland, *Haggai and Zechariah 1–8: A Handbook on the Hebrew Text*, Baylor Handbook on the Hebrew Bible (Waco, TX: Baylor University Press, 2016), 72. The NRSVue and NABRE use the term "sorrel," which is another name for a chestnut-colored horse.

meanings in the colors of the horse is likely the most prudent path. The number of horses in the vision is not clear. It is tempting to assume that the four colors mentioned mean that the prophet saw four horses. As David Petersen notes, the text does not indicate the number of horses, only that the horses the prophet saw were of four different colors.[39] The horses are identified by their color, and the horses of each color—except for the horse with the rider—are plural in number. The text, then, implies the prophet saw more than four horses in his vision though it mentions only one with a rider. Some interpreters insist there was more than one rider, a view that Lena-Sofia Tiemeyer is right to criticize.[40] There is no hint in the text that there was more than one rider.

The literature and art of the ancient Near East associate horses with war. Horses pulled the chariots and carried the cavalry into battle. It is likely that columns of Persian chariots and cavalry forces were a common sight in Zechariah's time as they passed through Yehud on their way to Egypt to strengthen Persian control of that valuable part of the empire. Viewing these forces must have brought unpleasant memories to the people of Yehud—memories of the devastation of the kingdom of Judah by Babylonian cavalry and chariots. Indeed, Jerusalem and the other cities of Yehud had not yet fully recovered from that trauma. Women, in particular, almost always suffer outrages at the hands of military forces passing through their villages and towns. The sight of troops marching through Yehud must have been terrifying.

Horses in Persia's military machine also highlighted the economic disparity between Yehud and the rest of the empire. Horses were the property of monarchs and their armies. Ordinary folk could not afford to keep such animals. The peasant farmers of Yehud had to be content with donkeys and mules, which were hardier and less expensive to maintain. At first glance, a vision of horses was not at all reassuring; it could have been a painful reminder of Yehud's military impotence and economic weakness in the face of Persian power. Second Kings 23:11 notes that the kings of Judah used horses and chariots as part of an idolatrous cult in a temple, so a vision of horses could also be a reminder of Judah's idolatrous past.[41]

39. Petersen, *Haggai and Zechariah 1–8*, 143.

40. See her *Zechariah and His Visions: An Exegetical Study of Zechariah's Vision Report*, LHBOTS 605 (London: Bloomsbury, 2015), 81–82.

41. Petersen, *Haggai and Zechariah 1–8*, 141, notes that the Assyrians considered horses to be sacred and assigned them a role in the cult of Ashur.

The interpreting angel, however, turns a potentially disturbing vision into a comforting one. The angel suggests that the horses are not a sign of impending conflict between peoples. Rather, the horses are emissaries sent by God "to patrol the earth" (v. 10; see also 6:1-8). Zechariah uses this martial imagery to announce that "the whole earth remains at peace" (v. 11). Thus, this vision reverses the common biblical image of horses as powerful war machines and turns them into messengers of comfort and reassurance.[42]

Horses in the Ancient World

Instead of focusing on the phrase "an eye for an eye, a tooth for a tooth" as *lex talionis* (law of retaliation), we can appreciate it in a new light, namely, one regarding equine vision and dentition. Did you know that horses' laterally set eyes allow for a 350-degree field of vision and that their teeth continuously erupt through their adult life? These fun facts are often covered in veterinary school where people learn to take care of horses. Let us delve into ways that horses have come to take care of us.

A horse represents different things to different people. To the farmer, a Clydesdale horse can be viewed as a source of income, a means to pull a wagon, a livelihood. The parent of a child with cerebral palsy may look at a thoroughbred mare and see her as an agent of hippotherapy. A dressage rider peers into the eyes of her Trakehner and sees a partner in the arena. No matter the breed of horse, its status as wild, purebred, or hybrid, or its traditional usage in society, it is very likely that our lives or those of our forebears have been impacted in some shape or form by these special creatures. The dog may be "man's best friend" and domesticated earlier in history, but the horse has come a long way since its domestication thousands of years ago in Eurasia.

Because of equids' sheer size and strength (essentially, their horsepower), people have utilized them for agricultural and military

---

42. In the view of some early Jewish readers of Zechariah, the horses are angelic warriors who execute the decisions of the divine council. Garrick V. Allen has shown that early Jewish reconceptualizations of the visions in Zechariah 1 and 6 conflate "horse visions" with traditions about angels as members of the divine council (Ps 82:1; 1 Kgs 22:19; 2 Chr 18:18; Isa 6:1-8) and as heavenly warriors (Isa 13:3-4; 40:26; 45:12; Joel 3:9-11; Ps 103:20-21; Zech 14:5). See Allen's "Zechariah's Horse Visions and Angelic Intermediaries: Translation, Allusion, and Transmission in Early Judaism," *CBQ* 79 (2017): 237.

purposes for millennia. The age-old association between human beings and the horse is evident in a number of ancient artifacts, whether found on a Mesopotamian stela or in Indian medicinal treatises. Even going as far back as 1750 BCE, we can appreciate the value placed on beasts of burden and the importance of caring for their health. Hammurabi's Code (224–225 BCE) describes the costs associated with an ox or donkey, e.g., the payment to a physician treating an animal for a serious wound as well as a fine due to accidentally killing it. Elsewhere in the world, Vedic literature from around 1500 BCE records a list of ointments that could be applied to the lesions of horses and cattle. The *Atharvaveda* posited that the knowledge for treating horses and elephants was divinely revealed to people.

It was not just in ancient India that horses brought to mind ideas of a higher power. Horses appear in a number of religious texts, including the Bible. The prophet Zechariah speaks of four separate chariots being drawn by red, black, white, and ash-colored horses. "The angel answered me, 'These are the four winds of the heaven going out, after presenting themselves before the Lord of the whole earth'" (6:5). This imagery is also seen in the Apocalypse of John (6:1-8). Whether pulling chariots across the heavens or wagons on earth, horses have always captivated our minds. How blessed are we to share this planet with them!

Max Vizelberg

In the second part of the first vision report, Zechariah refers to God three times as יהוה צבאות (vv. 12, 14, 17). Like his treatment of the horses, the prophet ironically uses this martial language to express a message of comfort. The words that יהוה צבאות speaks to Jerusalem and the other cities of Yehud are comforting, gracious, and compassionate (vv. 13 and 16). The interpreting angel instructs the prophet to deliver a comforting message, beginning with God's assertion, "I am very zealous [קנאתי] for Jerusalem and for Zion" and "extremely angry" with the nations that have exploited Jerusalem's weakness (vv. 14-15).

An oracle of salvation promises that God will return to Jerusalem, the temple will be rebuilt, and reconstruction of the city's walls will begin (v. 16). In addition, the prophet is to announce that the cities of Yehud will enjoy prosperity because of God's compassion toward Jerusalem and its election as God's dwelling (v. 17). Restoration will have important religious and political impact as well as economic benefit by offering financial stability to people who have been struggling (see Hag 1:5-6). This news will be welcome for the women of Yehud, who were responsible for the welfare of their families. No longer would the people be threatened by the specter of food shortages because the cities of Yehud "shall again overflow with prosperity" (v. 17). The word עוד ("again") appears three times in verse 17, underscoring the vision's message of the resurgence that Jerusalem and its people will experience in the near future. This resurgence is the result of God's passionate concern for the city.

Zechariah's first vision provides good news for all the people of Yehud—women and men, young and old. It allows them to resume their lives with a new sense of purpose, enthusiasm, and hope. The vision transforms the people of Yehud from victims, burdened with the consequences of their own failures and those of their forebears, into agents actively creating a future for themselves. In sum, Zechariah's first vision assures the people of Yehud that their long national "winter" is at an end and a springtime of peace and prosperity will soon begin.

TRANSLATION MATTERS

The word קנא (1:14), translated as "zealous" in the NRSVue, comes by way of the LXX, which renders קנאתי as εζήλωκα. The Vulgate follows suit with *zelum*; Carol Meyers and Eric Meyers (*Haggai, Zechariah 1–8*, 120) suggest "great zeal." There does not appear to be a satisfactory English equivalent for קנא. A circumlocution like "I am passionate about Jerusalem's welfare" is necessary to convey the meaning of verse 14b. This phrase reflects the importance that the city of Jerusalem came to have in Second Temple Judaism. Jerusalem was no longer the political center of the kingdom of Judah. The city's religious significance is its only claim to importance. It is the setting for the temple whose holiness becomes extended to the entire city so that even after the Romans destroy the temple, Jerusalem's significance for Judaism does not diminish. On the contrary, it only increases.

The Second Vision: Scattering Horns (1:18-21 [2:1-4])

Despite several problems of vocabulary, grammar, and imagery that complicate any attempt at interpretation, the basic thrust of this cryptic account of the second vision is clear: the vision points to the defeat of the nations that were responsible for the fall and/or subordination of Israel and Judah. Though Assyria, Egypt, and Babylon may have been God's instruments of judgment against sinful Israelites, what they did to the two former Israelite kingdoms was excessive in the extreme. Though

Zech 1:18-21

[18] And I looked up and saw four horns. [19] I asked the angel who spoke with me, "What are those?" And he answered me, "Those are the horns that have scattered Judah, Israel, and Jerusalem." [20] Then the LORD showed me four blacksmiths. [21] And I asked, "What are they coming to do?" He answered, "Those are the horns that scattered Judah, so that no head could be raised, but these have come to terrify them, to strike down the horns of the nations that lifted up their horns against the land of Judah to scatter its people."

Persia may have been God's instrument to defeat the Babylonians, its failure to reconstitute the Judean state and reinstate the Davidic dynasty stopped short of complete restoration for the people of Yehud. The prophet's second vision asserts that these nations would face judgment for their cruelty toward Israel, Judah, and Jerusalem.

Israel fell to Assyria in 721 BCE. The Israelite national state ceased to exist and its territory was incorporated into the Assyrian provincial system. The Assyrians compelled many of the people of Israel to leave their homeland and settle in various places in Mesopotamia (2 Kgs 17:23), replacing them with other peoples from various parts of the empire on whom Assyria was imposing a similar fate. Judah became a vassal state first to Assyria, then to Egypt, and finally to Babylon. An ill-advised revolt against Babylonian hegemony ended with the destruction of the temple, the scattering of its priesthood, the end of the national state and Davidic dynasty, the incorporation of Judah's territory into the Babylonian provincial system, and the forced migration of Judah's elite to agriculturally marginal regions in Mesopotamia (2 Kgs 25:1-12). Though the fall of the Israelite kingdoms had happened before most of Zechariah's audience had even been born, these tragic events became part of the collective memory of the Jewish people. The second vision testified to the lingering resentment against the nations that subjugated the two Israelite kingdoms and scattered their people.

There is some ambiguity regarding the fourth horn, which represents Persia in this vision. On the one hand, some biblical traditions look upon the rise of the Persian Empire as a blessing from God. For example, Isaiah 45:1 calls Cyrus the Great, who founded the Persian Empire, God's anointed, and the Chronicler and Ezra note that, after defeating Babylon and seizing its empire, Cyrus encouraged the Jews who were in Babylon to return to their homeland and rebuild the temple of Jerusalem (2 Chr 36:23; Ezra 1:1-4). On the other hand, the Persians did not permit the reconstitution of Judah—even as a vassal state—with a Davidic king as its head. By encouraging the rebuilding of the temple in Yehud, the Persians were contributing to their own economy, since temples in urban centers like Jerusalem administered tax collection on behalf of the empire.[43] In addition, constructing a temple to the patron deity of the former kingdom of Judah was tantamount to the Persian king's claim upon the throne of Judah. In the face of Persian hegemony over Yehud, Zechariah's vision affirms that *all* nations are subject to God's judgment. Yehud's subordination to Persia expresses itself in the burden of taxation that the people of Yehud had to bear.

Community Power Dynamics

The return of Judah's elite to the territory of the former kingdom of Judah, which began under Cyrus, created a social conflict between the returnees and those who had not been forced to migrate. The returnees considered themselves to be the religious elite, having been purified by the exile.[44] Ezra 4:4 alludes to this conflict within the community as it speaks of "the people of the land" and the "people of Judah," with the former discouraging the latter from rebuilding the temple.

A similar pattern of social and religious elitism led Francis of Assisi to align his community of "brothers" with the lower class of Assisi's population. He wanted his community of brothers to stand with the *minores* of Assisi, so he called his community the *Ordo Fratrum Minorum* ("The Order of Lesser Brothers"). The determination to identify his fraternity with the *minores* endeared Francis and his community to ordinary folk of the towns of Umbria. Francis and Clare laid the foundation of an order of cloistered nuns who lived a life of prayer in poverty and simplicity. Francis composed a rule of life for people who remained "in the world" but were inspired by Francis's lifestyle of poverty and

---

43. Meyers and Meyers, *Haggai, Zechariah 1–8*, 41–42.

44. Nicolae Roddy, "Exile as Identity in Persian Yehud," *Journal of Religion and Society* Supplement 13 (2016): 43–44; see also John Kessler, "Diaspora and Homeland in the Early Achaemenid Period: Community, Geography and Demography in Zechariah 1–8," in *Approaching Yehud: New Approaches to the Study of the Persian Period*, ed. Jon L. Berquist, SemeiaSt 50 (Atlanta: SBL, 2007), 137–66; Dalit Rom-Shiloni, *Exclusive Inclusivity: Identity Conflicts between the Exiles and the People Who Remained (6th–5th Centuries BCE)*, LHBOTS 543 (New York: Bloomsbury, 2013).

humility. This rule forbade the bearing of arms. The popularity of the Franciscan movement in Italy effectively ended its feudal system because the ethos of the movement deprived warring lords of soldiers for their armies. When members of the nobility (the *majores*) of the medieval community began joining the Franciscan movement, the *minores* and the *majores* of Italian society began drawing closer to one another, beginning the Franciscan social reform.[45]

The Jews who returned from exile in Babylon claimed for themselves the identity of "true Israel" along with ownership of Yehud's agricultural land and control of the economy and Judaism's principal religious symbol: the temple and its priesthood. The עם־הארץ ("people of the land") found themselves reduced to strangers in their homeland. The only alternative left to them was to recognize the authority of Jerusalem's priests since they had the support of the Persian authorities, who wanted to hasten the economic recovery of Yehud that was left in shambles after years of Babylonian control. An important function of the prophet's vision accounts is to assure the people of Yehud that better times were coming. Those ushering in those better times were the priests and their supporters. The book of Zechariah was a significant instrument of social control as the temple priests assumed the leadership of the Jewish community of Yehud.

Essential to the priests' claim on the symbols of Jewish religion was control of the temple and associated institutions. It was during the reign of Darius I that work on rebuilding the temple resumed (Ezra 4:24). When the regional Persian governor tried to halt the project, Darius decreed that the reconstruction of the temple should continue. He also ordered imperial officials to help expedite the rebuilding project (Ezra 5:1–6:15). The reconstruction of the temple provided the priestly class with a foundation for their leadership role in the Jewish community and solidified the dominance of the male Jewish priesthood in the post-exilic community. The destruction of the temple by the Romans in 70 CE deprived the priests of the base of the operations, and their importance diminished. Religious leadership in the Jewish community passed to the

45. Theodore A. Zaremba, *Franciscan Social Reform: A Study of the Third Order Secular of St. Francis as an Agency of Social Reform according to Certain Papal Documents*, Studies in Sociology 26 (Washington, DC: Catholic University of America Press, 1947).

rabbis, who were predominately laypeople. The role of women in the religious sphere was confined to the home. Still, the home was the setting for important religious observances such as the sabbath and Passover. It was not until the late twentieth century that some Jewish communities began to recognize women's gifts for communal religious leadership by ordaining women as rabbis.

Zechariah 1:18-19 [2:1–2] states that the prophet saw "horns" that symbolized four nations. Horns of large bovines were symbols of power and victory (see Deut 33:17 and 1 Kgs 22:11).[46] Although both male and female cattle have horns naturally, it is likely that Zechariah had bulls' horns in mind, since the male of the species more often displays aggressive power. In this vision, the horns represent the militarily and politically powerful nations that reduced the kingdom of Judah to vassalage (Assyria and Egypt), brought an end to the kingdom of Judah and its ruling dynasty (Babylon), and turned Yehud into a colony (Persia). The presence of "blacksmiths" in verse 20, however, suggests that the horns in the prophet's vision were not natural objects but fabrications made by blacksmiths. That the horns were made of metal (probably iron, as in 1 Kgs 22:11) accentuates the destructive power of the nations that they represent.

The key words in God's explanation of the vision's meaning are זרו and לזרותה (1:21 [2:4]), both of which are from the Hebrew root זרה ("scatter"). This word alludes to the effects of the dispersion of the people of Israel and Judah following their defeat at the hands of Assyria and Babylon; these words may also be a play on זר, the participial form of זור ("to be a stranger"), and may be an implicit criticism of the colonization of Yehud by the Persians. Under the Persians, the "scattering" took the form of keeping the people of Yehud subjugated as foreigners in their own land. The primary goal of Yehud's Jewish leadership was to create a collective identity of people who were connected to their homeland, their God, and their laws and customs. The Persian policy of keeping people of Yehud

---

46. Petersen, *Haggai and Zechariah 1–8*, 165–66, identifies the horns that the prophet sees as horns of an altar, which are places of refuge. The effect of the vision is to reverse the imagery so that horns become symbols of the destruction of the nations that have destroyed the Israelite kingdom. Robert Good suggests that "horns" here are a synecdoche for plow animals and the חרשים of v. 20 are ploughmen who come to drive the animal, i.e., the nations hostile to Yehud, back to their proper place, thus portending Judah's restoration; see "Zechariah's Second Night Vision (Zech 2, 1-4)," *Bib* 63 (1982): 58–59. Good bases his views of lexical and grammatical issues of this passage on the historical context to suggest that the "horns" of vv. 2 and 4 have a military-political significance.

as colonized in their own land undermined this project; it embodied the very opposite of what the leaders of the Jewish community were striving to achieve. The "horns," then, are acting in opposition to the will of God and the leadership of the Jewish community by depriving the people of their collective identity through policies that kept the Jewish people politically and economically subject to the Persian Empire. The former kingdom of Judah, with its reduced territory, was just a colony of Persia. Zechariah's second vision promises an end to this situation.

TRANSLATION MATTERS

Scholars have debated how best to translate חרשים in Zechariah 1:20 [2:3]. The NRSVue and Carol Meyers and Eric Meyers read this word as "blacksmiths."[47] The NABRE also follows the BHS but renders the Hebrew word as "workmen." Robert M. Good also follows the BHS pointing but asserts that this noun can mean "ploughmen."[48] Mark Boda accepts Good's reading and suggests emending the BHS to חורשים, a participle from חרש, which can mean to plough.[49] Those who advance either position engage in emendations to the text of verse 20 to support their respective readings. Still, the agricultural imagery that Good sees here is in tension with the martial imagery of Zechariah's first and last visions (1:7-17 and 6:1-8) and the oracles against the nations that subdued and "scattered" Judah with their overwhelming military might. The second vision foresees a reversal of fortunes. The blacksmiths will fashion four horns that will defeat the nations responsible for scattering Israel, Judah, and Jerusalem. The image of ploughmen obscures the prophet's vision, which sees the nations being repaid in kind.

TRANSLATION MATTERS

The meaning of the idiom כפי איש לא נשא ראשו ("so that no head could be raised," 1:21b [2:4]) is not self-evident. The words that make up the phrase are common enough, but the phrase is grammatically difficult, so it is sometimes emended.[50] Carol Meyers and Eric Meyers argue that the phrase speaks of individuals in Yehud whose personal autonomy has been compromised by the exile, i.e., "so

---

47. Meyers and Meyers, *Haggai, Zechariah 1–8*, 139.
48. Good, "Zechariah's Second Night Vision," 58.
49. Boda, *The Book of Zechariah*, 164–65.
50. Max Rogland, "'The Horns That Scattered Judah': The Vision of Zechariah 2:1-4," *BZ* 58 (2014): 93n6.

that no head could be raised."[51] Their view, which is reflected in both the NRSVue and the NABRE, is representative of the scholarly consensus. Alternatively, based on a similar phrase in Exodus 30:12, which refers to the taking of a census, Max Rogland suggests that Zechariah 1:21b says, "as a man who has not been counted." Rogland sees the text as describing how the "scattering" of Israelites by the "horns" (symbolizing ruling nations) has undermined Israelites' legal claims to the land, if census records, which should have demonstrated their ownership rights, were not properly maintained.[52]

It is possible, then, to see this phrase as veiled criticism of the Persian authorities. The effect of the failure to maintain census records complicated the restoration of the returnees. Their questionable legal status may have led to disputes about land ownership, resulting in great harm to the social fabric of Judahite society.[53] The significance of records providing support for people's claims to land ownership remains to this day in the state of Israel. Though individuals or families claim ownership of land, without deeds to attest to ownership, the possession of real property is often in dispute and subject to confiscation by the state.

Conclusion

The number four, which often symbolizes universality (reflected, for example, in the idea of the four corners of the earth), appears several times in the prophet's dreams (see 2:6 [2:10]; 6:1; 6:5). Zechariah's second vision of the four nations (Assyria, Egypt, Babylon, and Persia) that "scattered" and subjugated the people of Israel and Judah conveys the idea that God controls the destiny of all the nations of the earth. The imagery suggests that the military and political powers that brought about the collapse of the two Israelite kingdoms were about to end. Emphasis on the vast expanse that God controls is in tension with the angel's reference to Jerusalem, which, of course, is of primary concern to the prophet. In later prophecies, Zechariah resolves this tension by arguing that God's power emanates from Jerusalem and connects the destiny of Israel to

51. Meyers and Meyers, *Haggai, Zechariah 1–8*, 141. "To lift up one's head" is taken to mean restoring a person to his or her rightful position (e.g., Gen 40:13, 19, 20).

52. Rogland, "The Horns That Scattered Judah," 96–97; Mark C. Love makes a similar suggestion in his *The Evasive Text: Zechariah 1–8 and the Frustrated Reader*, JSOTSup 296 (Sheffield: Sheffield Academic, 1999), 189, 196, though he does not develop it to the extent that Rogland has.

53. Meyers and Meyers, *Haggai, Zechariah 1–8*, 145, 147, however, see the Persians as the "smiths" that destroy the destructive power of the Babylonian Empire as God's agents. They do see, however, an implicit critique of the Persians in the second vision because of Darius I's use of deportation practices as a response to rebellion.

that of the nations. The image of God reflected here is benevolent but patriarchal. God is acting to avenge the disasters that the nations brought on Jerusalem and the temple. The people of Yehud are not able to reverse their fortunes. God will accomplish this.

The aggressive and expansionist policies of the neo-Assyrian and neo-Babylonian Empires led to the fall of the kingdoms of Israel and Judah, but at the time of Zechariah's writing, it was Persia that controlled the life and destiny of the peoples of the ancient Near East. Darius maintained Persian hegemony by exercising tight control through a carefully crafted and implemented administrative structure throughout the vast territories that Persia governed.[54] For example, the return of the Judahite exiles suited Persia's strategic purposes, and granting partial autonomy to designated leaders in Yehud aligned with Persia's policy of pacification. Although Persia's policies benefitted Yehud to some extent, Zechariah was not fooled by Persia's apparent benevolence. Instead, the prophet dreams of a future when empires will no longer intrude into the lives of the people of Yehud or any other people by "scattering" peoples, denying them the opportunity to create a cohesive and independent collective identity, and preventing them from having access to the means to support themselves with dignity. Zechariah envisions a world where God, not Darius, will reign over all peoples, to the four corners of the earth.

Unlike the colonization of Africa and southern Asia by European powers from the seventeenth to the early twentieth centuries, the colonization of Yehud by the Persians did not attempt to assimilate the colonized people into the culture of the imperial power, though Aramaic did replace Hebrew as the everyday language in Yehud. The Persians encouraged and supported the building of a temple for God in Jerusalem, and they authorized the Torah as imperial law for Yehud. From a purely political perspective, Persia was able to exercise complete control over Yehud. The empire was principally concerned with Yehud's economy, since a robust economy meant that Persia could extract more from Yehud through taxation. Nevertheless, the Jews were able to establish a communal identity and determine their own values and goals without significant interference from imperial authorities as long as taxes from Yehud continued to flow into the imperial treasury.

Colonization in the modern states has been harsher. In the eighteenth century, Spanish colonizers in what is now California effectively turned

---

54. John M. Cook, *The Persian Empire* (New York: Schocken Books, 1983), 41.

the indigenous population into slaves within their own homeland. Also in the eighteenth century, Austria, Russia, and Prussia dismembered Poland, with each taking a portion. Poles were forbidden to use their own language, and members of the educated and leadership classes were either expelled or fled to other countries. Both in Canada and in the United States, children from indigenous tribes were taken from their parents and permitted to speak only English, causing the children to lose their connection to their own language and culture. By the beginning of the twentieth century, most of Africa and south Asia had been colonized by Europeans, who appropriated the natural resources of those regions and treated the indigenous peoples there with paternalism and disdain. Nazi Germany attempted to colonize Poland and the Soviet Union to provide "living space" for the growing population of Germany, considering Poles and Russians as "subhuman" to justify Nazi expansionism. In each of these cases in the modern era, colonial powers imposed laws that forbade the use of local languages, suppressed expressions of local culture, and subjugated local populations within their own homelands. It seems we have yet to learn that a society whose foundation is built on repression and injustice cannot endure.

The limited autonomy granted by the Persians to Yehud gave a certain sense of political stability. Still, the assurance that God was about to "strike down" the horns that symbolized the imperial powers that subjugated Judah is evidence that the political stability of Yehud was a veneer behind which the desire for a free and independent Judah was strong. The book of Zechariah is a testament to the hope of the Jewish people that colonization of their homeland would end through a manifestation of God's liberating power.

Zechariah 2:1-13

Daughter Zion

The books of Kings present the fall of both Israelite kingdoms and the exile of their elite classes as divine judgment on those kingdoms (2 Kgs 17:7-20; 21:10-15). For those who endured the siege and fall of Jerusalem to Nebuchadnezzar in 587 BCE, the experience must have been traumatic in the extreme. The subsequent deportation to Babylon only added to the trauma. Those people lost their collective identity and their possessions. They were forced to settle in an unfamiliar place with an unfamiliar cultural environment. The book of Lamentations and Deuteronomy 28:65-67 are testaments to that trauma. Most of the people whom Zechariah addressed did not experience that trauma personally, but the literature of the books of Jeremiah, Ezekiel, and Kings whose final form comes from the postexilic period testifies that the events associated with the fall of Jerusalem continued to have traumatic effects on the children and grandchildren of those who had firsthand experience of those events.[1]

Following the fall of Jerusalem, the Judeans felt alone, abandoned, and vulnerable. One task Zechariah gave himself was to convince the people of Yehud that their collective nightmare was over. The third vision suggests that Jerusalem will enjoy unprecedented growth. This is followed

---

1. Dominik Markl, "The Babylonian Exile as the Birth Trauma of Monotheism," *Bib* 101 (2020): 13–14.

by God's assurance that "daughter Zion" will experience God's renewed presence and protection. This experience will enable the people of Yehud to overcome the lingering effects of their collective trauma and embark on the reconstitution of their community.

The Third Vision: The Measuring Line (2:1-5 [2:5-9])[2]

The account of Zechariah's third vision is brief but packed with characters, all of whom are male. There is a man measuring Jerusalem; two angels, one of whom is likely a periphrasis for God; a young man; and the prophet. Together these characters convey a message about Jerusalem's bright future when the city will be repopulated and safe from threats from foreign enemies. The portrait of God here differs markedly from that in the first two visions, where the title יהוה צבאות identifies God, who, as the leader of cosmic and human armies, is intent on ending the threat to the existence of the Jewish people. In this third vision, God is not a conquering avenger but a determined protector, who promises to keep Jerusalem safe from harm. God is a glorious presence within the city and acts as a "wall of fire all around it" (2:5 [2:9]).

In contrast to the first vision, which uses martial imagery, the third vision uses language of architecture and urban planning. An unidentified man uses a cord to measure the length and breadth of Jerusalem, presumably to plan for the reconstruction of the city's walls to accommodate an increase in population that was sure to come once the exiles returned from Babylon. A similar image of a person measuring Jerusalem is found in Ezekiel 40:3-4, and a detailed description of the city's physical dimensions appears in Ezekiel 48:30-35.[3] Unlike Ezekiel, whose primary concern is the placement of the temple in Jerusalem, Zechariah is concerned about the city itself in anticipation of an unprecedented period of population growth. The interpreting angel appears to inform the prophet of the significance of the vision. At the same time another angel comes forward and instructs the interpreting angel about what to

---

2. The versification of Zechariah 2 in the NRSVue differs from that of the BHS. In the commentary to this chapter all references will be to the versification in the NRS-Vue with the BHS versification in parentheses. The NABRE follows the versification in the BHS.

3. According to Ezekiel 48:30-35, there will be three gates on each side of the city. Although a wall is not mentioned, the gates imply one. The length of each side of the wall will be 4,500 cubits (7,652 feet) so that Jerusalem will be a perfect square.

¹I looked up and saw a man with a measuring line in his hand. ²Then I asked, "Where are you going?" He answered me, "To measure Jerusalem, to see how wide and how long it is." ³Then the angel who spoke with me came forward, and another angel came forward to meet him ⁴and said to him, "Run, say to that young man: Jerusalem shall be inhabited like unwalled villages because of the multitude of people and animals in it. ⁵For I will be a wall of fire all around it, says the LORD, and I will be the glory within it."

say to the "young man" (נער).[4] Measuring for a wall at this point is futile since Jerusalem's imminent growth spurt will cause the city's burgeoning population to spill into the nearby unwalled villages (פרזות).[5] Rebuilding the city's wall will limit its growth so care must be taken to ensure that the area enclosed by the walls is sufficient. This message affirms that Jerusalem's population is growing and that that population needs protection from military attack.

Normally, urban centers like Jerusalem were walled as a defense against military incursions. A city's wall, along with its gates and towers, also had symbolic value, reflecting the city's status as a self-sustaining political and economic entity. In addition, during the monarchic period Jerusalem was supported by a network of towns and villages outside its city walls that contributed to the city's viability. In Zechariah's day, however, Jerusalem's walls were still in ruins.[6] The meager revenue from

4. The identity of the נער ("young man," 2:4 [2:8]) and his relation to the איש ("man," 2:1) is not clear. Albert Wolters (*Zechariah*, HCOT [Leuven: Peeters, 2014], 76) suggests that נער refers to a person assisting the איש of v. 1 with the measuring line, since taking a measurement of a city's dimensions would normally require at least two people. Carol L. Meyers and Eric M. Meyers (*Haggai, Zechariah 1–8: A New Translation with Introduction and Commentary*, AB 25B [Garden City, NY: Doubleday, 1987], 149, 154–55) and Mark J. Boda (*The Book of Zechariah*, NICOT [Grand Rapids: Eerdmans, 2016], 169, 178–79) render נער as "official" and identify him as the person with the measuring line. The NABRE follows suit. Also, reading נער as a reference to the prophet is plausible. In all these scenarios, the reference to a נער could reflect the power and status of the divine speaker in this verse and the human (probably adult male) referent.

5. The NRSVue treats פרזות as a noun, i.e., "villages without walls" (2:4 [2:8]). The NABRE treats פרזות as an adjective so it renders v. 8 as "Jerusalem will be unwalled."

6. According to Neh 2:1-8, Jerusalem's walls were in ruins and remained so until Artaxerxes I gave permission for their reconstruction in 444 BCE—seventy-five years after Zechariah's ministry.

the villages surrounding Jerusalem was taken as taxes to support the Persian administration of the region, leaving Jerusalem barely able to survive economically.[7] Rebuilding the city's walls required permission from the Persian authorities. Initiating such a project without proper authorization could have been viewed as an act of sedition.[8]

The state of Jerusalem's walls represented the tension that the people of Yehud experienced between their desire to live as a politically independent community responsible only to God and the reality of Yehud's subordination to the Persian government that had little concern for the religious and political hopes of the Jews. Prosperity and self-determination were just dreams for the people of Jerusalem whose survival required the efforts not only of Yehud's male population but of women and children as well. It comes as no surprise that the people of Yehud probably wanted to control their own destiny so that they would no longer be forced to hand over the bulk of what they had produced to Persia's coffers. Meanwhile, the Jerusalem of the prophet's vision would have no walls. Still, the city would not be defenseless since God would be "a wall of fire all around it" (v. 5a).[9]

Zechariah 2:1-5 [2:5-9] ends with a declaration that the כבוד ("glory") of God will be within Jerusalem. The term כבוד does not point to an attribute or an aspect of the deity; rather, it is nothing less than God's very self. Unlike Ezekiel, who emphasizes the presence (or absence) of God's כבוד in the temple,[10] Zechariah makes no mention of the temple in the third vision but instead affirms that God's presence in the city will be the source of its safety and autonomy. In addition, כבוד significantly

---

7. Oded Lipschits, "Persian Period Finds from Jerusalem: Facts and Interpretations," *JHebS* 9 (2009): 18.

8. Carroll Stuhlmueller, *Rebuilding with Hope: A Commentary on the Books of Haggai and Zechariah*, ITC (Grand Rapids: Eerdmans, 1988), 75.

9. The prophet employs an image that most likely was derived from knowledge of Pasargadae, the capital of Cyrus the Great and the location of his tomb. That city, important as it was strategically and politically, had no walls; instead, the city was surrounded by fire altars in honor of Ahura Mazda, the benevolent deity of Persian religion. See David Stronach, *Pasargadae: A Report on the Excavations Conducted by the British Institute of Persian Studies from 1961 to 1963* (Oxford: Clarendon, 1978), cited in David L. Petersen, "Zechariah's Visions: A Theological Perspective," *VT* 34 (1984): 201.

10. The כבוד of God leaves the temple (Ezek 9:3; 10:4; 11:23), rendering the city defenseless; its return to the temple signaled Judah's restoration (Ezek 43:2-5; 44:4). Unlike Ezekiel, Zechariah did not think that the future of Jerusalem was dependent on the presence of the temple in its midst, though the prophet did hope that the temple would be rebuilt (Zech 1:16).

transforms Jerusalem's identity; the sphere of holiness is no longer limited to the temple, but it spans the city in its entirety. Zechariah's third vision reflects the transformation of Jerusalem from a royal capital to a purely religious center. The prophet expected some sort of restoration of Jerusalem's political and religious institutions although the precise shape of that restoration was not clear. When the political restoration failed to materialize, the prophet's vision of a city without walls helped the people of Yehud remain confident about the presence of God in their midst. Jerusalem's restoration, made possible by God's כבוד within the city, transcended the old political and religious institutions. The Divine Presence (כבוד) served to transform Jerusalem into "the Holy City" (Isa 52:1; Dan 9:24)—an identity the city still bears.[11]

TRANSLATION MATTERS

The portrait of God in the third vision differs markedly from that of the first two visions. The title יהוה צבאות does not appear in chapter 2. God is not presented as the one who leads armies in defense of the people of Yehud. Verse 5a [9:a] simply says ואני אהיה לה . . . חומת אש סביב ("I will be an encircling wall of fire for her [Jerusalem]"). Unfortunately, English translations of this verse find it difficult to render the nuances of the Hebrew. First, the presence of the subject pronoun אני ("I") is not grammatically necessary. Its presence underscores God's intention to *personally* protect Jerusalem as a God who is deeply invested in Yehud's welfare. Second, the verb אהיה is reminiscent of the divine name as it appears in Exodus 3:14 and Hosea 1:9 and further intensifies the divine commitment to restore a covenantal relationship with the people of Yehud and Jerusalem.[12] God promises to be present within the city and to provide all the protection it needs.

The prophet's vision of Jerusalem spilling over into its dependent villages because of the city's growing population is all too real today. In the decades following the establishment of the state of Israel in 1948 and especially after the Six Day War in 1967, the borders of Jerusalem have

---

11. Unfortunately, contemporary religious rivalries and political conflicts make that identity Jerusalem's burden as well as its glory as Jews, Christians, and Muslims make competing claims to religious primacy there.

12. Meyers and Meyers, *Haggai, Zechariah 1–8*, 156, note that David Noel Freedman, their editor, suggested that v. 9a be translated as "As for me, I am EHYEH for her."

indeed been extended at the cost of Arab villages like Silwan, Ain-Karim, Ras al-Amud, and al-Azarieh that are now part of the municipality of Jerusalem. The annexation of these villages has complicated the peace process and has made both Arabs and Jews feel less secure in their daily lives. It appears that the vision of Zechariah has portended both a blessing and curse for the modern city of Jerusalem.

An Intermezzo: Daughter Zion Restored (2:6-13 [2:10-17])

The account of the prophet's first three visions is interrupted by the threefold repetition of the Hebrew interjection הוֹי in verses 6-7 [vv. 10-11], which shifts the tone of the text from narration to urgent exhortation.[13] The exhortation shifts from the first to the third person, making it difficult to determine who is speaking—God or the prophet.[14] The message, though, is clear: those Jews still living in Babylon are to return to Jerusalem immediately. The prophet signals the importance of his message by employing a messenger formula four times and by asserting three times that God has sent him.[15] The urgent message entrusted to the prophet is that God will reclaim Jerusalem and rebuild the temple. Zechariah 2:6-10 [10-14] reiterates the theme of the first three visions—God's special concern for Jerusalem, God's judgment on the nations that have oppressed Judah, and the restoration of Jerusalem to God's favor—all seen against the backdrop of God's universal sovereignty. Zechariah 1:19, 21 claim that foreign nations were responsible for the dispersion of the people of Judah, but Zechariah 2:6 [10] asserts God's agency in the exile of Judah and likewise God's determination to reverse the fortunes of the exiles and their oppressors (2:12 [16]).

---

13. Bruce K. Waltke and Michael O'Connor (*An Introduction to Biblical Hebrew Syntax* [Winona Lake, IN: Eisenbrauns, 1990], sec. 40.2.4a) assert that הוֹי is a summons to action. Meyers and Meyers, *Haggai, Zechariah 1–8*, 161, 173, render the expression as "Hey! Hey!"; the NABRE and the NRSVue have "Up! Up!" Another possibility is "Attention, please!" Zech 2:6 is the only biblical text where הוֹי is repeated three times in succession. This repetition increases the sense of urgency.

14. First-person forms: vv. 6 [10b], 8b [12b], 9a [13a], 10 [14], 11a [15a]; third-person forms: 8a [12a], 9b [12b], 11b [15b], 12 [16], 13 [17].

15. The messenger formulas are נְאֻם יהוה ("says YHWH," v. 6 [10] twice and v. 10 [14]) and כֹּה אָמַר יהוה צְבָאוֹת ("Thus says YHWH of armies," v. 8 [12]). The prophet asserts that God had sent him in vv. 8 [v. 12], 9 [13], and 11 [15].

Zech 2:6-13

⁶Up, up! Flee from the land of the north, says the LORD, for I have spread you abroad like the four winds of heaven, says the LORD. ⁷Up! Escape to Zion, you who live with daughter Babylon. ⁸For thus said the LORD of hosts after his glory sent me to the nations who plundered you: Truly, one who touches you touches the apple of my eye. ⁹For I am going to raise my hand against them, and they shall become plunder for their own slaves. Then you will know that the LORD of hosts has sent me. ¹⁰Sing and rejoice, O daughter Zion! For I will come and dwell in your midst, says the LORD. ¹¹Many nations shall join themselves to the LORD on that day and shall be my people, and I will dwell in your midst. And you shall know that the LORD of hosts has sent me to you. ¹²The LORD will inherit Judah as his portion in the holy land and will again choose Jerusalem.

¹³Be silent, all flesh, before the LORD, for he has roused himself from his holy dwelling.

The prophet calls the exiles from Judah who have chosen to remain "in the land of the north" to return to their ancestral homeland.[16] That was not an easy decision for the exiles to make—to choose to leave their homes in Babylon for a land few remembered. Most of the exiles from Judah had grown up in Babylon and had lived and worked in agriculturally marginal areas. Still, they managed to do well. Some Judahites even became civil servants and led reasonably comfortable lives. Leaving all that behind was not easy. The prophet, however, believed that the exiles needed to escape the judgment that God was about to bring upon the nations—including Babylon—that had "plundered" Judah and Jerusalem.[17] Today political, religious, economic, and environmental pressures

---

16. The expression ארץ צפון ("land of the north") appears five times in Jeremiah (3:18; 6:22; 16:15; 23:8; 31:8) and three times in Zechariah (2:6 [10]; 6:6, 8). In all eight occurrences it clearly refers to Babylon. While Babylon is not directly north of Jerusalem, any military advance toward the city from Mesopotamia would come from the north because the direct route from the east passes through a desert that would make the movement of an army practically impossible. Similarly, any immediate attack on Jerusalem would come from the north—the one side of the city that was vulnerable since deep ravines on three sides of the city made an attack from any other side impractical.

17. Persia's policy of allowing and even encouraging the repatriation of Jews to Jerusalem (see 2 Chr 36:23 and Ezra 1:2-4) may have added impetus to the prospect of returning to Judah.

in some countries lead to the reverse. Difficult situations in their native lands lead people to abandon homes to settle in countries that are free of such pressures. The economic and psychological consequences of such moves can take a heavy toll on families. Women and children in such situations are vulnerable to abuse and exploitation, but often they have little choice but to emigrate.

Verse 7 [11] employs a distinctive metaphor in speaking of Babylon, Judah's conqueror. The expression "daughter Babylon" occurs only four other times in the Hebrew Bible (Ps 137:8; Isa 47:1; Jer 50:42; 51:33). Isaiah 47:1-3 describes Babylon's humiliation and loss of status as it depicts "daughter Babylon" as an elegant queen who is deposed, stripped of her finery, sexually abused, and forced to perform menial tasks. Because of "her" hubris (Isa 47:8) and "her" reliance on divination (47:9),[18] Babylon is condemned to widowhood and childlessness. Likewise, Psalm 137:8-9 threatens "daughter Babylon" with the loss of her children as a punishment for the treatment of the Judahites by their Babylonian captors (Ps 137:3). Similarly, "daughter Babylon" appears twice in Jeremiah (50:42 and 51:33) as experiencing military defeat as a divine punishment. By way of contrast, Zechariah 2 does not exploit the personification of Babylon and avoids describing the humiliation and degradation of Babylon portrayed as a woman.[19] Instead, Zechariah 2 focuses attention on the future of בת ציון ("daughter Zion," 2:10 [14]).

The phrase בת ציון ("daughter Zion") appears twenty-six times in the Hebrew Bible.[20] The similar phrase, בת ירושלם ("daughter Jerusalem") appears seven times—often parallel to "daughter Zion."[21] Some ancient

18. Babylonian diviners and astrologers were well-known and respected in antiquity. See Stefan M. Maul, *The Art of Divination in the Ancient Near East: Reading the Signs of Heaven and Earth*, trans. Brian McNeil and Alexander Johannes Edmonds (Waco, TX: Baylor University Press, 2018). The Deuteronomic tradition is adamantly opposed to the use of divination by the people of Israel (Deut 13:2-4).

19. 2 Kgs 19:21; Ps 9:14; Isa 1:8; 10:32; 16:1; 37:22; 52:2; 62:11; Jer 4:31; 6:2, 23; Lam 1:6; 2:1, 4, 8, 10, 13; 4:22; Mic 1:13; 4:8, 10, 13; Zeph 3:14; Zech 2:10; 9:9.

20. The phrase "daughter Zion" has been the subject of several recent studies. See Boda, *The Book of Zechariah*, 193n113.

21. 2 Kgs 19:21; Isa 37:22; Lam 2:13, 15; Mic 4:8; Zeph 3:14; Zech 9:9. These expressions can be translated as "daughter of Zion" and "daughter of Jerusalem." In that case the expressions would refer to female inhabitants of the city. Both expressions should be taken as appositional genitives. See William F. Stinespring, "No Daughter of Zion: A Study of the Appositional Genitive in Hebrew Grammar," *Encounter* 26 (1965): 133–41; F. W. Dobbs-Allsopp, however, asserts that the expressions are examples of genitive of location, reflecting Babylonian usage in which it serves as a divine epithet.

Near Eastern texts use בת ("daughter") with a geographical name as a title for a goddess.[22] The title "daughter Zion/Jerusalem," though influenced by the usage, does not appear as a goddess in the Hebrew Scriptures. Aloysius Fitzgerald traces the female personification of ancient Near Eastern cities such as Jerusalem and Babylon to the grammatical gender of city names in Western Semitic tradition.[23] Gina Hens-Piazza disagrees and asserts that, like women in hierarchical societies, cities "were managed, controlled and useful in providing food and a habitable place for life."[24] Christl M. Maier offers support for both positions and adds that another reason may be the ancient Near Eastern city-lament that deplores the destruction of cities.[25] Maier then asserts that prophetic texts do not portray a city as a woman per se but as exhibiting a particular female role, e.g., a daughter. In the ancient Near East, a daughter was socially and economically dependent on her father who kept her from sexual contacts with men prior to her marriage. Maier characterizes this as an example of an "androcentric notion of gender relations."[26] What Maier neglects is the affective dimension of the father-daughter relationship, i.e., that this relationship is about more than social status, economic dependence, and preservation of virginity. Parents love their children; fathers love their daughters. Julia O'Brien does note this affective dimension of the father-daughter relationship, though she nonetheless concludes that the expression and image of בת ציון is based on the circumstances of "defenseless" daughters, who need the protection of their fathers.[27] In addition, there is a type of permanence to the father-daughter relationship unlike that of husband and wife. The latter can be broken by divorce. Analogously, God will always be the parent of "daughter Zion/Jerusalem" and Zion/Jerusalem will always be God's

---

See his "The Syntagma of *bat* Followed by a Geographical Name in the Hebrew Bible: A Reconsideration of Its Meaning and Grammar," *CBQ* 57 (1995): 451–70.

22. Katheryn Pfisterer Darr, *Isaiah's Vision and the Family of God*, Literary Currents in Biblical Interpretation (Louisville: Westminster John Knox, 1994), 126–29.

23. See his "*BTWLT* and *BT* as Titles for Capital Cities," *CBQ* 37 (1975): 168–70.

24. Gina Hens-Piazza, "Zion's Destiny as Theological Disclosure: Mapping of a Metaphor across Isaiah," *CBQ* 84 (2022): 12.

25. See her "Daughter Zion and Babylon, the Whore: The Female Personification of Cities and Countries in the Prophets," in *Prophecy and Gender in the Hebrew Bible*, ed. L. Juliana Claassens and Irmtraud Fischer, BW 1.2 (Atlanta: SBL Press, 2021), 257–58.

26. Maier, "Daughter Zion," 259.

27. Julia M. O'Brien, *Challenging Prophetic Metaphor: Theology and Ideology in the Prophets* (Louisville: Westminster John Knox, 2008), 133–39.

daughter despite temporary alienation and separation. This enables the prophet to be confident about Zion's future. The dispersion of the people of Judah and Jerusalem across Babylon was a tragic interlude in Judah's relationship with God. Zechariah announces that this interlude is now over. Of course, some fathers abuse or abandon their daughters. Women who have had such traumatic experiences will find it difficult to think of the "daughter Zion" personification in a positive way. Still, the reprehensible actions of some fathers and people's utter contempt for such behavior only serve to underscore the expectation that people have of the affective bonds that should bind father and daughter.

As Marie-Theres Wacker notes, "daughter Zion" is one of several female personifications of Jerusalem. The city is depicted as the wife or former wife of God, who has been widowed or defiled. Jerusalem is also portrayed as the mother who has lost her children but who will ultimately be reunited with them. These metaphors are "inspired by concrete women's lives and play on the roles of women in patriarchal societies."[28] Because these metaphors so vividly mirror people's social framework, Wacker warns they might be misconstrued by some readers as reflecting how real-life women should be treated in their relationships with men. In other words, the embodiment of Jerusalem as mother, wife, or daughter has led some people to suggest that these are the only proper roles for women in society.

Beate Schmidtgen picks up on this problem when she notes that, while, on the one hand, descriptions of Jerusalem as a daughter, wife, and mother encompass the whole of a woman's familial experience in the ancient world, such descriptions also convey to the reader a sense of expectation regarding how women should act. Just as mother/daughter/ wife Jerusalem will be rewarded for particularly good behaviors and punished for particularly bad behaviors according to norms set by her husband/father God, so too will women be rewarded and punished should they not follow the normative behaviors set for them by the men of their communities.[29] This, of course, exploits the metaphor in a way that distorts its use in its literary context. For example, Zechariah

28. Marie-Theres Wacker, *Baruch and the Letter of Jeremiah*, WCS 31 (Collegeville, MN: Liturgical Press, 2016), 68–69.

29. Beate Schmidtgen, "Haggai and Zechariah: A New Temple—New Life for All," in *Feminist Biblical Interpretation: A Compendium of Critical Commentary on the Books of the Bible and Related Literature*, ed. Luise Schottroff and Marie-Theres Wacker, trans. Martin Rumscheidt et al. (Grand Rapids: Eerdmans, 2012), 469.

employs the image of "daughter Zion" to insist on the permanence of the relationship between the people of Jerusalem and God. To see this imagery as determining the social role and status of real-life women requires that the text bear a burden that it was not meant to bear. One illustration of this danger comes from the late seventeenth century, when Puritans arrived in the New World seeking to establish what they termed a New Jerusalem or a New Zion. This new community was intended to be a haven of purity and piety, purged of all evil consorts with the devil. Unfortunately, this zeal for sexual and religious purity found expression in the Salem witch trials, which demonized women as consorting with the devil. Even today, some readers of the Bible associate the restoration of Zion and the end of days with the restoration of strict sexual chastity, which requires suppressing female involvement from public life.[30]

The image of daughter Zion in Zechariah may have been intended to function as a response to Lamentations 2, in which daughter Zion's walls are about to be destroyed. The book of Lamentations describes the chaos and devastation left in the wake of the Babylonian destruction of the Jerusalem temple in 587 and 586 BCE:

> The LORD determined to lay in ruins
>   the wall of daughter Zion;
> he stretched the line;
>   he did not withhold his hand from destroying;
> he caused rampart and wall to lament;
>   they languish together.
> Her gates have sunk into the ground;
>   he has ruined and broken her bars;
> her king and princes are among the nations;
>   guidance is no more,
> and her prophets obtain
>   no vision from the LORD. (Lam 2:8-9)

Lamentations 2 gives daughter Zion a voice to lament her predicament and to challenge God to intervene in her situation. While in passages such as Hosea 1–3 and Ezekiel 16 and 23, God is the actor who "acts upon" daughter Zion, in Lamentations the daughter asserts her right to question God. If Zechariah is indeed responding to Lamentations, it is no surprise

---

30. One extreme example of people who adhere to such beliefs is the Heaven's Gate Community. See Benjamin E. Zeller, "Apocalyptic Thought in UFO-Based Religions," in *End of Days: Essays on the Apocalypse from Antiquity to Modernity*, ed. Karolyn Kinane and Michael A. Ryan (Jefferson, NC: McFarland, 2009), 342.

that the author gives daughter Zion a voice in this passage by inviting her to "sing and rejoice" (v. 10 [14]) at the prospect of her restoration. The invitation extended to daughter Zion to celebrate stands in contrast with the devastation that will be wrought upon daughter Babylon, but it is also in tension with the command given to "all flesh" to be silent as God is about to end daughter Zion's alienation (v. 13).

Maier finds that the personification of cities such as daughter Zion is a patriarchal construct that leads people to think of God as a male who protects and corrects his daughter. She suggests that this reflection on this metaphor can serve as "a critique of dominant images of God and hierarchical gender relations."[31] By reflecting on the affective dimension of the daughter Zion personification, one can recognize the positive value of this metaphor. Rather than simply a product of the social dynamics of Persian-period Yehud, it points to renewal of the covenant between the people of Yehud and their ancestral deity. It speaks of a God who wished to be reunited with the people who were returning to Jerusalem and reconstituting Jewish life there.

TRANSLATION MATTERS

The English translation of 2:8b [12b] makes it clear that an attack on Jerusalem is an attack on God, but the Hebrew text is not so clear. The note to verse 12b in the BHS suggests that עינו ("his eye") is an example of *tiqqun soferim* ("a correction of the scribes"), made because the scribes considered "my eye" to be an unacceptable anthropomorphism. Max Rogland, *Haggai and Zechariah 1–8*, 103, notes that the Dead Sea Scrolls read עינו ("his eye"), and the Targum Jonathan, LXX, Syriac support this reading. He also notes the copyists sometimes confused the ׳ and the ו and some Greek and Latin manuscripts do support the reading of "my eye." Lena-Sofia Tiemeyer also accepts the correction to עיני, though she admits that text-critical evidence favors עינו.[32] It is possible that both readings existed at one time. The NRSVue has "my eye" but includes a footnote indicating the Hebrew reads "his eye." The NABRE uses a paraphrase to avoid the problem: "Whoever strikes you strikes me directly in the eye."

Although Zechariah's message to the people of Yehud is positive, his attitude toward "the nations" is ambivalent. On the one hand, Zechariah

31. Maier, "Daughter Zion," 271–72.
32. See her "Compelled by Honour: A New Interpretation of Zechariah ii 12a (8a)," *VT* 54 (2004): 357.

2:6-13 [9-17] reflects the view expressed in the prophet's second vision, i.e., that God would bring about the destruction of "the nations that lifted up their horns against the land of Judah to scatter its people" (1:21). The anthropomorphism in 2:8-9 [12-13] serves to suggest that an attack on Jerusalem is an attack on God. In response to such an attack, the fortunes of Jerusalem and its oppressors will be reversed, and the nations will "become plunder for their own slaves" (v. 9 [13]). When this reversal takes place, the prophet's readers will recognize that he is an authentic prophet. On the other hand, Zechariah introduces universalist and eschatological notes in 2:11: "Many nations shall join themselves to YHWH on that day and shall be my people."[33] This statement is not so much about the nations as it is about the restoration of Jerusalem. The fall of the city, the destruction of its temple, and the scattering of its priests, no doubt, led to the belief that God had rejected Jerusalem and its people (see Lam 5:22). As a challenge to that belief, the prophet asserts that God will reclaim Yehud in the "holy land" (v. 12 [16])[34] and reaffirm the election of Jerusalem, thus reversing the harm done by the Babylonians. The bold assertion that there will come a time when even the "nations" will join themselves to God and become God's people (2:11) does not compromise Israel's unique status as the elect people of God. Zechariah elevates Jerusalem's status with the universalist assertion. The prophet's words will leave his audience—composed of both Jew and gentile—speechless in awe (v. 13). Such a universalist vision hardly seems possible in view of the political and economic status of Yehud in the late sixth century BCE. Still, the prophet is confident that God will reverse the circumstances of the exiles who will return to Jerusalem from exile in Babylon.

The chapter's final verses call for two seemingly contradictory responses. Verse 10 [14] exhorts daughter Zion to "sing and rejoice, O daughter Zion! For I will come and dwell in your midst." Then verse 13 [17] calls the nations who have joined themselves to God to "be silent . . . before the Lord, for he has roused himself from his holy dwelling." Both responses to God's renewed presence in Zion are expressions of reverential awe. The population of Jerusalem, swelled by the returnees from Babylon, will be transformed and reconstituted as the people of God protected by God's כבוד dwelling among them (2:4-5 [8-9]).

33. A similar motif appears in Isa 2:2-4; 56:6-7; and Mic 4:1-2.
34. This is the only occurrence of this phrase in the Hebrew Bible though it does appear in Wis 12:3 and 2 Macc 1:7.

Conclusion

Weaving together martial, feminine, eschatological, and mythological imagery with the language of covenant renewal, with an added twist of universality, the prophet assures his people that they can look to the future with confidence. He announces that God, whom he calls יהוה צבאות three times in chapter 2 (vv. 8 [12], 9 [13], 11 [15]), will end Judah's subjugation and reverse the harm done to Jerusalem by the militarist and expansionist Babylonian Empire.

Although Zechariah addressed the challenges faced by the people of Yehud as they were attempting to restore Jewish life in the ancestral homeland with the encouragement of Persian kings, appropriating the prophet's perspectives and their underlying theological assumptions needs to be done with care. The prophet's vision of the expansion of Jerusalem following the return of the exiles and the resurgence of Yehud's economy should not be taken as support for the unchecked growth of cities without concern for the impact on the environment.[35] Without environmental impact studies, irreparable damage could harm both the flora and fauna. Human beings need to live in harmony with other creatures. That is the message of Carolyn Merchant's *Reinventing Eden*.[36] Solidarity with nature must replace domination over nature. This has been an emphasis of papal teaching on the environment from Pope St. Paul VI to Pope Francis.[37]

In the foregoing discussion of "daughter Zion," this commentary suggested that this feminine image drawn from the experience of familial relations may suggest that the bond between God and the people of Yehud is a bond that has survived temporary alienation caused by the idolatry and injustice that was the subject of prophetic criticism. Still, it is possible to take that metaphor in another direction. The words of judgment on "daughter Zion" (e.g., Jer 6:23; Lam 2:1, 8; 4:22) can lead people to think of God as an authoritarian, abusive parent who brutalizes his disobedient daughter, who should remain loyal and submissive. This "daughter Zion" imagery is especially problematic for those who have been abused and brutalized by a parent. Zechariah's use of this imagery,

---

35. Sallie McFague, *The Body of God: An Ecological Theology* (Minneapolis: Fortress, 1993), 198–202.

36. Carolyn Merchant, *Reinventing Eden: The Fate of Nature in Western Culture* (New York: Routledge, 2004), 223–27.

37. Pope Francis, *Laudato Sì: On Care for Our Common Home* (Vatican City: Vatican Press, 2015), sec. 4–5, 67; and his more recent Apostolic Exhortation on the climate crisis, *Laudate Deum*, issued October 4, 2023.

however, carries no such overtone. The "daughter Zion" personification appears only twice in Zechariah:

> Sing and rejoice, O daughter Zion! For I will come and dwell in your midst, says the LORD. (2:10)

> Rejoice greatly, O daughter Zion!
>   Shout aloud, O daughter Jerusalem!
> See, your king comes to you;
>   triumphant and victorious is he,
> humble and riding on a donkey,
>   on a colt, the foal of a donkey. (9:9)

In neither case is there any intimation of the submission, humiliation, or degradation of a daughter to her abusive parent. Quite the opposite—it is God who takes the initiative in demonstrating loving care for daughter Zion. It is unfortunate that the experience of some women has made it difficult if not impossible for them to find this personification of Jerusalem as "daughter Zion" anything but horrific because of memories of abuse by someone whose sole responsibility was to love and care for them. At the very least, their experience calls for a critique of the ways believers speak about God.

The universalist dimension of the prophet's vision of Jerusalem's future is also easily misconstrued by readers today. The prophet does not envision gentiles becoming Jews or the obliteration of religious differences. Still, Zechariah suggests that the future of the Jewish community should be seen against the wider backdrop of the future of all peoples (v. 11 [15]). The latter part of the book (chaps. 9–14) will develop this thought further. The Bible recognizes that Abraham was the father of many nations (Gen 25). The prophet's vision of the future is not that all the gentiles will become Jews but that the destiny of all peoples is the same, i.e., to live in peace with one another as intended by God. Unfortunately, the universalism expressed by prophets such as Isaiah and Zechariah has served as justification for forced conversion, intolerance, and the attempts to stamp out the culture and religion of indigenous peoples by colonizers. Of course, none of this is about religion. Rather, it is about political and economic control.

Another one of the prophet's motifs that can be misconstrued is the reversal of fortunes theme in 2:8-9 [12-13]. This theme became a staple of the apocalyptic worldview and literature. The problem with the apocalyptic worldview is that it sees people as either good or evil and affirms that evil people will one day get their due and good people will reap the benefits that come from the downfall of evil people. But reality is not that simple. In Zechariah's attempts at describing a new and better future for a people who lived under political and economic oppression since the eighth century BCE, the prophet suggests that one group of oppressors be replaced by another. The people of Yehud should not themselves become oppressors. This is a special concern in the current conflict between the Israelis and Palestinians. The key to a future characterized by just relationship among people is not domination but mutual respect and inclusion.

Are we expecting too much from Zechariah? The prophet had a difficult task, i.e., to encourage people who knew little of self-determination since they had been a subject people for hundreds of years. In describing the contours of the future that the prophet believed God had in store for the people of Yehud, the prophet draws on their experience of familial relationships and their religious traditions. Evidently, Zechariah was successful since people thought it important to preserve his words. When believers pick up his book today, some find the temporal and cultural gap difficult to bridge because of their experience and their worldview that is so different from that of the prophet. They see the metaphors and imagery used by the prophet as supporting a concept of the deity that is abhorrent and human relationships that are hierarchic and oppressive. At the very least, what the prophet contributes to today's readers is the opportunity to offer a critique of religious language and the theological fallout from a reading that does not consider the experience of the oppressed, the kind of relationship that people need to have with Earth and the other creatures who inhabit it, and the contours of a future in which all people are respected.

Zechariah 3:1-10

Restoring the Priesthood

Among the leaders of the Judeans-in-exile who accepted Cyrus's invitation to return to Jerusalem and rebuild the temple to YHWH, there was Joshua, son of Jehozadak and grandson of Seraiah, the chief priest killed by the Babylonians following the destruction of Jerusalem and its temple (2 Kgs 25:18-21; 1 Chr 6:15). It is likely that Joshua was born in Babylon and was among the first group of Judeans to make their way to what was the Persian province of Yehud. His descent from the last high priest of Solomon's temple probably established Joshua as an important figure in the Jewish community. Indeed, Ezra 3:8 identifies Joshua as a leader of the returning exiles but does not call him "the high priest."[1] Mark Boda claims that both Zechariah 3:1-10 and 6:9-15 support the notion that Joshua had a significant role in both the sacral and political spheres.[2] Actually, prior to the building of the second temple, Joshua had

---

1. Sara Japhet notes that this may reflect the tendency in Ezra to avoid the use of titles. See her "Sheshbazzar and Zerubbabel: Against the Background of the Historical and Religious Tendencies of Ezra-Nehemiah," *ZAW* 94 (1982): 66–98. Note that although Zechariah uses the name יהושע (Joshua), Ezra and Nehemiah use ישוע (Jeshua) a variant of that name. See Ezra 3:8 and Neh 12:26.

2. Mark J. Boda, "Perspectives on Priests in Haggai–Malachi," in *Prayer and Poetry in the Dead Sea Scrolls and Related Literature: Essays in Honor of Eileen Schuller on the Occasion of Her 65th Birthday*, ed. Jeremy S. Penner, Ken M. Penner and Cecilia Wassen, STDJ 98 (Leiden: Brill, 2012), 23.

no institutional authority, though as a descendant of the last high priest, he was a member of the Judean elite. Also, he had no political authority. Zerubbabel was a Persian appointee; Joshua was not. Joshua did, however, have standing in the Jewish community. His political "authority" was, at best, informal. It came not from a royal appointment but from popular consent. Joshua's standing within the Jewish community of Yehud was an example of incipient "democratization" developing within that community.

The prophet Haggai delivered his message to Zerubbabel, the returning exile appointed as פחה ("governor") of Yehud by the Persians and to Joshua, the high priest (הכהן הגדול) (Hag 1:1; 2:2). The biblical text does not clarify the relationship between the two, leading scholars to suggest that they formed a "diarchy" in which they shared leadership responsibilities in the Jewish community. Describing the contours of the supposed diarchy in Yehud involves a reconstruction that is based more on speculation than on evidence. The biblical witness offers little information on the activities of Joshua, the high priest, other than his participation in the reconstruction of the altar and temple (Ezra 3:1-13; 5:1-2). Though Haggai mentions Joshua five times (1:1, 12, 14; 2:2, 4) along with Zerubbabel, the prophet does not describe Joshua's activities or his relationship with Zerubbabel. Zechariah offers a little more information about Joshua in chapters 3, 4, and 6. Chapter 3 lists some of Joshua's responsibilities as high priest. Chapter 4 implies that he is one of the two "sons of oil" (v. 14), though Joshua is not explicitly named. Zechariah 6:9-15 speaks of crowns for Joshua and for someone identified as "Branch" (צמח), whom some identify as Zerubbabel. It is this text that has led to the notion that Joshua and Zerubbabel were dual heads of the Jewish community of Yehud.

Whatever the form the community's leadership may have taken, Joshua and Zerubbabel probably did have prominent roles in the community. No woman receives any mention as playing a role comparable to that of Joshua or Zerubbabel. Still, the contribution of women to the restoration of Jewish life in Yehud was crucial to the success of the Judean restoration. With the collapse of the central authority of the Judean state, the family as a socio-economic entity rose in significance.[3] Women as managers of the family's resources exercised considerable influence in the development of Yehud's economy. Rebuilding the city's homes as well as the temple required women's participation (Neh 3:12). That

---

3. Claudia V. Camp, *Wisdom and the Feminine in the Book of Proverbs* (Decatur, GA: Almond Press, 1985), 263.

women also participated in the complex political life of the community is evident by reference to the opposition of the female prophet Noadiah to the policies of Nehemiah, an appointee of the Persian government (Neh 6:14). That she is mentioned along with Sanballat, the governor of Samaria, testifies to her prominence. Although the biblical accounts of the restoration do not highlight the role of women in the Judean restoration, they do reveal women's presence that is significant and effective.[4]

Zechariah 3 and the Women of Jerusalem

The vision account in Zechariah 3 provides a glimpse of the heavenly court where the high priest Joshua stands accused. When we first encounter Joshua, he is dressed in "filthy clothes" (בגדים צואים), which appears to symbolize his state of guilt. As the attendants subsequently take away these clothes, the angel of YHWH tells Joshua that he has removed his guilt (העברתי מעליך עונך, v. 4). Joshua is then being dressed in new clothes: a "fine robe" (מחלצות, v. 4b) and a "pure turban" (צניף טהור, v. 5).

Both sets of clothing evoke passages in Isaiah that feature women. Beginning with the filthy clothes, I suggest that Zechariah 3, as well as the wider Zechariah 1–8, contains a sustained allusion to Isaiah 4:1-4.

- Isaiah 4:1 speaks of seven women taking hold of (החזיקו) one man and asking him to take away their disgrace.

Zechariah 8:23 transforms this notion as it speaks about ten men who will grab hold (החזיקו) of one Jewish man.

- Isaiah 4:2a speaks about "that day" when "the Branch of YHWH" will be beautiful and glorious (ביום ההוא יהיה צמח ה' לצבי ולכבוד). The notion of a coming Branch is strongly reminiscent of Zechariah 3:8-10, when God will bring forth his servant "the Branch" (v. 8) on "that day" (v. 10).

- Isaiah 4:3 shifts the focus to Zion and proclaims that those remaining in Jerusalem will be called holy. Zechariah 3:2 echoes these sentiments as God proclaims his choice of Jerusalem.

- Isaiah 4:4 concludes the pericope by declaring that God will "wash away the filth of the women of Zion" and cleanse the bloodstains from Jerusalem by a spirit of judgment and a "spirit of fire." The term for

---

4. Tamara Cohn Eskenazi, " 'Out from the Shadows': Biblical Woman in the Post-exilic Era," *JSOT* 54 (1992): 41.

"filth" here in Isaiah 4:4 is the same as in Zechariah 3:4, and the reference to "fire" conjures up the imagery in Zechariah 3:2 of a "stick saved from fire" (אוד מצל מאש).

Turning to Joshua's clean clothes, the only other people in the Bible that wear both a מחלצות and a צניף are the women of Jerusalem in Isaiah 3:16-23. These women are described as "haughty" or "proud" (גבהו), and they behave in a flirtatious and alluring manner (v. 16). Therefore, God will snatch away their finery, including both their "fine robes" (המחלצות, v. 22) and their "turbans" (צניפות, v. 23). What do these allusions in Zechariah 3 to the women of

Jerusalem accomplish? In my view, the allusions to Isaiah 4:1-4 emphasize not only the culpability of these women but also that they will be included in God's cleansing of the land. Whatever the women's sins were, they will be exonerated. "On that day" in Zechariah 3:8-10 when God will "depart with the guilt of that land" (משתי את עון הארץ ההיא), the women's guilt will also be removed. As to the allusion to Isaiah 3:22-23, the fact that the cleansed high priest is portrayed as wearing finery associated with women may be taken as an additional sign of their rehabilitation.

Lena-Sofia Tiemeyer

The Fourth Vision: New Clothes for a New Day (3:1-5)

At the beginning of the restoration (the late sixth century BCE), Yehud's Jewish community faced the formidable task of having to reconstitute itself in the wake of the collapse of Judah's political and religious institutions earlier in the century. The new shape that the ancestral religion of the Jews would take was still unclear. Would the temple be rebuilt? Would its priesthood be revived? Would the Jewish people and their ancestral religion survive the political, economic, and social pressures that would be brought to bear on them? Would the national state and dynasty be reestablished? The visions recounted in Zechariah 3–4 focus on the religious and civic leadership of the Jewish community in Yehud as crucial steps in establishing Jewish life in Yehud. At the highest levels, that leadership was exercised by men. Still, the women of the Jewish community played an indispensable role in the Judean restoration, especially in the family and in the economy of Yehud. They had to find a way to make use of the limited resources available to most of Yehud's people to feed and clothe their families. The success of the Judean restoration depended on the women of Yehud.

Zech 3:1-5

¹Then he showed me the high priest Joshua standing before the angel of the LORD and the accuser standing at his right hand to accuse him. ²And the LORD said to the accuser, "The LORD rebuke you, O accuser! The LORD who has chosen Jerusalem rebuke you! Is not this man a brand plucked from the fire?" ³Now Joshua was wearing filthy clothes as he stood before the angel.

⁴The angel said to those who were standing before him, "Take off his filthy clothes." And to him he said, "See, I have taken your guilt away from you, and I will clothe you with festal apparel." ⁵And he said, "Let them put a clean turban on his head." So they put a clean turban on his head and clothed him with apparel, and the angel of the LORD was standing by.

Two figures are featured in Zechariah's fourth vision: the high priest Joshua and someone, probably Zerubbabel, whom the prophet refers to as צמח ("Branch," v. 8).[5] According to Ezra 2:2 and Nehemiah 12:1, Joshua and Zerubbabel led the first group of Judean exiles from Babylon to Judah. Haggai mentions Joshua alongside Zerubbabel, the governor of Yehud (Hag 1:12-15). These texts suggest that Joshua and Zerubbabel had important roles in the Judean restoration, though they offer few specifics and do not describe the relationship between the two.

The setting for the prophet's fourth vision (vv. 1-5) is the divine court, with the high priest Joshua,[6] an angel, and the accuser standing before God. The theme of God's choice of Jerusalem appears for the third time in the book (3:2; see also 1:17 and 2:12). Jerusalem played a central role in the religious life of all Jews—both the men and women returning from exile and the Judeans who had remained in the land—since God chose the city as God's dwelling place on earth (see Zech 2:10-12 [14-16]). Jerusalem, then, was the most appropriate setting for Zechariah's vision of the high priest, who will lead the efforts to return the people to God's

5. Mark J. Boda, "Oil, Crowns and Thrones: Prophet, Priest and King in Zechariah 1:7–6:15," *JHebS* 3 (2001): sec. 4.3.3.4. The identification of Zerubbabel as Branch is not without problems. Also, Beate Schmidtgen considers the oracle to Joshua in 3:7-8 to be an addition to the text by those interested in supporting the authority of the priesthood in the Jewish community. See her "Haggai and Zechariah: A New Temple—New Life For All," in *Feminist Biblical Interpretation: A Compendium of Critical Commentary on the Books of the Bible and Related Literature*, ed. Luise Schottroff and Marie-Theres Wacker, trans. Martin Rumscheidt et al. (Grand Rapids: Eerdmans, 2012), 460–72, at 462.

6. Unlike the other visions that are full of strange or obscure figures, the high priest Joshua is a historical figure who was a contemporary of the prophet.

good graces. The prophet reveals his hopes for the future of the Jewish people in the account of the fourth vision (vv. 1-5) and the related oracle (vv. 6-10). Joshua was to have a central role in fulfilling those hopes.

Reconstructing the development of the Israelite priesthood in the postexilic period is not a simple matter.[7] The primary designation for "priest" in biblical Hebrew appears only in the masculine form: כהן.[8] The feminine form, *khnt*, appears in cognate languages but is not found in the Hebrew Scriptures. Tamar Kamionkowski suggests that, while the role of priest was probably limited to men even before the creation of the Aaronide priestly tradition in the late Second Temple period, women in priestly families may have enjoyed higher social status relative to other women in Israelite and early Jewish society.[9] According to Wilda Gafney, women in priestly families (for example, the daughter of a priest) may have performed special functions, such as examining sick women and then reporting findings to the male priest, in order to maintain propriety in the priest's role of diagnosing skin conditions and other health concerns.[10]

While the Hebrew Bible does not refer to female priests, there are several women who exercise leadership roles in communal worship.[11] For example, Exodus 15:20 identifies Miriam, sister of Moses and Aaron, as

7. Aelred Cody's *A History of Old Testament Priesthood*, AnBib 35 (Rome: Pontifical Biblical Institute, 1969) remains a helpful treatment of this topic. See also Deborah Rooke, *Zadok's Heirs: The Role and Development of the High Priesthood in Ancient Israel*, Oxford Theological Monographs (Oxford: Oxford University Press, 2000); and Gary A. Anderson and Saul M. Olyan, eds., *Priesthood and Cult in Ancient Israel*, JSOTSup 125 (Sheffield: JSOT Press, 1991). For the postexilic period, see Martha Himmelfarb, *A Kingdom of Priests: Ancestry and Merit in Ancient Judaism*, Jewish Culture and Contexts (Philadelphia: University of Pennsylvania Press, 2006).

8. Another term for priest is כמר, which appears only rarely (1 Kgs 13:33; 2 Kgs 23:5; Hos 10:5; Zeph 1:4). In modern Hebrew usage, this word is used for priests of religions other than Judaism.

9. S. Tamar Kamionkowski, *Leviticus*, WCS 3 (Collegeville, MN: Liturgical Press, 2018), xlii–xlviii.

10. Wilda C. Gafney, *Womanist Midrash: A Reintroduction to the Women of the Torah and the Throne* (Louisville: Westminster John Knox, 2017), 114, cited in Kamionkowski, *Leviticus*, 118–19.

11. Phyllis A. Bird, "The Place of Women in the Israelite Cultus," in *Ancient Israelite Religion: Essays in Honor of Frank Moore Cross*, ed. Patrick D. Miller et al. (Philadelphia: Fortress, 1987); and Richard A. Henshaw, *Female and Male: The Cultic Personnel; The Bible and the Rest of the Ancient Near East*, Princeton Theological Monograph Series 31 (Allison Park, PA: Pickwick Publications, 1994).

a נביאה ("prophetess") who leads women in music and dancing in a cultic setting;[12] Exodus 38:8 mentions הצבאת ("the ministering women") who serve at the entrance of the tent of meeting, though the text provides no details about what that service entailed. Women also appear as singers (Ezra 2:65; Neh 7:67) and dancers (Exod 15:20; Jdt 15:12) in cultic settings. Although women may not have been priests in ancient Israel, they did serve in several capacities in the community's cultic life.[13]

TRANSLATION MATTERS

One of the characters in Zechariah's fourth vision is השטן (literally, "the satan"), which NRSVue renders as "accuser," a proper name. The presence of the definite article in the MT implies that השטן is a title in 3:1, not a proper name. The NABRE renders השטן as "the adversary." Both the NRSVue and NABRE translations of 3:1 suggest a judicial setting in which השטן is a type of prosecuting attorney, though there is no evidence that the word comes from a judicial context.[14] Ryan Stokes suggests that השטן is violently opposed to the individuals he attacks.[15] In Zechariah 3, השטן has set his eyes on Joshua.

The prophet's fourth vision depicts Joshua standing before the divine court, attired in filthy clothing, which symbolizes the ritual impurity of the exiles who have returned to Jerusalem after living outside of "the holy land" (see Zech 2:12). The accusation made by השטן is not stated explicitly, but God's response makes the meaning clear. Joshua is the

---

12. Perhaps also in her prophetic role Miriam, together with Aaron, rebuked Moses for marrying a Cushite woman, challenging Moses's authority as the sole spokesperson for God (Num 12:1-2).

13. See further Bernadette J. Brooten, *Women Leaders in the Ancient Synagogue: Inscriptional Evidence and Background Issues*, BJS 36 (Chico, CA: Scholars Press, 1982).

14. The BDB, 966, understands שטן to be a denominative verb שטן and renders it as "be or act as an adversary," while William Holladay's *A Concise Hebrew and Aramaic Lexicon of the Old Testament* (Grand Rapids: Eerdmans, 1988), 350, renders the verb as "bear a grudge against, harbor animosity toward." Holladay reads the noun as "accuser, adversary" and identifies the שטן of Zech 3:1 as a "supernatural figure." Carol L. Meyers and Eric M. Meyers (*Haggai, Zechariah 1–8: A New Translation with Introduction and Commentary*, AB 25B [Garden City, NY: Doubleday, 1987], 184) observe that the noun appears in a judicial context in Ps 109:6 while the verb usually designates "personal adversaries."

15. Ryan Stokes, "Satan, YHWH's Executioner," *JBL* 133 (2014): 251–70.

"brand plucked from the fire" of forced migration to Babylon (v. 2). Julia Foote (1823–1900), an African American evangelist, used this phrase in her autobiography to speak of the perils she experienced during her 1849 preaching tour. She believed that God preserved her from danger just as God protected Joshua.[16]

Joshua did not cause the impurity he contracted; rather, he remained faithful when the adversary tested his loyalty. God is determined to change the condition of impurity that Joshua "wears," first by ordering the adversary to cease his attacks on Joshua and then by directing the angel to exchange Joshua's filthy clothes for festal apparel.[17] In verse 5, the prophet himself calls for the placement of a turban on Joshua's head—an item that carries political as well as sacral significance. The vision appears to endorse hierocracy as an essential component of the Judean restoration.

Joshua's filthy garments likely reflect perceptions of the priesthood in Zechariah's day as tainted with ritual impurity that resulted from the destruction of the temple and the shame of the exile that lasted almost seventy years.[18] The high priest's rehabilitation begins as an angel orders unnamed associates of Joshua, who are standing before him, to remove his filthy clothes and replace them with "festal apparel." The divine declaration that, through this act, "I have taken your guilt away from you" points to a restoration of the priesthood and its religious standing (v. 4). As high priest, Joshua is a stand-in for all the returned exiles; therefore, their guilt also is removed by God. The exchange of filthy garments for festal ones confirms the legitimacy of Joshua as high priest and of other returning exiles (i.e., "those who were standing before him") in the restoration of Jerusalem.

The process of dressing, undressing, or changing one's clothes is a symbolic act in biblical literature. In some passages, putting on or taking off a

---

16. Joy A. Schroeder and Marion Ann Taylor, *Voices Long Silenced: Women Biblical Interpreters through the Centuries* (Louisville: Westminster John Knox, 2022), 158–59.

17. Janet E. Tollington, *Tradition and Innovation in Haggai and Zechariah 1–8*, JSOT-Sup 150 (Sheffield: JSOT Press, 1993), 156, points out that the emphasis here is on the defiled clothes that Joshua wears and not the defilement of Joshua himself. Had Joshua himself contracted impurity, he would have had to cleanse his own body, but because he "wears" the impurity of the people, he is unable to remove it himself.

18. Joseph Blenkinsopp maintains that Joshua's filthy garments represent some infidelity on Joshua's part. See his *A History of Prophecy in Israel* (Philadelphia: Westminster, 1983), 238. This is disputed by David L. Petersen, *Haggai and Zechariah 1–8: A Commentary*, OTL (Philadelphia: Westminster, 1984), 194–96; and Peter Ackroyd, *Exile and Restoration: A Study of Hebrew Thought of the Sixth Century B.C.*, OTL (London: SCM Press, 1968), 184. It is unlikely that Zechariah engages in a polemic against the priesthood here.

robe is associated with the donning or shedding of a leadership position, as exemplified by the narratives of Joseph (Gen 41:14) and David (1 Sam 17:38). The implied symbolism of being clothed by God, or by an angel who acts as a divine emissary, is even more significant. When a divine figure changes someone's clothes, it indicates a change in destiny. According to Phyllis Trible, God takes on a maternal role in the act of dressing or undressing a biblical figure.[19] Seen from this perspective, Zechariah 3:1-5 presents Joshua metaphorically in the role of a child being nurtured by his mother. Extending this point further is the fact that the "filthy clothes" that God orders be removed are not simply dirty laundry; rather, they are, like a soiled diaper, filled with excrement. This image highlights Joshua's vulnerability and his dependence on God to achieve the catharsis that the high priest and the people of Yehud all need as the Judean restoration begins.

Biblical texts involving dressing and undressing often reflect traditional gender roles in the ancient world. In the case of both men and women, dressing usually symbolizes taking on authority and power, and undressing symbolizes vulnerability. When men dress and undress, it often signifies a change in military or leadership roles; for example, in 1 Samuel 24:4-11, David rips off Saul's cloak to signify David's taking the monarchy from Saul. When women dress and undress, it usually indicates their sexual power or powerlessness.[20] For example, in the second-century BCE book of Judith, the author describes Judith bedecking herself so that she can seduce and kill the Assyrian general Holofernes, thus saving her city (Jdt 10:1-10). In these texts, donning beautiful clothes symbolizes power, authority, and sometimes religious purity. Removing these clothes, or wearing filthy clothes, symbolizes vulnerability, submission, and impurity.

The terms used in Zechariah 3:4-5 for Joshua's new garments suggest a sense of ambiguity regarding his gender and leadership roles.[21] First, the word מחלצות ("festal apparel" in v. 4) refers to a long robe that can be

19. Phyllis Trible, "Depatriarchalizing in Biblical Interpretation," *JAAR* 41 (1973): 32–33.

20. Shahram Jalilian and Seyed Ali Fatemi, "Women's Clothing in Ancient Iran (Case Study: Achaemenid Period)," *Journal of Iranian Cultural Research* 4 (2011): 1–22; Marie Johnson, Ethel B. Abrahams, and Maria M. L. Evans, *Ancient Greek Dress* (Chicago: Argonaut, 1964); Kristi Upson-Saia, Carly Daniel-Hughes, and Alicia J. Batten, eds., *Dressing Judeans and Christians in Antiquity* (Surrey: Ashgate, 2014).

21. Julia O'Brien, "Zechariah," in *Women's Bible Commentary*, ed. Carol A. Newsom, Sharon H. Ringe, and Jacqueline E. Lapsley, 3rd ed. (Louisville: Westminster John Knox, 2012), 346, points out that there are "ways in which gender assignments in the book of Zechariah are unstable. In Zechariah 1–8, men do not always speak with authority, and women's power refuses to be contained."

worn by women. In fact, the only other occurrence of this word in the Hebrew Bible is in Isaiah 3:22, where it refers to fine apparel worn by the "daughters of Zion," i.e., the proud women of Jerusalem's elite class.[22] Second, the word used for Joshua's turban (צָנִיף) reflects ambiguity in his role as high priest. The two Hebrew words for "turban" are etymologically related. מִצְנֶפֶת is far more common and is, with one exception, used to speak of priestly headgear.[23] For example, Exodus 28:3-4 includes a turban (מִצְנֶפֶת) among the items of Aaron's dress that "consecrate him for [the] priesthood." But the word for turban in Zechariah 3:5 is צָנִיף, which is always used in reference to the garments of royal (e.g., Sir 11:5 and 47:6) or noble (e.g., Job 29:14) figures.[24] Given the royal connotations of צָנִיף elsewhere in the Hebrew Bible, it is significant that Zechariah refers to Joshua's priestly turban as a צָנִיף instead of מִצְנֶפֶת. This may be a subtle way of indicating that Joshua's leadership of the restored community would extend beyond the sacral realm into the political as well.[25]

Zechariah's fourth vision may reflect internal conflicts in the Jewish community regarding the pattern that Yehud's leadership should take. On the one hand, there were those who wished for the return of the dynasty of David, but Darius's order to resume the rebuilding of the temple in Jerusalem was, in effect, his claim on the throne of Judah since the building and restoration of temples were royal prerogatives. Apparently, Zechariah accepted the political reality that the restoration of the Davidic dynasty was not possible. The prophet points to the high priest Joshua as the most likely candidate to lead the community into a new era. On the other hand, there were likely Jews who opposed the restoration of the office of high priest and investing the occupant of that office with authority over the Jewish community. Also, it is possible that some may have opposed returning Jerusalem to a place of prominence, arguing that the fall of the city and the destruction of its temple meant

22. According to BDB (323–24), חלץ, the root of מַחֲלָצוֹת, has two meanings, both of which carry interesting connotations for a feminist reading of Zech 3:4. One meaning has to do with taking off or stripping away, as in plunder (e.g., 2 Sam 2:21); the other refers to equipping (outfitting, empowering) for war (e.g., several times in Num 32:16-32) or a spiritual ordeal (e.g., Isa 58:11).

23. That exception is Ezek 21:26 [21:31], where it appears in parallelism with עֲטָרָה ("crown"). This word appears in the plural in Zech 6:11, which speaks of crowns made for Joshua.

24. Isa 3:23 includes צָנִיף as well as מַחֲלָצוֹת ("festive apparel") in the list of clothing worn by Jerusalem's affluent women.

25. Meyers and Meyers, *Haggai, Zechariah 1–8*, 192.

that God had permanently rejected the city. Rebuilding the temple and investing its priesthood with the leadership of the Jewish community may have been seen by some as patently contrary to the divine will.[26] Zechariah's fourth vision, however, counters such opposition by a strong affirmation of God's choice of Jerusalem (v. 2) and investiture of Joshua as high priest.

An Omen of Things to Come (3:6-10)

The reference to an inscribed stone in Zechariah 3:9 raises several questions. First, is the stone part of the vesture of the high priest or is it part of the new temple still under construction?[27] Both options are possible but, given the focus in the prophet's fourth vision on Joshua's garments, it is more probable that the stone is part of the high priest's vestments. Second, how many facets (עינים) does the stone have? As Max Rogland points out, the word עינים can serve as both a dual and a plural.[28] The NRSVue reads it as a plural ("seven facets"), while the pointing in the BHS has it as dual form, suggesting a reading of "seven pairs of facets." If the latter is intended, then the fourteen facets on the stone could recall the twelve stones (one for each of the Israelite tribes) on Aaron's breastplate (Exod 28:9-10), plus the *urim* and *thummim*. The single stone in Zechariah 3:9 probably symbolizes Judah as the only one of the tribes to experience the restoration. Third, it is unclear what God will inscribe on the stone. Is it, perhaps, a religious designation for this sacral object? Or is it a reference to the high priest or to Branch? What is clear is that the investiture of the new high priest signals the beginning of a new age. Just as God has restored Joshua's status by changing his filthy clothes for festal apparel, so God will remove Judah's accumulated

---

26. This opposition to the status of Jerusalem and its political and religious leaders is reminiscent of an oracle of the populist prophet Micah two hundred years earlier (Mic 3:9-12). Alternatives to Jerusalem were Bethel and Mizpah. Both towns were within the territory allotted to Yehud. Mizpah served as the administrative center of Judah under the Babylonians (2 Kgs 25:22-23). Bethel has a long pedigree as a Yahwistic shrine (Gen 31:13; 35:1). The temple built by Jeroboam (1 Kgs 12:25-33) managed to survive the destruction brought by the Babylonians.

27. See James VanderKam, "Joshua the High Priest and the Interpretation of Zechariah 3," *CBQ* 53 (1991): 562–67 for a discussion of these two options.

28. See his *Haggai and Zechariah 1–8: A Handbook on the Hebrew Text*, Baylor Handbook on the Hebrew Bible (Waco, TX: Baylor University Press, 2016), 126.

[6]Then the angel of the LORD warned Joshua, saying [7]"Thus says the LORD of hosts: If you will walk in my ways and keep my requirements, then you shall rule my house and have charge of my courts, and I will give you the right of access among those who are standing here. [8]Now listen, Joshua, high priest, you and your colleagues who sit before you! For they are an omen of things to come: I am going to bring my servant the Branch. [9]For on the stone that I have set before Joshua, on a single stone with seven facets, I will engrave its inscription, says the LORD of hosts, and I will remove the guilt of this land in a single day. [10]On that day, says the LORD of hosts, you shall invite each other to come under your vine and fig tree."

guilt in a single day (v. 9) and will usher in a time of peace and prosperity for the people of Yehud (v. 10).

The connection between the kingship and priesthood may have emerged more strongly in the late second century BCE, when some Hasmoneans were laying claim to both the high priesthood and kingship. But the connection between these two positions was already in place by the time Zechariah 3 was written. The role of the high priesthood was broadened to encompass many civil responsibilities as the community had to find a pattern of leadership.[28] Some scholars do not take this passage as historical evidence that the role of the high priesthood was being expanded in the early Second Temple period. Michael Segal argues that the focus in this chapter is on God's promised protection of Joshua and his priestly dynasty, which would occur only on the condition that Joshua properly maintained the temple.[29] According to Segal, Zechariah 3 reflects, not an expansion of Joshua's role, but rather a limitation on it, since the high priest's relationship with God was contingent on keeping God's requirements. The conditional aspect of God's promise to Joshua suggests that the high priesthood could move from family to family, which might indicate instability in the temple's administration. The text of Zechariah does not give any civil responsibilities to Joshua. Attention centers on Joshua's religious responsibilities.

28. Meyers and Meyers, *Haggai, Zechariah 1–8*, 182.

29. Michael Segal, "The Responsibilities and Rewards of Joshua the High Priest according to Zechariah 3:7," *JBL* 126 (2007): 724.

The focus of both the vision (3:1-5) and the oracle (3:6-10) is on Joshua, the high priest. The vision of Joshua's investiture and the significance of his vestments, however, point to the larger reality of the Judean restoration: the removal of Judah's guilt and the resumption of temple service that will follow. These developments will lead to a new era in Judah's life—an era of peace and prosperity, symbolized by the vine and fig tree mentioned in 3:10. It is likely that some Jews expected that this new era would be marked by the restoration of the Davidic dynasty. But two *Persian* kings, Cyrus the Great and Darius I, ordered the temple of Jerusalem to be rebuilt. Their actions, in effect, served as a claim to the throne of Judah. Zechariah accepted that reality and saw the resumption of priestly service by Joshua and his associates as the harbinger of the new era now that God had decided to dwell once again among the people of Yehud (Zech 2:10).

Without a doubt, leadership of the Jewish community in Yehud was a matter of great concern. With encouragement from Darius I and from Haggai and Zechariah, the Jewish community did complete work on the second temple in 516 BCE. It should not be surprising that the book of Zechariah accords the high priest Joshua and his fellow priests a prominent place in the Judean restoration. God promises to bring another person, referred to as צמח ("Branch"), which Isaiah 4:2; 11:1; Jeremiah 23:5; 33:15 associated with the Davidic dynasty, to give rise to hopes for a restoration of the dynasty and the kingdom of Judah. Zechariah does not make such an association explicit, since the Persian authorities would not have tolerated anything that might incite rebellion in Yehud. Rather, the text intimates that there was a cooperative relationship between the high priest and the Branch, marked by the invitation that each extended to the other "to come under your vine and fig tree" (v. 10). Still, it appears that the high priest was the senior partner—at least in Jewish eyes—because of the significance of the religious sphere of activity for the Jewish community.

The vision of God exchanging Joshua's filthy clothes for festal apparel (vv. 3-5) shows Joshua's (and Yehud's) dependence on God's forbearance to further the Judean restoration. Deuteronomic language in verse 7 gives shape to Joshua's (and Yehud's) response to God's mercy and reflects the growing influence of Deuteronomic theology in the Persian period. Zechariah 3 closes with a reference to the enigmatic figure צמח ("Branch"), whose arrival marks the imminent end of the Jewish people's alienation from God and anticipates a time of peace.

Conclusion

Ingrid E. Lilly describes Zechariah 3 as an instance of "innovative masculinity of messianic priesthood."[30] This makes possible reconciliation among the people at large. An effect of Joshua's leadership is peacebuilding so that the post-conflict Jewish community in Yehud will be characterized by reconciliation. Lilly's view of the leadership provided by Joshua asserts that it is not about control and domination but about the restoration of social peace expressed in traditional terms (see 1 Kgs 4:25; 2 Kgs 18:31) by the final verse of Zechariah 3: "On that day, says the LORD of hosts, you shall invite each other to come under your vine and fig tree." This is not a matter of restoring the social order of preexilic Judah but a new social order that was not to be marked by oppression of the ordinary folk by those who controlled the economy and politics of the kingdom of Judah.

Women had no explicitly stated role in Yehud's restoration as Zechariah described it in chapter 3 because of the centrality of the priesthood that, in Yahwistic religious practice, was limited to males. That limitation was reinforced by the prophet's apparent assumption that the gender as well as the leadership status of the high priest was the result of an exercise of divine sovereignty. That does not mean, however, that women had no role in cultic life once the temple had been rebuilt, nor does it necessarily mean that the gender roles that Zechariah assumed in his own social and historical context must be maintained in different contexts today.

Leadership roles and the status of women are significant issues in both Judaism and Christianity today. Women serve as rabbis in both Reform and Conservative congregations in the United States. Even some Orthodox congregations in Israel, the United States, and elsewhere, have begun to ordain women. While organizations such as the Rabbinical Council of America and the Orthodox Union officially oppose this practice, they have not expelled any member synagogues who have hired female clergy.[31] Almost all Christian denominations in the United States ordain women as congregational leaders. Even in churches that do not permit the ordination of women, women serve in important leadership

30. Ingrid E. Lilly, "Zechariah's Gendered Visions: A Feminist Biblical Theology of Reconciliation," in *After Exegesis: Feminist Biblical Theology; Essays in Honor of Carol A. Newsom*, ed. Patricia K. Tull and Jacqueline E. Lapsley (Waco, TX: Baylor University Press, 2015), 207.

31. https://www.jta.org/2018/01/31/news-opinion/united-states/orthodox-union -will-not-penalize-synagogues-with-women-clergy.

positions.[32] Women hold significant positions as administrators in some Jewish and Christian religious institutions, as administrators and faculty members in denominational colleges and universities, seminaries, and schools of theology. Women have been founders and directors of faith-based organizations across the United States and in other countries.[33]

As Tamara Eskenazi and other scholars have demonstrated, women played a significant role in the Judean restoration, although Zechariah's vision of the restored priesthood and, specifically, of the role of the high priest does not offer information on women's roles in the religious life of Yehud during the Persian period. Zechariah offers us a glimpse at the transition from Judah's monarchical leadership structure, when the king had primary responsibility over the temple as well as the state, to the independence of priestly leadership. Though "the Branch" does have some role to play, Zechariah's vision of the cleansing and investiture of Joshua signals that the high priest would not have to share authority over the temple with a civil power.

32. One example is the predominantly African American holiness denomination, the Sanctified Church. See Cheryl Townsend Gilkes, *If It Wasn't for the Women: Black Women's Experience and Womanist Culture in Church and Community* (Maryknoll, NY: Orbis Books, 2001).

33. Lisa K. Johnson, *Keeping Women Silent: A Study of Female Leadership in Faith-Based Institutions* (PhD diss., Capella University, 2011).

Zechariah 4:1-14

Leadership for a New Day

Zechariah 3 centers its attention on the high priest Joshua while chapter 4 focuses on Zerubbabel, referring to him by name four times (vv. 6, 7, 9, 10). Haggai identifies Zerubbabel as the פחה ("governor") of Yehud (Hag 1:1, 14; 2:2, 21) though Zechariah does not.[1] Nonetheless, Zerubbabel was a key figure in the Judean restoration. The role he played in the restoration and Darius's policy of encouraging the development of local law codes may have fueled expectation that some form of the old Judahite political structures would reemerge in Yehud.

Who was Zerubbabel? The simple answer is that Zerubbabel was a Jew from Babylon who relocated to Yehud in the early years of Persian rule. His name, which means "seed of Babylon" in Akkadian, suggests that he was born in Babylon during the exile. According to Ezra 5:14 and Haggai 1:1, Zerubbabel held the position of פחה of Yehud during the reign of Darius I. This simple answer, however, does not do justice to the complex biblical portrait of this enigmatic figure. Ezra (3:2, 8; 5:2) and Haggai (1:1, 12; 2:2, 23) identify Zerubbabel's father as Shealtiel, while 1 Chronicles 3:16-19 names Pedaiah, Shealtiel's brother, as Zerubbabel's father. In either case, the genealogy in 1 Chronicles asserts that Zerubbabel

---

1. פחה is masculine, though nouns ending in ה are usually feminine. Here the ה is not the feminine ending. פחה is an Akkadian loan word. See Paul Joüon and Tamitsu Muraoka, *A Grammar of Biblical Hebrew* (Rome: Gregorian Biblical BookShop, 2006), 89b.

was the grandson of Jeconiah (Jehoiachin), Judah's young king whom the Babylonians led into exile following an unsuccessful revolt against the empire in 597 BCE (2 Kgs 25:1-12) and who apparently died while still in Babylon (2 Kgs 25:30). There is no other evidence that Zerubbabel might have been a member of the Judean royal family (and Zechariah never suggests it).[2] Still, the presence of Zerubbabel in the New Testament genealogies of Jesus (Matt 1:12 and Luke 3:27) indicates that there was a popular belief that Zerubbabel was a member of the Davidic line—a belief that persisted into the Roman period.

Jewish tradition remembers Zerubbabel as serving in the royal court of Persia and having been appointed governor of Yehud by Darius I. First Esdras (3 Ezra) 3–4[3] preserves a delightful and imaginative legend about Zerubbabel and two other guards in Darius's court. In that story, these three members took part in a test of wits to "identify the strongest thing of all" (1 Esd 3:5, NRSV). One of the guards claimed that wine is the strongest thing, and the other, that the king is the strongest. Zerubbabel, however, argued that women are the strongest since they give birth both to kings who rule the world and to men who plant vineyards to produce wine (1 Esd 4:13-41). The Zerubbabel character added that a man will give up silver and gold for the love of a woman and so he concluded to his implied male audience, "You must realize that women rule over you!" (1 Esd 4:22). This story provides some insight regarding views about women among Jews of the Persian period. On the surface, 1 Esdras states that women are the "strongest of all" and that men are subordinate to women. Still, the story reflects an assumption that men are, nonetheless, superior to women, and it suggests that women are a threat to men. The story teaches that men must not let themselves be overtaken by women's sexuality, perhaps mocking Darius who, according to 1 Esdras 4:28-32, was under the spell of his concubine Apame.[4]

---

2. Jon L. Berquist, *Judaism in Persia's Shadow: A Social and Historical Approach* (Minneapolis: Fortress, 1995), 63; D. F. O'Kennedy, "Zechariah 3–4: Core of Proto-Zechariah," *OTE* 16 (2003): 384n39, considers the mention of צמח in Zechariah 3:8 as an oblique reference to Zerubbabel's status as a member of Judah's royal family.

3. 1 Esdras, also known as 3 Esdras in the Vulgate, is listed among the Old Testament Apocrypha. Except for the story of the contest won by Zerubbabel (1 Esd 3–4) the book rehearses 2 Chronicles, Ezra, and Nehemiah. An English translation of 1 Esdras is available in *The New Oxford Annotated Bible*, ed. Michael D. Coogan et al. (New York: Oxford University Press, 2001), 1633–54.

4. See Lewis John Eron, " 'That Women Have Mastery over Both King and Beggar' (*TJud* 15:5)—The Relationship of the Fear of Sexuality to the Status of Women

This engaging story provides a reason for Zerubbabel's appointment: he won the contest and got the appointment. Though this legend from 1 Esdras is without historical value, it is true that Zerubbabel owed his position in Yehud to his service to the Persians, not to his supposed relationship to the family of David. It is unlikely that the Persians would have provided for the restoration any hope for the Judahite monarchy by appointing a member of the former royal family of Judah as governor of Yehud. It is noteworthy that, unlike 1 Chronicles 3:17-19 and Haggai 2:21-23, Zechariah never alludes to any supposed royal connections for Zerubbabel, nor does the book explicitly identify Zerubbabel as the פחה of Yehud. Zechariah does not mention any of Zerubbabel's duties as the civil administrator of Yehud apart from his role in the reconstruction of the temple, nor does the book describe his relationship with the high priest Joshua. Zechariah focuses on Zerubbabel's connection with the building of the temple since this project was a central concern for the book as the centerpiece of the Judean restoration.

The complex structure of Zechariah 4, along with some challenging philological issues, makes the prophet's fifth vision one that is especially difficult to understand and appreciate.[5] To help simplify the analysis of the vision, the explanatory oracle in Zechariah 4:6b-10a will be discussed first, followed by commentary on the vision report in 4:1-6a and 10b-14.

"Grace, Grace to It" (4:6b-10a)

Unlike previous chapters, where the prophet's vision is followed by an explanatory oracle, the vision report in Zechariah 4 is interrupted by an oracle, leading some scholars to conclude that the oracle is a secondary insertion.[6] John Collins has pointed out that visions and oracles are intermingled in apocalyptic texts and that this phenomenon does not necessarily imply multiple authors.[7] Although Zechariah 4 is not an apocalyptic

---

in Apocrypha and Pseudepigrapha: 1 Esdras (*3 Ezra*) 3–4, Ben Sira and *The Testament of Judah*," *JSP* 9 (1991): 47–48.

5. Max Rogland, *Haggai and Zechariah 1–8: A Handbook on the Hebrew Text*, Baylor Handbook on the Hebrew Bible (Waco, TX: Baylor University Press, 2016), 130.

6. E.g., Martin Hallaschka, *Haggai und Sacharja 1–8: Eine Redaktionsgeschichtliche Untersuchung*, BZAW 411 (Berlin: De Gruyter, 2011), 222–28. There are oracles found in several places in 1:7–6:15. There is no reason to excise the oracles from the vision accounts.

7. John J. Collins, *The Apocalyptic Imagination: An Introduction to Jewish Apocalyptic Literature*, Biblical Resource Series, 2nd ed. (Grand Rapids: Eerdmans, 1998), 14.

Zech 4:6b-10a

Not by might, nor by power, but by my spirit, says the Lord of hosts. [7]What are you, O great mountain? Before Zerubbabel you shall become a plain, and he shall bring out the top stone amid shouts of 'Grace, grace to it!'"

[8]Moreover, the word of the Lord came to me, saying, [9]"The hands of Zerubbabel have laid the foundation of this house; his hands shall also complete it. Then you will know that the Lord of hosts has sent me to you. [10]For whoever has despised the day of small things shall rejoice and shall see the plummet in the hand of Zerubbabel.

text, the same principle can apply. The oracle is not a secondary insertion but introduces Zerubbabel, symbolized in verse 3 as one of the two "olive trees" that flank the menorah. The oracle also delineates his role in ceremonies connected with the temple's reconstruction, thus situating his place in the prophet's vision for the renewal of Jewish life in Yehud.

The words of God to Zerubbabel in verse 6—"Not by might, nor by power, but by my spirit"—do not form a complete sentence in Hebrew or in English; nevertheless, the meaning is clear. The oracle designates Zerubbabel as chosen by God to complete the construction of the temple (v. 8). The terms חיל and כח ("might" and "power") often refer to military power,[8] but Zechariah 4 asserts that the renewal of Jewish life in Yehud would not come about through the exercise of such power; rather, it would be God's רוח ("spirit," a word with feminine grammatical gender) that would enable Zerubbabel to complete his task.

Verses 7-9 describe a ceremonial role that Zerubbabel plays by setting a stone at the beginning of the reconstruction project. His actions generate exclamations of approval evidently on the part of the people of Yehud. The precise meaning of the exclamatory phrase חן חן לה (NRSVue: "Grace, grace to it"; NABRE: "Favor, favor be upon it") is unclear, but it likely

---

Although Zechariah 4 is not an apocalyptic text, it is an example of the same phenomenon that Collins sees in apocalyptic texts. Carol L. Meyers and Eric M. Meyers, *Haggai, Zechariah 1–8: A New Translation with Introduction and Commentary*, AB 25B (Garden City, NY: Doubleday, 1987), 267, describe chapter 4 as employing the "classic envelope construction" and also reject the view that the insertion is secondary.

8. The term כח generally refers to physical strength, sometimes coupled with moral rectitude; for example, it appears seven times in reference to Samson's strength in Judges 16. The term חיל has a wide range of meanings, including the strength of a warrior (see Judg 6:12 and 11:1); often חיל functions as a metonym for an army; for example, see Exod 15:4 and Jer 32:2.

expresses the people's approval of the progress in the temple project. This people's acclamation is followed by God's declaration that Zerubbabel's hands would complete what they had started (v. 9), reinforcing the confidence expressed in the rhetorical question and its answer in verse 7: "What are you, O great mountain? Before Zerubbabel you shall become a plain." The final verse of the oracle (v. 10a) encourages those who may not have believed that rebuilding the temple would have any real significance (i.e., would be a "small thing," v. 10) to recognize the importance of this achievement. In sum, the oracle in Zechariah 4:6b-10a insists that Zerubbabel's actions, empowered by God's spirit, would eventually bring about a change in Yehud's fortunes in accord with God's will.

The limited resources of the Jewish community and the extent of Persian hegemony prevented the complete fulfillment of Zechariah's vision of the Judean restoration. The fruits of Yehud's agricultural productivity were being siphoned off as taxes by the Persians. The politically powerless Jewish community had little control over its economic resources. Rebuilding the temple in Jerusalem, however, was one expression of imperial encouragement and support for the people of Yehud. A temple was not only a religious institution but also an important component of Yehud's economy since it made possible the efficient exchange of agricultural goods. Of course, Zechariah insisted that the rebuilding of the temple was not the work of human might and power but of the spirit of יהוה צבאות ("YHWH of armies," v. 6) and that Zerubbabel was God's designee to complete the project. In contrast to the conventions of the ancient Near East, where temple building was a royal responsibility and entitlement, Zechariah did not make any messianic claims or suggest royal status for Zerubbabel.[9] Similarly, the prophet does not provide justification for any attempt to reestablish a national state under Davidic rule.[10] On the contrary, Zechariah suggests an alternative meaning for the reconstruction project. Rebuilding the temple was not about legitimating Persian rule or supporting any messianic pretensions on Zerubbabel's behalf. It was about preparing a place for the Jewish people to have an authentic encounter with God. Zerubbabel may have been the governor of the Persian province appointed by a Persian king, but for Zechariah, Zerubbabel's role was limited to ceremonies connected to the reconstruction of the

9. *Pace* Daniel L. Smith-Christopher, "Zerubbabel," in *Eerdmans Dictionary of the Bible,* ed. David Noel Freedman, Allen C. Myers, and Astrid B. Beck (Grand Rapids: Eerdmans, 2000), 1419.

10. Compare Haggai's language in 2:20-23, which speaks of Zerubbabel as one who may restore the Davidic dynasty.

Jerusalem temple. Persian kings may have sponsored the reconstruction project as a clear claim to hegemony over Yehud, but for Zechariah it was all the work of God's spirit in accord with the divine will. The prophet was a strong advocate of the temple's reconstruction, but he was careful to avoid wading too far into political waters.

It is important to appreciate the difference between Zechariah's treatment of Zerubbabel and that of Haggai, who repeatedly calls attention to Zerubbabel's connection to the Davidic dynasty and to the position he held as a representative of the Persian king (see Hag 1:1, 12, 14; 2:2, 23). Only once does Haggai mention Zerubbabel without reference either to his Davidic connections or to his political office (Hag 2:4). Zechariah's avoidance of pedigrees and titles must have been intentional. Rather than suggesting the reconstitution of the kingdom of Judah with its Davidic dynasty, Zechariah focuses on the renewal of the people's identity as a worshiping community. The success of the temple reconstruction would provide the people of Yehud with assurance that there would be a restoration of that identity, despite Yehud's political and economic impotence.

The Fifth Vision: The Two Olive Trees (4:1-6a, 10b-14)

Because Zechariah's previous visions are at night, it is reasonable to think of them as dreams. In contrast, 4:1 specifies that the interpreting angel awakens the prophet, to clarify what the prophet has seen. The fifth vision speaks of two olive trees that flank a menorah (vv. 2-3, 11),[11] with two branches of the olive trees pouring oil into the menorah through two golden pipes (v. 12). In response to the prophet's claims that he has no idea of the significance of the numbers two and seven in the vision (vv. 5, 11–13), the angel explains them. The menorah represents the "seven . . . eyes of the LORD" (v. 10), and the two olive trees, branches, and pipes represent the "two anointed ones who stand by the Lord of the whole earth" (v. 14).

A principal motif of all of Zechariah's visions, including this one, is the sovereignty of "the Lord of the whole earth" (vv. 10b, 14). The image of

---

11. Both the NRSVue and NABRE use the word "lampstand" to translate מנורה in vv. 2 and 11. The lampstand or menorah that the prophet sees is one designated for use in the temple. Its description does not conform to that of the lampstand used in the wilderness tabernacle (Exod 25:31-40) nor of the lampstand of Solomon's temple (1 Kgs 7:49), but it contains elements of both. The menorah became a common motif of Jewish iconography. For a comprehensive study of this motif see Carol L. Meyers, *The Tabernacle Menorah: A Synthetic Study of a Symbol from the Biblical Cult*, 2nd ed. (Piscataway, NJ: Gorgias Press, 2003). The arch of Titus in Rome depicts the menorah the Romans took from the second temple. The menorah is the official emblem of the state of Israel.

Zech 4:1-6a, 10b-14

¹The angel who spoke with me came again and wakened me, as one is wakened from sleep. ²He said to me, "What do you see?" And I said, "I see a lampstand all of gold, with a bowl on the top of it; there are seven lamps on it, with seven lips on each of the lamps that are on the top of it. ³And by it there are two olive trees, one on the right of the bowl and the other on its left." ⁴I said to the angel who spoke with me, "What are these, my lord?" ⁵Then the angel who spoke with me answered me, "Do you not know what these are?" I said, "No, my lord." ⁶He said to me,

"This is the word of the LORD to Zerubbabel: . . . .

"These seven are the eyes of the LORD that range through the whole earth." ¹¹Then I said to him, "What are these two olive trees on the right and the left of the lampstand?" ¹²And a second time I said to him, "What are these two branches of the olive trees that pour out the oil through the two golden pipes?" ¹³He said to me, "Do you not know what these are?" I said, "No, my lord." ¹⁴Then he said, "These are the two anointed ones who stand by the Lord of the whole earth."

God's "seven eyes" (v. 10), symbolized by a menorah with seven lamps (v. 2), signifies belief in God's omniscience and universal sovereignty, which some in Zechariah's time might have interpreted as undermining the loyalty of the people of Yehud to the Persian Empire.[12] The "twos" (vv. 11, 12, 14) of the vision likely represent Zerubbabel and Joshua, who were leaders in the Jewish community of Yehud. The leadership they exercised in the community is a departure from ancient Near Eastern royal ideology, in which the king was the principal intermediary between the divine and human spheres and, consequently, responsible for building and maintaining temples and supervising the cult. It is also a departure from the practice during Judah's monarchic period when the Davidic king was considered God's anointed, and the chief priest was part of the king's entourage. Zerubbabel was an appointee of the Persian government. Joshua's descent from the last functioning Judahite high priest was the source of his position but Joshua's relationship to Zerubbabel is unclear. Still, it is likely that Zechariah presents this new arrangement as the divine will for the Jews of Yehud. Joshua and Zerubbabel have their respective responsibilities. Joshua's derive from the Torah and traditional religious practice. Zerubbabel's come from the warrant

---

12. Bart B. Bruehler suggests that the "exact referent and meaning of the 'seven eyes' seems to have been lost already in antiquity." See his "Seeing through the מיכיע of Zechariah: Understanding Zechariah 4," *CBQ* 63 (2001): 440.

he received from Darius I. This arrangement involves a "separation of powers" and responsibility. How this arrangement worked out in actual practice, however, is not clear.

TRANSLATION MATTERS

Zechariah 4:10b-14 has several translation issues that call for attention. First, the phrase כל־הארץ ("the whole earth") frames this passage (4:10b, 14). It is a phrase that occurs three other times in Zechariah (1:11; 5:6; 6:5). Here the phrase suggests that what is happening in Yehud has significance beyond Yehud. YHWH of verse 10b is not just the ancestral deity of the Jews. YHWH is the "Lord of the whole earth" (אדון כל־הארץ, v. 14). The effect of this identification is to provide the people of Yehud with confidence regarding the restoration that the prophet envisions. This universalizing phrase is the product of the move from "YHWH alone" of the preexilic prophets to the monotheism of the exilic and postexilic prophets. "The Lord of the whole earth" can and will bring an end to the humiliation and subjugation of the Jewish people and restore them to their homeland in peace and prosperity. There are no human powers that can prevent this.

Both the NRSVue and NABRE translate בני־היצהר (v. 14) as "anointed ones" although the word "anoint" does not appear in the Hebrew text. A more literal translation of this phrase is "sons of [olive] oil." This oil was used for food preparation, medicines, cosmetics, and fuel for lamps. The word for the oil used in anointing persons is always שמן (1 Sam 10:1; 16:13; 1 Kgs 1:39). The NRSVue and NABRE are misleading as they appear to invest verse 14 with messianic overtones that it does not have. Who are the two בני־היצהר? The common hypothesis is that they are Zerubbabel and Joshua[13] and that the text supports a supposed "diarchy" of the Persian-appointed governor and Jewish high priest. That is not self-evident. First, though 4:7-8, 10 do mention Zerubbabel, chapter 4 does not mention Joshua by name. Mark Boda suggests that the two "sons of oil" are likely Haggai and Zechariah, who are linked in Ezra 5:1-2 and 6:14.[14] It is an interesting suggestion. If correct, it would mean that the text is not speaking of a supposed "diarchy" of Zerubbabel and Joshua. On the contrary, the text highlights the role of prophets in the Judean restoration. Wolter H. Rose and Lena-Sofia Tiemeyer, however, suggest that the "two sons of oil" are members of the divine council.[15] Although they agree that the two "sons of oil" might be Zechariah and Haggai, they note that the book of Zechariah never mentions Haggai by name. They consider verses

13. E.g., Wilhelm Rudolph, *Haggai–Sacharja 1–8, Sacharja 9–14, Maleachi*, KAT 13/4 (Gütersloh: Mohn, 1976), 107–8; Michael R. Stead, *The Intertextuality of Zechariah 1–8*, LHBOTS 506 (New York: T&T Clark, 2009), 184.

14. Mark J. Boda, *The Book of Zechariah*, NICOT (Grand Rapids: Eerdmans, 2016), 315–16.

15. Wolter H. Rose, *Zemah and Zerubbabel: Messianic Expectations in the Early Postexilic Period*, JSOTSup 304 (Sheffield: Sheffield University Press, 2000), 204–7; Lena-Sofia Tiemeyer, *Zechariah and His Visions: An Exegetical Study of Zechariah's Vision Report*, LHBOTS 605 (London: Bloomsbury, 2015), 164–65.

10b-14 to be describing a session of the divine council and that the two "sons of oil" are members of the council who supply oil to the lampstands, i.e., support the community worshiping in the restored temple.

The imagery in chapter 4 is evocative. Readers are drawn in by the prophet's vision and must engage this imagery, using their imagination to make sense of this vision. The significance of this and the other visions is clear in a general way, i.e., the prophet is affirming that the Judean restoration is the working out of the divine will. The details of how this restoration will come about are less clear. Readers are invited to imagine, with the prophet, how this restoration is proceeding. Looking for precise referents for the characters in the accounts of the prophet's visions puts limits on the readers' engagement with the text. The identity of the "son of oil" remains ambiguous and allows readers to imagine several possibilities. The one limitation on the readers' imagination is the result of the phrase "the *sons* of oil." This may have led readers to imagine that the chosen instruments for the Judean restoration are males. Of course, women were indispensable in making that restoration a reality. Minimizing or, worse, ignoring, women's role in the religious and economic spheres in the postexilic period is a serious error.[16]

Verse 12 has its own set of problems that bedevil any translator. The NRSVue translates שבלי as "branches." In Genesis 41:5, the word refers to "ears" of grain. The NABRE has "streams," following the suggestion of Othmar Keel, who claims that שבלי is derived from שבלת ("stream").[17] These alternatives serve only to obfuscate an already difficult passage. צנתרות, the word the NRSVue renders as "pipes" and the NABRE as "taps," is a *hapax* and has proven to be difficult to translate. Not surprisingly, these problems have led to debates among scholars.[18] More recently, Max Rogland considers צנתרות to be a transliteration from Greek; thus, "centaurs," a composite human horse creature with wings similar to the cherubim.[19] None of the scholarly alternatives has achieved consensus. The NRSVue attempts to make this difficult text readable by having the two branches of the olives tree pour out "oil" through two golden pipes. The word "oil," however, does not appear in the Hebrew text, and the NRSVue notes that its reading is conjectural as it renders זהב ("gold") as "oil." There is no support for this conjecture in the ancient versions. Verse 12 may be a secondary addition to chapter 4. If it is, this addition did not make the vision described in chapter 4 more understandable; rather, it rendered the meaning of that vision more opaque.

16. Tamara Cohn Eskenazi has shed significant light on the role of women in the Judean restoration. See her "The Lives of Women in the Postexilic Era," in *The Writings and Later Wisdom Books*, ed. Christl M. Maier and Nuria Calduch Benages, BW 1.3 (Atlanta: SBL Press, 2014), 11–31, and "Out from the Shadows: Biblical Woman in the Postexilic Era," *JSOT* 54 (1992): 25–43.

17. Othmar Keel, *Jahwe-Visionen und Siegelkunst: Eine neue Deutung der Majestätsschilderungen in Jes 6, Ez 1 und 10 und Sach 4*, SBS 84/85 (Stuttgart: Katholisches Bibelwerk, 1977), 306–11.

18. Tiemeyer, *Zechariah and His Visions*, 165–70, provides a lucid summary of these controversies.

19. Rogland, *Haggai and Zechariah 1–8*, 131, 146–48.

That two olive trees stand on either side of the menorah (vv. 1-3) implies divine approval for the activity of both Joshua and Zerubbabel regarding the temple. The resumption of temple service that would be overseen by Joshua had a positive effect on the economy of Yehud. The repair of that economy was a primary goal of Persian policy since it would increase revenues from taxation, which was a principal responsibility of Zerubbabel. Women of Yehud, who were responsible for the feeding and clothing of their families, would have found their lives much easier with a functioning economy in Yehud. Though some people regarded the pace of the restoration too slow and the results too insignificant (v. 10), the prophet affirms that Zerubbabel's efforts are harbingers of better days for the people of Yehud.

This vision, like all the others, speaks to the experiences of the Jewish community in the last quarter of the sixth century BCE. The people of Yehud were subjects of the Persian Empire, and, as such, they had to bear the burden of taxation. A good portion of their economic resources was handed over to the Persians, creating financial hardship (see Hag 1:4-6), which undoubtedly led some people to wonder about the wisdom of initiating a major building project such as the reconstruction of the temple. There was also some tension between the Jews like Joshua and Zerubbabel, who had arrived from Babylon with imperial support and high social status, and Jews who had remained in Judah after 586 BCE, many of whom probably struggled just to survive in their devastated homeland during the neo-Babylonian era (see Lam 5).[20] These political, economic, and social problems were probably reflected in Zechariah's emphasis on the role of the temple in Judah's restoration. He was convinced that Jerusalem's future depended on maintaining a commitment to their ancestral religious traditions and faithfulness to their God, and he also was aware of the effects of the resumption of temple service on the daily life of the people.

Chapter 4's focus on the reconstruction of the temple appears to suggest that the prophet's horizons were far too limited. A comprehensive restoration of Jewish life in Yehud required more than the resumption of worshiping God in the temple. There were significant political, social,

---

20. Many of the descendants of the forced migration to Babylon chose not to make the journey to the land of their ancestors since they had accommodated themselves into the Babylonian economy and society. See Rainer Albertz, *Israel in Exile: The History and Literature of the Sixth Century*, trans. David Green (Atlanta: SBL, 2003), 101.

and economic challenges that needed attention (see Hag 1:5-6). The text seems to imply that once the temple was rebuilt, all else would fall into place. This narrow perspective led to an equally narrow focus on the responsibilities of leadership in Yehud's religious and political spheres. It is not surprising, then, that the prophet's visions pay almost no attention to the roles that women and most Jewish men would play in the Judean restoration. A feminist lens that focuses only on the role and status of women in postexilic Judah may reasonably take exception to the book's preoccupation with the leadership roles held exclusively by men when a successful resumption of Jewish life in Yehud required the participation of ordinary women and men.

Zechariah made no attempt to change the social and political landscape of Yehud. The religious and political leadership of the preexilic Judah and the postexilic Jewish community remained in men's hands. Athaliah ruled as queen of the kingdom of Judah from 841 to 835 BCE, however, and provided the precedent for leadership of the state by a woman. Salome Alexandra ruled the Hasmonean kingdom as queen from 75 to 67 BCE. (Since the priesthood was limited to men, Salome Alexandra appointed her son Hyrcanus II as high priest.) Salome Alexandra was the last woman to govern an independent Jewish state until the twentieth century, when Golda Meir assumed the role of prime minister of the state of Israel from 1969 to 1974. The social and political landscape of many modern, democratic societies has changed dramatically since the last half of the twentieth century. Women serving as heads of government are no longer seen as exceptional. The role and status of women in such societies is not limited to the familial sphere, as was the case during the Judean restoration.

The vision account and oracle in Zechariah 4 offered a "traditional" response to the circumstances in which the Jewish people found themselves at the end of the sixth century BCE. The temple was in ruins and its priesthood had been scattered; the national state and the Davidic dynasty were gone, and the likelihood of their restoration was extremely remote. Zechariah took a pragmatic route rather than an ideological one by asserting that the leadership provided by Zerubbabel, the Persian-appointed official, and Joshua, the high priest, would improve the circumstances of the Jewish people. Zechariah saw the future of the Jewish people dependent on the rebuilding of the temple and the resumption of worship there.

Zechariah does not call for the restoration of the Judean state and the Davidic dynasty. He supports Zerubbabel along with Joshua. Neither opposed Persian hegemony in part because the Persians granted the Jewish community limited autonomy as that community moved into an uncharted future. Unlike Haggai, Zechariah did not whip up enthusiasm for a restored Davidic monarchy. Instead, he focused on a single goal: the reconstruction of the temple, which Persian kings supported. Still, the prophet maintained that the leadership provided by the high priest and the governor was empowered not by human armies but by the spirit of God. The efforts of Joshua and Zerubbabel offered a promise of social cohesion and economic stability at a difficult time in the life of the Jewish community of Yehud. Zechariah provided the Jewish community with a viable alternative to both active resistance to Persian rule and complete assimilation. He deserves credit for contributing to the survival of the Jewish people at a critical moment in their history. At the same time, the book continues to see the formal leadership of the Jewish community in the hands of men. It does not see a Deborah on the horizon but is content with conventional gender roles, content to stick to "safer" solutions to the challenges faced by the people of Yehud. Women had few opportunities to exercise political leadership though they had a central role in family life. Their efforts provided stability for the Jewish community of Yehud. The value of this contribution cannot be overestimated. The Judean restoration could have failed. That it did not is, in great measure, due to the efforts of the ordinary women of the Jewish community of Yehud.

Conclusion

Zechariah 3–4 offers Yehud a model of leadership that responds to the economic, political, and religious realities of Persian hegemony in the early postexilic period. The pattern of leadership envisioned by Zechariah departed from the model set by earlier prophets who spoke out against royal authority and the priestly establishment in preexilic Judah. But it is important to remember that Yehud of the Persian period was not the Judah of the monarchic period. The national state and the Davidic dynasty were no more, and the likelihood of their restoration was remote. The temple was in ruins and its priesthood scattered. The vision of Zechariah 4 was a conventional response to the circumstances in which the Jewish people found themselves as they tried to reconstitute their community's religious life. Zechariah takes the pragmatic rather than the ideological route. The book asserts that the leadership provided by Zerubbabel as governor and Joshua as high priest would improve the circumstances of the Jewish people and lead to completing the reconstruction of the temple. Zechariah promotes a nonmonarchic form of leadership that did not threaten Persian hegemony, while it provided the Jewish community with leaders who had connections with the past but could help that community move into a future whose contours were unclear. Unlike Haggai, Zechariah was not whipping up enthusiasm for a restoration of the monarchy. He had more modest goals: cooperation with the Persians, a modicum of autonomy within the empire, and the construction of a new temple in Jerusalem.

The formal leadership of the Jewish community in Yehud was in the hands of two men. Still, it is essential to remember the role women had in the family, whose welfare was vital for the success of the Judean restoration. Zechariah did not provide a comprehensive plan for the restoration. Such a plan could not ignore the role of women in Jewish life in Persian-period Yehud, but Zechariah's horizons were limited by his single-minded focus on completing the temple's reconstruction. The successful completion of this project overseen by Zerubbabel was to revitalize Jewish religious life in Yehud. Of course, women maintained that religious life in their families under most difficult circumstances following the fall of Jerusalem. Without their efforts there was no point in rebuilding the temple since there could be no authentic Jewish community for Joshua and Zerubbabel to lead.

Today women hold positions of civic leadership and trust in their communities. They serve as heads of government, legislators, and judges on both local and national levels. They are also leaders in business, education, health care, science, the news media, and entertainment. Of course, the glass ceiling is still there, but it is not as impenetrable as it once was. Women today are doing for their communities what Zerubbabel did for his community when its future was uncertain. There needs to be new leadership for a new day in today's communities of faith, and women have been at the forefront of that new leadership.

Zechariah 5:1-11

Flights of Fancy

This commentary, like most others, divides Zechariah 5 into two visions: the flying scroll (vv. 1-4) and the flying basket (vv. 5-11).[1] These two vision accounts share some common words, such as כל־הארץ ("the whole earth" in vv. 3 and 6) and בית ("house" in vv. 4 and 11), as well as similar bizarre features, namely, flying objects. There is a significant shift in 5:5-6, 9 as the central image changes from a flying scroll to a basket that is being carried by two winged women. Though it is possible to see the two portions as parts of a single vision, it seems more likely that the chapter contains accounts of two separate visions.

Unlike the vision accounts, which speak positively about the prospects of Yehud's future, the two visions in chapter 5 refer to negative aspects of life in Yehud, such as a prevalence of theft, perjury, and idolatry. The vision of the flying scroll hints at the social unrest in the Jewish community of Yehud caused by acts of injustice. Mark Boda claims that the text may be a critique of the priests who have failed to provide moral

---

1. Max Rogland (*Haggai and Zechariah 1–8: A Handbook on the Hebrew Text*, Baylor Handbook on the Hebrew Bible [Waco, TX: Baylor University Press, 2016], 151–52) maintains that the chapter describes a single vision with two parts. See also his "Flying Scrolls and Flying Baskets in Zechariah 5: Philological Observations and Literary Implications," *JNSL* 40 (2014): 103–4. While Rogland's theory is possible, the two vision reports in Zechariah 5 make no explicit reference to each other.

leadership,[2] but Jon Berquist asserts that the text addresses problems associated with civil officials appointed by the Persian authorities to maintain social order in Yehud.[3] It is also possible that 5:1-4 reflects antagonism between descendants of the Judean exiles and those families that remained in Judah following the fall of Jerusalem in 587 BCE. Perhaps the former were resorting to theft, perjury, and other unethical behaviors as a means of gaining control over the land of Yehud and its resources. In any case, the first vision described in Zechariah 5 announces judgment upon the guilty (v. 4) and offers hope for a just social order to those on the margins of the Jewish community—those who lacked economic and political power. The second vision (vv. 5-11) suggests that idolatry must not find a home in Yehud.

The Sixth Vision: The Flying Scroll (5:1-4)

The first image in Zechariah 5 is of a flying scroll (מגלה עפה). מגלה, though a common word for "scroll" in rabbinic Hebrew, appears rarely in the Hebrew Scriptures: only in Jeremiah 36; Ezekiel 2:8–3:3; Psalm 40:7; and here.[4] In all four contexts, מגלה refers to a written document with moral instruction or a declaration of judgment for violation of that instruction. The participle "flying" (עפה) suggests that the scroll is not merely hovering above the prophet (as do the olive trees in 4:3) but is flitting about by its own power. The scroll's dimensions are unusual as well. According to 5:2, the scroll is twenty cubits (thirty feet) long and ten cubits (fifteen feet) wide, which is several times the size of ordinary scrolls.[5] (By way of comparison, Qumran's Isaiah scroll is twenty-four feet long and eleven inches wide.) The scroll's unusual dimensions have generated much

---

2. Mark J. Boda, *The Book of Zechariah*, NICOT (Grand Rapids: Eerdmans, 2016), 323.

3. Jon L. Berquist, *Judaism in Persia's Shadow: A Social and Historical Approach* (Minneapolis: Fortress, 1995), 166–67.

4. The LXX uses the word δρέπανον ("sickle") in vv. 1 and 2, apparently reading מגל in place of מגלה. Boda, *The Book of Zechariah*, 325, points out that in a consonantal text without *matres lectionis*, the two words would look alike. Of course, "sickle" does not fit the context. Other ancient versions (Targum, Vulgate, Peshitta) support the MT.

5. These dimensions have led David Noel Freedman to suggest that the prophet was looking at one column of a scroll. See his "The Flying Scroll in Zechariah 5:1-4," in *Studies in Near Eastern Culture and History: In Memory of Ernest T. Abdel-Massih*, ed. James A. Bellamy, Michigan Series on the Middle East 2 (Ann Arbor: MPublishing, 2011), 47.

¹Again I looked up and saw a flying scroll. ²And he said to me, "What do you see?" I answered, "I see a flying scroll; its length is twenty cubits and its width ten cubits." ³Then he said to me, "This is the curse that goes out over the face of the whole land, for everyone who has stolen, as is forbidden on one side, has gone unpunished, and everyone who has sworn falsely, as is forbidden on the other side, has gone unpunished. ⁴I have sent it out, says the LORD of hosts, and it shall enter the house of the thief and the house of anyone who swears falsely by my name, and it shall abide in that house and consume it, both timber and stones."

discussion among interpreters.[6] Although some visionaries claim to have eaten scrolls (see Ezek 2:8–3:3; Rev 10:8-11), which symbolizes the prophet's embodying the message he is to convey, the scroll in the sixth vision is not to be eaten but read.

Another anomaly is that the scroll has writing on both sides, unlike most scrolls that have text on just one side. The message written on the scroll asserts that the thief and the perjurer are under a curse imposed by God (vv. 3-4).[7] This explicit condemnation of theft and perjury implies that those actions were common in the Jewish community of Yehud. That such an enormous scroll is inscribed on both sides and flying about suggests widespread abuses of these ethical standards, subject to divine judgment throughout "the whole land" (v. 3). The association of scrolls and accompanying curses was commonplace when Zechariah was writing. For example, the scroll of Deuteronomy lists numerous curses for violations of the commandments (see Deut 27:15-26 and 28:15-68). The prophet Huldah calls attention to those curses when the scroll is found in the temple, according to 2 Chronicles 34:24.[8] Though not explicitly called a curse, the additional text that Jeremiah dictates on the scroll that

6. For example, see Carol L. Meyers and Eric M. Meyers, *Haggai, Zechariah 1–8: A New Translation with Introduction and Commentary*, AB 25B (Garden City, NY: Doubleday, 1987), 279–83; and Lena-Sofia Tiemeyer, *Zechariah and His Visions: An Exegetical Study of Zechariah's Vision Report*, LHBOTS 605 (London: Bloomsbury, 2015), 187–91.

7. Scholars have offered several suggestions as to what precisely is written on the scroll. For a convenient summary of these suggestions, see Tiemeyer, *Zechariah and His Visions*, 184–86.

8. In both Deut and 2 Chr, the term ספר ("book") appears instead of מגלה ("scroll").

replaces the one burned by King Jehoiakim essentially is a curse against the rebellious king and his doomed dynasty (Jer 36:30-31).

Zechariah envisions divine action against those who have been threatening the renewal of Jewish life during the Persian period by actions that undermine the viability of the Jewish community. Rebuilding the temple and restoring the community's religious practices were essential, but these efforts would bear no fruit without the restoration of the moral life of the community. Darius's policy of encouraging the development of local law led to the codification of traditional Israelite morality and provided the impetus for the renewal of the community's moral sense. Theft and perjury are examples of the kinds of activities that undercut that renewal. Moreover, the constant motion of the flying scroll, together with the phrase כל־הארץ ("the whole land," v. 3; see also 4:10, 14; 5:6; and 6:5), invokes the idea that God's power extends beyond the point where the prophet is viewing the scroll and applies universally. "Everyone" (כול) who steals or swears falsely will be subject to the curse uttered in 5:3-4. All must heed God's command to act with honesty and integrity.

The Seventh Vision: The Woman in the Flying Basket (5:5-11)

After failing to mention women in any of the preceding visions, Zechariah's seventh vision features three female figures in central roles. Consequently, feminine grammatical forms are prevalent in this passage. Every noun but three (מלאך in vv. 5 and 10, פיה in v. 8, and שמים in v. 9) is feminine in gender. The subject of the vision is the removal of a basket and its contents by two women with wings of a stork (vv. 9-11). The interpreting angel calls upon the prophet to see "what is leaving"[9] and explains that the flying object, which the prophet does not recognize, is a basket (איפה). Its leaden lid is lifted, revealing a woman sitting inside. The angel identifies the woman as הרשעה ("Wickedness," v. 8), puts her back in the basket, and seals it. Two women with wings of a stork appear, lift the basket, and begin a journey to "the land of Shinar,"[10] where it will be placed in a house that will be built for it.

---

9. The NRSVue translates v. 5b as "Look up and see what this is that is coming out" and considers the sentence declarative; the NABRE translates v. 5b as "Raise your eyes and look. What is this that comes forth?" and renders the passage as a question. The JPS has "Now look up and note this other object that is approaching." The phrase הזאת היוצאת can be translated as "what is leaving." This makes it clear that the vision is about the movement of the basket.

10. Gen 10:10; 11:2, 9; Dan 1:1-2 imply that the land of Shinar is Babylon.

Zech 5:5-11

⁵Then the angel who spoke with me came forward and said to me, "Look up and see what this is that is coming out." ⁶I said, "What is it?" He said, "This is a basket coming out." And he said, "This is their iniquity in the whole land." ⁷Then a leaden cover was lifted, and there was a woman sitting in the basket! ⁸And he said, "This is Wickedness." So he thrust her back into the basket and pressed the leaden weight down on its mouth. ⁹Then I looked up and saw two women coming forward. The wind was in their wings; they had wings like the wings of a stork, and they lifted up the basket between earth and sky. ¹⁰Then I said to the angel who spoke with me, "Where are they taking the basket?" ¹¹He said to me, "To the land of Shinar, to build a house for it, and when this is prepared, they will set it down there on its base."

The Place That Must Not Be Named

Babylon is made invisible: To return to Jerusalem from the exile in Babylon is the main aim the book of Zechariah wants to achieve for its readers. For that, Jerusalem is named very often (forty-one times) and in varied ways (daughter Zion, 2:11; Zion, eight times) as is the region (Israel, five times; Judah, twenty-one times; "the earth" [ארץ], 1:10-11; the cities of Judah, 1:12; my cities, 1:17; "Jerusalem . . . along with the towns around it, and . . . the Negev and the Shephelah," 7:7; "house of Judah and house of Israel," 8:13). One day Jerusalem will be named "faithful city" (8:3). In contrast Babel is nearly not mentioned at all (6:10) or differently (daughter Babel, 2:7), which is also true for the region (Shinar, 5:11). Naming Babylon seems to be avoided at any cost. Is Babylon among the four horns that have treated Israel violently (1:18-21) or the proud peoples that tortured Israel (1:15) or that robbed God's people (2:8-9)? Is Babylon the land of the north (2:6-10)? The speaker dates his prophecies to the day; he names himself in his genealogy back to his grandfather but does not give even a hint about from where he speaks. Probably he is in Babylon.

Still, the suppressed B-word dominates even more. Zechariah 1–8 includes many citations of and allusions to the books of Second Isaiah and Jeremiah, but neither of these explicitly deals with Babylon. This is especially striking since both books contain significant texts about the desired destruction of Babylon (Isa 46:8-10; 47; see also Isa 13; 14; 21:1-10; and Jer 25; 50–51) and deal with the threatened (Jeremiah) and actual (Second Isaiah) exile in Babylon. Furthermore, Babylonian culture may stand in the background of images appearing in Zechariah. The textual organization as a cycle of visions, the spatial structure of the text, the interpreting angel, the riders in the field are influenced by Babylonian art and culture.

Babylon is named only indirectly and not described. But Babylon is characterized: in a strange magical act without any detectable traditional symbols, a woman being "Wickedness" stuffed in a container for grain solidly enclosed—it is named "their iniquity in the whole land" (Zech 5:6)—is carried by two women with stork's wings between earth and heaven to Shinar, the old mythical name of Babylonia, and installed there on a worshiping device. This text leaves many questions and contains many remarkable details. In ancient Near Eastern elimination rites impurity, sins, divine wrath, and others can be put away by transferring them onto a living substitute or thoroughly enclosing them in a vessel and transporting it as far away as possible. This ritual is doubled in this text since "Wickedness" is transferred on the living substitute "woman" *and* enclosed thoroughly. This text has mainly two consequences for the image of Babylon and the image of women. What is to be worshiped in Babylon comes from elsewhere. The woman is evil. The vision in 5:5-11 aims at defaming female "Babylon" but strikes all women. The visionary image of Babylon is so powerful that it has to be treated with violence. The woman is so wicked that she has to be treated with violence.

Especially in Babylonian contexts the question of God's omnipotence becomes important: Does God's power reach as far as Babylon? Is God's power as great as Babylon's power and/ or as great as that of Babylon's gods? Zechariah has to use such exaggerated means because there are not many important reasons why any exiled person should leave the rich, peaceful, and infrastructural center of the world to settle in the poor and unsafe region of Israel. Babylon has become their home. The best evidence for this is the name "Zerubbabel" of a prominent leader of Yehud (4:6-10). Babylon is now exactly nowhere: scarcely mentioned, imprisoned in a vessel, carried by imaginary species, between earth and heaven, back to a destiny that became famous in the end of primeval history, in a sphere of hyperreality and installed in a mythical world. Babylon is dangerous: the place and the woman that must not be named.

Ulrike Sals

Several ambiguous terms and unclear referents (discussed below) render this the most obscure of the prophet's visions. The first of these words is איפה ("ephah," v. 6), which the NRSVue and the NABRE translate as "basket."[11] An ephah is both a dry measure of about six-tenths of a bushel and a vessel of that capacity used to store grain or other dry commodities. Zechariah 5 is the only text in the Old Testament where ephah refers to a vessel; in all other occurrences, it is a measure of volume. This vessel could hold little more than a half bushel and was too small for even a petite woman to fit in, so the contents of the ephah must have been something other than a person.

Scholars have proposed various ways to explain the presence of the woman in the ephah, all of which have some cultic significance, consistent with Zechariah's focus on temple-related matters. For example, Carol and Eric Meyers see verse 6 as a double entendre because of the etymological relationship between ephah and related words in Akkadian and other Semitic languages that signify a cult room or shrine (*"E-pa"*) that housed statues of gods worshiped in Babylon. According to this view, Zechariah is seeing such a room being transported to the land of Shinar, thus relocating "wickedness" to Babylon.[12] Along similar lines, Shlomo Marenof argues that in Zechariah 5, the word "ephah" refers to a shrine of the Astarte cult, which he maintains was widespread in Judah.[13] The woman in the ephah, according to Marenof, should be understood as an image of the goddess herself and the vision in Zechariah 5:5-11 as a denunciation of idolatry. A third perspective is offered by Mark Boda, who asserts that Marenof is misreading the Mesopotamian texts. Boda sees the ephah as having some connection with cult and worship, such as a vessel used to transport grain to be offered at sanctuaries as well as a measure of volume used to apportion grain offerings.[14]

A second ambiguous word in Zechariah 5:6 is עינם. The JPS, following the MT, has "their eye." The NRSVue follows the LXX, rendering ἀδικία αὐτόν as "their iniquity," while the NABRE translates the Greek phrase as "their guilt." Another challenge is that the masculine plural pronominal suffix ם ("their") has no antecedent. The only plural nouns in the passage are נשים ("women") and כנפים ("wings") of storks in verse 9. Boda suggests that

11. The JPS translates איפה as "tub" in vv. 6, 8, and 9.

12. Meyers and Meyers, *Haggai, Zechariah 1–8*, 296.

13. Shlomo Marenof, "Note Concerning the Meaning of the Word 'Ephah,' Zechariah 5:5-11," *AJSL* 48 (1932): 265, 267; Johannes Schnocks, however, points to a total lack of archaeological evidence of the veneration of a goddess in postexilic Judah. See his "An Ephah between Earth and Heaven: Reading Zechariah 5:5-11," in *Tradition in Transition: Haggai and Zechariah 1–8 in the Trajectory of Hebrew Theology*, ed. Mark J. Boda and Michael H. Floyd, LHBOTS 475 (New York: T&T Clark, 2008), 267.

14. Boda, *The Book of Zechariah*, 342–43.

the suffix is objective (i.e., "the eye that sees them").[15] A third challenge in this text concerns the word פיה ("its mouth" in v. 8). The antecedent of the feminine pronominal suffix ה can be either the ephah or the woman. If פיה refers to the woman's mouth rather than the opening at the top of the basket, then the image here is of a violent act being inflicted on the woman or the cult object in the ephah. The NRSVue assumes that the ephah is the antecedent of the pronominal suffix so that the leaden weight is placed on the mouth of the basket. The NABRE avoids making a choice and does not translate the suffix: "pushing the leaden weight into *the* opening."

Having noted these textual issues, we can take a closer look at the function of the ephah and identify its contents. When the prophet catches sight of the ephah, he asks, "What is it?" (5:6). Unfortunately, the interpreting angel's answer is unclear. The NRSVue and the NABRE base their translations of verse 6 on the LXX rendering of עינם ("their eyes") as ἀδικία αὐτόν ("their iniquity," NRSVue, and "their guilt," NABRE). These English translations imply that the ephah represents the sins of the Jews from Babylon who have returned to Jerusalem. That the possessive pronoun "their" refers to the returned exiles, however, is not evident from the Hebrew text.

In verse 8, the angel explicitly identifies the ephah (and, by implication, its contents) as הרשעה ("wickedness"), a noun that is feminine, instead of the more common, grammatically masculine term רשע. Meyers and Meyers claim that Zechariah's choice to identify the woman in the basket as הרשעה is "the key to understanding the overall meaning of the vision."[16] Max Rogland suggests that the word הרשעה connotes behavior rather than the abstract notion of "wickedness."[17] In addition, הרשעה is an anagram of "Asherah," the name of the Canaanite goddess some Israelites considered to be YHWH's consort.[18] According to Diana Edelman, worship of Asherah was popular in Judah in the preexilic and exilic periods.[19] Alliances made by Judah's kings and the vassal states of preexilic Judah to Assyria, Egypt, and Babylon created occasions for

15. Boda, *The Book of Zechariah*, 345.

16. Meyers and Meyers, *Haggai, Zechariah 1–8*, 302.

17. Rogland, *Haggai and Zechariah 1–8*, 160. Johannes Schnocks maintains that הרשעה should be understood as "an overall iniquity" that was characteristic of the people of Judah. It must be extinguished so that the restoration of Judah may go forward. See his "An Ephah between Heaven and Earth," 264.

18. Mark S. Smith, "God Male and Female in the Old Testament: Yahweh and His 'Asherah,'" *TS* 48 (1987): 333–40.

19. Diana Edelman, "Proving Yahweh Killed His Wife (Zechariah 5:5-11)," *BibInt* 11 (2003): 336.

the introduction of non-Yahwistic cults into the temple of Jerusalem. The temple restoration as envisioned by Zechariah was an appropriate time to rid Judah of the residual effects of those idolatrous entanglements. Judah's exiles returned to their homeland. The construction of the temple of YHWH is proceeding so the worship of foreign gods had no place in it. This supports the suggestion that the woman in the ephah was an image of that goddess. The choice of a grammatically feminine noun does not necessarily reflect misogynist tendencies on the author's part but rather reflects his insistence on removing a non-Israelite cultic object to Babylon since it did not belong in Yehud.[20]

One more object mentioned in this vision account must not be overlooked, namely, the "leaden cover" (ככר עפרת) placed on top of the ephah to seal "wickedness" inside. Ingrid Lilly sees the references to lead in verses 7 and 8 as an "allusion to concerns about economic justice."[21] Leaden weights were used in marketplaces to determine the pricing of commodities. Such weights were sometimes manipulated to extract higher prices than were just. Like the non-Israelite cult objects, unjust weights had to be expunged from the temple precincts where some taxes were collected and some commercial activity took place. Lilly suggests that the images in this passage are polyvalent, denouncing both non-Yahwistic worship and unjust commercial practices.

A significant point of comparison between the vision of the scroll (5:1-4) and the ephah (5:5-10) is the mobility of the two objects. Unlike the scroll of Zechariah 5:1-4, the ephah does not fly on its own; rather, the two winged women transport it to Babylon. These composite creatures are reminiscent of the cherubim that adorned the mercy seat covering the ark of the covenant (Exod 25:18-20; 37:6-9; Num 7:89; 1 Sam 4:4), reinforcing the association of the ephah with the cult of a deity whose proper place is in Babylon rather than in Yehud. The two women rid Yehud of an idolatrous cult by removing the contents of the basket to Shinar (Babylon).[22] The chapter's final verse states that the contents of the ephah will be placed on its own מכנתה ("base," v. 11) in a temple or

20. 2 Kgs 23:4, 6, 7 testifies to the popularity of the Asherah cult in preexilic Judah. Zechariah considered that cult incompatible with that of YHWH.

21. Ingrid E. Lilly, "Zechariah's Gendered Visions: A Feminist Biblical Theology of Reconciliation," in *After Exegesis: Feminist Biblical Theology; Essays in Honor of Carol A. Newsom*, ed. Patricia K. Tull and Jacqueline E. Lapsley (Waco, TX: Baylor University Press, 2015), 211.

22. According to Eibert J. C. Tigchelaar, the relocation of an idolatrous cult rather than its destruction is a unique feature of this passage; see his *Prophets of Old and the Day of the End: Zechariah, the Book of Watchers and Apocalyptic*, OtSt 35 (Leiden: Brill, 1996), 62.

shrine (בית, literally, "house") built for it.[23] In the end, Zechariah's seventh vision is not a denunciation of idolatry as such, though the text does call for a removal of idols from the temple in Jerusalem.

There is no question that Zechariah 5:5-11 is a perplexing passage. Obscure descriptions of a strange woman sitting inside an ephah borne by two women flying with stork-like wings leave the reader filling in gaps about the meaning of the vision. For example, who (or what) is the woman in the ephah? What is the significance of the two winged women? Why are the women carrying the ephah and its contents to the land of Shinar (Babylon)? Questions such as these have given rise to a variety of scholarly interpretations.[24]

For example, Ulrike Sals characterizes this passage as one of the Old Testament's "misogynist texts."[25] Sals asserts that this vision gives the overall impression that the woman in the basket symbolizes "Every Woman," thus intrinsically linking all women to unrighteousness.[26] According to this view, 5:5-11 weaves together "woman, unrighteousness, and Shinar," producing an "aetiology of woman as evil" and gendering unrighteousness as feminine. It is true that some interpreters have read the text in this way.[27] Although Sals is right in calling attention to

23. For Christoph Uehlinger this settled the question: the woman must be a goddess. See his "Die Frau im Efa (Sach 5,5-11): Eine Programmvision von der Abschiebung der Göttin," *BK* 49 (1994): 97; Ulrike Sals, "Reading Zechariah 5.5-11: Prophecy, Gender and (Ap)Perception," in *Prophets and Daniel: A Feminist Companion to the Bible*, ed. Athalya Brenner, 2nd ser., vol. 8 (Sheffield: Sheffield Academic, 2001), 190n12, observes that the "precise" meaning of מכנתה in Zechariah 5:11 is not clear, but the context does suggest a meaning related to the cult.

24. For a short description of the variety of approaches taken to this text, see Michael H. Floyd, "The Evil in the Ephah: Reading Zechariah 5:5-11 in Its Literary Context," *CBQ* 58 (1996): 51–52.

25. Sals, "Reading Zechariah 5:5-11," 186; Ben C. Ollenburger agrees with this assessment. See his "The Book of Zechariah," in *NIB*, ed. Leander E. Keck (Nashville: Abingdon, 1996), 7:781.

26. Sals, "Reading Zechariah 5:5-11," 189, 195.

27. For example, Wilhelm Rudolph, *Haggai–Sacharja 1–8, Sacharja 9–14, Maleachi*, KAT 13/4 (Gütersloh: Mohn, 1976), 120, identifies the woman with Eve, and David L. Petersen, *Haggai and Zechariah 1–8: A Commentary*, OTL (Philadelphia: Westminster, 1984), 257–58, appears to do the same; without offering any evidence to support this suggestion, Hinkley Gilbert Mitchell identifies the woman in the ephah as a cult prostitute in Hinkley Gilbert Mitchell, John Merlin Powis Smith, and Julius A. Bewer, *A Critical and Exegetical Commentary on Haggai, Zechariah, Malachi and Jonah*, ICC (Edinburgh: T&T Clark, 1912), 173, as does Gerhard Wallis, "Die Nachtgesichte des Propheten Sacarja: Zur Idee einer Form," in *Congress Volume 1977*, VT Sup 29 (Leiden: Brill, 1978), 388. There is no support in the text for this identification.

how easily Zechariah 5:5-11 can be used to legitimate unjust treatment of women today, such an interpretation does not reflect the historical context in which this passage was written.[28] Margaret Barker presents another view, namely, that the vision of the ephah has historical roots in the conflict between the descendants of the Judeans who were not exiled and who may have worshiped Asherah as YHWH's consort during the neo-Babylonian period and the returning exiles who did not.[29] This view is supported by the possibility that the popular cult of Asherah may have experienced a resurgence in Judah during the restoration period if non-Israelite women who came with their Jewish husbands returning from exile engaged in Asherah worship.[30] According to this view, the purpose of the ephah's flight was to rid Judah of the offending goddess cult. Both Barker and Sals maintain that the contents of the ephah embodied something foreign to Judah that posed a threat to authentic Yahwism and that had to be removed from the land in the process of Jerusalem's restoration.

It is likely that "the woman" in the ephah is an image of a goddess, perhaps Asherah, and Zechariah 5 is a condemnation of idol worship in Yehud.[31] Michael H. Floyd sees this text as suggesting that some people in Yehud supported the building of cultic sites, in addition to the temple in Jerusalem, where Asherah could be worshiped alongside YHWH.[32] If one reads Zechariah 5:5-11 through a lens of postexilic Judaism, the vision suggests that the temple needed to be purified, after having been polluted by the introduction of idolatrous cults. Zechariah envisions the expulsion of one such cult, that of Asherah, from Yehud and from the temple. What matters is not the gender reflected in the cult object but the fact that the object represented a threat in Yehud to the worship of YHWH alone.[33]

---

28. Sals, "Reading Zechariah 5:5-11," 195.

29. Margaret Barker, "The Evil in Zechariah," *HeyJ* 19 (1978): 12–27. Barker identified the woman as the "prostitute Jerusalem."

30. Beth Glazier-McDonald sees the woman as representing both idolatry and the danger of foreign women whose influence on their husbands can lead to idolatry. See her "Zechariah," in *The Women's Bible Commentary*, ed. Carol A. Newsom and Sharon H. Ringe (London: SPCK, 1992), 231.

31. Edelman, "Proving Yahweh Killed His Wife," 342; Mark C. Love, *The Evasive Text: Zechariah 1–8 and the Frustrated Reader*, JSOTSup 296 (Sheffield: Sheffield Academic, 1999), 212–13, asserts that the text reflects the abuse of a woman and identifying the woman as a goddess is tantamount to ignoring violence against women. There is no indication in the text that the issue is the abuse of women.

32. Floyd, "The Evil in the Ephah," 67.

33. The prophets often associated idolatry with sexual impropriety. If the woman in 5:5-11 is understood to be an idol, then it is reasonable to see this text as a polemic against idolatry and the women who practiced it.

Additional questions arise when we consider the role of the women with the stork-like wings in this vision. Are these women portrayed positively for their role in removing the ephah from Judah or negatively for their apparent association with "Wickedness"? Are they agents of YHWH, commissioned to transport the ephah and the idol it contains to Shinar, or are they evictees being cast out of Yehud for worshiping the goddess the idol represents? Floyd rejects the possibility that the women are commissioned by God since that interpretation would make God the "founder and patron of some idolatrous cult."[34] Meyers and Meyers suggest that the passage implies that foreign gods can rightly be worshiped "by their own peoples in their own territories."[35] This is supported by the fact that the woman in the ephah is not killed but simply contained physically and removed to Babylon, a city that, in prophetic literature, stands in contrast to Jerusalem with respect to culture and religion. The two women make the transport possible by airlifting the ephah and its contents back to Babylon where they properly belong. Jerome Kodell sees the two women who transport the ephah serving as a balance to the prophet's depicting the woman in the basket as "Wickedness."[36]

Was there any connection between the image of women carrying a non-Israelite cult object to Shinar and the lives of women and men of Yehud? Both Ezra (chaps. 9–10) and Nehemiah (13:23-29) call for Jewish men to divorce their foreign wives, implying that those women had introduced non-Yahwistic cultic practices into the temple and that sending them away would eliminate the problem. That assumption, however, amounted to little more than scapegoating those foreign women and casting them as a threat to Jewish religious identity and the source of Yehud's social problems. The "othering" of the woman in the ephah may reflect a society in which women were taken from the communities of their parents when they married and brought into the communities of their husbands. They may have been regarded with suspicion as outsiders who threatened the community's loyalty to their God. It may be that the vision described in Zechariah 5:5-11 reflected the distrust of foreign women that led to the mass divorces and deportations called for by Ezra.

34. Floyd, "The Evil in the Ephah," 62.

35. Meyers and Meyers, *Haggai, Zechariah 1–8*, 315.

36. Jerome Kodell, *Lamentations, Haggai, Zechariah, Malachi, Obadiah, Joel, Second Zechariah, Baruch*, OTM (Wilmington, DE: Michael Glazier, 1982), 78.

Elie Assis offers an idiosyncratic position, holding that the ephah represents the Samaritans.[37] Assis associates the vision of the ephah with the notion that originally the Samaritans were foreigners who had been settled in the territory of the former kingdom of Israel by the Assyrians in the late eighth century BCE (2 Kgs 17:24). He argues that the message of 5:5-11 is that the Samaritans ought to build their own temple in Shinar (i.e., Babylon), their original homeland. The key to this interpretation is a wordplay between חסידה ("stork") and צדיק ("pious person").[38] The stork-women, then, are not evil but rather very pious Jews whose task it is to remove idols (and the Samaritans who worship them) from the land. This hypothesis, though interesting, is also without basis in the text itself, though Assis maintains that the text was made purposely obscure to prevent Samaritans from discovering its true intent.

A minority of scholars sees Zechariah 5:5-11 as primarily a continuation of the social justice motif addressed in 5:1-4,[39] though some of those views are based on evidence that is not clear from the text itself. We read the vision as primarily a condemnation of foreign cults. It may reflect conditions that harmed women, particularly non-Israelite women in Yehud during the Persian period. Identifying the woman in the ephah as "Wickedness" may have reflected a view in postexilic Judah that wives of Jewish men were the source of religious and social problems challenging the Jewish community. This assessment aligns with descriptions in Ezra and Nehemiah of the expulsion of gentile women required by Yehud's male leaders as an act of loyalty to YHWH. These texts serve to transform an unjust policy of misogyny and xenophobia into an act of piety, as it wrongly lays the blame for the slow pace of the Judean restoration on the foreign wives of Jewish men.[40]

---

37. Elie Assis, "Zechariah's Vision of the Ephah (Zech 5:5-11)," *VT* 60 (2010): 15–32.

38. Assis, "Zechariah's Vision of the Ephah," 31–32.

39. Petersen, *Haggai and Zechariah 1–8*, 255–59; Carroll Stuhlmueller, *Rebuilding with Hope: A Commentary on the Books of Haggai and Zechariah*, ITC (Grand Rapids: Eerdmans, 1988), 92; Barker, "The Evil in Zechariah," 12–27; Dominic Rudman, "Zechariah 5 and the Priestly Law," *SJOT* 14 (2000): 194–206. Rudman, however, does acknowledge the cultic flavor of the text. Love, *The Evasive Text*, 212, suggests that the woman was forced into prostitution by poverty; the prophet envisions a life of prosperity for her once she settles in Babylon. The identification of the woman as a prostitute is purely speculative without support in the text.

40. Modern societies are guilty of similar acts of scapegoating. The Nazis identified the Jewish population of Germany as the source of the economic problems of Germany after World War I. Immigrants to the United States—those with documents

Finally, it is possible to assert that the vision of the ephah in Zechariah 5:5-11 is not as obscure as it first appears. The prophet sees a vessel in which an image, perhaps of a female deity, has been placed. That vessel and its contents are then borne on the wings of two composite creatures (women with stork's wings) to Babylon, where they are to be housed in a shrine. The ephah and its contents no longer have a home in Judah now that YHWH and the exiles have returned to reclaim Jerusalem as their home.

There is no question that the reader does not receive much help from the text itself in determining the meaning of the puzzling images that appear in Zechariah 5:1-11. We have a basket that is not really a basket, two composite creatures (women with wings of a stork), a woman who may (or may not) represent a goddess, and an interpreting angel that also plays a potentially misogynistic role in the vision by shoving the woman/goddess image back into the ephah and sealing it. Such ambiguity has been compounded by scholars who read into the text details that are simply not there. For example, Klaus Koch asserts that the woman is ugly[41] while Max Haller claims that she is beautiful,[42] but the text does not support either claim. On a different note, some scholars have criticized interpretations of this passage that label it as misogynistic and anti-Jewish. For example, Beate Schmidtgen suggests that this vision is about the expulsion of the image of a female deity, which must be escorted out of the land by the deity's female priestly attendants.[43] Assessing the text's purported misogyny, however, involves more than observing that the prophet identifies the woman in the ephah as "Wickedness." Such an assessment should take into consideration other details

---

and those without—are falsely blamed for taking jobs away from American citizens. Muslims are blamed for the terrorist acts perpetrated by a small percentage of their co-religionists. Ethnic and religious minorities are routinely the subject of scapegoating since they lack social status, political and economic power, and access to legal protection afforded to others in the countries where they live.

41. Klaus Koch, *Die Profeten II: Babylonisch-persische Zeit*, Urban-Taschenbücher 281, 2nd ed. (Stuttgart: Kohlhammer, 1988), 173; Eng. trans.: *The Prophets*, vol. 2: *The Babylonian and Persian Periods* (Philadelphia: Fortress, 1984), 169.

42. Max Haller, *Das Judentum: Geschichtsschreibung, Prophetie und Gesetzgebung nach dem Exil*, SAT 2.3, 2nd ed. (Göttingen: Vandenhoeck & Ruprecht, 1925), 104.

43. Beate Schmidtgen, "Haggai and Zechariah: A New Temple—New Life for All," in *Feminist Biblical Interpretation: A Compendium of Critical Commentary on the Books of the Bible and Related Literature*, ed. Luise Schottroff and Marie-Theres Wacker, trans. Martin Rumscheidt et al. (Grand Rapids: Eerdmans, 2012), 466.

in the text, such as the ambiguous role of the two winged women and their relationship to God.

Sals claims that this passage exemplifies the misogyny characteristic of the Old Testament. As noted above, however, there is no inherent misogyny in the text itself, but I acknowledge that it could have been interpreted by some readers as associating idolatry with women, especially foreign women.[44] Although Sals is correct that the text explicitly labels the woman as "fundamentally evil," it does not follow that the text is labeling all women evil. It is denouncing a non-Israelite cult object.[45] Unfortunately, however, the prophet's ambiguous and obscure imagery has opened the way for some readers today to find justification for their own misogynistic views and to minimize the role and status of women in synagogue, church, and society.

It is important to remember that the vision of the flying basket is only one component of the prophet's visions concerning Yehud's future. Zechariah's notion of that future is by no means comprehensive. Its principal components are the temple, the priesthood, and the creation of a just society with leadership roles filled by men. It is little wonder that women appear to be left out of Zechariah's picture of the Judean restoration and relegated to a minor and not explicitly positive role. Being present but not accounted for becomes more acute in Zechariah 5 since a woman is identified as the personification of the wickedness that threatens to undermine the Judean restoration. It is not surprising, then, that some interpreters who focus on the woman in the ephah see her as the archetype of evil.[46]

Conclusion

Zechariah 5 asserts that God will not tolerate injustice. Today injustice includes sexual harassment in the workplace and in academia, domestic violence and sexual assault, and other crimes against women. In

44. Marvin A. Sweeney maintains that misogyny is not inherent in the text but is a product of interpretation. See his *The Twelve Prophets*, Berit Olam (Collegeville, MN: Liturgical Press, 2000), 2:620.

45. Sals, "Reading Zechariah 5:5-11," 194–96. She sees the text as an etiology of evil with a description of evil's removal (204). That Zechariah 5:5-11 presents all women as "fundamentally evil" goes beyond the evidence. The female figure represents idolatry, not women or evil in the abstract.

46. Petersen, *Haggai and Zechariah 1–8*, 257–58, sees this as reflecting the popular understanding of Genesis 3, which thought of the "feminine as evil."

too many instances, employers, universities, police, judicial systems, and other institutions minimize or even ignore these crimes, becoming complicit by refusing to stand up for gender justice. One important contribution of the women's movement in general, and of movements such as #MeToo in particular, has been the demand to take seriously the experiences of women whose lives have been forever changed by such crimes. It is, of course, important that perpetrators be held accountable for their crimes. Equally important are proactive efforts to eradicate misogyny and violence against women from the fabric of our culture.[47]

People with political influence and economic power should challenge systems that are rigged to maintain the status quo at the expense of people on the margins of society. Voter suppression, tax loopholes, antiquated immigration laws, unrealistic property assessments, underfunded schools, unaffordable health care—these are just a few of the ways that "the system" harms those without power or influence. What threatens society today (as in biblical times) is the failure to ensure that all people—especially women and children and those without power—are treated justly. Tragically the attitudes of some people toward women are still fueled by ignorance and misogyny, and attitudes toward people who are poor are fueled by prejudice and falsehoods.

Biblical texts have an "afterlife" not foreseen or controlled by those who composed them. The account of Zechariah's vision of the woman in the ephah is one such text. It has contributed to the association of women with evil, and it has led to its author being labeled a misogynist. On the one hand, that label is understandable given the prophet's choice of imagery, which poses a serious challenge to a feminist reading of Zechariah. On the other hand, it is important to keep in mind the context that shaped the prophet's vision. His hope was in the rebuilding of the temple and the resumption of religious life for the people of Yehud. Like the preexilic prophets of Judah, Zechariah called for justice and challenged those who perpetuated unjust systems by dishonest means. He saw justice in the Jewish community as essential to its religious life. Thus, as worship was about to resume in the temple, Zechariah urged

47. An example of the sin of witnessing injustice and not acting has come to the fore in the recent trial of Larry Nassar, a doctor who molested hundreds of girls, including high-profile Olympic athletes such as Aly Raisman. According to Raisman and others, the girls had complained to parents, coaches, and other adults for years before the case was taken to trial. In her testimony, Raisman accused not only Nassar but also all the adults who heard these accusations and neglected to act.

the people of Yehud to embrace justice so that they could worship God with integrity.

A significant concern of Zechariah was the building of a new temple in Jerusalem. The completion of this project was an essential component of the Judean restoration. For that restoration to be successful the community had to recognize what brought it to the brink of extinction. At the very least, people who wish to live together need to be honest with each other, and they need to respect each other's property. Similarly, Jewish community life demands absolute commitment to God alone. The visions recounted in chapter 5 uphold the value of honesty within the community and the rejection of idolatry. In addition to building a temple for God in Jerusalem, the members of the Jewish community in Yehud had to strengthen their bonds with each other by committing themselves to honest interpersonal relations and maintaining their commitment to the God of their ancestors. Truth sustains community life. Readiness to speak the truth and a willingness to hear the truth and respond with appropriate action are the keys to life-giving community life. People who have been relegated to the margins of community need to speak the truth in love, and those in positions of authority need to recognize the truth before authentic reconciliation can begin. But both those on the margins and those at the center must be committed to a process that will lead to the reconciliation and the restoration of justice within the community. Also, there could be no further dalliances with the service of foreign gods. Their images need to be sent back to the places where they belong. They certainly do not belong in Yehud. The future of the Jewish people depends on their loyalty to YHWH alone.

The visions in Zechariah 5 reminded the people of Yehud that the rebuilding of the temple is central to the Judean restoration, but it does not comprise the whole of that restoration. The future of the Jewish community involves the people's commitment to each other and to God. Honesty and loyalty are the keys to securing the blessings of peace and prosperity for the people of Yehud.

Zechariah 6:1-15

Envisioning the Future

L ike all of Zechariah's visions, this final one reflects the unsettled times and difficult circumstances in which the prophet and his community found themselves. The Babylonians fared well following Cyrus's conquest of their kingdom in 539 BCE. They had welcomed the Persian king into their capital because they were certain that Cyrus was going to depose the unpopular Nabonidus and restore the cult of Marduk, the patron deity of the city of Babylon.[1] The people of Babylon, however, rebelled against Persian rule following the death of Cambyses in 522 BCE, and Darius put down that rebellion with great ferocity. Zechariah likely was convinced that the Babylonians brought disaster upon themselves by rebelling against Persia just as the Judeans did the same by rebelling against Babylon in the days of Zedekiah (2 Kgs 25). Although Yehud was drawn into political unrest in the Persian Empire to some extent, the Jewish community lacked the political, economic, or military power to do anything but be bystanders. One purpose of Zechariah's vision accounts in general and the final one in particular was to assure the people of Yehud that their God had matters in hand despite the

---

1. Nabonidus spent most of his seventeen-year reign in Tayma, a city in the Arabian Peninsula. He promoted the cult of Sin, the patron deity of Ur. This likely caused friction with the priests of Marduk. With a war with Persia on the horizon, Nabonidus called for several Babylonian cities to send the images of their patron gods to Babylon in the hope that the people would resist the Persian invasion to protect these images. This policy had the opposite effect and contributed to Nabonidus's unpopularity.

political and military problems facing the Persian Empire—problems that threatened to stall the Judean restoration.[2]

The Eighth Vision: The Four Chariots (6:1-8)

Zechariah's final vision bears some similarity to the first (1:8-11), since both visions depict horses patrolling the earth. In the first vision God sends the horses and their riders on a mission to prepare for judgment against the nations that had devastated Judah and Jerusalem. The oracle following that vision (1:12-17) promises to deal with the nations that had brought disaster on Jerusalem, so that the city could once again enjoy peace and prosperity. In this final vision (6:1-8), horses hitched to rider-less chariots are sent to the four corners of the earth (6:6), with a special focus on "the north country" (6:8; i.e., Babylon), which posed a threat to Judah's very existence.[3] Zechariah likely saw the fate of Babylon following its unsuccessful revolt against Persia as divine judgment that neutralized the threat from "the land of the north." Julia O'Brien suggests that the assertion in verse 8 that God's spirit is at rest signals the fulfillment of the promises of peace for Jerusalem made in 1:8-17.[4] Persia's response to Babylon's rebellion effectively ended any threat that Babylon posed to Yehud. No doubt the Jews of Yehud felt more secure as a consequence. The toppling of Judah's oppressor and the support of Persia meant that the reconstruction of the temple and restoration of the Jewish community in Yehud could proceed, reversing the damage done to Judah and Jerusalem.

Two important elements bring a sense of ambiguity to this passage. First is the function of the chariots. In a military context, chariots were mobile, horse-drawn platforms that carried a driver plus two or three archers (or soldiers using other weapons) into battle.[5] That the passage makes no reference to the soldiers riding in the chariots, but only

---

2. The account of his eighth vision is a good example of *vaticinium ex eventu*, a prophetic text that purports to predict an event but, in fact, is written after the event has occurred.

3. Carol L. Meyers and Eric M. Meyers, *Haggai, Zechariah 1–8: A New Translation with Introduction and Commentary*, AB 25B (Garden City, NY: Doubleday, 1987), 331, maintain that "the land of the north" refers to Persia, but Babylon is more likely since God has acted against "daughter Babylon" (2:6-13) and dispatched the image of the goddess Asherah there (5:5-11).

4. Julia M. O'Brien, *Nahum, Habakkuk, Zephaniah, Haggai, Zechariah, Malachi*, AOTC (Nashville: Abingdon, 2004), 202.

5. Chariots were also used occasionally for nonmilitary purposes. For example, royalty and the wealthy used chariots for ordinary transportation, hunting, and religious processions.

Zech 6:1-8

¹And again I looked up and saw four chariots coming out from between two mountains—mountains of bronze. ²The first chariot had red horses, the second chariot black horses, ³the third chariot white horses, and the fourth chariot dappled gray horses. ⁴Then I said to the angel who spoke with me, "What are these, my lord?" ⁵The angel answered me, "These are the four winds of heaven going out, after presenting themselves before the Lord of the whole earth. ⁶The chariot with the black horses goes toward the north country, the white ones go toward the west country, and the dappled ones go toward the south country." ⁷When the steeds came out, they were impatient to get off and patrol the earth. And he said, "Go, patrol the earth." So they patrolled the earth. ⁸Then he cried out to me, "See, those who go toward the north country have set my spirit at rest in the north country."

to the horses pulling them, is puzzling. That omission suggests that the impatient האמצים ("the strong [horses]")⁶ of verse 7 personify the unmentioned charioteers. The rhetorical effect is to amplify the sense of anticipation of the charioteers anxious to carry out their mission. Second is the multivalence of the poetic imagery used to describe God's presence and actions. In verse 5, the interpreting angel explains that the chariots are ארבע רחות ("the four winds"). רחות could also be translated as "spirits" (see v. 8 where the NRSVue translates רוחי as "my spirit"). These four winds (chariots) are going out after having presented themselves to "the Lord of the whole earth" (see 4:14). If understood as "winds," the רחות serve as the conduits that bring the celestial world of God into the physical world of human beings. If understood as "spirits," the רחות serve as God's agents ensuring justice in "all the earth," especially in the "north country," a reference to Babylon.⁷ In either case, the message of the vision is that God's promise to vanquish Yehud's enemies and restore peace will be fulfilled (see 2:6-13).

---

6. Verses 3 and 7 are the only times that האמצים appears in the Hebrew Bible. Mark J. Boda (*The Book of Zechariah*, NICOT [Grand Rapids: Eerdmans, 2016], 358 no. k) notes that this adjective likely describes the horses as strong. The NRSVue has the occurrence of האמצים in v. 3 refer to the horses' color (grey) while it translates the same word in v. 7 as a substantive, "steeds," implying their strength.

7. The Hebrew word רוח ("wind," "spirit") is feminine in grammatical gender. Several Hebrew words that are feminine in grammatic gender represent words that mediate the divine/human relationship, e.g., תורה (Torah), מצוה (commandment), שכינה (Presence), חכמה (Wisdom).

TRANSLATION MATTERS

Complicating the opaque imagery of the vision are two grammatical issues that lead to translation problems and interpretive difficulties. First is the question of how the phrase במרכבה in verses 2–3 is to be translated. Lena-Sofia Tiemeyer suggests that the phrase be translated as "in the chariot,"[8] but it is difficult to visualize horses that are described as "strong"[9] in verses 2 and 7 being small enough to fit inside a chariot. Alternatively, במכבה can be translated as "with the chariot" to specify which colored horses were with which chariot. This suggests that the horses drew the chariots—an image that is more easily visualized.[10] The NRSVue makes this clear.

A second problem is the meaning of the phrase אשר־בה, which appears at the beginning of verse 6. David Petersen asserts that there is something missing at the beginning of the verse.[11] Tiemeyer maintains that the feminine singular pronominal suffix on the preposition ב refers to one of the four winds (רחות) mentioned in verse 5, suggesting that the black horses are in one of the winds.[12] Carol Meyers and Eric Meyers suggest that בה refers to the chariot "specified before each horse group in verses 2-3 and which is feminine singular."[13] Max Rogland, however, asserts that the antecedent of בה is the abstract notion of rebellion alluded to in the phrase מהתיצב על־אדון כל־הארץ (v. 5), which Rogland translates as "on account of rebellion (lit., 'the taking of a stand') against the Lord of all the earth."[14] According to Rogland, the horses and their riderless chariots respond to a rebellion against "the Lord of the whole earth," and verse 8 declares that the rebellion has been quelled in the "north country." The translations in both the NRSVue and the NABRE are based on the position taken by the Meyerses.

---

8. Lena-Sofia Tiemeyer, *Zechariah and His Visions: An Exegetical Study of Zechariah's Vision Report*, LHBOTS 605 (London: Bloomsbury, 2015), 251. Tiemeyer recognizes the problem that this raises, but she sees the image of horses *inside* their respective chariots as no more bizarre than the talking horses of 1:11.

9. A word to translate ארמים ("strong" in vv. 2, 7) is missing from the NRSVue but is present in the NABRE.

10. See Meyers and Meyers, *Haggai, Zechariah 1–8*, 316; Max Rogland, *Haggai and Zechariah 1–8: A Handbook on the Hebrew Text*, Baylor Handbook on the Hebrew Bible (Waco, TX: Baylor University Press, 2016), 165; Paul Redditt, *Haggai, Zechariah, Malachi*, NCBC (Grand Rapids: Eerdmans, 1994): 75.

11. David L. Petersen, *Haggai and Zechariah 1–8: A Commentary*, OTL (Philadelphia: Westminster, 1984), 263–64.

12. Tiemeyer, *Zechariah and His Visions*, 261–62, though she admits it is not syntactically ideal.

13. Meyers and Meyers, *Haggai, Zechariah 1–8*, 324. Max Rogland considers their suggestion as "probably the most plausible interpretation of the MT as it currently stands." See his "Heavenly Chariots and Earthly Rebellion in Zechariah 6," *Bib* 95 (2014): 118.

14. Rogland, "Heavenly Chariots," 119–20 and 122. Both the NRSVue and the NABRE translate the phrase as "presenting themselves," without any allusion to rebellion.

A Coronation (6:9-15)

In Zechariah's night visions, God is the primary actor, and people are acted upon. The oracle that follows the final vision calls for a response from representatives of the Jewish community. Their response will help facilitate the restoration of the Jewish community in Yehud. Four returned exiles, who are otherwise unknown but who must have been people of means,[15] are to provide silver and gold for the preparation of two crowns. The prophet is to place one of the crowns on the head of Joshua, the high priest, informing him that there is "a man whose name is Branch [צמח]," who will rebuild the temple and eventually take up royal regalia. The oracle declares that Branch will sit on the throne of Yehud with a priest beside him. Harmony will exist between the two.

Zechariah 6:9-15 does not reveal the identity of Branch, but the contents of chapters 3 and 4 imply that the reader should understand Zerubbabel, the Persian-appointed administrator of Yehud, to be "Branch" (צמח). This epithet likely derives from Jeremiah 23:5 and 33:15, which speak of Branch as a descendant of David who will reign over Israel and Judah at some unspecified time in the future; Zechariah 3:8 and 6:12 imply that this person is Zerubbabel. Words in the same semantic field include חטר ("shoot") and נצר ("sprout"; NRSVue: "branch") that appear in Isaiah 11:1. William Holladay notes that צמח was a word used in northwest Semitic languages to designate the legitimate king.[16] Zechariah, however, foresees a delay of an indefinite period before "Branch" is crowned as the legitimate ruler of Yehud. During that delay, Heldai and the three others named in verse 14 will have the crown in their care. No doubt the prophet had no intention of stoking nationalistic fervor among the Jews. Although he may have favored the restoration of the Davidic dynasty, any attempt to do so would have been seen as rebellion against Persian rule, which Darius certainly would have suppressed as handily as he had the Babylonian rebellion in 522 BCE. In an admission of Yehud's

---

15. The names given of the four mentioned in v. 14 of the MT differ slightly from those given in v. 10. The four in v. 10 are Heldai, Tobijah, Jedaiah, and Josiah. In v. 14, the four are Helem, Tobijah, Jedaiah, and Hen. Both the NRSVue and the NABRE ignore the differences in the two lists and simply repeat in v. 14 the names given in v. 10. This reflects the opinion of most commentators that both lists refer to the same people. See O'Brien, *Nahum, Habakkuk, Zephaniah, Haggai, Zechariah, Malachi*, 206. The JPS translation follows the MT.

16. William Holladay, *Jeremiah 1: A Commentary on the Book of the Prophet Jeremiah (Chapters 1–25)*, Hermeneia (Philadelphia: Fortress, 1986), 617–18.

Zech 6:9-15

[9]The word of the LORD came to me: [10]"Collect silver and gold from the exiles—from Heldai, Tobijah, and Jedaiah—who have arrived from Babylon, and go the same day to the house of Josiah son of Zephaniah. [11]Take the silver and gold and make a crown and set it on the head of the high priest Joshua son of Jehozadak; [12]say to him: Thus says the LORD of hosts: Here is a man whose name is Branch, for he shall branch out in his place, and he shall build the temple of the LORD. [13]It is he who shall build the temple of the LORD; he shall bear royal honor and shall sit upon his throne and rule. There shall be a priest by his throne, with peaceful understanding between the two of them. [14]And the crown shall be in the care of Heldai, Tobijah, Jedaiah, and Josiah son of Zephaniah, as a memorial in the temple of the LORD.

[15]"Those who are far off shall come and help to build the temple of the LORD, and you shall know that the LORD of hosts has sent me to you. This will happen if you diligently obey the voice of the LORD your God."

subordinate status in the empire, the second crown was to be stored in the temple, therefore, until Branch was able to assert Yehud's political autonomy. Completion of the temple's reconstruction was to be the sign of Zechariah's authenticity and the harbinger of eventual restoration of Yehud's independence from foreign domination.

The rebuilding of the temple provided not only spiritual revival but political and economic stability for the Jewish community following the disasters of 597 and 587 BCE.[17] Resumption of temple services nourished their religious identity and life. Despite the royal imagery evoked by the sobriquet "Branch," however, the rehabilitation of Judah's priesthood was not accompanied by the restoration of the Davidic dynasty. The kings of Persia supported the rebuilding of the temple, probably as a means of advancing their own interests, but they did not permit Yehud to chart course toward political independence. The building of a temple was a royal prerogative as it served to legitimate the king's rule. Temples in the ancient Near East were state institutions. The temple that was being built in Jerusalem was an anomaly. It served to legitimate the rule of Persian kings over the Jewish community of Yehud instead of the rule of Judah's native dynasty. The oracle closes with a prediction that people

17. For the role of the temple in Yehud's economy, see Marty E. Stevens, *Temples, Tithes, and Taxes: The Temple and the Economic Life of Ancient Israel* (Peabody, MA: Hendrickson, 2006).

from near and far would come to help rebuild the temple (v. 15). This Zion-centered and universalist note echoes the reference in Zechariah 2:11 to the "Many nations [that] shall join themselves to YHWH" and reinforces the prophet's emphasis on the importance of the rebuilding of the temple as central to the Judean restoration.

Zechariah underscores the importance of the leadership of the Jewish community and the centrality of its principal religious institutions, i.e., the temple and its priesthood. For better or worse, the prophet sees the community's future as tied to both. The new temple led the Jewish people to define themselves as a worshiping community under the leadership of priests. The temple and its priesthood filled the void created by the loss of the state and dynasty. The prophet's message is that YHWH has set in motion a process to provide the Jewish people with appropriate leadership despite the impossibility of the Davidic dynasty's restoration. Also, though the impetus for and the determination to complete the reconstruction of the temple came from the Persian kings, Zechariah insists that it is by God's spirit that the temple will be rebuilt (see Zech 4:6).

Zechariah's vision of the leadership of the Jewish community of Yehud was restricted both by gender and by social class. The priesthood was limited to males of Levitical descent. The priests controlled access to the temple since they determined who was ritually clean and therefore fit to participate in the community's worship. Women were subject to the priests' control since menstruation rendered them ritually impure and, therefore, unable to join in the community's worship in the temple. Since ritual impurity could be passed on by touch, this led to the notion that women had to be carefully monitored to ensure that they would not pass on their impurity. This contributed to the notion that women posed a danger to anyone wishing to worship. Social control of women was the inevitable consequence of such notions.

All the individuals named in Zechariah 6 are male, and the text suggests that Jews arriving from Babylonia, who thought of themselves as a purified remnant, had a dominant role in the Judean restoration. Unlike Haggai (e.g., Hag 1:5-11), Zechariah did not focus on the challenges that most people in Yehud faced. Ordinary folk—especially the women of Yehud—appear to be just onlookers as the restoration was unfolding, though, of course, the restoration could not succeed without their contributions. Zechariah focused on those who inhabited the rarified atmosphere of Yehud's religious and political leadership: the high priest and "Branch." Zechariah envisioned a world whose leadership was male and in which women and most men remained on the periphery. To be fair to the prophet, 6:15 appears to recognize that all the people of Yehud had responsibility for making the restoration possible. Only through the people's obedience would the rebuilding be complete. Still, as Julia O'Brien observes, Joshua and Zerubbabel "are exalted in chapters 3 and 4 and deemed 'anointed ones' in 4:14."[18] Thus, they served as symbols of patriarchal power that apparently ensured political and economic stability—even if circumscribed by Persian hegemony—in Zechariah's vision of a restored Yehud.

Although Zechariah was probably effective in assuring his community that their God willed its well-being, the prophet's rhetoric may not speak well to a war-weary world today. In the 2020s, there were several major armed conflicts in Afghanistan, Yemen, Somalia, Gaza, and Ukraine, with each one resulting in at least ten thousand combat-related deaths, along with thirty-two smaller conflicts that caused thousands more deaths in that same year. Women, children, and other noncombatants are caught up in these conflicts, suffering serious injuries and death. Given that each of these contexts was rooted in complex political and cultural circumstances, martial imagery may not be the most appropriate way to speak of God for communities today in need of healing and hope.

In all of Zechariah's night visions, the men and women living in Yehud are passive recipients of the words of assurance that God is returning to Jerusalem, that God is ensuring the completion of the temple's reconstruction and is providing strong religious and political leadership exercised solely by men. According to Zechariah, God would ensure that justice prevailed, in part by banishing the last vestige of idolatrous worship from Yehud. The visions, then, underscore the priority of God's activity in Yehud's restoration. Both the men and women of Yehud are simply witnesses to and beneficiaries of what God is doing for the Jewish community. Apart from rebuilding the temple in Jerusalem, they have no personal agency in this major transformation in their lives. The prophet must have recognized that if Yehud's future depended on the potential of the Jewish community alone to effect genuine political and economic change, the people could have no hope. The people of Yehud may have been inspired by the prophet to reembrace authentic Jewish life, confident that God would bring about victory on their behalf. Male

18. Julia M. O'Brien, "Zechariah," in *Women's Bible Commentary*, ed. Carol A. Newsom, Sharon H. Ringe, and Jacqueline E. Lapsley, 3rd ed. (Louisville: Westminster John Knox, 2012), 347. The word "anointed," however, does not appear in 4:14; rather, the text refers to the two leaders as "sons of oil."

leadership, empowered by God and approved by the Persians, would reestablish the temple as the symbol of the restoration.

Zechariah's focus solely on the leadership of the Jewish community may provide us with a narrow lens through which to see communal life in Yehud. Conflicts rose within the Jewish community (see Isa 58 and 66). It was only when the entire Jewish community accepted responsibility for the past (Neh 9) and was committed to restoring Jewish life in Yehud (Neh 8) that there was a real possibility for the future of the community. The prophet's limited perspective may not resonate well today. It is becoming increasingly apparent that political, economic, social, and religious systems must be equitable and inclusive for justice to be served. That means in part that people must have a role in shaping the decisions and actions that impact their lives. This is particularly true of women whose voices have been muted by cultural prejudice and religious practice but whose leadership is reshaping society for the better in countries throughout the world.

The potential for restoration of the Jewish community in what remained of their ancestral homeland was limited, since the Persian rulers, though more benign than their Assyrian and Babylonian predecessors, were nonetheless insistent that the people of Yehud respect imperial authority. Zechariah's vision of leadership within the Jewish community helped the people of Yehud to rebuild their faith and their lives within Persia's carefully determined parameters. Readers of Zechariah today ought to look beyond the "high priests" and "Branches" of their political and religious institutions and rebuild those structures to support the inclusion and active participation of all members of society. With that participation comes responsibility to act in a way that serves the common good.

Conclusion

The accounts of Zechariah's visions end where they began: with the images of horses patrolling the earth, ensuring the peace of Jerusalem. The prophet foresees the city's repopulation, the return of YHWH to the city and the restoration of the Jewish people's relationship to their God, and the end of injustice and idolatry. The visions underscore the importance of the priests' role in the temple that is to be rebuilt. The high priest will oversee the rituals and ministers of that temple. The prophet is prudent enough not to challenge the rule of the Persian king over Yehud. He speaks of Zerubbabel with measured affirmation of his role in the

Jewish community of Yehud. Zerubbabel's principal task in Zechariah's view is to direct the completion of the temple in Jerusalem. The prophet is silent about Zerubbabel's political role, though, by implying that he is the "Branch" spoken of by his prophetic predecessors, Zechariah offers a hint of his hopes for Yehud's future.

Zechariah's vision for the future of Yehud is far from comprehensive. The prophet all but ignores whole segments of Jewish society: the poor, women, those who remained in the land during the exile. The prophet's principal concerns revolve around the security of Jerusalem and the reconstruction of the temple. This leads him to highlight the community's leaders: Zerubbabel, who will oversee the temple project, and Joshua, who will serve as the high priest. Zechariah describes the parameters of their leadership in muted and vague assertions. We know who they were, but we know little of their relationship. The narrow focus of Zechariah's visions did not diminish the Jewish community's respect for his prophetic ministry. His words are included in the scroll of the Twelve. Still, this narrow focus of the prophet's visions complicates the appropriation of their significance by contemporary believers—especially women. The one time that female characters receive some attention in Zechariah, these characters represent idolatry. Zechariah's use of the well-worn trope that has a female character represent "Wickedness" is regrettable since it makes it easy to dismiss the book's message as irrelevant or even detrimental to women. The most significant of the prophet's messages for believers today is that judgment is not God's last word. It was not God's last word to Judah and Jerusalem, and it will not be God's last word to believers today. The accounts of the prophet's vision, as bizarre as they may be, are clear about one thing: there is a future for the people of God—a future that is not dependent on what they can do. It is dependent on what God can do.

Zechariah 7:1-14

Creating New Possibilities

Two superscriptions (7:1 and 9:1) set off Zechariah 7–8 as a distinct unit within the book. The first includes a date like the superscriptions found in 1:1, 7; the second begins with the word מַשָּׂא ("burden," "oracle") as does 12:1. The two chapters are further delineated as a unit by references to fasting at the beginning (7:1-3) and end (8:18-19). Similarly, 7:2 mentions a person with a foreign name (Sharezer) who comes to Jerusalem "to entreat the favor of YHWH" while 8:20-23 describes the arrival at Jerusalem of "many peoples and strong nations . . . to entreat the favor of YHWH." Finally, chapters 7–8 recapitulate some of the motifs found in the vision accounts in chapters 1–6, while asserting that the restoration of the people's relationship with God is dependent on their response to the call for repentance and obedience that is found in 1:1-6.[1] Zechariah 7–8, then, plays a significant role in the book. The phantasmagoric visions recounted in chapters 1–6 serve to engage the reader's imagination about possibilities for the future, while assertions in chapters 7–8 remind the reader that the people of Yehud cannot simply remain passive beneficiaries of God's benevolence. They must actively participate in the creation of new possibilities for Yehud by upholding justice and compassion in their community (7:8-10; 8:16-17).

1. Michael R. Stead, *The Intertextuality of Zechariah 1–8*, LHBOTS 506 (New York: T&T Clark, 2009), 230. Elie Assis, however, limits this recapitulation to chapter 8. See his "Zechariah 8 as Revision and Digest of Zechariah 1–7," *JHebS* 10 (2010): 25.

Scholarly consensus maintains that chapters 7–8 complete the first half of the book of Zechariah and that chapters 9–14 come from a different hand.[2] Similarities between chapters 7–8 and both halves of the book indicate that chapters 7–8 serve to connect the two halves; for example, chapters 7–8 and 1–6 share a concern about the leadership of the Jewish community,[3] and both 1:4 and 7:12-14 contain rebukes of the people's ancestors who had refused to heed the words of the prophets. The three references to peace (שלום) in 8:12-19 are reminiscent of the reference to a tranquil earth in 1:11. Although the vocabulary in chapters 7–8 is like that of chapters 1–6, the literary form of chapters 7–8 more closely resembles that of chapters 9–14.

A Question about Fasting (7:1-7)

Zechariah 7 opens with a reference to "*King* Darius," in contrast to Zechariah's other two references to the Persian ruler simply as "Darius" (1:1, 7). The royal title in 7:1 is an acknowledgment that the kingdom of Judah being ruled by a scion of the Davidic dynasty was part of Yehud's past but not of its present. Recognition that Darius, a successor of Cyrus the Great, God's anointed (Isa 45:1), was sovereign in Yehud is consistent with Haggai and Ezra, who regularly use the expression "King Darius."[4] Zechariah's adoption of this title likely sought to prevent readers from getting the wrong idea about Zerubbabel from the vision described in chapter 4. Of course, Zerubbabel's role in the construction of the temple was in accord with the divine will (Zech 4:6-7, 9-10), but it was not an exercise of any royal prerogative. Zerubbabel was Darius's project manager—nothing more. The kingship was firmly in Persian hands.

The date provided in 7:1, which is equivalent to December 7, 518 BCE, is the third and final date mentioned in the book of Zechariah. It is also the last date to appear in the prophetic corpus of the Hebrew Bible. The other dates mentioned in Zechariah are October 520 BCE (1:1) and February 15, 519 BCE (1:7). Such specific dates are rare in prophetic literature,

---

2. Mark J. Boda, "From Fasts to Feasts: The Literary Function of Zechariah 7–8," *CBQ* 65 (2003): 390–407.

3. For a detailed comparison between Zech 7–8 and 1:1-6, see Boda, "Zechariah: Master Mason or Penitential Prophet?," in *Yahwism after the Exile: Perspectives on Israelite Religion in the Persian Era; Papers Read at the First Meeting of the European Association for Biblical Studies, Utrecht, 6–9 August 2000,* ed. Rainer Albertz and Bob Becking, Studies in Theology and Religion 5 (Assen: Van Gorcum, 2003), 49–69.

4. Ezra 4:5, 24; 5:6, 7; 6:1, 13, 15; Hag 1:1, 15; 2:10.

Zech 7:1-7

¹In the fourth year of King Darius, the word of the Lord came to Zechariah on the fourth day of the ninth month, which is Chislev. ²Now the people of Bethel had sent Sharezer and Regem-melech* and their men to entreat the favor of the Lord ³and to ask the priests of the house of the Lord of hosts and the prophets, "Should I mourn and practice abstinence in the fifth month, as I have done for so many years?" ⁴Then the word of the Lord of hosts came to me: ⁵"Say to all the people of the land and the priests: When you fasted and lamented in the fifth month and in the seventh for these seventy years, was it for me that you fasted? ⁶And when you eat and when you drink, do you not eat and drink only for yourselves? ⁷Were not these the words that the Lord proclaimed by the former prophets, when Jerusalem was inhabited and in prosperity, along with the towns around it, and when the Negeb and the Shephelah were inhabited?"

so these dates must have had special significance. It is likely that the people of Yehud were keenly aware of Jeremiah's prediction that the Babylonian exile, the first phase of which began in 597 BCE, was to last for seventy years (Jer 29:10-14). With the period of exile coming to an end, Zechariah's visions reflect the belief that a new moment in the life of the Jewish people was about to begin—a time of great transformation. Indeed, Michael Fishbane has suggested that knowledge of Jeremiah's prediction is the very thing that propelled the Jews to complete the rebuilding of the temple.[5] The reconstruction of the temple was completed by 516 BCE— seventy-one years after the Babylonians demolished Solomon's temple.

The shift in tone and content between Zechariah 1–6 and Zechariah 7–8 reflects markedly different historical circumstances although the dates preserved in these sections are only two years apart. Carol Meyers and Eric Meyers suggest that there was an important shift in the political sphere between 520 and 518 BCE. During this brief period, the Persian Empire encouraged its subjects to codify their ancestral laws and to begin working on organizing their local governments.[6] Persian records

---

* It is possible that Regem-melech was a title borne by Sharezer, i.e., "the king's spokesman," rather than a proper name. See Mark J. Boda, *The Book of Zechariah*, NICOT (Grand Rapids: Eerdmans, 2016), 431 no. c.

5. Michael Fishbane, *Biblical Interpretation in Ancient Israel* (Oxford: Clarendon, 1985), 481.

6. Carol L. Meyers and Eric M. Meyers, *Haggai, Zechariah 1–8: A New Translation with Introduction and Commentary*, AB 25B (Garden City, NY: Doubleday, 1987), 390.

have been discovered that are directed toward Egyptian officials that require them to codify their legal records. Given the proximity of Egypt to Yehud, it is possible that the Persians issued a similar edict to the Jews, or at least that the Jews were aware that the Persians expected them to exercise limited autonomy according to their ancestral laws. The Persian strategy of pacification in their vast empire involved granting limited autonomy to subject peoples, with the proviso that they would respect the Persian authorities and pay their taxes.

As the people of Yehud began to reconstitute their community life, they realized that they had to reconsider the fasting that the community had been observing to mark the events surrounding the fall of Jerusalem and the destruction of the temple. Decisions regarding whether to keep or do away with fasting depended on whether the observance of Jerusalem's fall remained relevant. It is not surprising, then, that chapter 7 opens with a question about the fast "in the fifth month" (v. 3).[7] Pious observance of that fast had been a sign of mourning over the tragic fate of Jerusalem and its temple, but now, with support from the Persians, that fate was being reversed. Was the fast, therefore, still relevant?

According to 7:2-3, the people of Bethel sent emissaries to ask the priests and prophets of Jerusalem whether observing the fast "in the fifth month" should continue now that the rebuilding of the temple was nearly complete. This is the earliest allusion to the fast observed on the ninth day of Av (תשעה באב), a practice that traditional Jewish communities continue to observe. It marks the day when the Babylonians destroyed Solomon's temple. The question posed by the people of Bethel implies uncertainty about the significance of the reconstruction project the Persians were supporting. Was the building of a new temple a sign of the coming redemption, perhaps signaling a new age when God would end foreign occupation and restore the kingdom of Judah? Or, since many Jews remained in Babylon and the Davidic kingdom and dynasty was not restored, was it possible that God had not sanctioned the rebuilding of the temple at all but desired that the people continue living in an unredeemed state?[8]

The date of the fast in question is also confusing. Why would the people of Bethel send emissaries in the ninth month (Kislev) to ask about

7. The Hebrew Bible usually refers to months by an ordinal number rather than the month's proper name. The name of the fifth month is Av.

8. Hayyim Angel, *Haggai, Zechariah, and Malachi: Prophecy in an Age of Uncertainty* (New Milford, CT: Maggid Books, 2016), 76.

what they must do in the fifth month (Av)? One option is that this exchange occurred just before the tenth month (Tevet), which marked the date when the walls of Jerusalem were breached in 587 BCE (2 Kgs 25:1). The Jews had likewise established a fast day on the tenth day of Tevet to commemorate the date of the Babylonian siege of Jerusalem (Zech 8:19). Perhaps the two fast days were conflated in Zechariah 7. In any case, both of these fast days commemorated events connected with the fall of Jerusalem to the Babylonians in 587 BCE. They were signs of mourning that sought to induce a sympathetic response from God and to persuade God to reverse Jerusalem's tragic fate; fasting then was probably not an ascetical practice.[9] Since the temple was being rebuilt with the support of the Persians, some members of the Jewish community may have considered mourning over its destruction by the Babylonians no longer appropriate.[10] Still, the question posed by the people of Bethel implied that some Jews of Yehud believed that Persian hegemony posed a continuing danger to the Jewish people.

That the delegation comes from Bethel is significant. Just nineteen miles north of Jerusalem in the ancestral territory of Benjamin, Bethel was the site of a temple built by Jeroboam I to deter people of the kingdom of Israel from going to Jerusalem for worship (1 Kgs 12:27-30). After the kingdom of Israel fell to Assyria in 722 BCE and most of its territory was absorbed into the Assyrian provincial system, Bethel found itself annexed to the territory of Judah. The people of Bethel came to recognize Jerusalem's unique status and the religious authority of its priests and prophets.[11] Rebuilding the Jerusalem temple was a key part

9. Some people in the ancient world did believe that abstaining from the indulgences of the physical world enabled them to communicate more intensely with the world of the divine. See David L. Petersen, *Haggai and Zechariah 1–8: A Commentary*, OTL (Philadelphia: Westminster, 1984), 286. Some rabbis also embraced an ascetic approach to the physical world, although this approach is not widely appreciated by modern scholars. See Eliezer Diamond, *Holy Men and Hunger Artists: Fasting and Asceticism in Rabbinic Culture* (New York: Oxford University Press, 2004). On the cultural sharing between rabbinic and Christian monastic communities, see Michal Bar-Asher Siegal, *Early Christian Monastic Literature and the Babylonian Talmud* (New York: Cambridge University Press, 2013). Fasting came to be considered a way to call on God in times of great danger; see Ezra 8:21-22 and Esth 4:15-16.

10. Wilhelm Rudolph, *Haggai–Sacharja 1–8, Sacharja 9–14, Maleachi*, KAT 13/4 (Gütersloh: Mohn, 1976), 62, 151; Petersen, *Haggai and Zechariah 1–8*, 122; Mike Butterworth, *Structure and the Book of Zechariah*, JSOTSup 130 (Sheffield: Sheffield Academic, 1992), 70–72.

11. 2 Kgs 23:4, 15 implies that Bethel was under the control of Josiah, king of Judah.

of reestablishing Jerusalem's status as chosen by God as a holy place (Zech 2:12; 3:2; 8:3), the religious center for the Jewish people, and the appropriate place to seek advice on proper religious observance. The inquiry by the emissaries from Bethel was about more than practical advice on pious acts by individuals or households. The people of Bethel needed to know how to handle communal observances of fast days that were instrumental in fashioning a collective memory and narrative about the fall of Jerusalem.[12]

Had the people of Bethel failed to observe the fast days that had been established by Jerusalem's leaders of an earlier generation, divergent sets of collective memories regarding the people's history might have emerged. This, in turn, almost certainly would have caused splintering in the Jewish community. Not all Judeans were forced to migrate to Babylonia (2 Kgs 25:12). Still, it is likely that all Judeans mourned the loss of the national state and the temple, and a fast day to commemorate that loss would have resonated with the entire community. The emissaries from Bethel likely understood what was at stake. To ensure unity among all those who worshiped YHWH, the community had to agree on how to commemorate major events in its history. That the emissaries came from Bethel, the location of a temple of the former kingdom of Israel, signaled a desire for unity that would overcome past divisions. Observance of common fast days was an expression of that desire.

There are two surprising features of the question posed in Zechariah 7:1-7. First, the emissaries from Bethel ask a question in the first-person singular: אבכה בחדש החמשי הנזר ("Should I mourn and practice the abstinence the fifth month?," 7:3b, NRSV)—not in plural, as one expects. Perhaps this indicates that the emissaries speak only on behalf of the people of Bethel and not for all Jews. It is possible that the way in which the question is framed reflects a lack of unity regarding how the people of Yehud observed their ancestral traditions. This view is reinforced by the claim in 7:3 that the people of Bethel had commemorated the fall of Jerusalem by observing the annual fast for a period of "many years." Perhaps that statement was to demonstrate to the leaders in Jerusalem, some of whom may have been returned exiles like Joshua and Zerubbabel, the continuity and authenticity of the practice by the people of

---

12. Yosef Hayim Yerushalmi addresses the question of how to "form" memories on a national level and what these memories meant to the people's national identity in *Zakhor: Jewish History and Jewish Memory* (Seattle: University of Washington Press, 1996). Cf. Duncan S. A. Bell, "Mythscapes: Memory, Mythology, and National Identity," *The British Journal of Sociology* 54 (2003): 63–81.

Bethel. In contrast, regardless of the peculiar form of the question, the answer is unequivocally meant for all the people. The phrase "Say to all the people of the land [אֶל־כָּל־עַם הָאָרֶץ] and the priests" (7:5a) indicates that the observance of the fast applies to all Jews. A single policy regarding the fast, sanctioned by the priests and prophets of Jerusalem, would manifest unity among the Jews of Yehud. Unity among all Jews, regardless of age, gender, and religious standing, becomes a key theme in Zechariah 9–14.

The second observation is that the response is not straightforward; rather, it is in the form of three rhetorical questions. These questions probe beyond the question of whether to fast. They challenge the people's motivation for keeping the tradition. A reference to "the former prophets" (הַנְּבִיאִים הָרִאשׁנִים) in verse 7 functions similarly to the first reference in 1:4. The prophet calls the people of Bethel to reflect on the instruction their ancestors had received and, unlike the earlier generations, to respond with faithfulness and obedience. (See discussion of 7:8-14 below.)

It may seem strange to the reader that the question in verse 3 is directed toward priests and prophets and that the answer is likewise directed to the people of the land and priests (v. 5). A likely explanation may be that temple administration was conducted by groups of priests who served twice a year and who represented one out of twenty-four priestly groups. At any given time, therefore, most of Yehud's priests were dispersed throughout the land, and only a few were serving in Jerusalem. In that sense, the priestly community of Yehud was not synonymous with temple administration. The priests were both part of the community's leadership and the recipients of priestly leadership. The continual rotation of priestly service in Jerusalem, moreover, ensured that no single individual besides the high priest had the task of leading the people in an ongoing manner. First Chronicles 24 provides a list of the rotation of duties among priestly families.[13] Jews in the Second Temple period were aware of the priestly rotations. Josephus speaks of the practice in the late first century CE, as do the rabbis.[14] The fluidity of taking on priestly roles for a few weeks a year and shedding them when "off-duty" contradicts the image of a society that has been presumed by some scholars to have fixed social strata that featured insular priests at the top of the political hierarchy.

---

13. According to 1 Chr 24, these divisions were organized by David, though they probably were set during the Persian period. Also, Deuteronomy 18:6-8 assumes that not all cultic personnel resided in Jerusalem.

14. On the priestly cycles, see Josephus, *Ag. Ap.* 2.108; cf. t. Ta'an. 4:2, and y. Ta'an. 4:2, 67d.

Compassion for the Poor (7:8-14)

Despite the urgent nature of the question about fasting that opens this chapter, the prophet asserts that God is indifferent to the fasts that mark the fall of Jerusalem (vv. 4-7; see also Isa 58:1-14). The oracle in 7:8-14 asserts, however, that God is not indifferent to injustice toward and neglect of the poor. The observance of formal fast days is not as important to the life of the Jewish community as is care for economically dependent people of Yehud—specifically the widow, orphan, and the resident alien. The book of Deuteronomy mandates special concern for these *personae miserabiles* (Deut 10:18; 14:29; 16:11-14; 24:17-21; 26:12-13; 27:19). Social and economic structures and practices made it almost impossible for those people to own land so that they could support themselves. In the agricultural economy of Yehud, being landless meant being poor. The deaths of husbands made their widows and their children particularly vulnerable since they were no longer members of their husband's family. They were left without economic support. Similarly, the resident alien was not part of a typical family structure that provided economic protection. Traditional Israelite morality embodied in Deuteronomy and in much of prophetic literature calls the people of Israel to embrace the poor as if they were close relatives.

Verses 8-14 include motifs that appear in several preexilic prophets. Among these are the call to justice and compassion toward widows, orphans, aliens, and the poor.[15] In verse 12 Zechariah acknowledges his debt to his prophetic predecessors and asserts that the difficulties the people of Yehud are experiencing are a direct result of their failure to heed the message of "the former prophets." The prophet equates ethical concern for the vulnerable members of society (vv. 8-10) with observance of the entirety of the law (vv. 11-12). Thus, Zechariah stands firmly in the prophetic tradition, which locates care for those in need at the center of Israelite ethics. Like earlier prophets, Zechariah maintains that the people's greatest flaw was their failure to create and maintain a society based on justice and compassion. The injunction in verse 10 forbids the plotting of evil איש אחיו ("against one another"), which literally means "a man (to) his brother." This kinship language reinforces the notion that the basis of the Jewish community and morality is the familial relationship that should exist among the members of the Jewish community. Zechariah often emphasizes the importance of family

15. Also Isa 1:16-17; Jer 7:5-7; Hos 6:6; Amos 5:14-15, 21-24; Mic 6:8.

Zech 7:8-14

⁸The word of the LORD came to Zechariah, saying: ⁹"Thus says the LORD of hosts: Render true judgments, show kindness and mercy to one another; ¹⁰do not oppress the widow, the orphan, the alien, or the poor; and do not devise evil in your hearts against one another. ¹¹But they refused to listen and turned a stubborn shoulder and stopped their ears in order not to hear. ¹²They made their hearts adamant in order not to hear the law and the words that the LORD of hosts had sent by his spirit through the former prophets. Therefore great wrath came from the LORD of hosts. ¹³Just as, when I called, they would not hear, so, when they called, I would not hear, says the LORD of hosts, ¹⁴and I scattered them with a whirlwind among all the nations that they had not known. Thus the land they left was desolate, so that no one went to and fro, and a pleasant land was made desolate."

structure throughout his book. We will see those references to kinship and the mutuality that flows from it are especially emphasized in the second half of the book (Zech 12:12, 14; 14:17).

Grammatical forms of the root שמע ("hear") appear four times in this passage—three times in reference to the people of Yehud (vv. 11 [משמוע], 12 [משמוע], 13 [לא שמעו]) and once in reference to God (v. 13 [אשמע]). Because the people did not listen to the cry of the poor, or to the words of the Torah and the message of the prophets, or to God's call, God will not hear them when they call upon God. The writer's emphasis on the people not listening to the prophets is meant to awaken readers, who ought to learn from the mistakes of the past. They must heed the words of the prophets. If the readers choose to hear the words of the Torah and the prophets, they will bring blessing rather than judgment on the Jewish community.

Verse 12 speaks of a "great wrath" (קצף גדול) that will be directed against the people of Yehud because they have ignored the words of "the former prophets." The phrase "great wrath" was used by earlier prophets, particularly Jeremiah, who predicted that the Babylonians, who had made the people of Judah suffer so much, would ultimately incur God's great wrath (Jer 21:5; 32:37). According to Jeremiah, God would return the people to their land, and a period of worship and universal peace, characterized by a "new covenant," would follow (Jer 31–32). The use of the phrase "great wrath" in Zechariah, therefore, is ironic. The people of Yehud have now been restored to their land, and Babylonian hegemony is a thing of the past. Still, the people have not repented; they have not returned to God in the way that Jeremiah foresaw. The great wrath, therefore, that was once reserved exclusively for Judah's enemies will now be directed against the people of Yehud themselves. The Jews, in effect, have become one of the nations whom God promised to bring to judgment. This is what makes the final verse of the chapter, which speaks of God having scattered the people of Judah across the earth, so poignant and disturbing. What God had done in the past God can do again. The fluidity with which the people can be either called by God or spurned by God reminds them that their future depends on their fidelity to the covenant and obedience to God's commandments.

Conclusion

Chapter 7 marks a significant turning point in Zechariah. The reader has now entered a new historical moment, a moment in which the people of Yehud must unite and agree on a common set of rituals that reflect a common set of values despite the differences among them. Above all, they must listen to the Torah and the prophets. Failure to do so will bring the kind of disasters that they have commemorated by their days of fasting. The message of the Torah and prophets is a familiar one: create and maintain a just and compassionate society.

Two central issues addressed in Zechariah 7—fasting traditions (vv. 1-7) and social ethics (vv. 8-14)—present a variety of considerations for feminist readers today. First, regarding fasting, this was a practice observed by both men and women according to several biblical texts. For example, Hannah abstained from eating out of grief for her barrenness (1 Sam 1:7). Esther fasted for three days before approaching King Ahasuerus on behalf of the Jews of his kingdom, and she called for the Jews of Susa to fast with her (Esth 4:16). Judith fasted all days except holidays and the day before holidays as an expression of piety (Jdt 8:6). The New Testament presents the prophet Anna devoting her time to fasting and prayer (Luke 2:37). These biblical examples suggest that fasting as a religious practice is not associated with a specific gender but is a religious observance common to all adult Jews. Also, here fasting serves to commemorate events in Jewish history, supporting a common narrative and building community cohesion. The people of Bethel demonstrate their desire to be included in the common narrative of the postexilic Jewish community by seeking guidance from Jerusalem's priests and prophets regarding proper observance. Yair Hoffman has argued that throughout the centuries and to the present, establishing a single date to commemorate a certain event can help to solidify collective memory and establish a set of values that all members of a community can accept. He calls attention to the attempt in the late 1990s to establish a "Fast of Yitzchak" to commemorate the assassination of Israel's Prime Minister Yitzchak Rabin.[16] To establish a day of commemoration that would be observed in all Jewish communities in perpetuity requires Jews to agree on a common narrative and on the meaning of major turning points in that narrative. Whether it was the late sixth century BCE or recent decades of the Common Era, establishing days of remembrance that an entire community accepts is a way to build cohesiveness and a sense of national memory. For Jews, a common interpretation of past events is linked to a common interpretation of the people's present circumstances and the way in which those circumstances reflect their relationship with God.

Although Zechariah does not mention the roles of women in fasting rituals or the historical events they marked, some biblical narratives do recount significant events in the story of ancient Israel in which both men and women play important roles. For example, when the Israelites leave Egypt, Moses's sister Miriam leads the women in song and celebration. And when the people are told to gather at the foot of Mount Sinai to experience their first communal divine revelation, Moses is told to gather all of the nation, which presumably includes women and children (Exod 15:20-21, 19:11).[17] The idea that the entire nation, regardless of age and gender, should forge a common religious experience is also projected into the future, when Moses instructs the Israelites to gather

16. Yair Hoffman, "The Fasts in the Book of Zechariah and the Fashioning of National Remembrance," in *Judah and the Judeans in the Neo-Babylonian Period*, ed. Oded Lipschits and Joseph Blenkinsopp (Winona Lake, IN: Eisenbrauns, 2003), 212–13. The attempt to establish such a date was not successful among Jews living in Israel and elsewhere, perhaps because of the wide variety of emotions toward what Rabin stood for. According to Hoffman, Jews living both in Israel and in the Diaspora held wide-ranging opinions about Rabin's legacy and about the historical events that Rabin was instrumental in piloting. Because Jews could not agree on a common historical narrative, and the *meaning* of that narrative, the effort to establish a permanent annual fast day in honor of Rabin was ultimately unsuccessful.

17. According to Midrashic tradition (m. Mek. 87a) the use of parallelism in the command to Moses, "Thus you shall say to the house of Jacob and tell the Israelites" (Exod 19:3), reflects God's intent to include both men and women as recipients of revelation. "The Israelites" stands for the men while "the house of Jacob" stands for the women.

all the people, explicitly including women and children, once a year to listen to the king read aloud from the Torah (Deut 31:12).

Regarding the issue of social justice, a feminist reading of Zechariah 7 raises important questions about values, practices, and policies and the leadership structures that support them. For example, the chapter depicts the priests and prophets of Jerusalem as collaborators in decision-making about the observance of fasting in Persian period Yehud. This collaboration challenges a popular notion that, in this period, priests and prophets were at odds with one another, with the priests defending an older cultic infrastructure that supported a hierarchical elite and the prophets arguing for a more democratic and ethical society. For Zechariah, no such binary exists. The prioritization of ethical concern (indicated in vv. 9-10) over ritual observance (addressed in vv. 3-7) implies that the priests and prophets agreed that religious ritual was meaningless unless accompanied by ethical behavior. This is consistent with Zechariah's generally favorable view of the role of the priesthood in Yehud's restoration.

The leadership roles that Zechariah speaks of are all held by men. The prophet's intended audience probably consisted of men who were forming Yehud's ruling class. The appeal to respond to the needs of those without access to property and livelihood demonstrates that Zechariah does not call for changes in Yehud's economic structures, which would have made it possible for those who were vulnerable to achieve autonomy and financial security. In Zechariah 7, widows and orphans, non-Israelites, and all others living in poverty are reduced to objects of charity, dependent on the largesse of people of means, most of whom were men. A critical reading today challenges both men and women who have access to power and influence to change unjust structures and systems so that all in the community have access to the resources they need to live in justice and dignity.

Zechariah 7 asserts that new possibilities lie open for the people of Yehud, who have been returned to their homeland. A new temple is under construction. Priests are ready to resume their service. The Jewish community enjoys some control over their daily lives. The task ahead is to create a society of equals in which all the poor, the widow, the orphan, and the alien enjoy the blessings that all other people enjoy. The future of the Jewish community is in the hands of that community. The keys to that future are compassion and justice.

Zechariah 8:1-23

Creating a Just Community

As noted in the previous chapter, Zechariah 7–8 should be read together. Chapter 7 opens with a question directed to priestly and prophetic leaders based in Jerusalem about whether the fast in remembrance of the fall of Jerusalem should continue to be observed. After all, circumstances have changed. The Persians encouraged Judeans in Babylon to return to Jerusalem and rebuild the temple. Chapter 8 forms an *inclusio* with chapter 7 by closing with a reference to the transformation of fast days into "cheerful festivals" (v. 19). Furthermore, chapter 8 brings closure to the seven chapters that precede it with a new and distinct message.[1] This new message is conveyed by ten prophecies. Nine of the ten prophecies in this chapter (the oracle in vv. 7-8 is the exception) paraphrase statements in earlier chapters to summarize, clarify, or modify them. Elie Assis identified these ten prophecies as verses 2, 3, 4-5, 6, 7-8, 9-13, 14-17, 19, 20-22, and 23.[2] Each begins with the formula

---

1. Mark J. Boda, "From Fasts to Feasts: The Literary Function of Zechariah 7–8," *CBQ* 65 (2003): 398. Some interpreters have suggested that chapters 7 and 8 have a chiastic structure, but these suggestions are not compelling; e.g., see Ben C. Ollenburger, "The Book of Zechariah," in *NIB*, ed. Leander E. Keck (Nashville: Abingdon, 1996), 7:789–90.

2. See his "The Structure of Zechariah 8 and Its Meaning," in *Perspectives on Hebrew Scriptures IX: Comprising the Contents of Journal of Hebrew Scriptures, vol. 12*, ed. Ehud Ben Zvi and Christophe Nihan (Piscataway, NJ: Gorgias Press, 2014), 353.

"Thus says יהוה צבאות [YHWH of armies]" except for verse 3, which has the abbreviated form "Thus says יהוה [YHWH]." Chapter 8 functions as an accessible digest of the book's earlier material and offers a comforting, optimistic message regarding the restoration of Jerusalem and its people at the eschaton.[3]

A Street Scene (8:1-8)

The chapter describes a scene in the future that associates YHWH's zeal (קנאה) for Zion with God's return to the city and God's anger toward the nations. By reversing Jerusalem's fortunes, God restores God's honor, making the city a fit place for God to reside (8:1-3). This association has led Erin Villareal to define God's jealousy as a response to the threat to divine prerogatives posed by the nations.[4] At the same time, there is a human element at play in God's jealousy since it is concerned about justice and stability in the Jewish community of Yehud. The purpose of God's "jealousy" for Jerusalem is not only to restore God's honor but also to restore justice in the Jewish community.

The image of elderly men and women sitting in the streets of Jerusalem, while boys and girls are playing in those streets, provides a charming vision of life in a community at peace. Zechariah 8:4-8 is not the only passage from the exilic and postexilic periods that specifically refers to women in the community. For example, Nehemiah 8:1-2 ("all the people . . . men and women") and Jeremiah 44:24 ("the people and all the women") state that women are to participate in communal assemblies, perhaps alluding to Deuteronomy 31:12, which specifies that women must attend the annual gathering of Israel to hear the Torah read to the assembly. The image in Zechariah, however, is distinctive because it is not about the public assembly, but it depicts women and girls in everyday life. While the rules of Hebrew grammar allow for third-person masculine plural nouns, such as זקנים ("old men") and ילדים ("boys"), to include females as well as males, words that explicitly mention females suggest that the inclusion of these words was intentional. References to women and girls in Zechariah 8:4-5 underscore the inclusive nature of the prophet's vision of the restored Jerusalem.

---

3. Elie Assis, "Zechariah 8 as Revision and Digest of Zechariah 1–7," *JHebS* 10 (2010): 25.

4. Erin Villareal, *Jealousy in Context: The Social Implications of Emotions in the Hebrew Bible* (University Park, PA: Eisenbrauns, 2022), 128.

¹The word of the Lᴏʀᴅ of hosts came to me, saying: ²"Thus says the Lᴏʀᴅ of hosts: I am zealous for Zion with great zeal, and I am zealous for her with great wrath. ³Thus says the Lᴏʀᴅ: I will return to Zion and will dwell in the midst of Jerusalem; Jerusalem shall be called the faithful city, and the mountain of the Lᴏʀᴅ of hosts shall be called the holy mountain. ⁴Thus says the Lᴏʀᴅ of hosts: Old men and old women shall again sit in the streets of Jerusalem, each with staff in hand because of their great age. ⁵And the streets of the city shall be full of boys and girls playing in its streets. ⁶Thus says the Lᴏʀᴅ of hosts: Even though it seems impossible to the remnant of this people in these days, should it also seem impossible to me, says the Lᴏʀᴅ of hosts? ⁷Thus says the Lᴏʀᴅ of hosts: I will save my people from the east country and from the west country, ⁸and I will bring them to live in Jerusalem. They shall be my people and I will be their God, in faithfulness and in righteousness."

The description of old men and women relaxing while girls and boys play in the streets paints an idyllic picture of life in Jerusalem following God's reversal of the city's fortunes. These images, coupled with an emphasis on the family in later chapters (Zech 12:12, 14; 14:17), lend a sense of inclusion and completeness to Zechariah's vision of the restored Jewish community—something missing in the vision accounts of chapters 1–6. *All* Jews, regardless of gender or age, will enjoy life in Jerusalem, whose people live together "in faithfulness and in righteousness" (8:8). Jerusalem will be home, both to the "remnant" who did not leave Judah as exiles and to the people returning from east and west (vv. 6-7). They will be a united people with their God dwelling in their midst (v. 3).

Rabbinic tradition regards Zechariah 8 as looking forward to the time when the fallen temple will be restored and a period of communal harmony will ensue. One especially popular tale appears in slight variation in numerous rabbinic texts. This story is about Rabbi Akiva (c. 50–135 CE) laughing as he walks past the destroyed ruins of the second temple. Horrified, his fellow rabbis ask him the reason for his laughter. Akiva answers that God had clearly fulfilled the words of the eighth-century prophet Micah, that Zion would be "plowed as a field" (Mic 3:9-12, cited in Jer 26:18). Also, according to Jeremiah 26:20, a prophet named Uriah expressed fundamental agreement with Jeremiah's announcement of judgment against Judah. Akiva tells his friends that the words of the prophet Zechariah, who is described as Uriah's colleague and fellow witness to Isaiah's words in Isaiah 8:2, will also be fulfilled. Specifically,

Akiva tells his colleagues, Zechariah's prediction in 8:4-5 that "old men and old women shall again sit in the streets of Jerusalem," and the image of the boys and girls playing in the streets, will become a reality following the fulfillment of the judgment against Jerusalem announced by the prophets. This, Akiva explains, is why he has laughed. The rabbi's friends respond, "Akiva, you have given us comfort."[5]

Early Christian readings of this passage differ from those of the rabbis. Jerome sees this text as speaking about the New Jerusalem that will be revealed at the end of the age. Although neither the MT nor the LXX states that the young people mentioned in Zechariah 8:5 were virgins, Jerome asserts that those young people would be filled with the spirit of chastity and virginity in the eschaton.[6] Perhaps Jerome felt that the image of young people cavorting together in the street implied behavior that he felt was inappropriate to the image of universal peace or perhaps he felt that the end time could not be characterized by lowering moral standards, particularly in matters of sexuality. Either way, this fourth-century Christian theologian insisted that Zechariah 8:5 had to be speaking about virgins striving to maintain their virginal status.

The horizon of these two eschatological visions inspired by verses 4-5 could not be more different. The rabbinic text sees the restoration taking place in this time while the patristic text envisions the restoration in the age to come. A feminist reading does not see the present age as beyond redemption. The message of Zechariah in chapter 8 provides the assurance that the struggle for inclusion and equity is not in vain. It is confident that justice will be the consequence of the efforts of people of good will to end marginalization and exclusion of people because of their gender, race, and social status. Like Akiva, they can see struggles of the present as harbingers of eventual triumph.

Zechariah's description of Jerusalem's vibrant, gender-inclusive, multi-generational community is framed by 8:1-3 and 7-8, which employ several words and phrases associated with covenant renewal. In 8:3 God promises to return (שבתי) to Zion and to "dwell [שכנתי] in Jerusalem," while in 8:8 God says, "I will bring them [i.e., the scattered Jews from east and west] to live [שכנו] in Jerusalem." Although it is not evident in the English translation, both phrases use the same verb, שכן (live, dwell). In verse 3, God will return to Zion and *dwell* in Jerusalem, and in 8:8,

5. Sifre Deut. 43:3; b. Mak. 24a–b; Lam. Rab. 5:18.
6. Jerome, *Jov.* 1.30, in Philip Schaff, ed., *Nicene and Post-Nicene Fathers*, 2nd ser., vol. 6 (Edinburgh: T&T Clark, 2009), 369.

the scattered Jews will be brought back by God to Jerusalem and will *dwell* there. God and God's people will both reside in Jerusalem. In the Hebrew Bible, the root שכן appears principally as a verb and refers to God's dwelling among the Israelites, providing them with protection because of their covenantal relationship.[7] Repetition of שכן in 8:3 and 8:8 expresses a sense of belonging, of being at home.

TRANSLATION MATTERS

The NRSVue's translation of Zechariah 8:6 includes a rhetorical question that suggests that the restoration of Jerusalem will astonish the people but will not astonish God:

> Thus says the LORD of hosts: Even though it seems impossible to the remnant of this people in these days, should it also seem impossible to me, says the LORD of hosts?

There is no interrogative marker in the Hebrew text, making it possible to read this verse as a simple declarative statement. Hayyim Angel, for instance, maintains that the verse should be rendered as something akin to "Just as it will seem impossible to you, the remnant of the people whom I exiled, so will it seem impossible even to me."[8] Instead of focusing on the difference between the reaction of the people and of God to Jerusalem's restoration, Angel's reading draws attention to the remarkable transformation that Jerusalem will experience: even God will be surprised that the reversal of Jerusalem's fortunes has occurred in such a swift and stunning manner. This translation presents God as an intimate participant in a covenantal relationship with the men and women of Yehud.

A related term, שכינה (*Shekinah*), first appears in rabbinic literature to refer to the divine presence. Jewish feminist scholar Judith Plaskow notes that שכינה, a grammatically feminine word, conveys the idea of divine nearness, the notion that God can be manifest in a tangible way and in a way that invites humankind to encounter the divine. Plaskow argues that this way of representing the divine naturally associates itself with feminine— and, more specifically, with maternal—characteristics of closeness and

---

7. Examples of texts that use the word שכן in relation to covenant renewal include Exod 25:8; 29:45; 1 Kgs 6:13; Ezek 43:9; Jer 7:7; and Zech 2:10-11.

8. Hayyim Angel, *Zechariah, and Malachi* (Jerusalem: Malbim al Nakh, 1992), 80.

protection.[9] The *Shekinah* suggests an image of God acting as a mother to provide safety, comfort, and assurance to the people of Yehud.[10]

TRANSLATION MATTERS

Isaiah 1:21 refers to Jerusalem as קריה נאמנה, which could be translated as "trusted town." Zechariah 8:3 says it will be called עיר־האמת ("the city of truth"). NRSVue renders both Hebrew phrases as "faithful city." The two Hebrew words translated as "faithful" differ slightly in nuance. The niphal participle נאמנה suggests reliability or dependability, such as one would attribute to a trusted friend. Isaiah's choice of this term amplifies the accusation in 1:21 that Jerusalem had broken God's trust by becoming a prostitute. In Zechariah 8, the NRSVue juxtaposes the reference to Jerusalem as a "faithful city" (v. 3) with a description of YHWH as a God of "great zeal" and "great wrath" (v. 2). The Hebrew word translated as "zeal" (קנאה) simply connotes passion and could easily be translated as "zealous." חמה (NRSVue's "wrath") refers to heat or rage, though Zechariah offers no explanation or further discussion of why YHWH would be angry. The NRSVue's rendering of verses 2-3 suggests a similar dynamic in Zechariah 8 to the one in Isaiah 1, where Jerusalem as the "faithful city"-turned-prostitute is condemned by God. Zechariah 8, however, is not a judgment oracle and the message it conveys about Jerusalem is more positive than that in the preexilic text. The use of אמת ("truth") to describe the "faithful city," then, is appropriate in the context of this chapter, which focuses on the prophet's view of restored Jerusalem where women as well as men participate in a life that reflects covenantal ideals of truth (אמת in vv. 3, 8, 16, 19), righteousness (צדקה, v. 8), and peace (שלום, vv. 12, 16, 19).

This maternal view of God stands in sharp contrast to the martial language used in reference to God in verses 1-3 and 7-8. The divine epithet יהוה צבאות occurs seven times in this passage, including four times in these framing verses. Repetition of this title, reinforced by the reference to God's mountain (v. 3), underscores God's power (conceived in martial

9. Judith Plaskow, *Standing Again at Sinai: Judaism from a Feminist Perspective* (San Francisco: HarperCollins, 1991), 165–66.

10. On the image of God as mother in the Bible, see Leila Leah Bronner, "The Motherly Role of God," in *Stories of Biblical Mothers: Maternal Power in the Hebrew Bible* (Lanham, MD: University Press of America, 2004), 106–17; Peter Schäfer, *Mirror of His Beauty: Feminine Images of God from the Bible to the Early Kabbalah*, Jews, Christians, and Muslims from the Ancient to the Modern World (Princeton: Princeton University Press, 2002).

terms) to demand obedience and loyalty from Israel and to impose terrible consequences on those who are disobedient and unfaithful. Still, the dominant imagery in chapter 8 is covenantal, as is evident from the appearance of the word אמת (literally, "truth"). Verse 3 speaks of a time when Jerusalem will be called עיר־האמת (NRSVue's "the faithful city"; literally "the city of truth"), and verse 8 states that God will dwell in Jerusalem with אמת ("truth"; NRSVue's "faithfulness") and צדקה ("righteousness"), another covenant-related term.[11] The covenant formula, "They shall be my people and I will be their God," closes the passage with a declaration of a covenantal bond sealed by patriarchal power and possession.

Zechariah 8:1-3 bears some similarities to Isaiah 1:21-26. Both passages assert that Jerusalem will be renamed as a "faithful city" once יהוה צבאות has restored righteousness (צדק / צדקה) in the city. Both prophets complain that the people of Jerusalem had abandoned any concern for social justice, a theme that Zechariah addresses more fully in 8:14-17 (see discussion below).[12] Still, there are several differences between Isaiah 1:21-26 and Zechariah 8:1-3 that account for a less challenging message, from a feminist perspective, in the latter. First, Isaiah's image of Jerusalem as a "faithful city" (קריה נאמנה) is juxtaposed with an accusation that "she" "has become a prostitute [זונה]!" (Isa 1:21).[13] In addition, the martial overtones of the divine epithet יהוה צבאות are complemented in Isaiah 1:24 by two additional patriarchal titles for God: האדון ("Sovereign") and אביר ישראל ("Mighty One of Israel"). Isaiah's negative female metaphor for Jerusalem draws a sharp contrast to the positive male titles for God in this preexilic judgment oracle, suggesting that Jerusalem, behaving like a prostitute, had strayed from "her" Warrior-God but is expected to return and remain faithful once again. In contrast, the rhetoric in Zechariah 8:1-3 is much

---

11. The term אמת ("truth") also appears twice in Zech 8:16; see discussion below.

12. Andrew E. Hill develops this claim by arguing that Isaiah and Zechariah 8 both suggest that the exile occurred because the people of Judah had violated God's call for social justice. See his *Haggai, Zechariah, Malachi: An Introduction and Commentary*, TOTC 28 (Downers Grove, IL: IVP Academic, 2012), 200.

13. Several prophets, e.g., Amos 4:1-3, cited the failure to care for vulnerable members of society as the reason for God's destruction of the Israelite kingdoms as punishment for their sins. Several biblical prophets, however, including Hos 1–2; Ezek 16; and Isa 1:21, use the prostitute metaphor to condemn Israel/Judah for idolatry; see also 2 Kgs 17:16-18. (2 Kgs 21:1-15 blames the fall of Judah on the sins of Manasseh.) Still, it is important to note that there is no formal distinction in the Hebrew Bible between violations against God and violations against humanity. Idolatry and social injustice both threaten the covenantal bond between Israel and God.

less polemical than in Isaiah 1, perhaps reflecting a postexilic perspective that acknowledges that punishment of Judah's sins has already occurred and that restoration now is on the horizon. The section ends with two prophecies: verse 2 is a veiled threat against the nations, and the second (v. 3) promises that God will return to Jerusalem. The third prophecy describes one consequence of the divine presence in the city: the joy of its inhabitants (vv. 4-5) as it depicts life in Jerusalem after the restoration, in which people—young and old, male and female—fully participate. That prophecy is framed by covenantal language in verses 1-3 (the first and second prophecies) and verse 8 that joins YHWH and Zion in a relationship of faithfulness and righteousness. The fifth prophecy (vv. 7-8) describes the ingathering of the exiles from east and west to Jerusalem. The thrust of chapter 8 is decidedly positive. God's residing in Jerusalem signifies a change in the relationship between the Jews and God. Using the traditional covenant formulary (see Exod 6:7), Zechariah 8:8 affirms that once again YHWH and the Jews will belong to one another in a relationship characterized by righteousness and truth. Similarly, this affirmation serves to cement the special place of Jerusalem as a faithful city in Jewish thought. The fourth prophecy (v. 6) asserts that what seemed impossible (the restoration of Judah and Jerusalem) is happening.

A Future of Peace (8:9-19)

The sixth prophecy (vv. 9-13), the longest of all, encourages the people of Yehud by assuring them that their economic situation will improve following the renewal of the covenant and the rebuilding of the temple. The oracles that follow in verses 13-19 offer guidelines for how to prevent repeating disasters that befell Judah and Jerusalem "in the former days" (v. 11). These guidelines focus on God's instruction regarding life in the Jewish community. They draw the reader back to Zechariah 7 by emphasizing that the people are to speak the truth to each other, to render just judgments that bring peaceful resolutions to disputes, and, finally, to continue observing certain fast days. The repeated references to God as יהוה צבאות (vv. 9, 11, 14, 18) give a sense of the power that God exercised when punishing the sins of previous generations (see also 7:11-14). Verse 14 reinforces that sense by speaking of God's anger at the failure of earlier generations to heed the prophets who had called them to observe the Torah.

Echoing guidance offered in Zechariah 7:9-10, 8:16-17 specifies what actions the people are to take in restoring their relationship with God.

⁹"Thus says the LORD of hosts: Let your hands be strong—you who have recently been hearing these words from the mouths of the prophets who were present when the foundation was laid for the rebuilding of the temple, the house of the LORD of hosts. ¹⁰For before those days there were no wages for people or for animals, nor was there any safety from the foe for those who went out or came in, and I set them all against one another. ¹¹But now I will not deal with the remnant of this people as in the former days, says the LORD of hosts. ¹²For there shall be a sowing of peace; the vine shall yield its fruit, the ground shall give its produce, and the skies shall give their dew, and I will cause the remnant of this people to possess all these things. ¹³Just as you have been a cursing among the nations, O house of Judah and house of Israel, so I will save you, and you shall be a blessing. Do not be afraid, but let your hands be strong."

¹⁴"For thus says the LORD of hosts: Just as I purposed to bring disaster

Zech 7:9-10	Zech 8:16-17
Render true judgments, show kindness and mercy to one another; do not oppress the widow, the orphan, the alien, or the poor; and *do not devise evil in your hearts against one another.*	Speak the truth to one another, *render in your gates judgments that are true and make for peace, do not devise evil in your hearts against one another,* and love no false oath.

Both texts instruct the people of Yehud to render "true judgments" and not to plot against one another. Subtle differences suggest, however, that the two texts were composed with different audiences in mind. On the one hand, Zechariah 7:9-10 is a more explicit, impassioned plea for all Jews to protect and care for the *personae miserabiles:* "the widow, the orphan, the alien, or the poor." This Deuteronomic language casts a retrospective view on how the behavior of previous generations had ignored God's instruction to protect vulnerable members of the community.[14] Zechariah 8, on the other hand, seems to be directed more toward the community's leaders, whose responsibility it is to "render in your gates judgments that are true and make for peace" (v. 16). These verses are more forward-looking, guiding the (presumably male) leaders in

---

14. Zech 7:9-10 bears striking parallels to Deut 10:18. Cf. Deut 14:29; 16:11, 14; 24:17-21; and 26:12-13. Note that most of these verses refer to setting aside food from one's agricultural produce for those without the necessary resources of their own.

Zech 8:9-19 (cont.)

upon you when your ancestors pro-
voked me to wrath, and I did not re-
lent, says the LORD of hosts, ¹⁵so again
I have purposed in these days to do
good to Jerusalem and to the house of
Judah; do not be afraid. ¹⁶These are the
things that you shall do: speak the truth
to one another, render in your gates
judgments that are true and make for
peace, ¹⁷do not devise evil in your hearts
against one another, and love no false
oath, for all these are things that I hate,
says the LORD."

¹⁸The word of the LORD of hosts
came to me, saying: ¹⁹"Thus says the
LORD of hosts: The fast of the fourth
month, and the fast of the fifth, and
the fast of the seventh, and the fast of
the tenth shall be seasons of joy and
gladness and cheerful festivals for the
house of Judah; therefore love truth
and peace."

how to establish a stable society that espouses common values that will
unite and protect all those living in Yehud. Repeating the instruction in
7:10 not to "devise evil in your hearts against one another," 8:14-17 (the
seventh prophecy) affirms that just and honest social relationships are
the condition for the realization of the good that God promises in the
other prophecies. These verses bring the reader full circle to the beginning of the chapter, which envisions Jerusalem renamed as "the faithful
city," where old women and men, and young girls and boys dwell in
faithfulness and righteousness with their God.

Zechariah follows the idyllic scene in 8:5-8 with a call for just governance in 8:9-19. This suggests that most of the people of Yehud lived in
difficult economic circumstances. Although some may have enjoyed a
measure of prosperity, most of the region's population probably worked
on small farms and bore the weight of heavy taxes. Zechariah resists the
temptation, however, to describe Judah's restoration in economic terms.
For example, unlike the prophets of the Isaianic tradition, Zechariah
does not envision the wealth of the nations coming into Jerusalem's
coffers (e.g., Isa 61:5-6). Rather, for Zechariah, Jerusalem's wealth is its
people—men and women and children. In 8:5-8, the prophet paints a
picture of Jerusalem's streets alive with people of all ages. In the mean-
time, the people's standing before God is a result of their commitment
(or failure) to live according to God's instruction. Those principally
responsible for maintaining a just and equitable social and economic
order are charged with upholding ideals of justice that would "make
for peace" in Yehud.

TRANSLATION MATTERS

Explicit references to both genders in Zechariah 8:5-8 give way in 8:16-17 to gender-specific language that is obscured in the NRSVue translation. Verses 16-17 speak of desired behaviors between איש את רעהו (literally, "a man with his neighbor"). The NRSVue sanitizes this gender-specific Hebrew phrase, rendering it as "to one another." Considering that we know of no women in Zechariah's time, for example, who undertook a formal position of local judge, it is reasonable to assume that 8:16-17 would apply only to men—in particular, male leaders in Yehud charged with maintaining a just and peaceful social order. Ingrid Lilly sees Zechariah's reference to men as peacebuilding in 8:16 as misogynist because nouns and pronouns that are grammatically masculine are used exclusively in this verse.[15] The NRSVue suggests a level of gender inclusion that the Hebrew idiom does not support. The text reflects its ancient Near Eastern cultural setting in which the public sphere was the domain of men while the domestic sphere was the domain of women. Today the gender differentiation between these two spheres is much more fluid. The enduring value of these texts, of course, is their concern for a just society.

Zechariah 8:16 is likely the source of one of the most foundational rabbinic statements found in the Mishnah.

Zech 8:16	m. Avot 1:18
These are the things that you shall do: Speak the *truth* [*dabru emet*] to one another, render in your gates judgments that are true and make for *peace*	Rabban Simeon b. Gamaliel says, "On three things the world stands: On justice, *truth*, and *peace*."

These texts attest to the centrality of ethical behavior in Jewish tradition and have inspired modern Jewish leaders as well. For example, in September 2000, over two hundred Jewish leaders signed a document that affirmed the importance of Jewish-Christian dialogue. The document was called *Dabru Emet* ("Speak Truth"), a title taken from Zechariah 8:6. It was the work of four professors of Jewish studies—Tikva Frymer-Kensky, David Novak, Peter Ochs, and Michael A. Signer—who published it in

15. Ingrid E. Lilly, "Zechariah's Gendered Visions: A Feminist Biblical Theology of Reconciliation," in *After Exegesis: Feminist Biblical Theology; Essays in Honor of Carol A. Newsom*, ed. Patricia K. Tull and Jacqueline E. Lapsley (Waco, TX: Baylor University Press, 2015), 201–16.

the *New York Times*. The document asserts that Jews and Christians serve the same God and share common Scriptures and values. Given these commonalities, the statement calls for collaboration between Jews and Christians toward social justice and world peace.

While *Dabru Emet* reflects a significant step forward in Jewish-Christian dialogue, some Jewish scholars considered it problematic. Some think the statement denies the historical roots of anti-Semitism, particularly Nazism, in Christian theology, thus inappropriately exonerating Christians who espouse anti-Jewish sentiments in formal settings such as churches and schools.[16] Others maintain that *Dabru Emet* implies a "theological reciprocity" that downplays essential differences between Jews and Christians. According to David Berger, for all its exquisitely skillful formulation, *Dabru Emet* suggests that Jews should reassess their negative views of Christianity considering Christian reassessments of Judaism.[17] Some Jews see the notion of theological reciprocity as fraught with danger: although Christians indeed "worship the God of Abraham, Isaac, and Jacob, creator of heaven and earth," they also worship Jesus of Nazareth as a manifestation or component of that God—a practice that constitutes what Jewish law and theology call עבודה זרה ("strange worship" or idolatry), at least when applied to a Jewish context. Many Jews have died to underscore this distinction, which is obscured in *Dabru Emet*, by a bland and inadequate assertion that "Christian worship is not a viable choice for Jews." Finally, some argue that *Dabru Emet* downplays the view that neither faith community "has interpreted Scripture more accurately than the other." While intended for the laudable purpose of discouraging missionizing (especially by Christians of Jews), this assertion conveys an uncomfortably relativistic message.

Despite these reservations, *Dabru Emet* continues to have a significant impact as Christian and Jewish clergy and scholars work to build bridges between their respective communities. It is important to note the statement's authors looked to Zechariah for its title. The writers of

16. Jon D. Levenson, "How Not to Conduct Jewish-Christian Dialogue," *Commentary* 112 (2001), https://www.commentarymagazine.com/articles/how-not-to-conduct-jewish-christian-dialogue/; cf. Jon D. Levenson and critics, "Jewish-Christian Dialogue," *Commentary* 113 (2002), https://www.commentarymagazine.com/articles/jewish-christian-dialogue/.

17. For the text of David Berger's statement, see "Statement by Dr. David Berger Regarding the New York Times Ad by Dabru Emet, Orthodox Union Advocacy Center, September 14, 2000, https://advocacy.ou.org/statement_by_dr_david_berger_regarding_the_new_york_times_ad_by_dabru_emet/.

Dabru Emet did not simply use a phrase from Zechariah because it had a nice ring but because it appears in a biblical context that emphasizes the importance of peacebuilding and reconciliation. While many prophets implored the people of Israel to pursue truth, the phrase *"dabru emet"* as articulated in Zechariah 8 is significant because of its context: verse 16 proclaims that all people should speak truth and seek justice as a strategy for making peace.

Jewish-Christian Relations

First published on September 10, 2000, as a full-page ad in the *New York Times* and *Baltimore Sun*, *"Dabru Emet*: A Jewish Statement on Christians and Christianity" is a milestone in Jewish-Christian relations. Never before has a group of Jews attempted to address the Christian world in this manner. *Dabru Emet* was endorsed by some two hundred rabbis and scholars representing a broad spectrum of the Jewish community, including Reform, Conservative, Reconstructionist, and Orthodox perspectives. It generated international media attention and was subsequently translated into at least nine languages.

Dabru Emet begins with a two-paragraph preamble. It acknowledges the changes in Christian theology since the Shoah as seen in *Nostra Aetate* (Vatican II's Declaration on the Relation of the Church to Non-Christian Religions), in various Protestant statements, and in the work of individual theologians (such as Paul van Buren, Alice and Roy Eckhardt, Fr. John Pawlikowski, and Sr. Mary Boys) whose writings "put them at odds with many of their colleagues and with the consensus of many people who were within their Church."[18] It proposes that, in light of these changes, Jews might begin to reassess their relationship to a Christianity that was no longer hostile.

Dabru Emet then makes eight points, each followed by a brief but essential explanatory paragraph:

- Jews and Christians worship the same God.

- Jews and Christians seek authority from the same book—the Bible (what Jews call Tanakh and Christians call the Old Testament).

- Christians can respect the claim of the Jewish people upon the land of Israel.

18. Michael A. Signer, "Some Reflections on Dabru Emet," (July 26, 2001), Jewish-Christian Relations, https://www.jcrelations.net/articles/article/some-reflections-on-dabru-emet.html.

- Jews and Christians accept the moral principles of Torah.
- Nazism was not a Christian phenomenon.
- The humanly irreconcilable difference between Jews and Christians will not be settled until God redeems the entire world as promised in Scripture.
- A new relationship between Jews and Christians will not weaken Jewish practice.
- Jews and Christians must work together for justice and peace.

Dabru Emet was part of larger project that included the publication of two books, a scholarly volume, *Christianity in Jewish Terms* (Tikva S. Frymer-Kensky, David Novak,

Peter Ochs, Michael Signer, David Fox Sandmel [Boulder, CO: Westview Press, 2000]), and a more popular volume targeted at congregational study, *Irreconcilable Differences? A Learning Resource for Jews and Christians* (David F. Sandmel, Rosann M. Catalano, and Christopher M. Leighton, eds. [Boulder, CO: Westview Press, 2001]).

Some have compared *Dabru Emet* to *Nostra Aetate*. *Nostra Aetate* carries the authority of a conciliar document of the Catholic Church, while *Dabru Emet* represents the opinions of only its authors and signers. Nonetheless, just as *Nostra Aetate* has come to represent the new era of Christian rapprochement with Judaism, *Dabru Emet* has achieved a similar stature.

David F. Sandmel

Finally, there is an interesting connection between Zechariah 8:18-19 and the book of Esther. In the face of the plans of the villain Haman, who sought to have the Jews of Susa massacred, Queen Esther (whose identity as a Jew is hidden) calls for a three-day fast (Esth 4:16). In the end, her uncle Mordechai was able to foil Haman's plot, thus ending the threat to the Jews. The book of Esther ends with a celebration of the feast of Purim to commemorate the deliverance of the Jews (Esth 9:19-32). Esther commands that the holiday of Purim be observed each year to celebrate that what could have been a disaster instead became an occasion for "gladness and feasting" (Esth 9:19).

Both Zechariah 8:18-19 and Esther 9 recount how fast days were established long ago to commemorate tragedies that had befallen the Jews that became occasions for celebration, which is the message of the eighth prophecy (v. 19). There is, however, a remarkable distinction between implied gender roles and women's agency in the two texts. In Zechariah, the prophet speaks as יהוה צבאות commands him, thus reinforcing a view of the authority bestowed by God on a designated male leader. In Esther, the Jewish queen herself calls for the fast (Esth 4) and establishes the feast of Purim (Esth 9). This story suggests that women in postexilic Yehud not only participated in public rituals of mourning and celebration but also could be credited with establishing them. Noting this distinction between Zechariah 8 and Esther 4 and 9 raises curiosity about the role of Jewish women in public rituals in Zechariah's time and in generations since. In growing Jewish congregations, women serve as rabbis and cantors. Women have also taken some roles of liturgical and pastoral leadership in Christian churches, though complete equality of men and women in these areas remains something that has yet to be achieved.

Grasping the Garment (8:20-23)

The closing verses of Zechariah 8 contain some of the earliest kernels of universalist thought in Jewish literature. The ninth and tenth prophecies (vv. 20-22, 23) assert that the redemption of Israel will lead to the gentiles going to Jerusalem to worship יהוה צבאות. Though there is no indication that they will become members of the Jewish community,[19] phrases such as "seek YHWH" and "entreat the favor of YHWH" (vv. 21-22) suggest that these people are engaged in a process of establishing an intense and ongoing encounter with the God of Israel and not simply a cursory or one-time worship experience. Passages like this one are rare in biblical prophetic literature. Many prophetic texts envision a time when the nations will acknowledge the God of Israel, but only a few passages predict that all nations will actively serve Israel's God in the end time.[20]

Zechariah 8:20-23 bears important similarities with Isaiah 2:2-4. Both passages speak of a time when gentiles will look to Jews for guidance as they seek to worship the God of Israel in Jerusalem:

19. Some scholars have presumed that this verse predicts the conversion of gentiles to Judaism. See, for example, Jacob Neusner, *Zephaniah, Haggai, Zechariah and Malachi in Talmud and Midrash: A Source Book*, Studies in Judaism (Lanham, MD: University Press of America, 2007), 85.

20. Isa 2:2-4//Mic 4:1-5; Isa 11:6-13; 27:6-13; 60:1-22; Zeph 3:9-19; Ezek 29:9; 34:30-31; 36:33-37; 37:26-27; 39:21-22; and 44:6-9.

Zech 8:20-23

²⁰"Thus says the Lᴏʀᴅ of hosts: Peoples shall yet come, the inhabitants of many cities; ²¹the inhabitants of one city shall go to another, saying, 'Come, let us go to entreat the favor of the Lᴏʀᴅ and to seek the Lᴏʀᴅ of hosts; I myself am going.' ²²Many peoples and strong nations shall come to seek the Lᴏʀᴅ of hosts in Jerusalem and to entreat the favor of the Lᴏʀᴅ. ²³Thus says the Lᴏʀᴅ of hosts: In those days ten men from nations of every language shall take hold of a Jew, grasping his garment and saying, 'Let us go with you, for we have heard that God is with you.'"

Zechariah 8:22	Isaiah 2:3
Many peoples and strong nations shall come to seek the Lᴏʀᴅ of hosts in Jerusalem and to entreat the favor of the Lᴏʀᴅ.	*Many peoples* shall come and say, "Come, let us go up to the mountain of the Lᴏʀᴅ, to the house of the God of Jacob, that he may teach us his ways and that we may walk in his paths." For out of Zion shall go forth instruction, and the word of the Lᴏʀᴅ from Jerusalem.
Zechariah 8:23	**Isaiah 2:4**
Thus says the Lᴏʀᴅ of hosts: In those days ten men from nations of every language shall take hold of a Jew, grasping his garment and saying, "Let us go with you, for we have heard that God is with you."	He shall judge between the nations and shall arbitrate for many peoples; they shall beat their swords into ploughshares and their spears into pruning hooks; nation shall not lift up sword against nation; neither shall they learn war anymore.

Neither passage mentions women explicitly as they speak of participation in the encounters that gentiles will seek with Israel's God.

According to Zechariah 8:23, the gentiles hold on to a garment that Midrashic literature consider to be the distinctive Jewish garment known as *tzitzit* ("fringes"). Jewish men began wearing *tzitzit* at the beginning of the rabbinic period.[21] The Hebrew word used in 8:23 is not בגד, the

---

21. On *tzitzit* in rabbinic literature, see b. Šhabb. 22a, 25b and b. Sukkah 9a–11a. The rabbis exempted women from the obligation to wear *tzitzit* since it is a positive command occasioned by time (t. Qidd. 1:10). Some Jewish women have taken to wearing *tzitzit* as part of their desire for equality in prayer and observance. See Pamela Barmash, "Women and Mitzvot," *Yoreh Deah* 246 (2014): 4–5.

more common word for "garment," but כנף, which refers specifically to the corner edge of a garment where the fringes are found. Since the word כנף is rarely used in the Hebrew Bible to mean "garment," its appearance in 8:23 suggests that Jewish dress was distinctive in the early postexilic period. This distinctiveness made it possible for gentiles to identify Jews. That gentiles (presumably men) were grasping at the כנף where the *tzitzit* were found implies that the Jew mentioned in 8:23 was a male.[22]

Similarly, Isaiah 2:4 envisions a time in which the gentiles' instruments of warfare, usually associated with men, will be transformed into farming tools. In Isaiah 2:4, references to weapons act as a gendered marker in a way like the dress worn exclusively by men in 8:23. The implications of these details are significant for a feminist critique. Gender-specific clothing (Zechariah) and weapons (Isaiah) seem to suggest that these prophets envision a time of universal kinship; however, the images are depicted in the language of universal brotherhood, not sisterhood. Furthermore, although both men and women are affected by this movement toward universal recognition of Israel's God, neither Zechariah nor Isaiah specify that women have any agency in that movement. Today, of course, women have a significant and vital role in the quest for peace based on the belief of a common humanity.[23]

Another significant feature in Zechariah 8:20-23 is the importance of language and communication. For example, the text describes ten gentile men "of every language" asking Jewish men to escort them to Jerusalem. The text implies these men, some of whom are gentiles and some of whom are Jews, are unable to communicate clearly with one another; therefore, accompanying their speech ("let us go with you," v. 23) with a gesture (grasping the Jews' garments) facilitates communication between gentiles and Jews. The statement, "we have heard that God is

---

22. It is also possible that Jewish dress including the *tzitzit* was somewhat like the dress of gentiles in the Persian period. For example, the rabbinic *tzitzit* were likely modeled after a Persian garment call a *kustīg*, which was a cord woven from seventy-two strands of wool. Pious Zoroastrians wore this cord around their waist. Garments worn by Jewish men could have been both an identity marker and a sign of their integration of the dominant Persian culture. See Yishai Kiel, "Redesigning Tzitzit in the Babylonian Talmud in Light of Literary Depictions of the Zoroastrian Kustig," in *Shoshanat Yaakov: Jewish and Iranian Studies in Honor of Yaakov Elman*, ed. Shai Secunda and Steven Fine, BRLA 35 (Leiden: Brill, 2012), 185–202.

23. See Lisa Leitz and David S. Meyer, "Gendered Activism and Outcomes: Women in the Peace Movement," in *The Oxford Handbook of U.S. Women's Social Movement Activism*, ed. H. J. McCannon et al. (New York: Oxford University Press, 2017), 708–28.

with you" (v. 23), likewise indicates that the word of God has transcended language barriers since these men have already heard about the God of Israel, and they seek to experience this God themselves. Indeed, these men are separated both by language and by dress, but worshiping the God of Israel together enables them to transcend cultural differences without erasing them.

Some interpreters regard Zechariah 8:20-23 as an exclusivist text with a missionary dimension, since it speaks of gentiles seeking to worship God as Jews do.[24] Scholars who read the text this way maintain that the foreign nations want to shed their ethnic and religious identities and enter fully into the Jewish community. There is no indication, however, that the nations as envisioned by Zechariah seek to assimilate into the Jewish community: they do not wish to *be* Jews; they only want to worship God *alongside* Jews.[25] The concept of Jews engaging in missionary activity to persuade foreign nations to assimilate into their community is foreign to the Hebrew Bible in general and to this passage in particular.

Other scholars have emphasized universalist elements in this text. When universalist elements in a biblical passage are present, it is important to avoid the assumption that these elements lie in direct opposition to a particularistic view. Contrary to what some scholars and readers assume, universalism and particularism are not necessarily in conflict with one another.[26] In biblical prophetic literature, the ideas that Israel is the elect nation of God and that all people may acknowledge and worship this God in an engaged manner are often complementary. This is especially the case in Isaiah 40–55, which emphasizes both the covenantal relationship between God and the Israelites and the concern that God has for all people.[27]

24. Hill, *Haggai, Zechariah, Malachi*, 200.

25. Julia M. O'Brien, *Micah*, WCS 37 (Collegeville, MN: Liturgical Press, 2015), 69. O' Brien cites Rabbi Aaron Lichtenstein as interpreting this passage as a reference to the Seven Noahide Laws. Aaron Lichtenstein, *The Seven Laws of Noah* (New York: Rabbi Jacob Joseph School Press, 1981).

26. See Malka Z. Simkovich, *The Making of Jewish Universalism: From Exile to Alexandria* (Lanham, MD: Lexington Books, 2016); Joel Kaminsky and Anne Stewart, "God of All the World: Universalism and Developing Monotheism in Isaiah 40–66," *HTR* 99 (2006): 139–63.

27. See Isa 42:5-17; 43:1-10; 44:3-5; 45:1-14; and 49:1-23.

Conclusion

This chapter includes ten prophecies about the restoration and its consequences. These prophetic statements speak of the return of God to Jerusalem and the renewal of the covenant with Israel. They assert that the return of the exiles and the rebuilding of the temple will have positive political and economic effects that will benefit the Jews of Yehud. Still, all this will take place only if the Jewish community establishes and maintains a just and equitable social order. On the surface, Zechariah 8 seems to envision a time of gender equality, universalist inclusion, and well-being (שלום) for all peoples once Jerusalem's restoration is complete. Also, a closer look at the prophet's utopian view of the community's future suggests that it is tinted by an androcentric lens. For example, in the street scene (8:4-5), "old women" are joined to "old men" and "girls" to "boys" in a parallel structure that keeps the genders in lockstep: male and female elders sit while male and female children play. There is no valuing of diverse expressions of gender nor any hint of agency for either gender; there is no sense of meaningful, real-life activity in which women and girls might participate quite independent of men and boys who, not surprisingly, return exclusively to center stage, dominating the rest of the chapter, once this brief glimpse of idyllic life has faded.

Another feminist consideration is that Zechariah remains attached to a social structure that wrongly assumes that male leadership will necessarily ensure justice and well-being for all members of the community. The prophet envisions a society that depends on a stable, traditional family unit, including a mother, father, sons, and daughters; anyone who does not fit into this structure may be on the margins but is not to be ignored. The prophet insists in 7:9-10 that the orphan, widow, and resident alien must be cared for and given financial provisions to ensure that they live and retain some dignity. In 8:16-17, however, the focus shifts in nuance, from ensuring the well-being of the community's most vulnerable members to safeguarding fairness and integrity among Yehud's male citizens. Concern for the widow and orphan in 7:10 gives way to cautions about comportment at "your gates" (the designated site of judicial proceedings) in 8:16. Furthermore, Zechariah does not go a step further to envision a time when non-Jews might live in peace alongside Jews and people of other nations. The message of hope is limited to those living in Yehud or its immediate vicinity. The prophet's vision focuses on the destiny of the Jewish people, stopping short of a universal scope.

This androcentric perspective is apparent in later portions of the chapter as well. While Zechariah 8 ends with universalist elements that envision men from all nations and religious communities seeking to worship the God of Israel (without implying that these gentile men assimilate into the Israelite religion), the chapter presents idealized notions of religious life in Persian-period Yehud that are based exclusively on men's experience. Gentile men seek out Jews (identified by clothing worn only by men) to help steer them toward Jerusalem to worship the God of Israel.[28] The interest among the nations in serving this God through patterns of religious worship is reserved exclusively for Jewish men; the author does not make space for expressions of religious life experienced by Jewish women. Their participation in Jewish worship (i.e., the experiences of half the population) is overlooked.

Zechariah 8 closes the middle section of the book of Zechariah, a section that moves the readers from experiencing Zechariah's prophecies as outsiders privy to private and obscure visions to insiders who will experience the end time themselves. Readers must be "insiders" in the second half of Zechariah, especially in its closing chapter, for, as we will see, the restoration will affect all the nations, all humankind, and all God's living creatures. Chapter 8 brings us closer to this moment by imagining a time when God will dwell among boys and girls, old men and old women (8:3-5). The world will be ruled with trust and righteousness. While nations will seek to worship Israel's God, Jews will still maintain distinctive status as God's covenanted people. Themes of universal truth and justice, introduced in these earlier chapters, will be further developed in the rest of the book.

28. See the prohibition in Deuteronomy 22:5 from women wearing men's clothing and men wearing women's clothing. This verse presumes that Israelite men and women dress differently.

Zechariah 9–14

Introduction

C hapter 9 marks a turning point in the book of Zechariah. From this point forward, the prophet makes no appearance in the book that bears his name. New terminology and vocabulary are introduced that do not appear in Zechariah 1–8. Instead of recounting visions that an interpreting angel explains to the prophet, the text speaks directly to readers as it identifies the internal and external forces that have impeded the Judean restoration. Chapter 9 begins with an introductory formula that recurs in 12:1 and in Malachi 1:1: משא דבר־יהוה ("An oracle—the word of YHWH . . ."). The repetition of this phase at these three places suggests that Zechariah 9–14 is a discrete literary unit within the book of Zechariah. The introductory formula of 9:1 and 12:1 differs markedly from the introductory formulas that appear in the earlier part of the book (1:1, 7; 7:1). The latter provide precise dates when the "word of YHWH" came to Zechariah. Chapters 9–14 contain no specific dates.

Some interpreters sought to identify the literary forms in these chapters. There are no reports of visions or dreams in chapters 9–14, but genres found elsewhere in prophetic literature such as the oracle of judgment against Judah's enemies and the proclamation of deliverance for Judah and Israel do appear. More recently, interpreters have attended to the overall literary shape of these chapters. For example, Paul Lamarche has asserted that they display a chiastic structure though Carol Meyers and Eric Meyers have rejected this suggestion as flawed and unpersuasive because Lamarche is able to identify a chiasm only through overmanipulation of the text.[1] Paul Hanson regards chapters 9–14 as the result of combining the divine warrior of Canaanite mythology with Israelite conquest traditions. This combination then became the core of later apocalyptic thought.[2] The recurrence of these martial motifs likely had little resonance with the experience of most Jews in Yehud because of Yehud's military and political impotence. By projecting God's victory and the restoration of the kingdom into an indefinite eschaton, apocalyptic found a way to appropriate the divine warrior motif, though it is unlikely that Yehud's war-weary women who had to bear the brunt of war's effects on the social and economic fabric of Yehud found comfort in this message. Too much had happened from the eighth century BCE onward. Another claim that YHWH will defeat all Judah's enemies and restore the kingdom to Judah would likely have fallen on deaf ears.

There were some in Yehud in the middle of the fifth century BCE who managed to find some solace in the old mythological imagery that the book of Zechariah employs. Certainly the image of God as a mother who cares for and comforts her children (Isa 49:14-15; 66:13) offers more possibilities in speaking to the Jews of Persian-period Yehud than the well-worn divine warrior metaphor. Still, Zechariah is content with re-using this ancient metaphor in speaking about God's actions on behalf of God's people. This is one consequence of the political and economic situation in which the people of Yehud found themselves. The people of Yehud were surrounded by more powerful enemies who sought to control the southern Levant and its resources. Speaking of God defeating Yehud's enemies is understandable.

The recurrence of imagery such as the divine warrior motif throughout the book of Zechariah has led some interpreters to argue for the unity of the book. Mark Boda is one such scholar.[3] Byron Curtis recognizes the change in tone and content that begins in chapter 9, but he asserts that such changes do not necessarily reflect different authorship and a

---

1. Paul Lamarche, *Zacharie IX–XIV: Structure Littéraire et Messianisme* (Paris: Libraire Lecoffre, J. Gabalda et Compagnie, 1961), 112–13; Carol L. Meyers and Eric M. Meyers, *Zechariah 9–14: A New Translation with Introduction and Commentary*, AB 25C (New York: Doubleday, 1993), 33.

2. Paul D. Hanson, *The Dawn of Apocalyptic: The Historical and Sociological Roots of Jewish Apocalyptic Eschatology*, rev. ed. (Philadelphia: Fortress, 1979). Though Hanson's hypothesis about the origins of apocalyptic has been called into question, it has identified an important motif in Zech 9–14.

3. Mark J. Boda, *The Book of Zechariah*, NICOT (Grand Rapids: Eerdmans, 2016), 28–29, 521.

different historical context. He maintains that such changes could have occurred in the lifetime of a single prophet.[4] Curtis supports his hypothesis by citing five case studies of twentieth-century societies from Africa that have experienced rapid social changes. He argues that the Jewish community of Yehud experienced changes that shifted its social dynamics in a relatively short time. This explains the difference between the prophet's words at the beginning of his career and those that came later. Though chapters 1–8 were written prior to the completion of the temple's reconstruction and chapters 9–14 come from the years following the completion of the temple project, both were the work of the same prophet.[5] Though the positions of both Boda and Curtis are reasonable, and their arguments are well thought-out, the indications of a fundamental difference between the two parts of the book are too strong to sustain the hypothesis of unity. Indeed, the overwhelming scholarly consensus holds that the canonical book of Zechariah is composed of two separate prophetic works.[6] Scholars usually refer to chapters 9–14 as "Deutero-Zechariah." Characters like the interpreting angel, Zerubbabel, and Joshua—so important in the first part of Zechariah—are missing from its final chapters. Deutero-Zechariah's eschatological orientation is much stronger than that of chapters 1–8. What, then, drew these two apparently independent texts together? Both chapters 1–8 and 9–14 affirm, though in different ways, that judgment was not God's last word to Israel. Both affirm that there is a future for Israel beyond judgment—that the people of Israel will live. Zechariah 1–8 appears to be more hopeful about the present as the setting for the restoration of Israel while Deutero-Zechariah describes that restoration in eschatological terms.

There are some interpreters who speak of a "Trito-Zechariah" that is made up of chapters 12–14. This hypothesis is associated with the work of Otto Plöger, who sees these chapters as containing eschatological perspectives absent from the rest of Zechariah.[7] In addition, the heading of 12:1 serves to set off these chapters. Although Plöger is correct in recognizing the pronounced eschatological rhetoric in these chapters,

4. Byron G. Curtis, *Up the Steep and Stony Road: The Book of Zechariah in Social Location Trajectory Analysis*, AcBib 25 (Atlanta: SBL, 2006), 4–5.
5. Curtis, *Up the Steep and Stony Road*, 277.
6. Meyers and Meyers, *Zechariah 9–14*, 15.
7. See his *Theocracy and Eschatology*, trans. S. Rudman (Richmond: John Knox, 1968). Eng. trans. based on 2nd ed. of *Theokratie und Eschatologie*, WMANT 2 (Neukirchen Kreis Moers: Neukirchener, 1962).

he goes too far in suggesting that there were groups with apocalyptic leanings who were responsible for the three final chapters of Zechariah. There is no doubt that there were different religious groupings in Yehud. Still, additional fragmentation of the book of Zechariah is unnecessary, and this commentary will treat chapters 12–14 as components of Deutero-Zechariah.

Steven J. Schweitzer has suggested another way of seeing a connection between Zechariah 1–8 and 9–14. He has applied utopian literary theory to Zechariah. This theory sees utopias not as blueprints for ideal societies but rather as revolutionary texts designed to challenge the status quo and question the way things presently are being done. Thus, utopias depict the world "as it should be," not "why it is the way it is."[8] "In other words, *utopias are not works of legitimation* (providing a grounding for the present reality), *but works of innovation* (suggesting a reality that *could* be, if its parameters were accepted). . . . The methodology of utopian literary theory contends that utopian and dystopian literature function more as a rejection of the present status quo than as a blueprint for the future."[9]

Chapters 9–14 come from circumstances that were different from those reflected in chapters 1–8. The temple has been rebuilt. The community is functioning, though not at an optimal level. The Persians are still in charge, and Yehud's economy is hampered by the demands for the payment of taxes by the Persians. The dream of a restored kingdom of Judah has faded. The leadership of the community is still problematic. Jewish religious traditions are in danger of sinking into irrelevance. In such circumstances, Zechariah 9–14 serves as a reaffirmation of a future for the Jewish people. It is more of a dream than a blueprint, but it serves the needs of a community that is not in control of its political and economic life. It offers a picture of possibilities. That picture may be indistinct, but it is one that is firmly based on the belief in the commitment of YHWH to the people of Yehud.

8. Steven James Schweitzer, "Visions of the Future as Critique of the Present: Utopian and Dystopian Images of the Future in Second Zechariah," in *Utopia and Dystopia in Prophetic Literature*, ed. Ehud Ben Zvi, Finnish Exegetical Society 92 (Göttingen: Vandenhoeck & Ruprecht, 2006), 250–59.

9. Steven James Schweitzer, "Utopia and Utopian Literary Theory: Some Preliminary Observations," in Zvi, *Utopia and Dystopia in Prophetic Literature*, 13–26, emphases original.

Chapters 9–14, which anticipate the purification and glorious restoration of "daughter Zion/Jerusalem," are framed by oracles against gentile nations that will face judgment as an integral element of Yehud's promised salvation (9:1-8; 14:12-15). The martial imagery employed in 9:1-8 probably was inspired by political developments in the Persian Empire at the end of the sixth century BCE. The Persians sought to extend their empire into Europe, which led to a series of wars with the Greeks that continued sporadically for one hundred years until the victory of Alexander the Great over Darius III at the battle of Issus in 333 BCE. Egypt and Babylon sought to take advantage of Persia's preoccupation with the Greeks by attempting to throw off Persian rule. Though Yehud remained fully under Persian control, this political situation probably led some in Yehud to speculate about their future. In Zechariah 9–14, this speculation takes on a distinct eschatological flavor since the prophetic circles responsible for these chapters believed that it was unrealistic to hope that the restoration would be completed during their own lifetimes. Still, the martial imagery used to portray God's actions on Yehud's behalf seems to fit the circumstances in which the Jewish people found themselves at the beginning of the fifth century BCE. The Judean restoration and the redemption of the Jewish people remained objects of hope. The whole of the book of Zechariah affirms that the basis for this hope is God's commitment to daughter Zion.

Zechariah 9:1-17

YHWH and Daughter Zion

The principal concern in Zechariah 9 is the recovery of ancient Israel's homeland and the return of the Judeans from Babylon. God's victories over various nations are the principal mode of expressing that concern. Images of wars that YHWH will wage for the benefit of the Jewish people dominate this chapter. Also central to this chapter is the metaphor "daughter Zion/Jerusalem," first introduced in Zechariah 2:10. Use of this metaphor, coupled with martial imagery, reflects the political and economic standing of Yehud in the Persian period. Like real-life women in every generation whose worlds are overturned and shattered by war, Yehud, a small Persian province, had little opportunity to shape its own destiny. Zechariah 9:16 offers hope by raising an expectation that ביום ההוא ("on that day") God will take decisive action on behalf of the people of Jerusalem, restoring them "like the jewels of a crown." That action will entail the vilification and defeat of enemy nations (a central motif in chapter 9), making it virtually impossible to establish a basis for genuine peace. This chapter exemplifies the belief that peace comes through war, i.e., that peace results from the military defeat of the enemy, though experience has shown that war brings not peace but only more war.

It is best to read Zechariah 9 in a postexilic context, although we cannot be certain when it was written with any precision. Like other oracles against the nations, e.g., Isaiah 13–23, Jeremiah 46–51, and Ezekiel 25–32, this chapter makes mention of divine judgment on the nations to underscore God's imminent universal reign. The author's reliance on Ezekiel 16 (see discussion below), which was written in the exilic period, supports dating Zechariah 9 to the postexilic period. This chapter reflects an awareness of earlier prophetic passages that affirmed God's lasting commitment to the people of Israel and appears to address apparent concerns that the predictions of earlier prophets had not yet been actualized.

Three subunits make up this chapter. Verses 1-8 deal with the restoration of the land of Israel while verses 11-17 are concerned with the restoration of the people of Israel. These two units are joined in verses 9-10 by a description of the person whom God will designate to rule over both Israel and the nations. Because warfare is identified in this text as the primary means of establishing God's rule, a critical reading must consider even more carefully how modern warfare, as well as political oppression, uncontrolled extraction of natural resources, and gross inequities in wealth and well-being, negatively impact women in countries around the world today. Such considerations can help stimulate readers to develop thoughtful approaches to achieving gender equity and social justice in their own contexts.

Against Oppressors (9:1-8)

Zechariah's announcement of the restoration of Judah's land and people begins with an oracle[1] of judgment against some of Yehud's neighbors in the Levant. Cast as a warrior moving from place to place, God marches in a geographic arc,[2] subjugating important Aramean, Phoeni-

---

1. The word מַשָּׂא ("An oracle" in 9:1 and 12:1, NRSVue) is a superscription that introduces several oracles in prophetic literature. (See also Isa 13:1; 15:1; 17:1; 19:1; Hab 1:1; Nah 1:1; Mal 1:1.) It is derived from the root נשׂא whose basic meaning is "carry" or "bear"; hence, it is sometimes translated as "burden." The root also means "lift up," so an "oracle" is "that which is lifted up." The term indicates that what follows is an account of divine speech. This word also appears in Zech 12:1 and Mal 1:1. This has led some interpreters to suggest that it introduces independent oracles that were added to the books of Zechariah and Malachi when the scroll of the Twelve (minor prophets) was put in its final form. For the translation and use of מַשָּׂא in the Hebrew Scriptures, see Mark J. Boda, "Freeing the Burden of Prophecy: Maśśaʾ and the Legitimacy of Prophecy in Zech 9–14," *Bib* 87 (2006): 338–57.

2. David L. Petersen, *Zechariah 9–14 and Malachi: A Commentary*, OTL (Louisville: Westminster John Knox, 1995), 46. There have been attempts to link the itinerary in vv. 1-8 to that of some historical conquest of the Levant, e.g., that of Alexander the Great. See Carol L. Meyers and Eric M. Meyers, *Zechariah 9–14: A New Translation with Introduction and Commentary*, AB 25C (New York: Doubleday, 1993), 260, and Karl Elliger, "Ein Zeugnis aus der jüdischen Gemeinde im Alexanderjahr 332 v. Chr.," *ZAW* 62 (1950): 63–115. These proposals, though interesting, are speculative.

Zech 9:1-8

¹An Oracle.

The word of the LORD is against the land of Hadrach
and will rest upon Damascus.
For to the LORD belongs the capital of Aram,
as do all the tribes of Israel;
²Hamath also, which borders on it,
Tyre and Sidon, though they are very wise.
³Tyre has built itself a rampart
and heaped up silver like dust
and gold like the dirt of the streets.
⁴But now, the Lord will strip it of its possessions
and hurl its wealth into the sea,
and it shall be devoured by fire.
⁵Ashkelon shall see it and be afraid;
Gaza, too, and shall writhe in anguish;
Ekron also, because its hopes are withered.

The king shall perish from Gaza;
Ashkelon shall be uninhabited;
⁶a mongrel people shall settle in Ashdod,
and I will make an end of the pride of Philistia.
⁷I will take away its blood from its mouth
and its abominations from between its teeth;
it, too, shall be a remnant for our God;
it shall be like a clan in Judah,
and Ekron shall be like the Jebusites.
⁸Then I will encamp at my house as a guard,
so that no one shall march to and fro;
no oppressor shall again overrun them,
for now I have seen with my own eyes.

cian, and Philistine cities. The route of that military campaign, beginning in Aram to the northeast, moving west to the Phoenician coastal cities of Tyre and Sidon, then south to the Philistine cities, and northeast to Jerusalem, follows a path that an army invading from the north would have taken to attack the states of the Levant. The irony is that the "enemies list" is anachronistic, because it does not reflect the political reality of the region in the Persian period.[3] By the time the book of Zechariah made its appearance, the former Philistine city-states were just Persian towns under tight imperial control. None of the cities mentioned in verses 1-8 enjoyed freedom of action. Similarly, Yehud posed no military threat to

3. For example, the Philistine city-states that revolted against Nebuchadnezzar in the early sixth century BCE suffered a fate like that of the Judeans. To prevent further disruptions, the Babylonians deported the survivors of the war to Babylon. It was not long before evidence of the Philistine culture had all but disappeared from the Levant.

any of its neighbors; nor was it capable of mounting an effective defense if attacked since the walls of Jerusalem were not yet rebuilt.[4] That Yehud could enlarge its territory at the expense of its neighbors, therefore, was an impossibility. The text did serve a rhetorical function, however, by declaring that, when the nations will see what would happen to those who threatened Jerusalem, they would make no attempt to attack the city (v. 8b). Zechariah 9 thus assures the people of Yehud that their security—especially of those in Jerusalem—was in God's hands (v. 9a).

The oracle begins with a series of statements that address gentile city-states in a domineering and menacing tone. The text declares that God will move against the Arameans (in Hadrach[5] and Damascus, v. 1), the Phoenicians (Hamath, Tyre, and Sidon, v. 2), and the Philistines (Gaza and Ekron, vv. 4-5). In verse 4 this threatening rhetoric escalates to explicit expressions of violence. God will dispossess Tyre and will destroy its fleet, leaving it to "be devoured by fire" (v. 4). Gaza will "writhe in anguish," and its king shall perish (v. 5). God's violent actions will leave Ekron bereft of hope and Ashkelon terror-stricken and uninhabited (v. 5).

Verse 6a suggests that the violence that Ashdod will experience is of a sexual nature. The key word in this verse is ממזר.[6] The only other time this word appears in the Old Testament is in Deuteronomy 23:2, where it refers to a category of people excluded from the assembly of worshipers, though the text does not specify the reason for their exclusion. In the rabbinic period, ממזר referred to the offspring of an incestuous or adulterous union. When read through that lens, Zechariah 9:6 might imply that the people of Ashdod were conceived through rape, an act of terror often perpetrated by invading armies during times of war. Rape is a weapon of war whose horror continues beyond the brutal act itself. The victims and their children are often relegated to a permanent outsider caste (ממזר), though they bear no responsibility for the outrage committed against them.

---

4. Zech 9:1-8 suggests that the people of Yehud regarded their neighbors as enemies to be subdued by force to establish Israel's borders as delineated in Gen 15:18-21 and Exod 23:31. The Israelite kingdoms—even at the height of their power—never controlled the entirety of the region as set out in these texts.

5. Hadrach (v. 1a) was an Aramean city-state located on the Orontes River north of Damascus. It was an important member of a coalition that attempted to block Assyrian expansionism into the Levant during the eighth century BCE. Sargon II defeated the coalition. This is the only time Hadrach appears in the Hebrew Scriptures.

6. The NABRE softens the NRSVue's rendering "mongrel people" with "the illegitimate." Mark J. Boda, *The Book of Zechariah*, NICOT (Grand Rapids: Eerdmans, 2016), 544, has "the one of illegitimate birth."

TRANSLATION MATTERS

NRSVue's rendering of 9:4 is awkward and misses the point of the Hebrew original. First, the term יורשנה is more accurately understood as: "he will dispossess her/it." The NRSVue's "strip it of its possessions" supplies a verb with sexual connotations that are otherwise absent from this verse. Second, NRSVue translates הכה (Hebrew root is נכה) as "hurl" instead of its usual meaning: "smite," "attack," or "destroy," a term often used in the context of military activity.[7] This is true in Zechariah 9:4, though NRSVue's choice of "its wealth" instead of the equally plausible "its armed forces" for the direct object of הכה also obscures the martial allusion in the Hebrew original. Thus, a better alternative to "[God will] hurl its wealth into the sea" (NRSVue) is "[God will] defeat her forces at sea" (JPS), which declares God's decisive victory over Tyre's fleet. While the NRSVue adds sexual innuendo to 9:4 where it does not appear in the Hebrew, some might argue that this translation also obscures implicitly gendered references where they do appear in the Hebrew of 9:1-8. As is common in prophetic literature, Zechariah refers to "cities" (ערים, a feminine noun) as a synecdoche for "nations" (גוים, a masculine noun).[8] Thus, the text rhetorically emasculates the nations by referring to them with grammatically feminine forms and vocabulary.

Julia O'Brien suggests that the grammatically gendered forms in 9:1-8 are rhetorically significant, i.e., that using grammatically feminine terms to refer to the nations, particularly in the context of martial imagery, is intentional. She sees the statement that Gaza "will writhe in anguish" (a phrase that usually describes labor pains) as similar to feminine terms used to describe daughter Zion as vulnerable and dependent on God, who is portrayed as "king," a masculine metaphor of domination (see 9:9).[9] On the other hand, Tikva Frymer-Kensky notes that the biblical writers show little interest in gender stereotypes.[10] Gendered verb forms in texts like 9:1-8 simply reflect the conventions of Hebrew grammar. The NRSVue is consistent with this view, while JPS, which uses feminine pronouns to refer to cities in verses 1-8, aligns more closely with O'Brien's views.

---

7. For example, it appears frequently in Exodus to describe actions of YHWH toward the Egyptian oppressors of the Hebrew slaves and in Joshua and Judges, in accounts of armed conflicts between Israelites and gentile nations.

8. Synecdoche is a figure of speech in which a part stands for the whole or vice versa. In this case, "cities" (a part) stands for "nations" (the whole).

9. Julia M. O'Brien, "Zechariah," in *Women's Bible Commentary*, ed. Carol A. Newsom, Sharon H. Ringe, and Jacqueline E. Lapsley, 3rd ed. (Louisville: Westminster John Knox, 2012), 348.

10. Tikva Frymer-Kensky, *Reading the Women of the Bible* (New York: Schocken Books, 2002), xv.

Rape as a Weapon in War

Rape continues to be used as a weapon of war. During the Bosnian War between 1992 and 1995, for instance, the Bosnian Serb army raped between twelve thousand and fifty thousand women. These crimes are viewed by most analysts not only as brutal acts of gendered violence but as a military strategy to terrorize and convince the local population to avoid returning to their homes. It is also estimated that two hundred thousand women were raped during the Bangladeshi war for independence in 1971. More recently, ISIS (Islamic State of Iraq and Syria) captured hundreds of young Yazidi girls and forced them into sexual slavery, while killing thousands of other Yazidi people in northern Iraq. In 2008, the United Nations Security Council passed Resolution 1820, which identifies rape as a war tactic. This resolution galvanized several organizations to address the matter of wartime rape. Today, organizations such as the Nobel Women's Initiative are working to raise awareness about wartime rape, as well as to help protect women and children caught in war zones around the globe by providing them with safe harbors.[11]

Oracles against the nations are a feature of every prophetic book except for Hosea, so the presence of such oracles in Zechariah is not surprising. Wartime was the original life-setting for such oracles. Denouncing Israel's enemies was certainly part of preparing the armies of the Israelite kingdoms for battle against their enemies. The people of Yehud, however, had no army with which to face any hostile forces arrayed against them so it is unlikely that 9:1-8 anticipates actual military engagements. Another life-setting for oracles against the nations was cultic services of lamentation.[12] In such a context, oracles of judgment against the nations serve as oracles of salvation for Israel. Containing military vocabulary typical of such oracles, verse 8 affirms that God will guard the temple and protect it from harm.

A unique feature in Zechariah's oracle is the astonishing declaration that the Philistines, once intractable enemies of Israel, will become "like

11. Peter Moszynski, "Women Peace Laureates Urge Protection for Women in Armed Conflict," *British Medical Journal* 342 (2011), doi: 10.1136/bmj.d3373.

12. John H. Hayes, "The Usage of Oracles against Foreign Nations in Ancient Israel," *JBL* 87 (1968): 87.

a clan in Judah." With God speaking in the first person, 9:7 suggests that the Philistines will observe the Torah's dietary laws,[13] thus underscoring the transformation of the Philistines from Israel's enemies to the "remnant of our God." Use of the preposition "like" (כ) implies that the Philistines will not have the same status as Jews. Still, even asserting that the Philistines would be *"like* a clan in Judah" amazingly turns the oracle against the nations on its head. Thus, Zechariah not only transforms a literary form (an oracle against a nation becomes an oracle that incorporates that nation into the people of God) but also transforms the way the readers/hearers of this text are to look on those whom they have regarded as their enemies.

Zechariah 9:1-8 employs the geography and history of ancient Israel not to dwell on the past, but to speak about Israel's hoped-for future once Jerusalem has been restored. The text takes readers/hearers on an excursion through some of the more prominent cities of the Levant before bringing them to the temple of Jerusalem. The cities through which God marches represent nations that have been political and military opponents of the two Israelite kingdoms. The text calls attention to Israel's tribal traditions (v. 1) and invites readers/hearers to imagine a future that will see an ancient enemy becoming "like a clan in Judah" (v. 7). Zechariah promises that Israel's long history of military conflict will someday come to an end, once God has eliminated threats to Jerusalem and has taken up residence there again (v. 8).

The war God wages against Yehud's neighbors has as its goal the protection of Jerusalem and the guarantee of its peace. With God dwelling in the rebuilt temple, the city is safe (v. 8). Tragically, Jerusalem's safety comes at a high cost. As allusions in verses 4-6 suggest, violence directed at the nations inflicts terror and suffering on women and children living in gentile cities along the military route. The irony is, of course, that Zechariah, like many of the biblical prophets, sees warfare against Yehud's neighbors as a necessary pathway to Jerusalem's peace. Of course, history has shown that "peace through war" is illusory. Violence and war breed more violence and war. With only a brief respite under the Hasmoneans, the Jewish people remained subject to foreign domination. The two failed revolts against Roman rule in the first and second centuries CE left the temple in ruins and the Jewish people in dispersion. It was not until 1948 that a Jewish state reemerged in the southern Levant. Still,

---

13. See Gen 9:4; Lev 11:2-47; and Deut 14:3-21.

to the present day modern Israel has been in virtually a constant state of war with neighboring states and the Palestinians.[14] "Peace through war" is an illusion. One war simply sets the stage for the next.

YHWH and Daughter Zion (9:9-10)

Martial imagery continues in Zechariah 9:9-10, where it links two metaphorical figures: Jerusalem/Zion personified as a "daughter," and a "king" whose arrival in the eschaton will lead Jerusalem to shout and rejoice (v. 9). These two metaphors—a feminized city-woman greeting "her" king—evoke images from other biblical texts of women singing victory songs to celebrate the return of their men from battle.[15]

In Hebrew poetic texts, the word "daughter" (בת) followed by a toponym refers to the inhabitants of the place named.[16] The term "daughter Zion" (בת ציון) appears twenty-six times in the Hebrew Bible—all in poetic texts. Each of the seven occurrences of בת ירושלם ("daughter Jerusalem" [2 Kgs 19:21; Isa 37:22; Mic 4:8; Zeph 3:14; Zech 9:9; Lam 2:1, 15]) is paired with "daughter Zion," suggesting that the two terms are synonymous. In verse 9, then, the prophet calls on the people of Jerusalem/Zion, personified as the daughter of "her" patron deity, to celebrate YHWH's victories.[17] In the context of 9:9-10, the expression "daughter Jerusalem/ Zion" is ambivalent. On the one hand, it conveys a positive sense of comfort: daughter Jerusalem/Zion has an identity, a home, and a feeling of belonging, rooted in "her" familial bond with her king. Zechariah uses this idiom to affirm that Jerusalem is the setting for the divine-human encounter that is unique to Israel, God's covenant people. On the other hand, as a component of the Zion tradition and its association with military power, the "daughter Zion" metaphor bears a negative connotation by alluding to Jerusalem's vulnerability.[18] This literary metaphor reflects

---

14. Israel has signed peace treaties with Egypt and Jordan and has recognized the Palestinian National Authority. Still, the peace with these neighbors is fragile.

15. For example, see the celebration by Miriam and "all the women" in Exod 15:20-21 and the Song of Deborah in Judg 5.

16. H. Haag, *"bath," TDOT* 2:33.

17. The plural form בנות ציון ("daughters of Zion") appears four times (Song 3:11, Hebrew; Isa 3:6, 17, Hebrew; 4:4), always referring to the women living in Jerusalem, not to the personified city.

18. The JPS translation renders v. 9a as, "Rejoice greatly, Fair Zion; Raise a shout, Fair Jerusalem," eliminating the intimation of Jerusalem's vulnerability as a daughter needing her father's protection.

Zech 9:9-10

⁹Rejoice greatly, O daughter Zion!
Shout aloud, O daughter
Jerusalem!
See, your king comes to you;
triumphant and victorious is he,
humble and riding on a donkey,
on a colt, the foal of a donkey.
¹⁰He will cut off the chariot from
Ephraim

and the war horse from
Jerusalem;
and the battle bow shall be cut off,
and he shall command peace to
the nations;
his dominion shall be from sea
to sea
and from the River to the ends of
the earth.

the lived reality of unmarried daughters in ancient Israel who had no independent agency. They had to rely on their fathers and older brothers for protection. Daughter Jerusalem/Zion was vulnerable, unable to withstand military incursions by enemies or political oppression by imperial authorities. At the core of the Zion tradition, therefore, was a belief in Jerusalem's inviolability, not because of her own strength, but because she was the "daughter" of יהוה צבאות, who will defend "her" (for his own honor) and dwell in her midst (to guard her as "his" possession).[19]

The Zion tradition also has a strong connection with the Davidic dynasty.[20] Indeed, Jerusalem became known as "the city of David" after it was taken from its Jebusite inhabitants by David (2 Sam 5:7). Although Zechariah 9:9 is not explicit about the king's identity, it is likely that the people of Yehud would have assumed that such a king would come from the Davidic dynasty. Unlike Judah's earlier kings, however, the one described in 9:9-10 is a nonmilitary, eschatological figure who will inaugurate a period of peace by disarming those poised to attack Jerusalem. The "cutting off" of the chariot, war horse, and bow (v. 10) eliminates the most potent offensive weapons from the enemy's arsenal. Although Zechariah 3:8 and 6:9-15 may have aroused expectations that the Davidic dynasty might be restored in the person of Zerubbabel, 9:9 does not identify the future king by name, thus ensuring that readers/hearers understand that this king would come at the eschaton, not in the immediate future. This was a strategic move since the Persians certainly

19. For example, Ps 48. See John H. Hayes, "The Tradition of Zion's Inviolability," *JBL* 82 (1963): 419–26.

20. Jamie J. M. Roberts, "The Davidic Origin of the Zion Tradition," *JBL* 92 (1973): 329–44.

would not permit a member of the native Judean dynasty to claim the throne of David. Yehud will remain part of the Persian provincial system. Its civil leaders will be Persian appointees. The Persian king was the legitimate heir of David with prophetic designation (Isa 45:1).

TRANSLATION MATTERS

Verse 9 describes the king as צדיק ונושע, which the NRSVue translates as "triumphant and victorious." Following the LXX (δίκαιος καὶ σῷζων) the NABRE has "a just savior." Both Mark Boda and Carol Meyers and Eric Meyers have "righteous and saved."[21] This phrasing accurately renders the niphal (passive) form נושע. This phrase portrays the king as dependent on God (who is the victorious one), and the king's dependence on God, paired with his righteousness, makes him a suitable and appropriate viceroy for God. Thus, the Hebrew implies that the righteous king will be saved by God from his enemies through actions that bring peace to Jerusalem and to the world.

Zechariah also describes the king as עני ("humble" in v. 9), a word that is often (but not here) paired with אביון ("poor") to describe a person who lacks the resources necessary to be socially and financially self-sufficient. In 9:9 the emphasis is not on the king's economic status but on his social status within the Jewish community. Zechariah suggests that the relationship between the king and his people would be different from that of kings in the ancient Near East, where monarchy, as a political and social system, was based on domination over people as subjects. That form of monarchical power is the opposite of the ideal described in Deuteronomy's "law of the king" (Deut 17:14-20), which describes the relationship between the king and his people as familial, not hierarchical. Guided by "all the words of this law and these statutes, neither exalting himself above other members of the community[22] nor turning aside from the commandment" (Deut 17:19-20), the king was to regard the people not as subjects but as siblings.

Characterizing the king as humble balances the image of him seated on a donkey as he arrives in Jerusalem (v. 9). In ancient Near Eastern

---

21. Boda, *The Book of Zechariah*, 560; Meyers and Meyers, *Zechariah 9–14*, 4.
22. The phrase "other members of the community" is the NRSVue's attempt to have the text be inclusive at the cost of accuracy. The Hebrew has אחים ("brothers"), which makes the familial dimension clear.

societies, the donkey was a valuable animal that carried both people and cargo with ease. Because it was more suited than the horse to warfare in hilly regions, it became a symbol of military power in regions like the central highlands of the southern Levant. Zechariah's depiction of the king as humble and seated on a donkey suggests that, at the end time, the king will arrive in Jerusalem empowered by God, who will end all military threats to the city and establish peace (v. 10).[23]

While the Gospels present this passage as a prophecy of Jesus's triumphal entry into Jerusalem (Matt 21:5; John 12:15), the rabbis read this passage as a restoration of Judah's monarchy that will inaugurate a period of universal, permanent peace. This peace will come only after a large-scale military conflict. Also, rabbinic tradition associates this passage with the blessing of Jacob's son Judah in Genesis 49:8-12. According to Genesis, Judah is endowed with royal power that will enable him (and ultimately the tribe made up of his descendants) to rule over all nations. Zechariah 9:13-14 describes Judah as the "bow" that God uses to bring about that final victory. The military images associated with the royal figure who will save the people correlate well with an interpretation that either God is the king or a future unnamed monarch, a descendant of the patriarch Judah, will be victorious. This latter interpretation is the background of the gospel tradition concerning Jesus's entry into Jerusalem.[24]

Another rabbinic take on chapter 9 situates verse 13 within a second-century BCE context as the rabbis regard this text as a prediction of the conflict between Jews and the Seleucids between 175 and 142 BCE. Jews successfully achieved autonomy through this conflict and maintained that status until the Romans invaded Jerusalem in 63 BCE.[25]

God Restores Daughter Zion (9:11-17)

The final seven verses of chapter 9 supplement the martial imagery that is woven throughout this chapter with cultic, pastoral, and agricultural images. God is the implied speaker and daughter Zion the implied

---

23. Paul D. Hanson, "Zechariah 9 and the Recapitulation of an Ancient Ritual Pattern," *JBL* 92 (1973): 43–45; Frans du T. Laubscher, "The King's Humbleness in Zechariah 9:9: A Paradox?," *JNSL* 18 (1992): 126–27.

24. William J. C. Weren, "Jesus' Entry into Jerusalem: Matt 21:1-17 in the Light of the Hebrew Bible and the Septuagint," in *Studies in Matthew's Gospel: Literary Design, Intertextuality, and Social Setting* (Leiden: Brill, 2014), 162–85.

25. Pesiq. Rab. 2.

Zech 9:11-17

[11]As for you also, because of
the blood of my covenant
with you,
I will set your prisoners free from
the waterless pit.
[12]Return to your stronghold,
O prisoners of hope;
today I declare that I will restore to
you double.
[13]For I have bent Judah as my bow;
I have made Ephraim its arrow.
I will arouse your sons, O Zion,
against your sons, O Greece,
and wield you like a warrior's
sword.
[14]Then the LORD will appear over
them,
and his arrow go forth like
lightning;
the Lord GOD will sound the trumpet

and march forth in the whirlwinds
of the south.
[15]The LORD of hosts will protect them,
and they shall consume and
conquer the slingers;
they shall drink their blood like wine
and be full like a bowl,
drenched like the corners of the
altar.

[16]On that day the LORD their God will
save them,
for they are the flock of his
people,
for like the jewels of a crown
they shall shine on his land.
[17]For what goodness and beauty are
his!
Grain shall make the young men
flourish,
and new wine the young women.

addressee in 9:11-13,[26] which focuses on a specific segment of the Jewish people: the descendants of those who were forced to migrate to Babylon following the fall of Jerusalem in 587 BCE. God will begin the eschatological battle by sounding the trumpet (שׁופר, "shofar") and marching forward at the head of the sons of Zion (vv. 13-14). The epithet יהוה צבאות (v. 15) appears only once in chapter 9, where it affirms that God will protect "the flock of his people" (v. 16) during the eschatological battle. Speaking of the people of Jerusalem as "the jewels of a crown" (v. 16), the text points to the new status awaiting those whom God will lead to victory. The prophet employs metaphors from the cultic sphere (a bowl full of "blood like wine" and the corners of the altar, in v. 15) to describe the defeat of Jerusalem's enemies. Following the victory "on that day" (v. 16), all the people of Yehud—young men and young women—will

---

26. After v. 13, the text uses the third person in speaking of God, indicating that it is the prophet's voice that is being heard.

enjoy the fruitfulness of the land. God's eschatological victory will make it possible for people to enjoy the bounty of their homeland in peace.

God's blowing a shofar signals the beginning of an eschatological clash that will result in the destruction of Israel's enemies. The Hebrew Bible allots multiple functions to the shofar. In one case, the blowing of the shofar announces imminent communion with God (Exod 19:19). More often, though, the sounding of a shofar signals the onset or conclusion of a military battle (Josh 6:5; 2 Sam 20:22).[27] In these cases, it is not God who sounds the shofar, but military leaders who are signaling the beginning of military engagement. Finally, the shofar serves as a tool to announce the appointment of a new king (1 Kgs 1:34-39). All these functions would have been familiar to Jews who heard the prophet's message, a message that alludes to the military, monarchic, and spiritual uses of the shofar. Zechariah 9:14 mentions the shofar in an eschatological context, issuing a universal call to all who hear it. The prophet's eschatological call is gender-inclusive, explicitly pairing old men and women (8:4), young boys and young girls (8:5), young men and young women (9:17), and mothers and fathers (13:3). It is not coincidental, therefore, that Zechariah 9 closes with a reference to young men and young women blessed with a bounty of grain and new wine. The inclusion of young women in this verse emphasizes the totality of restoration and participation by people of both genders in Yehud's agricultural bounty.[28] This type of inclusion is expanded even further in some early commentaries on Zechariah 9:17. According to Leviticus Rabbah 1.2, the references to young men and young women here actually refer to men and women who will convert to Judaism in the end time. One feature of Zechariah's eschatological vision is the breakdown of social barriers such as gender, age, and wealth in the age to come. This suggests the relative value of such barriers in the present age.

An assortment of textual issues make understanding these verses a challenge. First is the phrase בדם בריתך, which the NRSVue emends and

27. On the symbolic meaning of the shofar in the Hebrew Bible, see Markus N. A. Bockmuehl, " 'The Trumpet Shall Sound': Shofar Symbolism and its Reception in Early Christianity," in *Templum Amicitiae: Essays on the Second Temple Presented to Ernst Bammel*, ed. William Horbury, JSNTSup 48 (Sheffield: JSOT Press, 1991), 199–225. In the rabbinic period, the shofar is refurbished into a symbol of peace and freedom. See Sifre Numbers 77:4.

28. References to agricultural products, especially grain and new wine, suggest both abundance of food to eat and resumption of Zion's cultic celebrations once God has defeated those who threaten Jerusalem.

renders as, "the blood of my covenant with you," despite the lack of the first-person possessive suffix on ברית. The pronominal suffix is second-person feminine singular: "*your* covenant." The antecedent is daughter Zion/Jerusalem (see v. 9). Exodus 24:8 is the only other occurrence in the Hebrew Bible of the expression "blood of the covenant." There it refers to the ratification of the covenant between God and Israel mediated by Moses in the wilderness of Sinai. By using this phrase, Zechariah 9:11 implies that the Zion tradition is a legitimate heir to the Sinai tradition. For the prophet, the fidelity of God to the blood-sealed covenant with Israel is manifest in the return of the exiles of Judah to Zion.[29]

A second textual challenge appears in verse 12, where Jews still living in Mesopotamia are referred to as prisoners who will return to בצרון ("fortress"; NRSVue's "your stronghold").[30] At the time this was written, Jerusalem could hardly have been considered a "stronghold" since its walls were yet to be rebuilt, but the text likely refers to the fortifications that the Persians built in the region to discourage Greek incursions into the Levant.[31] Verse 12 also speaks of hope in the reclamation of authentic Jewish identity by "prisoners" returning from exile to Zion. God will transform those returnees, including people from both northern (Ephraim) and southern (Judah) tribes, into armed forces to resist the Greeks attempting to expand into the Levant.[32] Ironically, for Jews in Babylon this meant that God would empower them to relocate to Yehud to become defenders of Persian hegemony. This text also implies that there was resistance to the cultural transformation that followed the Greeks into the Levant. That transformation was the product of the in-

---

29. Exod 24:8 and other texts in the Hebrew Bible that associate blood with the covenant likely influenced the New Testament narratives that has Jesus inviting his disciples to drink wine, saying, "This is my blood of the covenant, which is poured out for many for the forgiveness of sins" (Matt 26:28; Mark 14:24; some versions read this verse as, "This is my blood of the new covenant."). Christians take this gospel story to mean that the ancient, blood-sealed covenant between God and Israel would be extended to Jesus's followers. The idea of a new covenant being forged is not an invention by the New Testament authors but appears as early as Jer 31:31, which has God saying, "I will make a new covenant with the house of Israel and the house of Judah."

30. This is the only occurrence of בצרון in the Hebrew Bible. The NRSVue translates it as "your stronghold," though the word "your" is not present in the Hebrew text. NABRE has "a fortress" and suggests that it may be a wordplay on "in Zion" (בציון). JPS renders the word as a proper name: "Bizzaron."

31. Meyers and Meyers, *Zechariah 9–14*, 142.

32. As a province of the Persian Empire, Yehud would have been opposed to Greek expansionism; see Petersen, *Zechariah 9–14 and Malachi*, 62.

troduction of a new language into the regions accompanied by cultural institutions such as the gymnasium (see 1 Macc 1:11-15).

A third textual consideration is how to interpret Zechariah 9:15b. The Hebrew reads ושתו המו כמו יין (literally, "they shall drink, they shall rage with wine"). Consistent with the MT, JPS and NABRE render המו as "they shall rage" and "become heated," respectively. NRSVue follows some LXX manuscripts, which apparently read המו ("they shall rage") as דמם ("their blood"), thus rendering the phrase, "they shall drink their blood like wine."[33] It is easy to see how the lexical confusion may have occurred, but we cannot accept NRSVue's reading, because it suggests that Jews are to drink the blood of their enemies, an act which is strictly forbidden, according to Leviticus 17:10-12.[34] While there is much to be said about references to blood in Zechariah 9 (see below), including verse 15 in that discussion would be based on a misreading of this text.

Having sorted out several textual challenges, we can now proceed to explore feminist perspectives on Zechariah 9:11-17. The previous verses (9:9-10), address daughter Zion/daughter Jerusalem explicitly and assure her that her king will return to her, having conquered all her enemies. This "daughter" metaphor allows the reader to attribute to Jerusalem qualities expected of a "good daughter," such as being obedient to her father as a girl and being loyal to her husband as a young woman. Though the intended message may have been generally positive (i.e., Jerusalem would be restored as "the faithful city"; see discussion of Zech 8:8 above), the "good daughter" metaphor denies women and girls agency and characterizes them as subordinate to and dependent on their male "protectors." Like the stereotypical "damsel in distress," Jerusalem is told to do nothing but wait for her knight in shining armor. She is helpless but hopeful that the knight (God) would save her. Of course, one could understand this metaphor as identifying all the people of Jerusalem and Yehud—both men and women—with daughter Zion. This view suggests that all people manifest attributes associated with both genders. For example, not all women in the Bible are passive, and not all men in the Bible are active: one need only look at the

33. Some scholars view this alternate version as the *lectio difficilior*, the older text that was later smoothed over into a more agreeable phrase by a copyist. See Susan Niditch, "Good Blood, Bad Blood: Multivocality, Metonymy, and Mediation in Zechariah 9," *VT* 61 (2011): 642.

34. S. Tamar Kamionkowski, *Leviticus*, WCS 3 (Collegeville, MN: Liturgical Press, 2018), 170–74.

story of Deborah and Barak in Judges 4 or the story of Adam and Eve in Genesis 3 to find examples of women who take control while their male partners remain more passive. Indeed, there are no exclusively "female personality traits" in the Bible. While the metaphor is familial, it does not necessarily focus on daughter Zion's social position as subject to her father. There is also an affective dimension to the metaphor that should not be ignored. As daughter Zion's parent, God loves her and protects her. Like most metaphors the "daughter Zion" imagery is multivalent. Readers are well advised to keep this multivalence in mind.

A second concern is three references to blood in Zechariah. Each reference carries with it a distinctive meaning. The blood mentioned in verse 7 serves to depict the Philistines as carnivorous animals with the blood of their prey still in their mouths. In verse 11, blood is associated with the covenant that motivates God to release prisoners of Judah because of "the blood of the covenant." Finally, in verse 15, God's people will drink their enemies' blood as if it were wine. The image of God's people drinking their enemies' blood like wine presumably stands in stark contrast to Obadiah 16, which predicts that Judah's enemies will celebrate their victory by drinking wine on Mount Zion. In Obadiah, people of Judah are condemned for disobeying God, while in Zechariah, this condemnation is reversed into an image of victory for the Jews over their enemies. The presence of blood in Zechariah, moreover, adds a new and strange element to the motif of drinking wine in celebration that is absent in earlier prophetic literature.

Susan Niditch argues that Zechariah 9 is a single literary unit, and that the three occurrences of blood help to unify the chapter. She asserts that the varied allusions to blood reflect the symbolic meanings associated with blood in Israelite tradition. Also, Niditch cites anthropological research that concludes that humans see the world in binaries but that they use symbolic mediators that bridge the gaps between these binaries. Blood functioned as such a mediator in the ancient world. According to Niditch, "Blood links creation, sin, violent destruction, recreation, repair, purification, and redemption. Blood mediates between seeming opposites by partaking of both sides of the opposition."[35] In this way, Niditch argues, blood does not need to symbolize the same thing each time it is mentioned in Zechariah. The multiple and sometimes contrasting associations with blood provide cohesion to the chapter and point

35. Niditch, "Good Blood, Bad Blood," 643.

to multiple layers of meaning at the same time. This is another instance of the multivalence of biblical metaphors.

Ezekiel 16–17, a literary unit that also refers to blood in varied ways, seems to have served as an inspiration for Zechariah 9. Ezekiel 16–17 depicts God taking care of Jerusalem, which is personified as an infant girl abandoned in a field. God retrieves and nourishes this infant until she grows into a beautiful young woman. Once this woman is "at the age for love" (Ezek 16:8), God again washes blood from her and adorns her with fine clothes and jewelry. Ultimately, however, this woman sheds the blood of her own sons and daughters and offers them as sacrifices to images of her own making (Ezek 16:17-22). Thus, Ezekiel features the blood of childbirth and the blood of menstruation (if one is to interpret the blood that God wipes off the young woman as menstrual blood), as well as the blood of murder and idolatry. Like Zechariah 9, Ezekiel 16–17 alludes to varied associations with blood to link diverse themes within a single text.

Conclusion

The two central metaphorical figures in Zechariah 9—daughter Zion/ Jerusalem and צבאת יהוה—present challenges for a feminist reading of the text. Some readers will find the use of feminine imagery in Zechariah 9:9-17 a welcome change since men and male imagery dominate the biblical tradition in general and the book of Zechariah in particular. Still, the image of "daughter" can serve to perpetuate the stereotype of women as dependent and passive. References in this chapter to daughter Zion/ Jerusalem both convey an intimate covenantal relationship between God and God's people and reinforce a sense of God as someone who demands obedience, loyalty, and subservience. Of course, Zechariah 9 neither created, nor can it solve, problems surrounding the role and status of women in society today. Still, a feminist reading calls to mind the importance of questioning theological assumptions behind literary stereotypes and gender roles and of considering how best to interpret ancient texts in modern contexts.

Divine Warrior imagery is firmly embedded in biblical tradition, and it is not surprising that the book of Zechariah employs it. Unfortunately, readers in many generations and contexts have assumed that this metaphor both defines God as militaristic and prescribes war as a divinely ordained means of accomplishing God's will. Wars fought with that premise often involve the demonization of others as the "enemy," casting them as beyond God's compassion or concern. Zechariah 9:1-8 and 14:12-15 illustrate this problem. Although Zechariah 9 provides no explicit descriptions of the horrors that accompany war, its portrait of God as the Divine Warrior marching through cities (which are characterized by feminine grammatical gender) in the Levant can be troubling for a feminist reader.[36] Usually women are noncombatants,[37] but often they are targets in war because they carry the future of their people. They bear and raise children, passing on the values and traditions of their people; raping women and girls is often a military strategy for humiliating the men unable to protect their families. Pregnant women were targets of invading armies (see 2 Kgs 8:12; 15:16; Hos 13:16 [MT 14:1]; Amos 1:13). Without neutralizing the women of a nation, any victory over that nation is temporary. The task of contemporary hermeneutics, then, is to seek alternative approaches to affirming God's power to save without perpetuating the idea that war is the only effective means to do so.[38]

Most of the scholarship on the theme of blood in Zechariah 9 neglects to note that the reference to blood in 9:11 appears in a divine speech addressed to Jerusalem and that Jerusalem is personified as a young woman (daughter Zion).

> As for you also, because of the blood of my covenant with you,
> [literally, "in the blood of your (2nd fem. sg.) covenant,"]
> I will set your prisoners free from the waterless pit.

With Jerusalem/Zion addressed as a woman, the puzzling phraseology of chapter 9 can evoke a range of associations. For example, "the blood of

---

36. The violence of God in the Hebrew Bible has been the subject of several recent works: Renita J. Weems, *Battered Love: Marriage, Sex, and Violence in the Hebrew Prophets*, OBT (Minneapolis: Fortress, 1995); Eric A. Seibert, *The Violence of Scripture: Overcoming the Old Testament's Troubling Legacy* (Minneapolis: Fortress, 2012); Susan Niditch, *War in the Hebrew Bible: A Study of the Ethics of Violence* (New York: Oxford, 1993); Jerome F. D. Creach, *Violence in Scripture*, Interpretation: Resources for the Use of Scripture in the Church (Louisville: Westminster John Knox, 2013).

37. With a few notable exceptions, such as Deborah and Jael (Judg 4–5), biblical narratives virtually ignore the participation and even the presence of women in battles, and the image of the "woman warrior" presents its own challenges for feminist interpreters. See Gale A. Yee, "By the Hand of a Woman: The Metaphor of the Woman Warrior in Judges 4," in *Women, War, and Metaphor: Language and Society in the Study of the Hebrew Bible*, ed. Claudia V. Camp and Carole R. Fontaine, SemeiaSt 61 (Atlanta: Scholars Press, 1993), 99–132.

38. For example, the New Testament presents Jesus as a savior who is victorious in defeat.

your [2nd fem. sg.] covenant" could be read as an allusion to the blood of childbirth and a reminder of her children ("your [2nd fem. sg.] prisoners") lost in war. Or perhaps this reference could be associated with menstrual blood, which determines the schedule of impurity and purity that a married woman must follow in Israelite tradition to know when she can sleep with her husband (Lev 15:19, 25), who also might be among the prisoners for whom daughter Zion mourns. The blood mentioned in 9:11 might remind women readers of their own wounds incurred in war—the wounds of rape, sexual slavery, and abuse. God's promise in 9:11 (reaffirmed in 9:16-17) assures daughter Zion—and women reading this text—that a restoration of life is possible, although experiences of trauma, violence, and violation will leave them forever changed.

Zechariah 9 uses a variety of images to assure readers that Jerusalem will have a future of peace and security under God's sovereign rule. This chapter declares that God will act against the nations that pose a threat to Jerusalem's peace, thus extending God's rule to "the ends of the earth" (v. 10). But the idea that waging war will bring about peace is a way to justify war; in fact, war has never brought about lasting peace—especially not in contexts of modern warfare. With the ever-present danger of thermonuclear war threatening to end life on our planet, it is imperative to develop nonviolent approaches to settling disagreements between nations. The way to achieve peaceful relations among all nations is to work for economic, social, and political justice. Zechariah 9 offered hope to the people of Yehud for a future peace at a time when the prospects of peace were low. Likewise, readers today can find in these words the assurance that their work for peace and justice will not be in vain. Reimagining God, not as a relentless warrior, but as a compassionate, universal savior, will help bring God's gift of peace to the human family.

Zechariah 10:1-12

Returning Home

Zechariah 9 proclaims a vision of restoration for Jerusalem that ends with a promise that Judah's young people—women and men—will enjoy the produce of the land, especially the grain and wine. This is no idle promise. A principal anxiety among the people of Yehud during the Persian period was the possibility of food shortages and even famine (see Hag 1:6). The eschatological vision in chapter 9 provides assurance that people will not have to face that eventuality.

Chapter 10 begins by taking up that same motif. The prophet calls his readers/hearers to turn to YHWH with their prayers for rain. They are to abandon idolatry and divination to deal with the possibility of drought and the resultant food shortages (v. 1). The prophet assures the people that God will bring rain at the proper times to ensure that their harvests will sustain them. In addition, God will bring back both the exiles of the house of Joseph and the house of Judah (v. 6), reuniting all Israel (v. 6) and empowering the returnees to walk in God's ways, despite the failures of Yehud's leaders (v. 3). The martial imagery in this chapter is used of Judah and not of God, but God will prepare the house of Judah for the eschatological conflict with its enemies, promising victory over Egypt and Assyria and the return of all Israel to its ancestral homeland.

The House of Judah Will Come Home (10:1-6)

Zechariah 10 begins with a dramatic command—"Ask rain from YHWH"—followed by the assertion that YHWH makes the storm clouds

167

Zech 10:1-6

¹Ask rain from the L ORD
   in the season of the spring rain,
from the L ORD who makes the storm
     clouds,
    who gives showers of rain
      to you,
    the vegetation in the field to
      everyone.
²For the teraphim utter nonsense,
   and the diviners see lies;
the dreamers tell false dreams
   and give empty consolation.
Therefore the people wander like
    sheep;
   they suffer for lack of a shepherd.
³My anger is hot against the
    shepherds,
   and I will punish the leaders,
for the L ORD of hosts cares for his
    flock, the house of Judah,
   and will make them like his proud
    war horse.

⁴Out of them shall come the
    cornerstone,
   out of them the tent peg,
out of them the battle bow,
   out of them every commander.
⁵Together they shall be like warriors
    in battle,
   trampling the foe in the mud of the
    streets;
they shall fight, for the L ORD is with
    them,
   and they shall put to shame the
    riders on horses.
⁶I will strengthen the house of Judah,
   and I will save the house of
    Joseph.
I will bring them back because I have
    compassion on them,
   and they shall be as though I had
    not rejected them,
   for I am the L ORD their God, and I
    will answer them.

that bring the rains. Rain was an absolute necessity in the agriculture of the southern Levant. Unlike Egypt and Mesopotamia, the southern Levant did not have a river system to make large-scale irrigation possible. The water necessary for crops had to come in the form of precipitation, i.e., rain, snow, and dew. Also, to be beneficial, the rain had to come at the right time in the growing season. Verse 1 mentions specifically the late or spring rains (מלקוש). These rains fall in March and April and provide the moisture necessary for cereal crops to mature and be ready for harvesting.[1] If these late rains do not come, the crops will invariably fail. Since bread was the mainstay of the diet in ancient Israel, the failure of the barley and wheat crops meant, at the very least, food shortages, if not famine. The prophet then calls hearers/readers to petition YHWH

---

1. The early or fall rains (יורה) come in October and November and serve to soften the soil in preparation for plowing and sowing.

to provide the rain needed for a successful harvest (v. 1).[2] The admonition to ask YHWH for rain was necessary because some people did seek to assuage their anxiety about possible crop failure of their harvest by employing various mantic techniques and associated apotropaic idolatrous rituals to reassure themselves that the needed rains were coming (v. 2). Deuteronomy explicitly and forcefully forbids this (Deut 18:14).[3]

TRANSLATION MATTERS

Zechariah 10:2 mentions three mantic techniques employed by those wanting assurances that the rains would come: divination, dream interpretation, and the use of the *teraphim. Teraphim* is a Hebrew word of unknown etymology. The precise nature and function of the *teraphim* are uncertain, though this plural form appears fifteen times in the Hebrew Bible.[4] The NRSVue and the NABRE both suggest that the *teraphim* were images of deities or perhaps ancestors that were found in homes rather than in public shrines.[5] The NRSVue renders *teraphim* as "household

2. Dependence on God for rain is a prominent theme in the Bible; the patriarchs suffer from famine and must pray to God before receiving rain (Gen 43:1), Deuteronomy warns the people that they will not receive rain if they fall into idolatry (Deut 11:17), and prophets such as Samuel and Elijah ask God to bring rain or withhold rain as a means of showing the people what their standing is with God (1 Sam 12:18; 1 Kgs 17:1).

3. Deuteronomy does not claim that these techniques are ineffective but that Israel is not allowed to make use of them. Still, some of these techniques, such as dream interpretation (Gen 37:5-11; 41; 1 Kgs 3:5; Dan 4:18-27) and the lot oracle (Exod 28:30; Num 27:12-33; Deut 33:8; 1 Sam 14:41), were considered legitimate forms of divine/human communication. Zech 10:2 implies that divination and even dream interpretation cannot be relied on. The New Testament contains an instance of the employment of lots to determine the divine will, assuming that God controlled how the lots fall (Acts 1:15-26). Similarly, the New Testament reflects the belief that dreams were means by which God communicated with human beings (Matt 1:20; 2:12, 13, 19; 27:19). The oracle in Zech 10:1 suggests that the use of divination is a manifestation of Israel's lack of faith in God's promises and God's power to provide for their needs. These practices showed a blatant failure to trust God's promise to provide the early and late rains for the production of grain, wine, and oil, thus preventing famine and the consequent food shortages and starvation (see Deut 11:14-15).

4. Gen 31:19, 34, 35; Judg 17:5; 18:14, 17, 18, 20; 1 Sam 15:23; 19:13, 16; Hos 3:4; Zech 10:2. A singular form never appears in the Hebrew Bible.

5. 2 Kgs 23:24 appears to be citing Deut 18:11 while replacing necromancy ("spirits of the dead") with *teraphim.* This has led Karel van der Toorn to conclude that the *teraphim* were representations of deceased ancestors. See his "The Nature of the Biblical Teraphim in the Light of Cuneiform Evidence," *CBQ* 52 (1990): 203–22.

gods" in Genesis 31:19 and Judges 17:5, NRSV. In translating Genesis 31:19, the NABRE has "household images." Judges 17:5 associates the *teraphim* with the ephod, to which was attached the breastplate containing the *urim* and *thummim* (Exod 28:30). These two objects were part of the legitimate divinatory practice in the Israelite cult. Neither the NRSVue nor the NABRE translates *teraphim* in Zechariah 10:2, offering instead a transliteration of the Hebrew word. The Zechariah passage implies that the *teraphim* had some connection with divination. It is likely that the *teraphim* were employed in apotropaic rituals designed to reverse the effects of an unfavorable outcome in the use of divination. Josiah outlawed the *teraphim* along with other divinatory and idolatrous objects (2 Kgs 23:24).

Teraphim have a role to play in two stories featuring women. Genesis 31:19, 33-35 notes that Rachel took her father's *teraphim* when Jacob was leaving Laban and returning to Canaan with his family. She hides her father's *teraphim* in a camel's saddle and successfully prevents him from recovering them. First Samuel 19:11-17 tells how Michal helped her husband David escape from the soldiers that her father Saul sent to kill him. After David flees through a window, Michal places the *teraphim* in his bed, covering them with his clothes. She then tells the soldiers that David was ill. By the time the soldiers discovered her ruse, David successfully made his escape. This story suggests that the *teraphim* in the house of Michal and David were large enough to simulate a human body.

Neither story suggests what the function of the *teraphim* might be, though the story of Rachel implies that the *teraphim* were objects of some religious or economic value. In both cases, it appears that women had access to and control over the *teraphim*, suggesting that they were household images used in family rituals involving women. Also, in both stories the women use the *teraphim* to benefit their husbands to the disadvantage of their fathers. Rachel and Michal use the *teraphim* to act independently, cleverly, and decisively, shifting their loyalty from their fathers' houses to that of their husbands.

Zechariah 10:2 condemns the use of mantic techniques as an act of disloyalty since reliance on such practices showed that the people of Yehud lacked trust in their true shepherd, YHWH (Ps 28:9; Isa 40:10-11; Ezek 34:13-16). Using pastoral imagery, 10:2 laments that "the people wander like sheep; they suffer for the lack of a shepherd."[6] God is angry with both the shepherds (i.e., the high priest and governor) and the

---

6. Mark J. Boda, *The Book of Zechariah*, NICOT (Grand Rapids: Eerdmans, 2016), 595–96, notes that vv. 1-3 and Jer 14:1–15:4 both treat of the motifs of "drought, idolatry, and false prophetic activity" and suggests that the text from Zechariah is dependent on that passage from Jeremiah. The lexical connections that he adduces to support his suggestion should not be surprising since both deal with the same topics. Jeremiah asserts that the prophets engaged in divination, resulting in disaster for the people who consult them. Zechariah, however, makes no such accusation against any prophets but is content to condemn divination and those who make use of it.

people (עתודים, literally "young male goats").[7] The text is explicit neither about specific accusations against the leaders nor about their fate. Rather, the focus shifts in verse 3b to the future transformation of the people of Yehud, from a "flock" (צון, which can also mean "sheep") totally dependent in their relationship with God to something like a "proud war horse" (סוס הודו במלחמה) in service to יהוה צבאות.

The prophet resumes speaking in 10:3b, and martial imagery dominates verses 4-6. The prophet asserts that God will transform "the house of Judah" into a military force and lead them to a decisive victory over their enemies. The result of that battle will be the full restoration of the people of Israel—north and south—in the land promised to their ancestors (v. 8). Indeed, the central concern of Zechariah 9 and 10 is the restoration of all Israel to its homeland. This was a dream not only of Zechariah but also of Isaiah (Isa 11:11-16), Jeremiah (Jer 31:14-19), Ezekiel (35:10; 37:22), and the Chronicler (see, e.g., 2 Chr 30:1–31:1).[8] These texts look forward to a union of all Israel, north and south, with its center in Jerusalem. This will occur because of God's "compassion" for Israel (v. 6b).[9] The covenant formulary ("I am YHWH their God") in verse 6c confirms the reestablishment of the covenant relationship between God and all Israel.

The House of Joseph Will Come Home (10:7-12)

The remainder of chapter 10 shifts attention from "the house of Judah" to the "house of Joseph."[10] References to "the house of Joseph" (v. 6), "the people of Ephraim" (v. 7), and the territories of Gilead and Lebanon (v. 10) combine with allusions to two major migration traditions—the

---

7. This metaphor appears in Isa 34:6; Jer 51:40; Ezek 39:18, where it refers to princes and people. See fuller discussion in Carol L. Meyers and Eric M. Meyers, *Zechariah 9–14: A New Translation with Introduction and Commentary*, AB 25C (New York: Doubleday, 1993), 196–97.

8. For the Chronicler's attitude to the people of the former kingdom of Israel, see Mark J. Boda, "Identity and Empire, Reality and Hope in the Chronicler's Perspective," in *Community Identity in Judean Historiography: Biblical and Comparative Perspectives*, ed. Gary N. Knoppers and Kenneth A. Ristau (Winona Lake, IN: Eisenbrauns, 2009), 249–72.

9. The verb that speaks of God's compassion is רחמתים (NRSVue: "I will have compassion on them"). This verb is derived from the noun רחם ("womb"). This is one instance of feminine imagery used in connection with God in Zechariah.

10. Technically, the "house of Joseph" refers to the tribes of Ephraim and Manasseh whose eponymous ancestors were the two sons of Joseph (Gen 48:1). These two tribes were the largest and most important of the tribes that constituted the former kingdom of Israel. Ephraim is sometimes used as a synecdoche for the kingdom of Israel, e.g., Isa 7:2-17; 9:8, 20 (NRSVue 9:9, 21); 11:13; Jer 31:9-20; Ezek 37:16-19.

⁷Then the people of Ephraim shall
  become like warriors,
  and their hearts shall be glad as
    with wine.
Their children shall see it and
    rejoice;
  their hearts shall exult in the LORD.

⁸I will signal for them and gather
    them in,
  for I have redeemed them,
  and they shall be as numerous as
    they were before.
⁹Though I scattered them among the
    nations,
  yet in far countries they shall
    remember me,
  and they shall rear their children
    and return.

¹⁰I will bring them home from the land
    of Egypt
  and gather them from Assyria;
I will bring them to the land of Gilead
    and to Lebanon,
  until there is no room for them.
¹¹They shall pass through the sea of
    distress,
  and the waves of the sea shall be
    struck down,
  and all the depths of the Nile
    dried up.
The pride of Assyria shall be laid low,
  and the scepter of Egypt shall
    depart.
¹²I will make them strong in the LORD,
  and they shall walk in his name,
    says the LORD.

exodus (vv. 10-11) and the Assyrian conquest (v. 10)—to indicate that God is about to return the people of the northern tribes to their ancestral homeland. In verses 6-12 the voices of God and the prophet alternate in the description of the restoration of the house of Joseph. The readers/ hearers of these words are the people of Yehud. The people of the northern tribes are spoken of in the third person throughout the oracle. This may indicate that the people of Yehud may have needed to be persuaded to accept the prophet's announcement of what God intended to accomplish for the people of "the house of Joseph."[11] Still, it is amazing that the fate

11. The two Israelite kingdoms were long-time rivals. The kingdom of Israel fell to the expansionist policies of the Neo-Assyrian Empire in 721 BCE. Second Kings 17:7-18, however, claims the fall was due to the northern tribes' penchant for idolatry and their failure to listen to the prophets. The Jews regarded the people who lived in the territory of the former kingdom of Israel as descendants of intermarriage with the foreign population introduced into the north by the Assyrians (2 Kgs 17:24). The Deuteronomist referred to these people as השמרנים ("the Samaritans," 2 Kgs 17:29) while they call themselves השרים ("the Observant"). Rivalry between the Jews and the Samaritans grew intense during the Hasmonean period and continued into the Common Era; see John 4:9. Today the Samarian community in the state of Israel numbers about eight hundred.

of people from the kingdom of Israel, which fell in the eighth century, is a concern for the Jews of Yehud at least two hundred years later. The unity of the Israelite tribes appears to have been a concern despite the tensions that have existed between the two Israelite kingdoms over the centuries. Indeed, the central concern of chapter 10 is the eschatological recovery of the land of Israel and the return of its exiles.[12]

God promises to act with compassion by restoring the northern tribes to the land and, more importantly, to the covenant: "I will bring them [the house of Joseph] back because I have compassion on them . . . for I am YHWH their God" (v. 6b). Despite the previous rebellion of the northern tribes (because of which YHWH had rejected them, according to v. 6b), the people of the house of Joseph will again be numbered among the people of God. With God as the implied speaker, verses 8-10 describe how God will restore the house of Joseph by bringing the northern tribes back from exile. Several verbs that speak of returning—שׁוּב ("return" in v. 9 and "bring" in v. 10a), קבץ ("gather" in vv. 8 and 10), and בוא ("bring" in v. 10b)—echo the theme of restoration promised to Judah's exiles in 9:11-12. The return of the house of Joseph (10:9-10) is an essential component of the eschatological restoration of Yehud, according to Zechariah 9–10.

At first, the settlement of the returning northern tribes in Gilead and Lebanon (v. 10) seems odd since these two regions were on the periphery of the former kingdom of Israel. Gilead was in the Transjordan east of the Sea of Galilee. The tribes of Reuben and Gad and half of the tribe of Manasseh settled there. Lebanon was along the northern border of Israel, though the southern part of Lebanon sometimes came under Israelite control (see 1 Kgs 9:19). Both regions were mountainous. In addition, Lebanon was densely forested, and Gilead's soil was rocky; consequently, both were lightly populated since the regions' topography made farming very labor-intensive. Still, both regions were well-watered and blessed with fertile soil. Mentioning these regions by name may suggest that the restoration of Israel would include expanded territory. This will provide room for the burgeoning population of returnees from the house of Joseph: "I will bring them back to the land of Gilead and to Lebanon, until there is no room for them" (v. 10c).[13]

Martial imagery continues in the second half of chapter 10, which declares that "the people of Ephraim shall become like warriors" (v. 7)

12. Meyers and Meyers, *Zechariah 9–14*, 231.
13. See the vision report in Zech 2:1-5, which describes Jerusalem as so densely populated by the returning exiles that the city would be unable to accommodate them.

and that God "will make them strong in YHWH" (v. 12).[14] The description of the Ephraimites as warriors whose strength will deter any enemy that tried to threaten it is reinforced by the messenger formula, נאם יהוה ("says YHWH"), which concludes the chapter.

TRANSLATION MATTERS

The NRSVue renders the final verb in chapter 10 (יתהלכו) as "they shall walk." The translations offered by Mark Boda ("they will march")[15] and JPS ("they shall march proudly") provide better renderings of the hithpael of הלך—especially in view of the martial tone of this passage.

Zechariah 10 concludes with the common image of divine power that manifests itself in God's mastery over the waters (v. 11). This imagery is reminiscent of the story of Marduk's defeat of the Mesopotamian sea-goddess Tiamat, which results in the creation of the waters above and the waters below the earth, and of the Canaanite tale of Baal's battle with Yamm, the god of the sea. Genesis tells of a wind from God that swept over the face of the water and of the creation of a dome separating the waters above and below the dome (Gen 1:2, 6-8). Zechariah 10:10-12 makes clear allusions to the story in Exodus 14 of God's mastery of the Red Sea, which resulted in the deliverance of the Israelites from slavery in Egypt. Just as the Hebrew slaves had been an alien population in Egypt, so their descendants were now aliens among the nations (v. 10). And as the Israelites had walked through a sea that miraculously split for them at the moment of their greatest peril—a miracle celebrated in song and dance by the Israelite women led by Miriam (Exod 15:20-21)—so the prophet envisions a time when both the sea (perhaps the Red Sea or perhaps all seas) and the Nile would be tamed or dried up altogether, so that they would never again place God's people in peril (v. 11). The prophet assures his readers/hearers that God will restore all the people of Israel to their land. By invoking imagery of the exodus, the speaker

---

14. Words from the Hebrew root גבר ("strong," "mighty") occur four times in chapter 10: גבור ("warrior") in vv. 5 and 7; גברתי ("strengthen") in v. 6; and גברתים ("make them strong") in v. 12.

15. Boda, *The Book of Zechariah*, 619.

paints a picture at the end of this chapter of Yehud's restoration—perhaps an even greater wonder than the exodus itself.

The splitting of the sea and drying up of the Nile envisioned in 10:11 create a literary *inclusio* with the chapter's opening verse, where the people are commanded to petition YHWH for rain. Thus, Zechariah 10 begins and ends with a declaration of human dependence on God to control the forces of nature. The text assures the people of Yehud that God will both provide rainwater for crops at the proper time and over-power the waters of chaos in times of social, political, or economic peril.

Conclusion

There are two primary concerns that arise in this feminist reading of Zechariah 10. First is the denigration of those who practice mantic techniques and Zechariah's criticism of such activities as demonstrating disloyalty to YHWH (10:2-3). It is likely that many of those practitioners were women whose role within their households required making sure there was ample food to eat. It is likely that some women would resort to divination and the associated apotropaic activities to relieve the anxiety over the food supply available to them. The second concern is the persis-tent use of martial language in chapter 10, which both renders women invisible and relegates the earth—its waters, land, and produce—to be controlled, constrained, and modified by the צבאות יהוה and the armies God empowers. The rest of this chapter explores these two challenges.

Zechariah 10:1-2 exemplifies how a biblical text can tacitly invalidate women's leadership roles without explicitly mentioning women. In the ancient Near East, food insecurity was a constant issue. People found comfort in the employment of divination and associated apotropaic rituals to deal with the uncertainty of the weather and its effects on their crops. They needed assurance that the rains would come when they should, so that crops could mature and harvests could be sufficient to avoid famine. The vehemence of the Deuteronomic prohibition against divination (Deut 18:9-14) is evidence that the practice remained popular precisely because people believed that it was effective.

Zechariah 10:2 asserts that these mantic techniques were utter non-sense and that those who practiced them were charlatans offering empty consolation. Though the text does not specify that women were practi-tioners of these customs, it is reasonable to assume that women in an-cient Israel (as in many indigenous cultures even today) as well as men were practitioners of the mantic arts and were consulted by people who respected them as sources of wisdom in dealing with the uncertainties of life.[16]

Since the preparation of food was a principal responsibility of women in Yehud, they were the first to feel the effect of food shortages.[17] Families struggled to obtain the grain they needed for survival (see Neh 5). Their struggle was exacerbated by the fact that the Persian authorities imposed high taxes on the Jewish community. Maintaining a sufficient supply of grain to ensure the family's survival proved difficult in years when the rains were insufficient to guarantee a plentiful harvest. People—especially women—coped with their diminishing supply of staple foods in part by consulting diviners who would assure them that the rains would come in due course. The prophet's insistence that the people of Yehud look to YHWH for rain likely ran contrary to customs that many, especially Israelite women, had come to depend on.

The concern about the militarized views of the people of Israel arises in the context of Zechariah's vision of the restoration of all Israel—north and south.[18] The prophet imagines what the restored Israel will look like. It will include both the house of Judah and the house of Joseph. Animosity and distrust between the two regions in the past will be put aside, enabling a new Israel—a united Israel—to emerge. This new Israel will be able to hold its own against nations that threaten its existence. The people of the new Israel will enjoy the bounty of the land made fertile by the rains God will send. No longer will mothers need to worry about not having enough grain to make bread for their families. No longer will men have to face the armies of world powers (e.g., Egypt and Assyria) without competent leadership. The restored Israel can look forward to a future of peace and prosperity that befits the people of God.

This imagined future stands in contrast to the realities experienced by the people of Yehud. With no political or military power to speak of, Yehud was little more than a backwater province of the Persian satrapy of "Beyond the River." Persian policies and practices may not have been as

16. Esther J. Hamori, *Women's Divination in Biblical Literature: Prophecy, Necromancy, and Other Arts of Knowledge*, AYBRL (New Haven: Yale University Press, 2015), 3–19.

17. See Carol L. Meyers, "From Field Crops to Food: Attributing Gender and Meaning to Bread Production in Iron Age Israel," in *The Archaeology of Difference: Gender, Ethnicity, Class and the "Other" in Antiquity: Studies in Honor of Eric M. Meyers*, ed. Douglas R. Edwards and C. Thomas McCollough, AASOR 60/61 (Boston: ASOR, 2007), 68–71.

18. Note that in chapter 10 military language is used of Judah (vv. 3-5) and not of God. The title יהוה צבאות, used so frequently in Zechariah, does not appear in this chapter.

harsh as those of earlier empires that dominated the region, but Persian taxes imposed a heavy burden on Yehud's fragile economy. Although Zechariah viewed Yehud's religious and political leadership as weak and ineffective (10:2-3), the prophet boldly and creatively constructed the parameters of a new Israel, which he was certain would come about by the power of God. Zechariah's optimistic assessment of the future for the restored house of Judah and house of Joseph was rooted in the assurance that YHWH will bring the exiles back to their homeland (just as God had delivered their ancestors from Egypt) and empowered them to march in YHWH's name once again (10:12).

A critical reading with a feminist lens of biblical texts like Zechariah 10 challenges readers today to question how depicting the people of Yehud as "warriors in battle" (v. 5) can restore wholeness to communities of men, women, and children that have been torn apart by war.[19] It is also challenging to imagine how metaphors of a God that dominates the forces of nature can help readers today to rethink and reject extractive and exploitative practices that deplete natural resources, exacerbate climate change, and push Earth's ecosystems to the brink of disaster. In the context of the early Persian period in Yehud, the message of Zechariah 10 gave hope to the people of Yehud that, after many years marked by destruction, devastation, and dispersal, the descendants of the exiles from both the house of Judah and the house of Joseph would return to the land of Israel and flourish there. While appreciating the value of that message for Zechariah's earliest readers/hearers, audiences today must develop different visions for their future that call for healing for all people—a vision based on justice and compassion.

19. By way of illustration, "The UN estimates that there are now 281 million international migrants worldwide, or about 4 out of every 100 people. This is according to newly released data from the UN Department of Economic and Social Affairs (DESA), in its first major update to the dataset since the onset of the COVID-19 pandemic." This same UN report notes that about 48 percent of international migrants worldwide in 2020 were women and children, with a slightly higher percentage among those who migrated to Europe, North America, and Oceania. See IOM UN Migration, "COVID-19 Analytical Snapshot #64: Impact on International Migrant Numbers," January 18, 2021, https://www.iom.int/sites/g/files/tmzbdl486/files/documents/covid-19_analytical_snapshot_64_international_migrants.pdf.

Zechariah 11:1-17

When Leadership Fails

The transition from chapter 10 to chapter 11 is abrupt, as the subject changes from the restored Israel as it should be to the politically, socially, and economically struggling Yehud as it still is. The mood of the text shifts from hopeful anticipation to distressful gloom. In verses 1-3, the prophet suggests that the return of the house of Joseph and the house of Judah will not occur without problems. This does not mean that the restoration will not take place, but it does hint at the challenges that the Jews arriving from Babylon to Yehud will face when they encounter the people already living in the land. In verses 4-17, the prophet offers his hearers/readers another dose of reality as he turns to issues within the Jewish community that prevent the restoration from proceeding as envisioned in chapters 9–10. Also, the prophet seeks to undercut any false sense of security that people may have based on the promises found in earlier prophetic material, such as Isaiah 40–55.[1] The text focuses on the leadership, the economy, and the social elite. References to "shepherds" as a metaphor for Yehud's failed leadership link verses 1-3 and 4-17, as the prophet calls attention to the extended hardship that the people will endure because of their corrupt and worthless "shepherds."

---

1. Robert L. Foster, "Shepherds, Sticks, and Social Destabilization: A Fresh Look at Zechariah 11:4-17," *JBL* 126 (2007): 736.

Nature Suffers (11:1-3)

The first three verses of chapter 11 are connected to the closing section of chapter 10 by references to Lebanon (10:10; 11:1) and to the impact that Jews immigrating from Babylon will have on the population and the ecology of the region. Some of Lebanon's famed cypress and cedar trees (Ezek 31:3) will have to come down to make way for the farms that the newcomers will set up. Lebanon's cedars and oaks will join shepherds and lions in lamentation over the impending changes in the region's environment. Adding their voice to the lamentation are the "oaks of Bashan" (v. 2). Located east of the Sea of Galilee and north of Gilead, Bashan was a hilly region blessed with soil that was enriched by decomposed basalt, a volcanic rock rich in minerals.[2] This fertile soil supported flora like the trees of Bashan's forests (see also Isa 2:13; Ezek 27:6) and cultivated crops like cereal grains, olive trees, and grape vines (see Deut 32:14; Jer 50:19). In addition to the loss of its trees, Bashan's pasture lands whose nutritious grasses nourished sheep, goats, and cattle will be ruined, leading shepherds and herders to join in the lament. Even the young lions will bewail the loss of the undergrowth, trees, and thickets along the shore of the Jordan River (v. 3). This area had provided natural cover enabling lions to ambush their prey. It also was a good place to hide and rest. Verbs derived from שׁדד (destroy) appear three times in verses 1-3, underscoring the environmental devastation that would occur in Lebanon, Bashan, and the banks of the Jordan.

Although Bashan was only lightly populated, an increase in population would have disrupted the ecological balance in the region. Woodlands would disappear, grazing lands would diminish, and wildlife would suffer from loss of habitat.[3] Lebanon and Bashan could absorb a new population only at the cost of their fragile environments, leading to serious problems for their human populace. In sum, what the Jewish population arriving from Babylon would experience as redemption, the indigenous population of Lebanon and Bashan would regard as devastation. Most of Zechariah's intended audience were farmers or shepherds. They were aware of the effects on nature that a new human population

---

2. Harold Liebowitz and Robert L. Folk, "Archeological Geology of Tel Yin'am, Galilee, Israel," *JFA* 7 (1980): 28–29.

3. Dianne Bergant has studied how prophetic literature, particularly the books of Zephaniah, Jeremiah, Joel, and Isaiah, envisions the eschatological moment of the Day of the Lord and how this moment impacts the natural sphere. See her *The Earth Is the Lord's: The Bible, Ecology, and Worship*, AELS (Collegeville, MN: Liturgical Press, 1998).

Zech 11:1-3

¹Open your doors, O Lebanon,
  so that fire may devour your
      cedars!
²Wail, O cypress, for the cedar has
      fallen,
  for the glorious trees are ruined!
Wail, oaks of Bashan,

for the thick forest has been
      felled!
³Listen, the wail of the shepherds,
  for their glory is despoiled!
Listen, the roar of the lions,
  for the thickets of the Jordan are
      destroyed!

would have on the environment. The prophet gives voice to Bashan's trees, grasslands, and animals as they lament their losses. Concern for the environment is not a modern phenomenon.

The People Suffer (11:4-17)

Though some of the details are difficult to interpret, the basic thrust of the final verses of Zechariah 11 is clear enough—and it is not good news for Yehud's leaders.[4] Shifting abruptly from poetry to prose, the text reports that God is calling the prophet to take on the role of "shepherd" by joining the corrupt leadership class within the Jewish community (v. 4). In fulfilling his mission, the prophet deposes three other shepherds, but still, there is tension between the prophet/shepherd and the people/sheep. The prophet/shepherd performs a sign-act by breaking a staff. This prophetic sign-act serves to symbolize the annulment the covenant God made with the בני ישראל ("the children of Israel," v. 10). The prophet then accepts payment for his service, but, at God's command, he throws the coins into the temple treasury.[5] He then breaks a second

---

4. Commentators cite with approval S. R. Driver's assertion that Zech 11:4-17 is the most enigmatic passage in the Old Testament. See his *The Minor Prophets: Nahum, Habbakkuk, Zephaniah, Haggai, Zechariah, Malachi* (Edinburgh: T. C. and E. J. Jack, 1906), 23.

5. The word "treasury" results from emending MT's היוצר to read האוצר. Charles Cutler Torrey has shown that such an emendation is unnecessary. היוצר is a participle from יצר, which means "to fashion in a mold." היוצר was a temple official who melted down offerings from silver into bars for storage. See his "The Foundry of the Second Temple at Jerusalem," *JBL* 55 (1936): 250–58. See also Joachim Schaper, "The Jerusalem Temple as an Instrument of the Achaemenid Fiscal Administration," *VT* 45 (1995): 530–31. The LXX has χωνευτήριον ("melting furnace"), which suggests that the Hebrew text did refer to this temple official.

Zech 11:4-17

[4]"Thus says the LORD my God: Be a shepherd of the flock doomed to slaughter. [5]Those who buy them kill them and go unpunished, and those who sell them say, 'Blessed be the LORD, for I have become rich,' and their own shepherds have no pity on them. [6]For I will no longer have pity on the inhabitants of the earth, says the LORD. I will cause them, every one, to fall each into the hand of a neighbor and each into the hand of the king, and they shall devastate the earth, and I will deliver no one from their hand."

[7]So on behalf of the sheep merchants, I became the shepherd of the flock doomed to slaughter. I took two staffs; one I named Favor, the other I named Unity, and I tended the sheep. [8]In one month I disposed of the three shepherds, for I had become impatient with them, and they also detested me. [9]So I said, "I will not be your shepherd. What is to die, let it die; what is to be destroyed, let it be destroyed; and let those that are left devour the flesh of one another!" [10]I took my staff Favor and broke it, annulling the covenant that I had made with all the peoples. [11]So it was annulled on that day, and the sheep merchants who were watching me knew that it was the word of the LORD. [12]I then said to them, "If it seems

staff that symbolized the familial ties that bound Judah and Israel. God then commands the prophet to take up the implements used by worthless shepherds as a way of introducing the judgment oracle that condemns a leader guilty of abusing his power at the expense of the people/sheep (vv. 15-17). There have been some attempts at identifying the three shepherds of verse 8 with specific historical figures, though these attempts have proven fruitless.[6] It is likely that this passage simply was a denunciation of political corruption, human exploitation, and social injustice. Whatever the case, Zechariah lays the blame for Yehud's weak

---

6. For summary of proposed identifications and a critique of such efforts, see Paul L. Redditt, "The Two Shepherds in Zechariah 11:4-17," *CBQ* 55 (1993): 677–79; Carol L. Meyers and Eric M. Meyers, *Zechariah 9–14: A New Translation with Introduction and Commentary*, AB 25C (New York: Doubleday, 1993), 250, identify the shepherds as false prophets. Paul D. Hanson, *The Dawn of Apocalyptic: The Historical and Sociological Roots of Jewish Apocalyptic Eschatology*, rev. ed. (Philadelphia: Fortress, 1979), 345–46, identifies the shepherds with the Zadokite priestly hierocracy. Robert L. Foster asserts that the shepherds were the governors of Yehud. See his "Shepherds, Sticks, and Social Destabilization," 737–39, 743; Marvin A. Sweeney, *The Twelve Prophets*, Berit Olam (Collegeville, MN: Liturgical Press, 2000), 2:677, suggests that the three shepherds were the first three Persian kings: Cyrus, Cambyses, and Darius I; Mark J. Boda, *The Book of Zechariah*, NICOT (Grand Rapids: Eerdmans, 2016), 661, admits that the precise identification of the shepherds is not certain.

right to you, give me my wages, but if not, keep them." So they weighed out as my wages thirty shekels of silver. ¹³Then the LORD said to me, "Throw it into the treasury"—this lordly price at which I was valued by them. So I took the thirty shekels of silver and threw them into the treasury in the house of the LORD. ¹⁴Then I broke my second staff Unity, annulling the family ties between Judah and Israel.

¹⁵Then the LORD said to me: "Take once more the implements of a worth-

less shepherd. ¹⁶For I am now raising up in the land a shepherd who does not care for the perishing, or seek the wandering, or heal the maimed, or nourish the healthy, but devours the flesh of the fat ones, tearing off even their hoofs. ¹⁷Oh, my worthless shepherd,
who deserts the flock!
May the sword strike his arm
and his right eye!
Let his arm be completely withered,
his right eye utterly blinded!"

economy at the feet of the wealthy minority.[7] The prophet/shepherd is unwilling to be part of this system that feeds off ordinary folk to further enrich the wealthy.

The prophetic sign-acts described in Zechariah 11 are similar to Hosea's marriage to Gomer (Hos 1:2-11), Jeremiah's yoke (Jer 28), Isaiah's nakedness (Isa 20), and Ezekiel's sign-acts regarding Jerusalem (Ezek 4:1–5:12). The purpose of these actions is to dramatize and intensify the force of the prophet's message. In Zechariah 11:4-17, the prophet assumes the role of a "shepherd," i.e., a political leader. One of the principal duties of leadership is to oversee the economy to ensure the well-being of the people; however, Yehud's shepherds are corrupt. They buy and sell the people/sheep (11:5, 7), and they attempt to corrupt the prophet/shepherd to ensure that they continue profiting from exploiting the sheep (11:7, 12). The prophet/shepherd becomes a participant in an economic system of exploitation that treats people as commodities—a system in which a few get wealthy because of the labor of many.[8] In protest, the prophet/shepherd throws the silver coins that represented his wages into the temple treasury.

7. Foster, "Shepherds, Sticks, and Social Destabilization," 746, asserts that this exploitation, promoted by Yehud's political leadership, resulted in the enslavement of some Jews by wealthy Jewish merchants. Although this hypothesis may be accurate, it does go beyond what the text asserts.

8. Hag 1:5-11 also calls attention to the problems of Yehud's economy during the early Persian period.

TRANSLATION MATTERS

The phrase עֲנִיֵּי הַצֹּאן ("The poor of the flock") appears in the MT of Zechariah 11:7 and 11. Both the NRSVue and the NABRE accept an emendation (כְּנַעֲנֵיֵי הַצֹּאן) based on the LXX's εἰς τὴν Χαναανῖτιν and the context of the passage. The term כְּנַעֲנֵיֵי in the emended text literally means "Canaanites." Rendering this word as "merchants" makes sense in the context of chapter 11. Trade was a significant part of economic life in Canaan.

Because of the corrupt economic system that is the subject of 11:4-17 the promises made in chapters 9–10 are revoked, thus preventing the Judean restoration from proceeding. The breaking of the two staffs by the prophet/shepherd is the prophetic sign-act that effects that nullification. The first to be broken is the staff named "Favor" (נֹעַם). The Hebrew word carries with it the notion of something that is pleasant. The implication is that the staff refers to "the covenant [God] had made with all the peoples" (v. 10). The expression "all the peoples" (כָל־הָעַמִּים) as a reference to the peoples that made up Israel rather than foreign nations is unusual but plausible in this context.[9] The exiles of Israel were to return from all the nations where they were captive, but the breaking of the staff called "Favor" is the sign that God now dissociates God's self from the promise to bring back all the exiles because of the exploitation of the ordinary folk by the people of means in Yehud.

The prophet's breaking of the staff called "Unity" (הַחֹבְלִים) signals the end of any hope of reestablishing "family ties between Judah and Israel" (v. 14). Through this sign-act the prophet reverses the vision of Ezekiel 37:5-23, which describes the joining of the two sticks that represents the hoped-for unification of Judah and Israel. The people of these two regions believe in the one God. They both read the Torah and share the memory of their ancient ancestors. Until this point, the book of Zechariah anticipated a future in which Israel and Judah would be permanently joined. Unfortunately, old rivalries between the northern tribes and Judah did not dissolve but grew and eventually hardened into a permanent separation.

9. Meyers and Meyers, *Zechariah 9–14*, 269–71, assert that the בְּנֵי יִשְׂרָאֵל ("children of Israel") were not a homogenous group. Boda does not see the phrase as referring to Israel; see his *The Book of Zechariah*, 664–65. He sees it as referring to the nations who allowed the people of Israel to return to their homeland.

Prophets

The writings of the Holocaust survivor and scholar Elie Wiesel may help us to understand the contradictions that are brought to bear for this anonymous shepherd who, like other prophets before him, resisted the destiny that had been laid out for him. In an essay on the prophet Elijah, Wiesel writes that all prophets live an existence that does not exactly belong to them. Prophets intimately understand human nature and yet must remain separate from humanity. According to Wiesel,

> Who is a prophet? Someone who is searching—someone who is being sought. Someone who listens—and who is listened to. Someone who sees people as they are, and as they ought to be. Someone who reflects his time, yet lives outside time. A prophet is forever awake, forever alert; he is never indifferent, least of all to injustice, be it human or divine, whenever or wherever it may be found. God's messenger to man, he somehow becomes man's messenger to God. Restless, disquieting, he is forever waiting for a signal, a summons. Asleep, he hears voices and follows visions; his dreams do not belong to him. Often persecuted, always in anguish, he is alone—even when addressing crowds, when conversing with God or himself, when describing the future or evoking the past.
>
> There is sometimes a theatrical aspect to him; he seems to recite lines written by someone else. And yet, in order for him to be a prophet, he must descend into the very depths of his being. In order for him to be inhabited or penetrated—or invaded—by God, he must be truly, authentically, himself.
>
> Hence, a prophet's tragic dimension: having attained the highest degree of self-realization, he gives himself to God. The more he exists, the more he belongs to God, who speaks through his voice and uses him as a link, a bridge, an instrument. The prophet is at once an irritant and a simplifier. What others will think or learn the prophet already knows; he is the first to know. He is God's sounding board. But, at times, he is the last to know.[10]

10. Elie Wiesel, *Five Biblical Portraits* (Notre Dame, IN: University of Notre Dame Press, 1981), 38–39. Although Wiesel has male prophets in mind, there are several female prophets mentioned in the Old Testament who also show these same qualities: Miriam (Exod 15:20), Deborah (Judg 4:4), Huldah (2 Kgs 22:14; 2 Chr 34:22), the unnamed mother of Isaiah's child (Isa 8:3), Noadiah (Neh 6:14), and unnamed

This portion of Zechariah has significant connections to several other ancient texts. First, Zechariah 10–11 shares motifs with Micah 5. It is likely that the writer(s) of Zechariah 10–11 knew Micah 5, or at least that these texts reflected similar social and religious settings. Micah 5:5 asserts that God will bring against the Assyrians "seven shepherds and eight rulers." These shepherds will rule by the sword and defeat any Assyrian army that threatens the kingdom of Judah. The image of a shepherd holding a sword is incongruous with other depictions of shepherds whose weapons are staffs and slings in the defense of their flocks from predators. The image of a sword-wielding "shepherd" is consistent with the use of shepherd as a metaphor for king, and it is likely that that usage is reflected in Micah 5 and Zechariah 10–11.

Second, an allusion to Zechariah 11:12-13 appears in Matthew 26:15 and 27:3-10. The chief priests agreed to pay Judas thirty pieces of silver to betray Jesus into their hands.[11] Once Judas repented, realizing that he has betrayed "innocent blood," he threw the silver pieces into the temple (Matt 27:5; see Zech 11:13). Matthew interprets the action of the chief priests, who use the silver pieces to buy a place to bury foreigners, as the fulfillment of prophecy.[12]

Third, a rabbinic interpretation viewed Zechariah 11:15-17 as a prediction of the disastrous Second Revolt against Rome, also known as the Bar Kokhba Revolt (132–136 CE). Shimon bar Kokhba led an armed rebellion against Rome in response to the plans of the emperor Hadrian to transform Jerusalem into a Roman city with a temple to Jupiter at the very place that the second temple stood. Some rabbis considered the revolt a serious mistake that cost thousands of Jewish lives in the quix-

---

daughters who prophesy (Joel 3:1-2; Ezek 13:17; 1 Chr 25:3-5); in the New Testament: Anna (Luke 2:36-38), Philip's four daughters (Acts 21:9), and unnamed Corinthian women (1 Cor 11:5).

11. The phrase "thirty pieces of silver" appears in "The Curse of Agade," a Sumerian text from the third millennium BCE (*ANET*, 648, line 104). There the amount is considered a sign of contempt. See Erica Reiner, "Thirty Pieces of Silver," in *Essays in Memory of E. A. Speiser*, ed. W. W. Hallo, AOS 53 (New Haven: American Oriental Society, 1968), 186–90.

12. Matthew's citation is a combination of various prophetic verses, which explains why some ancient versions of this passage say that this act fulfilled the words of Jeremiah, while others state that it fulfilled the words of Zechariah or Isaiah. The connection of Judas's suicide to Zech 11:12-13 would have suggested to early Christians that the leaders who took Judas's money were the very ones who were condemned by the prophetic words of Zechariah.

otic attempt to end Roman rule.[13] They read Zechariah's lament—"Oh, my worthless shepherd, who deserts the flock!"—as a condemnation of Simon bar Kokhba.

Both Christian and Jewish traditions, then, resonate with the prophet's critique of leaders who were not concerned with the well-being of their people. In both traditions, the leaders were Jewish. Whereas the Jewish tradition uses Zechariah's prophecy as a tool to reflect on leadership, some Christian interpreters have used Zechariah's prophecy to advance anti-Judaism by claiming that Jewish leaders were responsible for the death of Jesus.

Conclusion

Zechariah 11 demonstrates that circumstances in Yehud were difficult at the beginning of the Persian period. The Jewish community was subject to foreign rule. Although that rule was benevolent compared to that of the Assyrians and Babylonians, foreign occupation was, nonetheless, a heavy strain on Yehud's struggling economy. But the villains of 11:4-17 are not foreigners but wealthy and powerful members of the Jewish community. They were oppressive and corrupted the community's leaders, e.g., the three shepherds of verse 8 who were responsible for maintaining the people's well-being but who failed miserably. The situation is so bad that the prophet/shepherd can do nothing but give up (v. 9). He would no longer be a part of a corrupt social, political, and economic system. He acted out his resolve by returning his wages. Through prophetic signs, he proclaimed the nullification of the covenant made with the Judeans in Babylon to reunite the houses of Joseph and Judah.

Throughout the biblical period, communities living in the southern Levant experienced social upheaval, political oppression, and economic hardship at the hands of empires asserting hegemony across the region. Imperial powers—Egypt, Assyria, Babylonia, Persia, Greece, and Rome—had a profound effect on the region's economy, culture, and way of life. Populations of women and men, elders and children, were destroyed, displaced, and dispersed by warring armies fighting for political and

---

13. Y. Tanit 4:5. Elsewhere in the Jerusalem Talmud, Zechariah's reference to the thirty shekels of silver is interpreted allegorically as the thirty commandments that gentiles are to observe or, alternately, as the thirty righteous people without whom the world cannot survive (see Y. 'Abod. Zar. 2:1). Both of these interpretations have a universalist tone.

economic gain. As empires rose and fell, people were on the move to escape political, economic, and religious oppression. Compounding this oppression by foreigners was a social and economic system that allowed people of means to exploit those members of the Jewish community without power. The community's leadership, which was exclusively male, became a tool in the hands of the wealthy in maintaining a social, political, and economic system of corruption and exploitation.

Situations like those described in Zechariah 11 continue to occur. Because of European antisemitism, the Zionist movement encouraged immigration into Palestine, and the region had to absorb a new population. Some of those immigrants settled in existing towns and worked as artisans or in the trades, while others established agricultural settlements (*kibbutzim*).[14] Over time, tensions arose between the Arab population, which sought to maintain the Arab character of the region, and the Zionist settlers who wanted to establish a Jewish homeland there. With the establishment of the state of Israel in 1948, the entry of an increasing number of Jewish immigrants from around the world has accelerated, causing the displacement of large segments of the region's Arab population, leading to several wars and continuing civil unrest. Like the cedars of Lebanon and the oaks of Bashan (Zech 11:2), the Arabs of Palestine lamented the arrival of Jewish immigrants who are returning to what these immigrants regarded as their ancestral homeland. In this situation, leadership is critically important. There is a need for Israeli and Palestinian leaders who are not afraid to look for ways to achieve peace among all the people of the region.

Human populations are not the only ones to suffer from the impact of wars, political conflicts, forced migrations, and economic policies that are exploitative. Nature suffers as land is deforested and animals' habitats are destroyed. Even more than at the time when Zechariah 11 was written, deforestation has reached a critical level because of the growth of the human population and dramatic increases in destructive human

---

14. These agricultural settlements drained swamps, planted trees, and took other measures to improve the ecological balance of the region to counter the neglect during the period of Ottoman rule. Still, the state of Israel, the Hashemite Kingdom of Jordan, and the Palestinian National Authority have significant environmental issues that need to be addressed in the peace process. For a discussion of "environmental peacemaking" issues in the region, see Marina Djernaes, Teis Jorgensen, and Elizabeth Koch-Ya'ari, "Evaluation of Environmental Peacemaking Intervention Strategies in Jordan-Palestine-Israel," *Journal of Peacebuilding & Development* 10 (2015): 74–80.

activity. Forests in South America, Africa, and Southeast Asia are rapidly disappearing as trees are cut down for timber and undergrowth is burned to clear the forest floor for industrial-scale agriculture. With the loss of woodlands, hundreds of plant and animal species are being pushed toward extinction. The twentieth century alone witnessed the loss of 3.9 million square miles—roughly the equivalent of the size of Europe—of forest lands with the concomitant loss of regional biodiversity. [15]

Also, deforestation is contributing to an alarming increase in greenhouse gas levels, leading to worldwide climate change. The violence that these destructive processes inflict on the earth and nonhuman species is matched by the injustice it causes for the world's most vulnerable human populations. Those who use the smallest portion of the earth's resources suffer the most devastating impacts of environmental degradation and climate change, driven by the activity of the wealthiest and most powerful people in developed countries.[16]

While the negative social and environmental impacts of Persian hegemony are implicit throughout Zechariah 11, the chapter's primary focus is not on foreign occupation but on domestic corruption. Terms describing the actions of the shepherd/leaders against the sheep/people are often associated either with war or with commerce (11:6-7),[17] suggesting a kind of "war on the poor" that usually results when corrupt leaders use their power to protect the interests of a wealthy minority. Not only do Yehud's own leaders exploit and abuse the community in their care, but they claim that the economic gain because of their evil deeds is a sign of God's blessing (v. 5). God calls the prophet to "be a shepherd of the flock doomed to slaughter" (v. 4). The act of breaking the staffs reflects the severed relationships—covenantal "Favor" with God and "Unity" with other Israelites—that patriarchal domination and exploitation inevitably produce. The payment and rejection of wages for participating in that corrupt system (vv. 12-13) is an episode that later generations of Jewish and Christian interpreters associate with leaders who betray God's covenantal bond.

---

15. Hannah Ritchie, Fiona Spooner, and Max Roser, "Forests and Deforestation," OurWorldInData.org (2021), https://ourworldindata.org/forests-and-deforestation.

16. Sallie McFague, *The Body of God: An Ecological Theology* (Minneapolis: Fortress, 1993), 4.

17. Commercial terms are "buy" and "sell" (vv. 7, 11), "wages," "shekels," "silver," and "treasury" (vv. 12-13); martial terms include "ruined" (v. 2), "despoiled" and "destroyed" (v. 9), "devastate" (v. 6), "sword" (v. 17).

It is a tragic reality that, when those entrusted to lead fail to carry out their responsibilities with integrity and compassion, the most vulnerable members of society—women and children and all who are systemically denied access to resources they need to thrive—suffer the most injurious consequences. In Zechariah 11, "the flock doomed to slaughter" is abandoned to the power of "a worthless shepherd . . . who does not care for the perishing, . . . but devours the flesh of the fat ones" (vv. 15-16). The violent retribution that the prophet declares in the chapter's final verse reflects the desperation of a community in anguish. A desire for vengeance is a common and understandable response to such suffering, but vengeance rarely guarantees a lasting solution capable of transforming systems that are inherently unjust.

What is needed to transform those systems is a new understanding of God as calling not for revenge but for repair of the harm done to the flock facing dissolution. The prophet's message and the actions that symbolize it today would need not only to disrupt and destroy the broken systems but to design and construct new ones that ensure equity, well-being, and justice, especially for society's most vulnerable members.

A feminist reading of Zechariah 11 challenges people living in democratically structured societies today to use governmental processes to create just and equitable policies and systems that ensure the health and well-being of the people and natural environment where they live. This challenge must be met both by shepherd/leaders responsible for maintaining a sound government and a strong economy, and by the people/sheep who elect them.[18] Zechariah 11 can serve as a warning to those tempted to participate in systems that oppress and exploit, and as an invitation to build a society that maintains favor with God and unity with one another.

18. McFague, *The Body of God*, 174–78.

Zechariah 12:1-14

Women and the Survival of the Jewish Community

The word מַשָּׂא ("oracle," "burden") at the beginning of chapter 12 signals the beginning of a new section of the book of Zechariah.[1] Chapters 12–14 constitute the final section of the book. As is the case with the rest of the book, chapter 12 deals with the challenges the people of Yehud face as they try to reconstitute their political, economic, and religious lives in their ancestral homeland after the fall of the kingdom of Judah and the trauma of their forced migration to Babylon. First, they had to accomplish this reconstitution as a subject people. Yehud was a small province of the Persian Empire. Persian policy supported both the building of a temple in Jerusalem and a measure of self-rule for Yehud, but the province's struggling economy had to bear the burden of the taxes demanded by the empire. Yehud's neighbors in the Levant also sought to control the region's limited resources. In addition to the external forces, the Jewish community of Yehud had to deal with social instability that was a serious threat to the survival of that community.

---

1. The term מַשָּׂא also appears in Zech 9:1 and Mal 1:1. Carol L. Meyers and Eric M. Meyers (*Zechariah 9–14: A New Translation with Introduction and Commentary*, AB 25C [New York: Doubleday, 1993], 359) suggest that the recurrence of this word in these texts is the work of redactors to introduce subunits of the second half of the Haggai-Zechariah-Malachi collection of oracles.

In these difficult circumstances, the women of Yehud made significant contributions that ensured the survival of their community.

A phrase that offers a key to understanding the thrust of chapter 12 is ביום־ההוא ("on that day"), which appears six times in the chapter and eight more times in chapters 13–14.[2] This expression serves to identify these final chapters of Zechariah as describing an eschatological event, i.e., God's decisive intervention on behalf of Judah and Jerusalem that will involve judgment on the nations and redemption for the Jewish people. Locating the final restoration of Judah and Jerusalem at a non-specified point in the future indicates that the prophet did not regard the present as the likely setting for the triumph of divine justice. On the contrary, at the time when Zechariah 12 was being written, Persian domination showed no signs of waning, as the empire built fortresses throughout the Levant to guard against incursions into the region by the Greeks and Egyptians. The sight of these Persian fortresses being built in Yehud must have been an intimidating sight, reinforcing belief in the permanence of Persian hegemony and Yehud's economic, military, and political impotence.[3] Hope for divine intervention provided the only way for the people of Yehud to feel as if they had any control over their destiny. Zechariah then provides the people with an eschatological vision of God's victory over their enemies. YHWH alone was able to provide Judah and Jerusalem with a path to freedom and prosperity in the land promised to their ancestors.

Zechariah 12 focuses on God's decisive intervention on behalf of Judah and Jerusalem that will enable the people of Yehud to chart their destiny by ending the threats posed by the nations arrayed against them. Speaking in first-person pronouns in 12:2-9, יהוה צבאות ("YHWH of armies" in v. 5) promises to transform Jerusalem into a powerful weapon ("a cup of reeling," v. 2, and "a heavy stone," v. 3) with which YHWH will bring judgment and destruction to "all the surrounding peoples" (v. 6), making "the house of David . . . like God, like the angel of YHWH, at the . . . head [of the inhabitants of Jerusalem]" (v. 8). The first-person address continues in 12:10-14, as YHWH promises to "pour out a spirit of compassion and supplication on the house of David and the inhabitants of Jerusalem" following the tragic death of "one whom they have

---

2. 12:3, 4, 6, 8, 9, 11; 13:1; 14:4, 6, 8, 9, 13, 20, 21.

3. According to Meyers and Meyers (*Zechariah 9–14*, 353), Yehud's territory covered only 660 square miles, with Jerusalem's area limited to just five acres at the beginning of the Persian period, and the city's population was just four hundred people. The people of Yehud simply lacked the resources to free themselves from Persian control.

pierced" (v. 10), perhaps a prominent member of Jerusalem's ruling class. The chapter's closing verses detail the significant role women had in the community's rituals of mourning. This chapter's message, however, presents challenges for feminist readers today, who view male images like יהוה צבאות and dynamics of patriarchal domination like those alluded to in Zechariah 12 as among the factors that perpetuate the kind of social instability and economic hardship that YHWH is to end "on that day."

Israel's Victory *on That Day* (12:1-9)

The opening line of chapter 12 establishes the prophet's authenticity and authority by identifying its משא ("oracle") as דבר־יהוה ("the word of YHWH") and נאם־יהוה ("an oracle of YHWH"). This assertion stands in contrast with the ridicule of divination expressed in 10:2. It is further re-inforced by the description of YHWH as the creator of the heavens, earth, and human beings in 12:1.[4] Christine Mitchell argues that Zechariah adopts this formula as an allusion to a Persian creation ritual text that affirms that the king rules by divine designation and reframes it as an affirmation of the divine origin of the prophet's message.[5] There is, however, a noticeable difference between the ideology behind the Persian creation formula and its reformulation in Zechariah. Whereas Persian creation theology assumed that the order established by the Zoroastrian deity Ahura Mazda was permanent—thus implying that Persian hegemony over the nations of the world would likewise be permanent—Zechariah 12:1-9 speaks of YHWH as disrupting Persia's dominance in the world for the sake of Judah and Jerusalem.[6]

---

4. Although similar language is used in other biblical texts, the only other occurrence of the sequence of heaven-earth-humanity is in Isa 42:5-6.

5. Christine Mitchell, "A Note on the Creation Formula in Zechariah 12:1-8; Isaiah 42:5-6; and Old Persian Inscriptions," *JBL* 133 (2014): 305–8. Meyers and Meyers, *Zechariah 9–14*, 29, claim that Zech 12:1 alludes to the order of creation found in Gen 2; Julia O'Brien sees the vocabulary of Zech 12:1 as like that of Gen 2, and she sees the Zechariah text as an oracle against Babylon. See her *Nahum, Habakkuk, Zephaniah, Haggai, Zechariah, Malachi*, ATOC (Nashville: Abingdon, 2004), 258.

6. Meyers and Meyers, *Zechariah 9–14*, 310, state that this eschatological vision of Yehud's future includes the restoration of the Davidic dynasty; Mark J. Boda, *The Book of Zechariah*, NICOT (Grand Rapids: Eerdmans, 2016), 692n30, cites their opinion with approval. Verses 1-6 make no mention of the Davidic dynasty; David and his house are first mentioned in v. 8. If the intent was to support the restoration of Judah's native dynasty, such an omission is mystifying.

Zech 12:1-9

¹An Oracle.

The word of the Lord concerning Israel: Thus says the Lord, who stretched out the heavens and founded the earth and formed the human spirit within: ²See, I am about to make Jerusalem a cup of reeling for all the surrounding peoples; it will be against Judah also in the siege against Jerusalem. ³On that day I will make Jerusalem a heavy stone for all the peoples; all who lift it shall grievously hurt themselves. And all the nations of the earth shall come together against it. ⁴On that day, says the Lord, I will strike every horse with panic and its rider with madness. But on the house of Judah I will keep a watchful eye, when I strike every horse of the peoples with blindness. ⁵Then the clans of Judah shall say to themselves, "The inhabitants of Jeru-salem have strength through the Lord of hosts, their God."

⁶On that day I will make the clans of Judah like a blazing pot on a pile of wood, like a flaming torch among sheaves, and they shall devour to the right and to the left all the surrounding peoples, while Jerusalem shall again be inhabited in its place, in Jerusalem. ⁷And the Lord will save the tents of Judah first, that the glory of the house of David and the glory of the inhabitants of Jerusalem may not be exalted over that of Judah. ⁸On that day the Lord will shield the inhabitants of Jerusalem so that the feeblest among them on that day shall be like David, and the house of David shall be like God, like the angel of the Lord, at their head. ⁹And on that day I will seek to destroy all the nations that come against Jerusalem.

The mention of "Israel" instead of Judah in verse 1 seems anomalous since the oracle concerns the future of Judah and Jerusalem alone. Recall that Zechariah 9–10 refers to the northern tribes as "Ephraim" (9:10, 13; 10:7) or "the house of Joseph" (10:6) rather than as Israel. In addition, the prophet already announced that he had broken a shepherd's staff marked "Unity" (11:14). This prophetic action marked the end of the hopes for unification of the house of Joseph and house of Judah into a single community. Referring to the recipient of the oracle in 12:1 as "Is-rael" suggests that by the time chapter 12 was written, those who were living in Yehud considered themselves to be *the* authentic Israel and those who were living in Samaria were among its enemies.[7] Although the Chronicler (e.g., 2 Chr 30:1; 35:16-20) and Zechariah 9–10 wished

---

7. 2 Kgs 17:29 is the only place in the Hebrew Bible that refers to these people as השמרנים ("Samaritans," i.e., "the people of Samaria"), a geographical designation. The northerners came to call themselves שמרים ("the Observant").

to include the people living in Samaria among the people of Israel, the Deuteronomistic tradition portrayed these people as idolaters who were descendants of intermarriage with gentiles and not authentic Israelites (2 Kgs 17:24-34).[8] The usage in Zechariah 12:1-14 may reflect the growing importance of Deuteronomic perspectives.

TRANSLATION MATTERS

The rendering of verse 2 in the NRSVue suggests that God's judgment will be directed toward Judah and Jerusalem instead of toward their enemies. Carol Meyers and Eric Meyers remark that some translators and commentators offer translations of verse 2 that do not agree with the thrust of the rest of the passage.[9] The awkward syntax of the Hebrew is the problem, offering a challenge to any translator who wishes to offer a literal translation of the Hebrew text. The NABRE makes the sense of this verse clearer while preserving its connection with the rest of chapter 12: "See, I will make Jerusalem a cup of reeling for all peoples round about. Judah will be besieged, even Jerusalem."

In speaking of God's eschatological victory over Jerusalem's enemies, the prophet employs new metaphors for Jerusalem and its people. Unlike feminine metaphors such as "daughter Zion" or "daughter Jerusalem," which appear in 2:10 and 9:9, Zechariah 12 refers to Jerusalem as סַף־רַעַל

---

8. Numbering the people of Samaria among the enemies of true Israel is consistent with the Deuteronomic portrait of the north as idolaters who were descendants of intermarriage with gentiles (2 Kgs 17:24-34). According to Ezra 4:1–24, Zerubbabel and the "heads of the families in Israel" rebuffed the people from the north who wished to join them in rebuilding the temple of Jerusalem. This, in turn, led the northerners to oppose the rebuilding project; however, neither Haggai nor Zechariah mention any opposition from the northerners. The narrative in Ezra 4 likely reflects the tensions between the Jews and the Samaritans when Nehemiah was governor of Yehud (465–424 BCE). From that time on, relations between the Jews and the Samaritans were acrimonious, and the possibility of reaching even a semblance of unity became practically nonexistent. The Samaritans built their own temple on Mount Gerizim. The Hasmonean king John Hyrcanus had that temple destroyed in 128 BCE, making the breach between Jew and Samaritan irreparable. The Gospel of John recounts a conversation between Jesus and an unnamed Samaritan woman. The conversation alludes to the animosity between Jews and Samaritans and their dispute regarding the proper place for worship (John 4:1-42).
9. Meyers and Meyers, *Zechariah 9–14*, 316.

("a cup of reeling," v. 2) and אבן מעמסה ("a heavy rock," v. 3), two images that carry martial implications. The "reeling cup" metaphor conjures up images of drunken soldiers unfit for military service; a similar image is found in Isaiah 51:17 and Jeremiah 25:15-29, although in those texts, Judah and Jerusalem are the ones who must drink from a "cup of judgment." Describing Jerusalem as a "heavy rock" implies that enemy soldiers will not be able to defeat the holy city as a military objective; their attempt to take Jerusalem will render them unable to continue the siege of the city (v. 3b). As Julia O'Brien points out, the martial connotations of these images suggest that they function as masculine metaphors because warfare is predominantly associated with men in biblical texts.[10] Furthermore, it is significant that, in switching from feminine to masculine metaphors, Zechariah also reverses Jerusalem's role, recasting the city as an active agent rather than a passive recipient of divine favor. God spoken of as יהוה צבאות also reinforces this masculine imagery. God, who once made Judah drink from the cup of judgment, now requires the nations to drink from that cup as they find Jerusalem a military objective that they will fail to take.[11]

Zechariah's continued reference to warfare reflects the likelihood that the people to whom the prophet preached were war-weary and discouraged. The people of Yehud found themselves at the crossroads of the ancient Near East. They witnessed caravans loaded with every sort of commercial goods, from perfumes and spices to ceramic wares and fine woven cloths, passing through the southern Levant on its trade routes. But armies also passed along these same highways, sent by monarchs who wished to control this commercial activity and the natural resources in the region. The two Israelite kingdoms collapsed under the weight of international rivalries and the miscalculations of their ruling elites. Ordinary folk had to pay the price of these machinations for which they had no responsibility. The people of Yehud certainly welcomed the news that God was going to reverse their fortunes, allowing them to see the final and decisive victory over the forces that prevented them from living at peace in their ancestral homeland.

10. Julia M. O'Brien, "Zechariah," in *Women's Bible Commentary*, ed. Carol A. Newsom, Sharon H. Ringe, and Jacqueline E. Lapsley, 3rd ed. (Louisville: Westminster John Knox, 2012), 346–49.

11. Paul Lamarche, *Zacharie IX–XIV: Structure Littéraire et Messianisme* (Paris: Libraire Lecoffre, J. Gabalda et Compagnie, 1961), 135–36.

The Rehabilitation of the House of David (12:10-14)

The message of comfort for the people of Yehud continues in the closing section of Zechariah 12. At verse 10, the focus shifts abruptly from the announcement of judgment against the nations, and final victory for the people of Judah and Jerusalem (12:1-9), to a promise of "a spirit of compassion and supplication on the house of David and the inhabitants of Jerusalem" in view of the tragic loss experienced by the community (12:10-14). Verse 10 is unclear about details of that loss. It might have involved the murder of an unnamed (but apparently prominent) member of the community—perhaps even a member of the house of David—killed during some internal power struggle. In this case, the death of a member of the former royal family of the kingdom of Judah could easily have been experienced as the loss of "an only child . . . [or] a firstborn" (v. 10). Some in Yehud believed that this "only child" was destined to reverse the fortunes of the house of David. Another possibility is that "the one whom they have pierced" may have referred to the Jewish community, suffering from a leadership crisis resulting in social instability and economic distress. In this case, the "spirit of compassion and supplication" may be understood as bringing about a change in the way members of the community, especially its leaders, would treat each other.[12]

Although the oracle in verses 1-6 emphasizes the priority of divine activity in the victory over the enemies of Jerusalem, the people of Yehud are more than passive witnesses of God's actions on their behalf. Verses 7-11 speak of God's empowerment of "the tents of Judah," "the house of David," and "the inhabitants of Jerusalem." All will have a role to play in the victory over "the nations that come against Jerusalem." The people of Yehud will be the instruments of their own liberation from foreign domination. The reference to the house of David is problematic since the former royal family apparently had no official role in the political organization of the Jewish community of Yehud, though individual members of the old royal house may have served as governors. The Persians granted that community some measure of self-rule, but

---

12. Zech 12 does not provide details of the circumstances alluded to in the text, but texts such as Isa 58:1-14 suggest that the actions of Judah's rulers that were condemned by the preexilic prophets were being repeated by later generations in the postexilic period. In Jewish tradition, public regret and mourning over a person (particularly a leader) who has been killed is followed by a period of public reconciliation, thus organizing a move toward repairing broken relationships and a framework of functional leadership to ensure the future of the community.

¹⁰And I will pour out a spirit of compassion and supplication on the house of David and the inhabitants of Jerusalem so that, when they look on the one whom they have pierced, they shall mourn for him as one mourns for an only child and weep bitterly over him as one weeps over a firstborn. ¹¹On that day the mourning in Jerusalem will be as great as the mourning for Hadadrimmon in the plain of Megiddo. ¹²The land shall mourn, each family by itself; the family of the house of David by itself and their wives by themselves; the family of the house of Nathan by itself and their wives by themselves; ¹³the family of the house of Levi by itself and their wives by themselves; the family of the Shimeites by itself and their wives by themselves; ¹⁴and all the families that are left, each by itself and their wives by themselves.

the community's internal affairs were managed by the high priest and the governor. This system worked well enough to see the construction of the second temple to its completion. Though the efforts of the high priest and governor did help the community preserve its religious and ethnic identity in the early postexilic period, there was no possibility of their leading any formal resistance to Persian rule. On the contrary, they helped facilitate the collection of taxes demanded by the Persians.

This does not mean that the "house of David" was completely eclipsed. Biblical tradition claims that in the early years of Persian rule, the governor was a member of the "house of David": Sheshbazzar (Ezra 1:8; 5:15),[13] Zerubbabel (1 Chr 3:16-19; Hag 1:1; 2:21), and possibly Elnathan. This Elnathan is unattested in the Bible. His name appears on bulla found in excavations near Jerusalem. Another bulla mentions Shelomith, his אמה ("servant"). Shelomith may have been a woman of influence, serving as Elnathan's administrative assistant. First Chronicles 3:19 identifies Shelomith as a daughter of Zerubbabel. Eric Meyers claims that Elnathan married Shelomith and so married into the Davidic family.[14] Sometime

13. There is no text that explicitly identifies Sheshbazzar as a Davidide, though Ezra 1:8 refers to him as הנשיא ליהודה ("the prince of Judah"). This title does not necessarily indicate that Sheshbazzar was of royal lineage. He may be the Shenazzar mentioned in 1 Chr 3:18 as Zerubbabel's uncle. If so, Sheshbazzar would be a member of the house of David.

14. See his "The Shelomith Seal and Aspects of the Judean Restoration: Some Additional Considerations," *Eretz Israel* 18 (1985): 33–38. See also Tamara Cohn Eskenazi, "Out from the Shadows: Biblical Women in the Postexilic Era," *JSOT* 54 (1992): 38–39.

in the early fifth century and without any explanation, the participation of a member of the Davidic family in the formal leadership of the Jewish community in Yehud came to an end. The attention given to "the house of David" in Zechariah 12 indicates that there were those in Yehud who believed that the future of the Jewish community and of Jerusalem was bound up with the fortunes of "the house of David." This notion eventually became the core belief of messianism.[15]

TRANSLATION MATTERS

Zechariah 12:10 is a particularly enigmatic verse in a book with many such verses. In fact, the rabbis used it as a paradigm for a biblical verse or passage that cannot be interpreted without supplemental tradition (b. Meg. 3). Identifying the victim of the stabbing mentioned in verse 10 is complicated by the difficult syntax of the Hebrew clause that reads: והביטו אלי את אשר־דקר. Both the NRSVue ("when they look on the one whom they have pierced") and the NABRE ("so that when they look on him whom they have thrust through") ignore the Hebrew term אלי ("to me" or "at me"), which is the crux of the translation issue. The presence of אלי is supported by practically all ancient versions, so it cannot be ignored. A common emendation is to change אלי to אלו ("to him" or "at him"). Such an emendation is reasonable since the Hebrew *yod* (י) and *waw* (ו) are easily confused by copyists.[16] Carol Meyers and Eric Meyers translate this clause as "so that they will look to me concerning the one they have stabbed."[17] This translation accounts for אלי but does not identify the victim of the stabbing, which leaves the enigmatic character of the verse unresolved.

The reason for the end of Davidic leadership of the postexilic Jewish community is not known for certain. The cryptic reference in 12:10 to the murder of an unnamed individual has led to speculation that the victim was killed during some internal power struggle that the house of David lost, thus ending the role of the dynasty in Yehud's political life. There is no evidence to support this. The assassination of Gedaliah (2 Kgs 25:22-26), however, may have inspired the imagery in 12:10. It is likely that the Persians thought better of relying on leadership exercised by a

15. The Synoptic Gospels apply the title "Son of David" to Jesus in their confession of Jesus as the Messiah sixteen times.

16. John 19:37 supports reading the third person as it sees the piercing of Jesus's side as a fulfillment of Zech 12:10.

17. Meyers and Meyers, *Zechariah 9–14*, 8.

member of the former royal family of Judah. The presence of a Davidide at the center of political activity in Judah could keep alive the hope for a restoration of the kingdom of Judah and the Davidic dynasty. This would only complicate matters for the Persians. The appointment of Nehemiah as governor in 445 BCE demonstrates a change in the Persians' strategy for the administration of Yehud. Nehemiah had been a member of the court of Artaxerxes (Neh 2:1) so the Persians thought that they could rely on his loyalty in his administration of Yehud without the danger of encouraging hopes for the restoration of the Davidic dynasty and the kingdom of Judah.

Despite the greatly diminished role of the former royal house in the administration of Yehud, the eschatological vision of chapter 12 provided a role for the house of David. Still, the oracle's vision of the future is not circumscribed by Judah's past. The kingdom of Judah was a small, insignificant Iron Age Cisjordanian state. The Babylonian Empire ended its existence and incorporated its territory into the Babylonian provincial system. The Judahite monarchy failed to prevent the collapse of the state. Almost all of Judah's kings come under judgment in the books of Kings. The reference to "the tents of Judah" and "the inhabitants of Jerusalem" broadens the horizons of the Jewish people regarding the shape of their community. The experience of the early years of the Persian period showed that the community could reconstitute itself without the institution of the monarchy and the associated bureaucratic elites. The book of Zechariah offers support to the priestly leadership that developed in the Jewish community that was without a king. Still, the belief that God had promised an eternal dynasty for David (2 Sam 7:5-17; Pss 89:28-37; 132:11-12) was too strong to be completely ignored in any vision of Judah's future, but the restoration of the Davidic dynasty became an element of an unspecified future when Judah will have a dominant role among the nations of the world.

Although the oracle offers a vision of the community's future that presents Yehud not only as independent but also as powerful, it describes its present circumstances as troubling. The text calls attention to an act of violence perpetrated by "the house of David" and "the inhabitants of Jerusalem" (vv. 10-11). At the very least, this violence reflects the social instability of the Jewish community in Yehud. It is difficult to be more specific without engaging in speculation. The community was in uncharted territory. The Persians gave the Jewish community of Yehud a measure of autonomy, but without precedents to guide the restoration of community life, there were the inevitable conflicts over how that life should be structured. The supporters of the Davidic dynasty likely wanted to restore the old political system as much as possible. The priests likely sought to take advantage of the Persian policy that favored the reconstruction of the temple and the resumption of activities there by offering themselves to fill the leadership gap in the Jewish community. Prophetic circles likely called attention to social inequities as they opposed structures and policies that put the poor at a disadvantage.

Amid social instability, the women of the Jewish community provided a measure of stability that made possible the survival of the Jewish community in Yehud. The people of Yehud experienced a trauma that undermined their basic beliefs and destroyed the infrastructure that made their lives possible. Upon the return from exile, their first task was to restore that infrastructure. It was the work of women that made it possible for that task to go forward. Their principal contribution was food preparation, though they contributed to every stage of the reconstruction.[18] The importance of food preparation in an ancient subsistence economy is difficult for people in a modern technological society to appreciate. Carol Meyers, among others, has shown that women made it possible for an ancient society to survive. Her work has helped scholars to recognize that they need to move women's work from the periphery to the center in their reconstructions of life in the ancient world.[19] Related to their work in food preparation was the maintenance of the family's supply of grain. This was also woman's responsibility. Women also prepared clothing for the members of their household. The skills of spinning and weaving were essential for families of limited means. Women were also influential in religious and cultic matters. That is the reason marriage outside the Jewish community became forbidden. The religious leadership recognized how easy it was for a woman to redirect her husband's religious commitments. Women continued to exercise the prophetic charism in the postexilic period. Nehemiah lists Noadiah among the prophets who opposed him (Neh 6:14). This is evidence of the activity of women. Their role and status

18. Tamara Cohn Eskenazi describes these contributions as delineated in Ezra and Nehemiah. See her "Out from the Shadows," 34–42

19. E.g., see her "From Field Crops to Food: Attributing Gender and Meaning to Bread Production in Iron Age Israel," in *The Archaeology of Difference: Gender, Ethnicity, Class, and the "Other" in Antiquity: Studies in Honor of Eric M. Meyers*, ed. Douglas R. Edwards and C. Thomas McCollough, AASOR 60/61 (Boston: ASOR, 2007), 68–71. See also her *Rediscovering Eve: Ancient Israelite Women in Context* (Oxford: Oxford University Press, 1988), 126.

within the community was independent of genealogical descent, as was that of the priests. Although there was some conflict within the Jewish community over matters of leadership, it was the work of women that kept the Jewish community functioning to reconstruct Jewish life in the land of their ancestors. This activity was centered in the family circle for the most part and made an essential contribution to the sustainability of the Jewish community—especially in the early years of the Persian period when the economy of Yehud was struggling.

Verses 12-14 mention four families by name that take part in a ritual of communal mourning. It is possible that these families were among Yehud's ruling class, or perhaps these references were more symbolic than historical and their specific referents are unknown. The first family mentioned is "the house of David," presumably descendants of the royal family of the former kingdom of Judah, who may have enjoyed pride of place in postexilic Yehud. The second is "the house of Nathan." It is unlikely that this refers to descendants of the prophet Nathan, since prophets typically did not establish dynasties.[20] Carol Meyers and Eric Meyers point out that one of David's sons was named Nathan (see 2 Sam 5:14), suggesting that the "house of Nathan" may have represented a subsidiary branch of the royal family.[21] The third family mentioned, "the house of Levi," probably does not refer to descendants of the tribe of Levi specifically but perhaps was associated with the sacral leadership of the community. Similarly, the Shimeites could have been another group of community leaders connected with the cult (see Num 3:21), though it is impossible to be more specific since textual details are lacking. Regardless of who these "families" or dynasties were, the text envisions a situation in which the community of Yehud would mourn publicly over a communal loss.

Both the community's leadership class ("the house of David") and "the inhabitants of Jerusalem" recognize that the community's instability can threaten not only the restoration but even the continued existence of the community. Verse 10b asserts that one can compare it with the loss of a child who was to be the key to the family's future. Unchecked, the community's social instability could lead to the community's self-destruction, so God imbues the community with the "spirit of compassion" that will bring about a change in the way members of the community treat one another. The "supplication" that verse 10 speaks of is likely a prayer for forgiveness that the elites offer because of the harm that they brought to

---

20. According to 2 Sam 7 and 12, Nathan was a key adviser to David who helped facilitate Solomon's succession to the throne.

21. Meyers and Meyers, *Zechariah 9–14*, 447.

the community. The text does not provide details of the conflict within the postexilic community, but a text such as Isaiah 58:1-14 affirms that the actions of the elite classes, condemned by the preexilic prophets, were being repeated in the postexilic period. The public regret and mourning over a person who has been killed and the period of public reconciliation that follows convey a move toward repairing broken relationships and organizing a framework of functional leadership to ensure the future of the Jewish community.

Hadad-rimmon

The lamentation over the sorry state of relationships within the community is compared to that of "the mourning for Hadad-rimmon in the plain of Megiddo" (v. 11). The precise referent of this phrase in unclear. The Bible gives the name "Rimmon" to three places, but none of these is located "in the plain of Megiddo" (Josh 19:7, 13 and Num 33:19-20). It is possible that verse 11 mentions an otherwise unknown place where periodic mourning rituals took place commemorating the tragic and untimely death

of Josiah during a battle with the Egyptians on the plain of Megiddo (2 Kgs 23:29-30; 2 Chr 35:22-24). Jeremiah began this custom that was taken up by "singing men and singing women" (2 Chr 35:25).[22] A village named Hadad-rimmon likely provided the venue for this observance. A less likely referent for the "mourning for Haddad-rimmon" is a Canaanite ritual of mourning over the death of Baal.[23] It is unlikely that the prophet would point to a Canaanite ritual as a model for the expressions of sorrow among the Jewish community.

The repetition of the phrase "their wives by themselves" (v. 12) points to the unique role that women played as mourners. Jeremiah 9:17 calls women mourners מקוננות, a word derived from קינה (lament, dirge).[24] Originally the

---

22. Benedikt Otzen maintains that the mourning ritual has nothing to do with the death of Josiah but with the fall of Jerusalem. See his *Studien über Deuterosacharja*, ATD 6 (Copenhagen: Munksgaard, 1964), 183.

23. See Boda, *The Book of Zechariah*, 718nn132, 133, and Meyers and Meyers, *Zechariah 9–14*, 343; Mark S. Smith, *The Origins of Biblical Monotheism: Israel's Polytheistic Background and the Ugaritic Texts* (Oxford: Oxford University Press, 2001).

24. William Holladay, *Jeremiah 1: A Commentary on the Book of the Prophet Jeremiah (Chapters 1–25)*, Hermeneia (Philadelphia: Fortress, 1986), 312.

קִינָה was a lament because of the death of a family member, i.e., a funeral song for an individual's death. The composition and performance involved a special learned skill, requiring training.[25] Indeed, Jeremiah also refers to the women mourners as הַחֲכָמוֹת ("skilled women," 9:17b). There have been proposals that these skilled, professional women might be responsible for formation of the book of Lamentations.[26] Although men almost exclusively formed the political, religious, and social leadership of the Jewish community of Yehud, it was "unofficial" leaders like women mourners who helped society cope when the failures of official leadership led to social instability. These women mourners expressed, in word and song, the community's response to the trauma that resulted from the type of intersocietal conflicts alluded to in verses 10-11. The מְקוֹנְנוֹת helped the community face what had happened as they named the problem in their laments.[27] As they led the community in lamenting the social problems in the Jewish community, women mourners had a powerful effect on that community. They found themselves at the center of the community's life in times of crisis and trauma. L. Juliana Claassens regards the actions of the women who stepped forward in helping the people of Yehud to deal with trauma and grief as important for feminist theology.[28] The woman mourner is an example of female agency and authority and is a metaphor for the feminist theologian, who leads the community not only in grieving but also in resisting what is responsible for the community's instability.

The early rabbis take a different tack in reflection on the women mourners. They regard 12:12-14 as concerned women and men mourning separately from one another. A historical reconstruction of this text's context sees the early Persian period as a time of social instability within the Jewish community, but according to the rabbinic reading, this period was characterized by a pious concern for modesty. That women and men worship separately to preserve proper decorum will be the norm "on that day."[29]

---

25. Athalya Brenner-Idan, *The Israelite Woman: Social Role and Literary Type in Biblical Narrative* (London: Bloomsbury, 2015), 37.

26. Nancy C. Lee, "Lamentations and Gender in Biblical Cultural Context," in *The Writings and Later Wisdom Books*, ed. Christl M. Maier and Nuria Calduch-Benages, BW 1.3 (Atlanta: SBL Press, 2014), 200–201, 212.

27. L. Juliana M. Claassens, "Calling the Keeners: The Image of the Wailing Women as Symbol of Survival in a Traumatized World," *JFSR* 26 (2010): 68–69.

28. Claassens, "Calling the Keeners," 76–77.

29. Gender separation for worship is practiced in Orthodox synagogues. When this practice became the norm is not certain.

The question of where women should pray in sacred spaces continues to be a relevant one, even today. The armistice following the 1948 war between the newly independent Jewish state and its Arab neighbors left the Hashemite Kingdom of Jordan in control of the Old City of Jerusalem. When Israel gained control of the Temple Mount following the Six-Day War in 1967, it enacted a ban on non-Muslim prayer at the site in the attempt to foster peaceful relations with the local Muslim community. The Israeli government designated the Western Wall (הכותל) as the place where Jews were permitted to pray. Separate sections of the wall were assigned for men and women, with the women's section being slightly smaller and further from the area where the temple was thought to have stood.

In recent years, some Jewish women have lobbied for a space to be made at the Wall for both women and men to pray together. Ultimately, however, the Israeli government bent to pressure coming from ultra-Orthodox coalition partners to reject the plan for an egalitarian prayer space and to maintain the separation of men and women at prayer in accord with the practice of Orthodox Judaism. Organizations such as Women of the Wall and the Jewish Orthodox Feminist Alliance (JOFA) have decried this decision, which was taken not only as a blow against women and men who wish to pray alongside one another but also as a blow against Diaspora Jews, who were largely responsible for the demand that there be a place for egalitarian prayer at the Wall. The entire incident touches on the ways in which sacred space continues to intersect with gender roles. The separation of gender on the part of Israeli religious authorities continues to make some Jewish women feel that they do not have a space to occupy in the religious realm.

Conclusion

Against this backdrop of the challenges the people of Yehud faced in the early years of the Persian period, the prophet offers a vision of Yehud's future that is nothing less than a complete reversal of its fortunes. From a small, impoverished town in an undistinguished province of the Persian Empire, Jerusalem will see the destruction of the nations allied against it. In addition, God will bless the Jews with a new spirit that will overcome the internal conflicts that are tearing apart the Jewish community. All this will take place "on that day" when God will bring about a remarkable reversal of fortunes for the Jewish community of Yehud. This does not mean that the Jews will be passive recipients of God's benevolence. On the contrary, God will empower them to take control of their destiny. The prophet's words assure the Jews that the outcome of their struggles is certain. Nothing they do to reconstitute their religious and political lives in their ancestral homeland will be done in vain. With the assurance that comes from God through the prophet, the people of Yehud can look to the future with confidence.

Zechariah 13:1-9

On That Day

Chapter 13 continues the prophet's depiction of the eschaton that will be the setting for the definitive Judean restoration. The eschaton will witness both the rehabilitation of "the house of David" and the cessation of prophetic activity. Such activity will no longer be necessary following the cleansing of Judah's royal house. This dark and enigmatic chapter ends with a rehearsal of Judah's fall and its devastating effects on both the leaders and ordinary folk along with an assertion that God and the Jewish people will recommit themselves to the covenant that defines them both. While that closing message was likely received as positive affirmation by Zechariah's earliest readers/hearers, images of God underlying that message convey a sense of a patriarchal deity that is destructive and domineering, which feminist readers today would find challenging.

Cleansing (13:1)

Zechariah 13:1 contains two phrases—"on that day" and "the house of David and the inhabitants of Jerusalem"—that appear in chapter 12, leading several commentators to consider 13:1 as the concluding line of a unit that begins in the previous chapter.[1] Whereas chapter 12 focuses on the restoration of the house of David and of Jerusalem, chapter 13

---

1. Robert Rhea ("Attack on Prophecy: Zechariah 13,1–6," *ZAW* 107 [1995]: 288) maintains that there is no compelling support for this view.

Zech 13:1

¹On that day a fountain shall be opened
for the house of David and the inhabitants of Jerusalem, to cleanse them
from sin and impurity.

reminds readers/hearers of the failures of the leadership of the former
kingdom of Judah, failures that will have to be rectified before God's
promise of restoration will be fulfilled.

The political and economic realities that the Jewish community of
Yehud faced determined the shape that the Judean restoration was to
take. These realities sometimes conflicted with Jewish religious tradition.
A case in point regards hopes for the reestablishment of the kingdom of
Judah and Davidic dynasty. At the beginning of the Persian period, it was
inconceivable that a new kingdom of Judah ruled by a member of the
old royal family could emerge following the return of the exiles. This is
something the Persians could not allow. Another complication was the
view of Deuteronomistic circles that regarded the monarchy as a failed
institution that was responsible for the fall of the Judean state (2 Kgs 21:1-
15). Still, belief that God promised David an eternal dynasty continued
to be strong (2 Sam 7:16; 1 Chr 17:11-14; Pss 89:28-29; 132:11; Amos 9:11).
Zechariah's solution to this conflict between religious belief and political
reality was to assert that the fulfillment of God's promises to David was to
be a component of the restoration that will take place "on that day" (Zech
12:7-9). In other words, the prophet's solution was to make the restoration
of the Davidic dynasty an eschatological reality. Remembering the failures
of Judah's kings and experiencing Persian hegemony did not lead to an
abandonment of belief in the promises made to David. The prophet offers
a surprisingly strong support for the monarchy, apparently believing that
the Judean restoration would be incomplete without the return of the
house of David to the leadership of the Jewish community. Still, it was
not possible to ignore the failures of the monarchy and the bureaucracy
associated with it so verse 1 offers the assurance that the system will be
cleansed from "sin and impurity."² The resumption of Davidic rule will
not restore the system as it was but as it should be.

---

2. The word translated as "sin" is חטאה, which usually refers to failures in the moral
realm, while the word translated as "impurity" is נדה, which refers to contact with a
person or object that renders one ritually impure, e.g., contact with a corpse or men-

The monarchy replaced the decentralized system of tribal governance with Jerusalem-centered polity and brought a stratified social and economic system along with it. A prebendal system of land ownership superseded familial inheritance. The story of Naboth's vineyard (1 Kgs 21:1-24) illustrates what happens when these two systems come into conflict. The monarchy upended the tribal political and economic system that had been in place since the Israelites emerged in Canaan's central highlands. Portraying the restoration of the monarchy following the ritual of cleansing "on that day" suggests that the prophet had no confidence that the monarchy could be reformed in the present age. Certainly the "house of David and the inhabitants of Jerusalem" will have recognized the failures of the royal establishment and repent of them (Zech 12:10), but that alone will not ensure that the monarchy will serve the benefit of the people rather than of the royal establishment. By having the restoration of the monarchy as an eschatological event, the prophet appears to give up on the possibility that the monarchy can be effective politically and morally in this age. The effect on the Jewish community in Yehud was to lower their expectations about their political status and economic prospects. For the foreseeable future, Yehud was to remain subject to a Persian king and forced to pay taxes that will go into the Persian treasury.

The eschatological dimensions of texts like Zechariah 13:1 can have two different effects on readers/hearers. The assurance that the prophet gives about the reformation of the monarchic system leading to its restoration may lead people to wait for God to deal with the inequities of economic and political systems that control their lives. This may appear to be the more prudent and realistic approach given Persia's power and Yehud's impotence. How can an individual or even a group change an entrenched social and political system like that of the Persian Empire? Such an attitude, of course, guarantees that little or no political and economic change that may benefit Yehud will take place. There is an inertia that pervades those in power when faced with the prospect of reform. Another response to the eschatological dimension of the restoration of the monarchy leads people to act to effect reform since they believe that nothing that they may do to hasten the day of Judah's restoration will be done in vain. The prophet has assured them that, in the end, God will act to cleanse the system of its inequities that it spawns, fulfilling God's promises to David while ensuring a just society. An eschatological vision can be a depressant or a

---

strual flow. Although drawing sharp distinctions between the two types of infractions is a mistake, here the usage of חטאה and נדה together, which occurs only one other time (Num 19:9), suggests that the monarchic system will be thoroughly reformed.

stimulant. It can lead people to accept an unjust social system, or it can urge people to reform such a system. Isaiah 58:1-14, for example, calls for action to ensure social justice within the Jewish community. The emphasis on the priority of God's activity in Zechariah 13:1 was a response to the community's political, economic, and military powerlessness. Despite this reality, the prophet affirms that the promises made to David will be fulfilled. The present is the time period for vestiges of the royal establishment that survived to recognize the monarchy's failure and repent, and "on that day," God will cleanse them of their "sin and impurity," leading to the hoped-for restoration of Judah and house of David.

TRANSLATION MATTERS

Verse 1 states that a מקור ("spring" or "fountain"; from the Hebrew root קור, which means "to dig," as in a well) will be opened to cleanse the house of David and the inhabitants of Jerusalem of "sin and impurity." Most translators supply a verb, although there is none in the Hebrew; for example, the NRSVue's "to cleanse" assumes that the purpose of the spring/fountain is to remove the effects of moral and ritual contamination from the people of Yehud so that their covenant with YHWH can be fully restored. No other occurrences of מקור in the Hebrew Bible focus on cleansing, however, ritual or otherwise. In most cases, the function of מקור is to quench thirst or nourish the land.[3] As a source of fresh, flowing water, מקור sometimes functions as a metaphor for YHWH.[4] Alternatively, מקור can be associated with the flow of blood during menstruation (Lev 20:18) or childbirth (Lev 12:7).

The choice to associate מקור with cleansing in Zechariah 13:1 is probably influenced by the reference to the "sin and impurity" of Judah's monarchy and related institutions, the failures of which are the focus of most of the chapter. The word translated as "sin" is חטאה, which usually refers to failures in the moral realm; the word translated as "impurity" is נדה, which refers to contact with a person or object (e.g., a corpse or menstrual flow) that renders one ritually impure.[5] Reference to חטאה and נדה as a word pair in Zechariah 13:1 emphasizes that God will thoroughly cleanse and reform the monarchic system so that it will be both ethically and ritually pure.

---

3. E.g., Ps 36:8-9; Joel 3:18.

4. E.g., see Jer 2:13 and 17:13. The Greek term for מקור is πηγή, which appears in John 4:14, where Jesus offers a woman from Samaria water that will become in her "a spring [πηγή] of water gushing up to eternal life" (NRSVue).

5. S. Tamar Kamionkowski argues that, in Leviticus, the term נדה simply refers to ritual impurity and that Zech 13:1 is influenced by Ezekiel, which "takes this innocuous term and extends its use figuratively to describe moral impurity (Ezek 7:19-20)." See her *Leviticus*, WCS 3 (Collegeville, MN: Liturgical Press, 2018), 143.

The End of Prophecy? (13:2-6)

The formulaic expressions ("on that day, says YHWH of hosts"), which begin the oracle in 13:2-6, set this section off from 13:1. The subject of this oracle is the place of prophecy in the utopian future described in chapters 9–14. In most emphatic terms, Zechariah asserts that prophecy will have no place in the eschaton. Prophets from Moses to Malachi and from Deborah to Huldah had had a significant role in the life of the people of Israel. They had a particularly important function during the period of the Israelite monarchy. A principal task of Israel's prophets was to remind the king to maintain the people's commitment to their ancestral deity in addition to ensuring a just social order. The prophets confronted Israel's kings and people, announcing the consequences of their failures to uphold traditional Israelite morality and to remain loyal to YHWH. Whether or not a prophet had a formal, officially recognized role in the royal administration, prophecy and monarchy frequently functioned as symbiotic institutions. Prophetic warnings and threats often went unheeded, leaving Israel's prophets unable to prevent the disasters that came upon both Israelite kingdoms. Another challenge to the reputation of prophets were the so-called false prophets who, according to the biblical writers, spoke in God's name without divine authority. (Jer 28:1-17 illustrates how difficult it was to identify such prophets because there were no practical criteria that were immediately verifiable.[6])

Like Deuteronomy 13:1-11, Zechariah 13:2 associates prophecy with idolatry, i.e., participation in the worship of other gods. At the very least, this association is evidence of a decidedly negative view of the behavior of some prophets or even of prophecy itself, but does Zechariah reject prophecy altogether as a legitimate component of Yahwistic religion? Both Mark Boda and Carol Meyers and Eric Meyers see the book of Zechariah as rejecting false prophets but not those who, like the book's own authors, were authentic Yahwistic prophets.[7] The end of the monarchy meant the elimination of what had been the principal concern of preexilic prophets, namely, the announcement of judgment to corrupt kings and those associated with them. Second, with the emergence of monotheistic rhetoric and theology in exilic and postexilic literature, a new awareness of the nature

---

6. The test for determining an authentic prophet given in Deut 18:20-22 is of no immediate use, since it calls for waiting to see if the prophet's words eventually come true.

7. Mark J. Boda, *The Book of Zechariah*, NICOT (Grand Rapids: Eerdmans, 2016), 726–27; Carol L. Meyers and Eric M. Meyers, *Zechariah 9–14: A New Translation with Introduction and Commentary*, AB 25C (New York: Doubleday, 1993), 399–40.

²On that day, says the Lᴏʀᴅ of hosts, I will cut off the names of the idols from the land, so that they shall be remembered no more, and also I will remove from the land the prophets and the unclean spirit. ³And if any prophets appear again, their fathers and mothers who bore them will say to them, "You shall not live, for you speak lies in the name of the Lᴏʀᴅ," and their fathers and their mothers who bore them shall pierce them through when they prophesy. ⁴On that day the prophets will be ashamed, every one, of their visions when they prophesy; they will not put on a hairy mantle in order to deceive, ⁵but each of them will say, "I am no prophet; I am a tiller of the soil, for the land has been my possession since my youth." ⁶And if anyone asks them, "What are these wounds on your chest?" the answer will be "The wounds I received in the house of my friends."

of deity was developing within the Jewish community. Persian tolerance of the worship of YHWH allowed Jewish religious life to be nourished by the restored temple and the ministry of its priests. Thus, in the context of the postexilic Jewish community, prophets as they had functioned in the monarchic period became obsolete, and they would not play an important role in the Jewish life "on that day." The need for prophetic activity given the community's present circumstance was negligible. Without the need for continuing further prophetic activity, the Jewish community honored the role of prophecy in Israel's past by collecting and preserving the words of earlier prophets. In addition, Jews in Yehud began looking to the written Torah as the authoritative guide to the divine will (see Neh 8:1-8), obviating the need for those who had claimed to be authorized intermediaries who communicate "the word of YHWH" to Israel.

The most troubling statement of the text's attitude toward prophetic activity is its assertion that parents will turn against their children who engage in such activity. Deuteronomy 13:6-11 calls for the execution of any family member who leads people into idolatry, and Deuteronomy 21:18-21 advises parents of a rebellious son to have him stoned by the townspeople. Still, the expectation of Zechariah 13:3 that parents will themselves kill a child who claims to be a prophet is shocking. Parents give life to their children—they do not take it away. It is inconceivable that the mothers who bore those acting as prophets will "pierce them through when they prophesy" (v. 3). Citing Amos 7:14, verses 4-5 depict those engaging in prophetic activity as rejecting the role and identity as prophets "on that day." The present age was witnessing diminished prophetic activity, and the eschaton would be an age when those who might have been prophets would neither speak nor even dress the part.

Prophetic activity may have diminished in the postexilic period, but did it cease entirely? The oft-cited rabbinic tradition that the holy spirit departed from Israel after the death of Haggai, Zechariah, and Malachi (T. Soṭa 13:2; b. Sanh. 11a) has been taken as evidence that Jews during the Second Temple period no longer thought that God communicated to Israel through prophets. Some scholars claim that prophecy ceased sometime after the Babylonian exile while others maintain that prophecy continued in both Judaism and Christianity.[8] Frederick Greenspahn maintains that there is little evidence that the Jews of the Second Temple period believed that prophecy had ceased. He suggests that the polemic against prophecy in Zechariah 13:2-6 was directed at self-styled prophets whom the author found unacceptable.[9] Greenspahn goes on to assert that the rabbinic dictum about the holy spirit departing from Israel does not specifically refer to prophecy and may simply have been an attempt to deny legitimacy to those who rejected the authority of the rabbis in favor of prophets.[10]

The decline in prophetic activity led to the diminishment of the role of women in religious leadership of the Jewish community. The charismatic nature of prophecy made it possible for women to have a recognized leadership role in ancient Israel. Judges 4–5 depicts the prophet Deborah as responsible for the victory that enabled the Israelite tribes to gain control of the vitally important Jezreel Valley. Second Kings 22 has the priest Hilkiah and other Jerusalem bureaucrats consulting the prophet Huldah regarding the authenticity of the lawbook found during repairs being made on the temple during the reign of Josiah. Her endorsement of the lawbook paved the way for Josiah's cultic reforms. In neither case did the actions of the women require some explanation or justification. Their actions were appropriate and effective. There is a female prophet named Noadiah mentioned in Nehemiah 6:14, who participated in a conspiracy to undermine Nehemiah.[11] He asks God to remember that she

---

8. See Benjamin D. Sommer, "Did Prophecy Cease? Evaluating a Reevaluation," *JBL* 115 (1996): 32nn2 and 3.

9. Frederick E. Greenspahn, "Why Prophecy Ceased," *JBL* 108 (1989): 40–41.

10. Greenspahn, "Why Prophecy Ceased," 45, 47–48.

11. The MT refers to Noadiah as הנביאה, identifying Noadiah as a female prophet. The LXX, however, refers to Noadiah as τῷ προφήτῃ, indicating that Noadiah was a

and other prophets opposed his mission. This text is another indication of the negative view of prophets and prophecy that was on the rise in the postexilic period. The New Testament mentions a female prophet named Anna (Luke 2:36-38). Although Luke writes that she spoke about the child Jesus, the evangelist does not cite what she said. Although Anna is otherwise unknown, the reference to her is evidence of a positive view of prophecy among early Christians.[12]

There are Jewish texts from the Second Temple period in addition to the New Testament that do speak of prophets and prophetic activity, suggesting that prophecy did not cease at some time following the return from Babylon.[13] Benjamin Sommer, however, asserts that most such texts reflect heightened messianic expectations. One feature of messianism was belief that prophecy would return with the coming of the messiah.[14] Prophecy began to decline in the early Persian period when it was clear that the restoration of the Judean state and Davidic monarchy were not on the horizon. Texts like Zechariah 13 and Deuteronomy 13 contributed to that decline. Still, prophetic activity continued in both Second Temple Judaism and early Christianity. Women such as Noadiah and Anna were remembered as prophets.

What the wounds mentioned in 13:6 refers to is not clear. Some prophets in an ecstatic state did sometimes inflict wounds on themselves (see 1 Kgs 18:28). Some early Christian theologians viewed verses 3 and 6 as prophecies of Jesus's crucifixion.[15] The early rabbinic tradition, however, reads these verses as a prophecy that Jews would be martyred at the hands of the Romans for violating laws prohibiting the study of

---

male. Since the prophet Noadiah is otherwise unknown, it is not possible to be certain about the prophet's gender. Following the MT, the NRSVue call her "the prophetess"; the NABRE calls her "the woman prophet." Ezra 8:33 mentions a Levite named Noadiah, the son of Binnui.

12. David Aune, *Prophecy in Early Christianity and the Ancient Mediterranean World* (Grand Rapids: Eerdmans, 1983), 36.

13. E.g., Alex P. Jassen has described the prophetic phenomena as depicted in the Dead Sea Scrolls in his "Prophecy after 'The Prophets': The Dead Sea Scrolls and the History of Prophecy in Judaism," in *The Dead Sea Scrolls in Context: Integrating the Dead Sea Scrolls in the Study of Ancient Texts, Languages, and Cultures*, ed. Armin Lange, Emanuel Tov, and Matthias Weigold, VTSup 140 (Leiden: Brill, 2011), 577–93. See also *Ant.* 18.85; 20.97, 167–70, 188; Matt 14:5; 21:11; Acts 3:22; Eph 4:11.

14. Sommer, "Did Prophecy Cease?," 37.

15. Justin Martyr, *Dialogue with Trypho* 53; Origen, *Homilies on Exodus* 11.6; Tertullian, *On Flight in Time of Persecution* 2.2.

Torah and the practice of Judaism. After Shimon bar Kokhba's unsuccessful rebellion against Rome in 135 CE, the Roman emperor Hadrian
enacted a series of oppressive laws that forbade the practice of Judaism.
One particularly wrenching Midrashic passage links these verses in
Zechariah to the Jews' suffering in the wake of bar Kokhba's rebellion:

> R. Nathan says, "'those who love me and keep my commandments'
> refers to those who dwell in the land of Israel and give their lives for
> keeping the religious duties. 'How come you are going forth to be put
> to death?' 'Because I circumcised my son as an Israelite.' 'How come
> you are going forth to be burned to death?' 'Because I read in the Torah.'
> 'How come you are going forth to be crucified?' 'Because I took up the
> palm branch [on Tabernacles].' 'Those with which I was wounded in
> the house of friends' (Zech. 13:6): these are the wounds that made me
> beloved to my father who is in heaven."[16]

The second-century CE rabbi Nathan imagines a conversation between
a gentile interlocutor and a Jew who has submitted to being tortured
and killed rather than ceasing to observe the Torah. The Jewish martyr
is asked three questions concerning the violations that he has committed. After the martyr answers the questions posed to him, he offers an
exposition of Zechariah 13:6 without being prompted. The phrase in
Zechariah, "Those with which I was wounded in the house of friends,"
alludes not to the suffering of the rabbi at the hands of the Romans but
the suffering that was the result of his fidelity to the Torah. The place
where the prophet suffers in 13:6 is בית מאהבי, which the NRSVue translates as the "house of my friends." The phrase can be rendered as "the
house of the one who loves me." This place is the land of Israel, and the
one who is beloved is none other than God. The very suffering of this
Jew is a means of expressing his love for God, the One who loves him.
The focus of this rabbinic interpretation of 13:6, then, is not on prophetic
activity but on the act of martyrdom.

Although prophetic activity may have continued in both Second
Temple Judaism and early Christianity, it appears that prophecy does
not have a place in Zechariah's eschatological vision as set out in 13:2-6.
"On that day," God will remove prophets (and the idols with which they
became associated) from the land (13:2), the parents of anyone claiming

16. Mekhilta de-Rabbi Ishmael 52.2, in Jacob Neusner, *Zephaniah, Haggai, Zechariah
and Malachi in Talmud and Midrash: A Source Book*, Studies in Judaism (Lanham, MD:
University Press of America, 2007), 95.

to be a prophet will kill them (at least metaphorically speaking, 13:3), and the prophets themselves will renounce any claims to prophetic inspiration (13:4-5). The role of prophets, whether male or female, was becoming increasingly marginal in Zechariah's vision of a restored Judah.

Recalling Judah's Devastation (13:7-9)

The final three verses of chapter 13 are a reflection on the fall of the kingdom of Judah, its aftermath, and its final resolution.[17] Maarten Menken argues that this text concerns "the time of the end." But, given the absence of any eschatological formulas such as "on that day," it is more likely that the prophet suspends looking to the future and instead looks back in time to offer a reminder of the events that brought the people of Judah to almost total destruction at the hands of the Babylonians. Reminding the Jewish community of those tragic events reinforces the hope that, despite the failures of the past, their relationship with God would be reestablished as part of the eschatological restoration of Judah.

For the fifth time in chapters 9–14,[18] the prophet employs the shepherd/flock imagery. In all of these texts, the image of the shepherd is negative (e.g., "worthless shepherd" in 11:15, 17), and the consequences of the shepherd's ineffectiveness are dire for the flock entrusted to the shepherd's care. As in several earlier chapters, God is portrayed as the Divine Warrior (יהוה צבאות, "Lord of armies") who, in 13:7, calls on a personified sword to strike and kill "my shepherd" and threatens to "turn my hand against the little ones." The identity of the shepherd in 13:7 is unclear. Mark Boda claims that the shepherd is a (presumably male) leader of the postexilic Jewish community, such as Zerubbabel or his son-in-law and successor Elnathan.[19] This is unlikely since Zechariah usually speaks of Zerubbabel in positive terms. Perhaps the unnamed shepherd is a personification of the Davidic dynasty itself, which had proven unable to maintain Judah's loyalty to YHWH alone. Indeed, most of Judah's kings either countenanced non-Yahwistic worship or promoted it. What is clear is that יהוה צבאות commands the sword to exe-

---

17. Maarten J. J. Menken, "Striking the Shepherd: Early Christian Versions and Interpretations of Zechariah 13:7," *Bib* 92 (2011): 41.

18. See 10:1-3; 11:1-3, 4-16, and 17.

19. Boda, *The Book of Zechariah*, 738.

Zech 13:7-9

7"Awake, O sword, against my shepherd,
against the man who is my
associate,"
says the LORD of hosts.
"Strike the shepherd, that the sheep
may be scattered;
I will turn my hand against the
little ones.
8In the whole land, says the LORD,
two-thirds shall be cut off and perish,

and one-third shall be left alive.
9And I will put this third into the fire,
refine them as one refines silver,
and test them as gold is tested.
They will call on my name,
and I will answer them.
I will say, 'They are my people,'
and they will say, 'The LORD is
our God.'"

cute divine judgment on Judah's political leadership, which had failed so miserably (recall 13:1).

Punishment of Judah's failed leadership is a common feature of pre-exilic judgment oracles. This message also presents a dramatic contrast to Zechariah 8:1-17 and 9:9-17, which declare that יהוה צבאות ("LORD of armies") would deliver Judah from its enemies. Perhaps this shift reflects the early stages of a transition from condemnation of failed leaders in the past to idealization of leaders who will successfully fulfill their responsibilities in the future. For example, Stephen L. Cook suggests that here Zechariah 13 combines a pessimistic attitude toward political leaders with a hopeful expectation of a messiah.[20] Cook argues that the wider eschatological contexts of chapters 12–14 hold out "bright hopes for the Davidides" (e.g., 12:8 and 13:1).[21] This may be an overstatement, however, since messianic expectations probably originated after Zechariah was written. The memory of the monarchy as a failed institution was still too fresh and the political realities of Persian hegemony too clear to give rise to a reasonable expectation that the future of Yehud would be tied up with an ideal king from the house of David. In fact, as the eschatological picture develops, the royal figure disappears altogether, and יהוה צבאות emerges in the forefront of activity that will bring about the Judean restoration in the final days.

20. Stephen L. Cook, "The Metamorphosis of a Shepherd: The Tradition History of Zechariah 11:17 + 13:7-9," *CBQ* 55 (1993): 459.
21. Cook, "The Metamorphosis," 461.

Zechariah 13:7 in the Gospels

Mark 14:27 cites Zechariah 13:7a, with significant alteration, to explain the defection of the disciples following Jesus's arrest in Gethsemane.[22] Mark changes the imperative singular הַךְ ("strike") to the first-person future πατάξω ("I will strike"), a reading that is supported by some LXX manuscripts, based on Psalm 69:27 (NRSVue 69:26), that has God as the implied subject who afflicts God's chosen one.[23] Matthew 26:31 borrows Mark's alteration of Zechariah 13:7a, and John 16:32 alludes to it but does not suggest that God does the striking. Both Mark 14:38 and Matthew 26:32 balance the desertion of Jesus by the apostles with the promise that Jesus will meet the apostles in Galilee after the resurrection.

Verse 9 shifts to different imagery to describe the impact the fall of the kingdom of Judah had on those who remained in the land. The text suggests that the population of Judah decreased by as much as two-thirds. People died during the invasion because of food shortages caused by disruption of agricultural activities and lawlessness that resulted from the nation's collapse. All this plus the forced migration of the elite classes had a severe negative impact on the population of Judah.[24] Those who remained in the land struggled to survive. The prophet compares their lives to the refining process that transforms ore into pure metals. Carol Meyers and Eric Meyers point out that refining gold was a difficult and expensive process.[25] The refining process was a most appropriate image to describe the experience of those who remained in the land of Judah following the fall of Jerusalem. Just as the refining produced precious metal, so also the result of Judah's fall and its consequences will be the recommitment of God to the people of Judah. The phrase "they shall

22. The citation of Zech 13:7 in Mark 14 is an example of what Charles H. Dodd (*According to the Scriptures: The Sub-structure of New Testament Theology* [New York: Scribner's, 1953], 107) sees as the pervasive influence of Deutero-Zechariah on Mark's passion narrative.

23. As with several texts in the Hebrew Bible, Christian interpreters tend to see Zech 13:7 as referring to Jesus's passion and death. According to that interpretation, Jesus acts in the role of God, thus "fulfilling" the message of the Jewish text.

24. Avraham Faust, "Deportation and Demography in Sixth-Century BCE Judah," in *Interpreting Exile: Interdisciplinary Studies of Displacement and Deportation in Biblical and Modern Contexts*, ed. Brad E. Kelle, Frank Ritchel Ames, and Jacob L. Wright, AIL 10 (Atlanta: SBL, 2011), 96–97.

25. See their *Zechariah 9–14*, 395.

be my people, and I shall be their God," or close variations of it, was a popular trope in early exilic prophetic literature. This axiom would have been meaningful to Jews who had experienced firsthand the trauma of being expelled from their land and who feared that the suffering that they had endured at the hands of the Babylonians might have signaled an irrevocable severance of their covenantal relationship with God.[26] The promise that the covenant with YHWH would someday be restored probably provided much-needed reassurance for the people of Yehud struggling to create a new way of living in their homeland under Persian rule. Still, words of possession and possessiveness, such as "I am yours; you are mine," coming from a domineering authority figure who threatens to "turn my hand against the little ones" can be disconcerting for a feminist reader today. This troubling text needs to be reimagined if a feminist reader is to affirm the mutuality and belonging that a covenant with God might entail.

Conclusion

A feminist reader recognizes that restoring a monarchy (or any other form of patriarchal, nonegalitarian government) will fail to eliminate the inequities, injustices, and oppression that such forms of government inevitably engender. Too often situations arise in which large segments of a population are denied access to freedom, safety, and a sustainable livelihood by politicians (and those who support them) dedicated solely to advancing their own interests. Such was the case in the sixth century BCE, when a substantial segment of Judah's citizenry (the scattered sheep of Zech 13:7) was forced to migrate to Babylon where most were settled in agriculturally marginal land. Similar examples of patriarchal abuse of power and authoritarianism abound today: persecution of women in Afghanistan under Taliban rule; occupation of the West Bank by Israel; ill treatment of people forced to leave their impoverished homelands and seek refuge and asylum in the United States and other developed countries that have comparatively such abundance; and attempted genocide of indigenous communities around the world so that the land and resources where they live can be extracted and exploited by those in power. Like the scattered sheep who had to endure the impacts of ineffectual leadership in Yehud, many peoples today are displaced,

26. For example, see Jer 24:7; 31:1, 33; 32:38; Ezek 14:11; 37:23, 27. These verses likely derive from Lev 26:11-12: "I will place my dwelling in your midst. . . . I will be your God, and you shall be my people."

disenfranchised, and destroyed by the unjust policies and practices of their own corrupt leaders and by exploitation and oppression by foreign powers. The prophet, however, is describing an eschatological reality in which the social, political, and economic problems of this age will no longer exist. The restoration the prophet envisions is not a restoration of the *status quo ante*. It involves a radical refounding of the kingdom of Judah. After thorough cleansing, the house of David will again provide leadership that ensures Judah's commitment to serve YHWH alone.

Zechariah 13 opens with an unexpected and devasting judgment on prophets. They who were to guide the people with the word of God became subject to physical harm by their own families. At the end of the chapter, God turns on the shepherd and the sheep. Nothing appears as it should. God appears as capricious and merciless. The end of the age will bring with it loss of meaning. The chapter, however, closes with the familiar election formula: "They are my people." Despite the disconcerting rhetoric of this chapter, it must end on a positive note since the prophet's message is that judgment is not God's last word. The bond between God and Israel is unbreakable. That assurance brings meaning and value to the lives of the believers of every age—to the children of Abraham and to those who have become his children through adoption.

Zechariah 14:1-21

A Universal Vision

The Day of YHWH (14:1-11)

The final chapter of Zechariah so mystified Martin Luther that he ended his 1526 commentary on Zechariah with chapter 13. A year later Luther wrote a second commentary on the book that did include a brief commentary on chapter 14 though he began his observations on this chapter by lamenting that he did not understand its meaning.[1] Zechariah 14 has also perplexed modern commentators.[2] What is it about this chapter that so mystified its interpreters? What makes it so difficult to unravel? The final chapter of Zechariah begins with an oracle announcing that a devastating siege of Jerusalem is coming. Such an oracle is the last thing the reader expects in a book that looks forward to the restoration of Judah and Jerusalem. Before the reader can process this unexpected and shocking vision of the city's future, the mood abruptly changes as the text affirms that God will fight against the nations arrayed against Jerusalem. The chapter and the book end with an assertion that even the cooking pots used by the people of Jerusalem will be holy. The puzzled

---

1. Albert Wolters, "Zechariah 14: A Dialogue with the History of Interpretation," *Mid-America Journal of Theology* 13 (2002): 40–41.

2. Some commentators see chap. 14 as distinct from the rest of the book. For a review of scholarly opinions on the distinctiveness of this chapter, see Konrad R. Schaefer, "The Ending of the Book of Zechariah: A Commentary," *RB* 100 (1993): 166 nos. 3–5.

Zech 14:1-11

¹See, a day is coming for the Lᴏʀᴅ, when the plunder taken from you will be divided in your midst. ²For I will gather all the nations against Jerusalem to battle, and the city shall be taken and the houses plundered and the women raped; half the city shall go into exile, but the rest of the people shall not be cut off from the city. ³Then the Lᴏʀᴅ will go forth and fight against those nations as when he fights on a day of battle. ⁴On that day his feet shall stand on the Mount of Olives, which lies before Jerusalem on the east, and the Mount of Olives shall be split in two from east to west by a very wide valley, so that one half of the mount shall withdraw northward and the other half southward. ⁵And you shall flee by the valley of the Lᴏʀᴅ's mountain, for the valley between the mountains shall reach to Azal, and you shall flee as you fled from the earthquake in the days of King Uzziah of Judah. Then the Lᴏʀᴅ my God will come and all the holy ones with him.

⁶On that day there shall not be either cold or frost. ⁷And there shall be continuous day (it is known to the Lᴏʀᴅ),

reaction of even the most sympathetic and perceptive readers to these abrupt shifts is understandable.

Though the vocabulary ("a day is coming," v. 1) and imagery of chapter 14 are eschatological in tone, the final chapter of Zechariah is based on existential experience of those who first heard or read this text.[3] The temple was rebuilt, but it was nothing like the one that the Babylonians destroyed (Ezra 3:12). A descendant of David (Zerubbabel) was the governor of Yehud, but the national state and the Davidic dynasty were not restored, and the likelihood of their restoration appeared to be remote in the extreme. Many people of both fallen Israelite kingdoms settled in various places in Mesopotamia and elsewhere—far from the land of Israel. Yehud was a minor province of the Persian Empire. Jerusalem's walls were in disrepair and its geographical footprint and population were much smaller than in the monarchic period. Though the Persians were far more benevolent rulers than either the Assyrians or the Babylonians, Persian hegemony did lead to a severe drain on the economy of Yehud. It was not possible to forget that the Judean restoration did not measure up to the expectations fueled by prophets such as

---

3. The eschatological nature of this chapter is underscored by the recurrence of the phrase ביום ההוא ("on that day") seven times (vv. 4, 6, 8, 9, 13, 20, and 21).

not day and not night, for at evening time there shall be light.

⁸On that day living water shall flow out from Jerusalem, half of it to the eastern sea and half of it to the western sea; it shall continue in summer as in winter.

⁹And the Lᴏʀᴅ will become king over all the earth; on that day the Lᴏʀᴅ will be one and his name one.

¹⁰The whole land shall be turned into a plain from Geba to Rimmon south of Jerusalem. But Jerusalem shall remain aloft on its site from the Gate of Benjamin to the place of the former gate, to the Corner Gate, and from the Tower of Hananel to the king's winepresses.

¹¹And it shall be inhabited, for never again shall it be doomed to destruction; Jerusalem shall abide in security.

Isaiah of Babylon, Jeremiah, and Ezekiel. The final chapter of the book of Zechariah envisions a Judean restoration beyond the expectations of earlier prophetic oracles, but it sees Judah's fall and the exile of its people as preludes to the final reconstitution of Judah's unique relationship with YHWH that it affirms in the end.

In this chapter, Zechariah once again couches his description of the Judean restoration in martial language and imagery. Although the chapter depicts God as acting on Jerusalem's behalf, the repeated use of martial imagery in the Bible in general and Zechariah in particular is off-putting. It serves to legitimate warfare as a means of fulfilling the divine will. The consequences of this legitimation have been tragic in the extreme over the centuries as both kings and revolutionaries insist that they are doing "God's work." Modern readers need to remember that war and its aftermath was an unfortunate part of the lives of people who lived in the southern Levant. It is unrealistic to expect that the literature of these people would not reflect the tragic circumstances of their lives.

The eschatological passages in prophetic literature are often enigmatic (e.g., Ezek 38; Joel 3:1-3; Mic 4:11-13), but Zechariah 14 is particularly difficult because it explicitly asserts that "a day is coming" when Jerusalem will be under a siege that God personally engineers. The vocabulary in verses 1-2 reflects the experience of a siege warfare: battle, plunder, looting, rape, and exile. The prophet gives no indication of when "that day" will be, but he does not spare his readers/hearers as he describes the horrors of a siege and its aftermath. The attack on Jerusalem foreseen by the prophet will result in the devastation and destruction of the city and the suffering of its people. The prophet focuses on what will happen after the city falls to the besieging army. The soldiers of that army are let loose on the fallen city. He identifies three progressively worsening levels of devastation: Jerusalem will fall, followed by the looting of its houses and the rape its women. The city, the houses, and the women are paired with verbs in the *niphal*, a passive Hebrew conjugation. This turns Jerusalem's women into objects like the city itself and its buildings, unable to offer any resistance. Women have been robbed of personal agency. They are compelled to submit.

Rape was the most common outrage committed when a besieged city was finally taken.[4] The city's conquerors believed that the right of the men of the fallen city—including those rights over the city's women—had come to them. The victorious soldiers did not regard their actions as sexual abuse but as their rightful due. The only other prophetic text that mentions the rape of women in wartime is Isaiah 13:16, which is part of an oracle against Babylon. That God speaks in the first person in Zechariah 14:2 intensifies the trauma that Jerusalem's women will experience. God is inflicting the same judgment on them as was inflicted on the women of Babylon. Ruth Poser suggests that men of the city likely experienced "sexual and sexualized violence" though the text is silent on that score.[5] Sexualized violence through the mutilation of the city's men by the enemy soldiers "feminized" them. The rape of the city's women and the mutilation of its men are assertions of the victors' power and dominance over those who managed to survive the siege. Most of the survivors would have been noncombatants. This "gendering of warfare" adds to the trauma of defeat. That the prophet explicitly mentions the rape of Jerusalem's women underscores the extent of the alienation between God and the people of Judah and Jerusalem. That God would explicitly claim responsibility for the devastation of the people of Jerusalem is unthinkable, but it will happen. Using this imagery has had a lasting effect on people's concept of their God who will bring such horrors upon the people of Jerusalem. Today some Jews maintain that it is impossible to believe in God after the Holocaust. The horrors perpetrated by the Nazis robbed many Jews of their loved ones but also

4. Paul B. Kern, *Ancient Siege Warfare* (Bloomington: Indiana University Press, 1999), 83.

5. Ruth Poser, "Embodied Memories: Gender-Specific Aspects of Prophecy as Trauma Literature," in *Prophecy and Gender in the Hebrew Bible*, ed. L. Juliana Claassens and Irmtraud Fischer, BW 1.2 (Atlanta: SBL Press, 2021), 343.

of the faith that was their inheritance from generations that extend to thousands of years.[6]

Medieval Jewish manuscripts of Zechariah reflect an attempt to avoid giving offense to readers/hearers when referring to the rape of the women of Jerusalem. A word written in the margins adjacent to verse 2 calls the reader of this passage in liturgical settings to chant תשכבנה ("lie down") in place of תשגלנה ("raped"), which appears in the text proper. This practice of substituting a form to be read, known as the *qere* (קרא), in place of the word that is written in the text, known as the *ketiv* (כתיב), is sometimes used to avoid giving offense. Carol Meyers and Eric Meyers suggest that שכב (to lie down) is often used as a euphemism for sexual intercourse and may have been a less offensive word than שגל.[7] Of course, no euphemism can hide the horror that victims of sexual violence experience.

The Jerusalem of Zechariah 14 is not inviolable. It will fall to nations that God has assembled for the task of subjecting the city to divine judgment. This is the opposite of the confidence that Psalm 46 expresses in God's protection of Jerusalem, for example. The prophetic tradition, however, does speak of a divine attack against Jerusalem, e.g., Isaiah 10:5-12; 29:1-8; Jeremiah 21:3-7; Ezekiel 24:3-14, but none is more explicit and direct than Zechariah 14:1-2. Still, God's war against Jerusalem is not a war of extermination. Its people will survive, though half will be sent away to exile. This detail also reflects the events following the fall of Jerusalem to the Babylonians in 597 and again in 587 BCE.

An unusual feature of this announcement of judgment on Jerusalem is the lack of any reference to the reason for the judgment against the city. Usually, a prophetic oracle of judgment begins with an "indictment" that lists the offense of the party under judgment. Apparently, the prophet assumes that his readers/hearers were aware of idolatry and injustice that brought down the two Israelite kingdoms according to prophetic tradition. This final act of judgment is a prelude to the final and decisive act of deliverance that will restore Judah and Jerusalem to God's good favor once and for all.

Verse 3 introduces this shift from the oracle of judgment in verses 1-2 and the oracle of salvation that takes up the rest of the chapter. God changes sides and turns against the nations that God had ordered to

---

6. Dan Cohn-Sherbok, "Jewish Faith and the Holocaust," *RelS* 26 (1990): 279–82.

7. Carol L. Meyers and Eric M. Meyers, *Zechariah 9–14: A New Translation with Introduction and Commentary*, AB 25C (New York: Doubleday, 1993), 415.

attack Jerusalem. The prophet offers no explanation for this sudden turnaround. The emphasis on YHWH as the one who will fight against the nations reflects the utter inability of Jerusalem to withstand the on-slaught of the nations that will attack it. The stronger the assurance of divine deliverance the less able Jerusalem is to defend itself. Once again, the text portrays God with martial imagery but now God goes into battle to prevent the total devastation of Jerusalem and its people.

The martial imagery of verses 1-3 gives way to theophanic imagery in verses 4-5. The prophet describes God's mighty acts that will rearrange the topography of Jerusalem. This rearrangement will facilitate the es-cape of the people of Jerusalem on the day of battle mentioned in verse 3 and then the agricultural productivity of the Jerusalem region. The prophet pictures YHWH as standing on the Mount of Olives, which splits in two with one part moving to the north and the other to the south. This will create "a very wide valley" running west to east between the two parts of the mountain. This valley will provide the people of Jerusalem a way to escape the siege of the city by crossing the Kidron Valley and making their way through the valley created by the splitting of the Mount of Olives to the safety of Azal.[8] Still, the splitting of the Mount of Olives and the creation of the valley were as unnerving as the earthquake that occurred during the reign of Uzziah (see also Amos 1:1).[9] God's actions to make it possible for the people of Jerusalem to escape the city are harbingers of the changing fortunes of Jerusalem as God, accompanied by members of the heavenly court (see Deut 33:2; Ps 89:5-7), appears on the scene.

The transformation of the topography of the region around Jerusalem will not only reveal the power of YHWH over the earth and the forces of nature but also provide the type of environment that increases the productivity of agricultural activity in the region. The central highlands of the southern Levant offered challenges to the subsistence farmers of Yehud who worked the land. If the rains did not come at the right time

8. Azal is an unidentified site that the text locates east of Jerusalem. There have been attempts to identify the "very wide valley" with an existing valley in the area, but none of these has found much support.

9. Uzziah ruled the kingdom of Judah from 785 to 733 BCE. The precise date of the earthquake, however, cannot be determined. The southern Levant is an earthquake-prone region because of the Great Rift Valley in its midst. In antiquity, earthquakes had disastrous effects on the region's buildings and infrastructure, leading people to flee out of fear as mentioned in v. 5.

and in sufficient quantity, the people faced shortages and even famine. Farming on the hills of the highlands was labor intensive, requiring the construction and maintenance of terraces that prevented erosion and made the best use of limited water resources. The effects of the Babylonian incursions on agriculture in the region were still being felt. The region's orchards and vineyards had yet to recover fully. Yehud's population still did not return to its preexilic level, so there was a shortage of agricultural workers. In addition, the taxes demanded by the Persian authorities led to the loss of a good portion of the harvest. The leveling of the land and the repopulation of the region will ease people's anxiety about the possibility of food shortages and famines.

TRANSLATION MATTERS

Both the NRSVue and the NABRE translations have verse 5 end with the phrase "with him." The MT reads instead עמך, "with you" (2nd fem. sing.). English translations except for the KJV follow the ancient versions, which have "with him." The MT presents the more difficult reading so the emendation to "to him" in the ancient versions and modern translations is understandable. The MT reading offers a contrast to verse 1 in the which the second feminine suffix appears in the text that describes the disasters that Jerusalem will experience (. . . שללך. . . בקרבך. . .). In verse 5 MT, the antecedent of the second-person feminine singular pronoun is Jerusalem, which will accompany its patron and God's heavenly courtiers: "Then YHWH my God will come, and all the holy ones *with you*." The MT reading makes sense from a literary perspective and the emendation found in the versions is unnecessary.

The principal challenge facing agriculture in the southern Levant has always been availability of water. Verse 8 testifies to the importance of water for the region's ecology. That text asserts the abundant runoff water from the rain falling on Jerusalem will flow into both the Mediterranean and the Dead Sea. The runoff water will continue to flow even after the rainy season has ended. Today's expanding population and the growth of tourism in the southern Levant have severely taxed the limited water supply in the region. The Israeli government has attempted to meet the increased demand for fresh water by drastically limiting the amount of water from the Sea of Galilee that is allowed to flow into the Jordan River, diverting that water into the Israeli National Water Carrier. This amount of water diverted for use in Israel has profound effects on the people of

Jordan and Syria who also depend on the Jordan River for water. The limited amount of water flowing into the Jordan has also changed the ecology of the Dead Sea and the land surrounding it. The Dead Sea is shrinking because 90 percent of the Jordan's water is siphoned off before it reaches the Dead Sea. The stability of the shoreline is eroding. Nearly three thousand sinkholes have developed along the shoreline of the Dead Sea because of its receding waters. The Dead Sea will not disappear, but it will shrink considerably. How much authority should human beings claim over the earth? Of course, the changes in Jerusalem's topography as described in verses 4-5 are the product of the prophet's imagination to speak of the restoration of Jerusalem that God will accomplish. Unfortunately, human beings have been able to turn such imagery into reality, e.g., the damming of the Colorado River to provide water for irrigation, the building of levees to control the spring flooding along the Mississippi River, the transformation of the Great Plains into farmland for the cultivation of grains, and the creation of the St. Lawrence Seaway to facilitate commerce in North America. Too often little, if any, attention is paid to the ecological consequences that result from people's attempt to refashion the earth—its land, water, and other resources—for their economic benefit. Technological advances have enabled human beings to change the face of their environment. Before attempting such changes, people should be conscious of the effects on the flora and fauna of the region whose ecological balance will be affected.

The eschatological vision in chapter 14 begins with a description of the fall of Jerusalem brought about by the nations summoned for this purpose by YHWH. It ends with a promise that such a thing will not happen again—Jerusalem will never again be subject to חרם, i.e., the total destruction, which the use of that term implies. A new era of peace will begin for Jerusalem, for the city "shall abide in security" (v. 11). History has painted a different picture of Jerusalem's fate. It was attacked and besieged scores of times since Zechariah expressed his confidence about the city's future. In 135 CE, the Roman emperor Hadrian destroyed it more thoroughly than did Nebuchadnezzar in 587 BCE. The city passed through the hands of the Greeks, the Romans, the Byzantines, the Arabs, the Crusaders, the Ottoman Turks, and the British—always managing to survive somehow. Today it is the principal flash point in the Palestinian–Israeli conflict. Zechariah's vision still awaits its fulfillment.

Ultranationalist Israelis and fundamentalist Christians oppose any compromise with the Palestinians over the status of Jerusalem. The ultranationalist Israelis want to end any Palestinian presence in East Jerusalem, which the Palestinians claim as the capital of the Palestinian state that they claim as their right. Fundamentalist Christians believe that Jewish rule over all Jerusalem is a necessary prelude to the Second Coming of Christ. It is incumbent on all believers—Jew, Christian, and Muslim—to collaborate in good faith to turn Zechariah's vision of a Jerusalem abiding "in security" (v. 11) into reality. The only other option is to continue the vicious cycle of occupation, oppression, violence, and terrorism.

In 1988, Israeli women formed the Women in Black in Israel. It is part of a worldwide women's antiwar movement.[10] The Israeli group was formed in response to the First Intifada. Women principally from the left of the political spectrum protested the violation of human rights in the Occupied Territories by standing in silence in the center of West Jerusalem. Soon similar silent vigils took place in other Israeli cities. In 2001, the movement was awarded the Millennium Peace Prize for Women given by the United Nations Development Fund for Women. The Women in Black vigils are a powerful statement made by women against oppression and injustice and for reconciliation and peace.

Zechariah asserts that manifestation of God's power over the nations and nature will extend beyond effects on Jerusalem: "YHWH will become king over all the earth" (v. 9a). This implies that in the eschaton the Israelite monarchy will not exist since YHWH will be king. Such a view is not surprising since the Israelite monarchy was a failed institution. Any hopes for a restoration of the Davidic dynasty disappeared with Zerubbabel. Jewish society in Yehud had become a hierocracy with the high priest of the Jerusalem temple taking on the principal position. Zechariah depicts YHWH as king over a secure Jerusalem (vv. 9-11). Such a portrait, of course, paints YHWH in masculine colors.

Zechariah 14:9 has been read as a Midrashic interpretation of the *Shema*, the passage in Deuteronomy 6:4-5 that became part of rabbinic Judaism's liturgical core.[11] A comparison of the passages underscores how the writer of Zechariah 14:9 employs foundational motifs of the *Shema* to make a new point:

> And the LORD will become king over all the earth; on that day the LORD will be one and his name one. (Zech 14:9)

10. Gila Svirsky, "Local Coalitions, Global Partners: The Women's Peace Movement in Israel and Beyond," *Signs: A Journal of Women in Culture and Society* 29 (2004): 545–46.
11. Carolyn Pressler, "The *Shema'*: A Protestant Feminist Reading," in *Escaping Eden: New Feminist Perspectives on the Bible*, ed. Harold C. Washington, Susan Lochrie Graham, and Pamela Thimmes (New York: New York University Press, 1999), 47–48.

> Hear, O Israel: The LORD is our God, the LORD alone. ⁵You shall love
> the LORD your God with all your heart and with all your soul and with
> all your might. (Deut 6:4-5)

While Deuteronomy instructs the Israelites to acknowledge YHWH as
their only God and to love their God, Zechariah precludes any possibility
of the existence of other gods. The question of whether Deuteronomy
6:4-5 is monotheistic or monolatrous is unclear, but it is probable that
the text reflects monolatry, not monotheism.[12] Zechariah, however, clari-
fies that in the end time, all creatures will worship only YHWH, which
implies that no other gods exist.[13]

The author's awareness of the *Shema* as a theological statement suggests
that, by the early Second Temple period, this passage was well known to
Jews and perhaps was even used liturgically. By the late Second Temple
period, the *Shema* would take pride of place in Jewish tradition: phylac-
teries found at Qumran include the *Shema* and the Decalogue of Exodus
20. In the view of the rabbis, the *Shema* would surpass the Decalogue as
the most theologically foundational text of the Pentateuch. References to
the *Shema* in the writings of Jewish thinkers who lived in the late Second
Temple period such as Josephus and Philo indicate that, by the first century
CE, it held an important place in Jewish thought. Zechariah's allusion here
might be the earliest Midrashic form of the *Shema* that has been preserved.[14]

Jew and Gentile (14:12-21)

The closing passage of the book of Zechariah comprises one of the
most universalist statements in the entire Hebrew Bible, though verses
12-15 suggest the opposite. The prophet reverts to matters associated
with warfare. This contrasts with the motif of a secure Jerusalem in
verses 10-11. The enemy soldiers besieging Jerusalem will suffer the
consequences of living in close quarters without proper sanitation and
other health measures. Disease flourishes in such conditions, potentially
rendering an army unfit for action. In the American Civil War, for example, more soldiers died in camp from disease than on the battlefield

---

12. Monotheism is the belief that only one God exists while monolatry is a religious system that permits the worship of only one God, though it holds that other
gods may exist.

13. Schaefer, "The Ending of the Book of Zechariah," 200.

14. On second temple sources that cite the *Shema*, see Sarit Kattan Gribetz, "The
Shema in the Second Temple Period: A Reconsideration," *Journal of Ancient Judaism*
6 (2015): 58–84.

Zech 14:12-21

¹²This shall be the plague with which the LORD will strike all the peoples who wage war against Jerusalem: their flesh shall rot while they are still on their feet, their eyes shall rot in their sockets, and their tongues shall rot in their mouths. ¹³On that day a great panic from the LORD shall fall on them, so that each will seize the hand of a neighbor, and the hand of the one will be raised against the hand of the other; ¹⁴even Judah will fight at Jerusalem. And the wealth of all the surrounding nations shall be collected: gold, silver, and garments in great abundance. ¹⁵And a plague like this plague shall fall on the horses, the mules, the camels, the donkeys, and whatever animals may be in those camps.

¹⁶Then all who survive of the nations that have come against Jerusalem shall go up year after year to worship the King, the LORD of hosts, and to keep the Festival of Booths. ¹⁷If any of the families of the earth do not go up to Jerusalem to worship the King, the LORD of hosts, there will be no rain upon them. ¹⁸And if the family of Egypt do not go

from enemy shot. The spreading of the plague in the camp will lead the enemy soldiers to become crazed with panic and to turn on each other. The army's livestock will also fall victim to disease. The Jewish resistance will take advantage of this situation and reverse the plundering that Jerusalem will have experienced during the siege. The flow of the nations' wealth in Jerusalem is the opposite of the situation at the beginning of the siege (vv. 1, 14). The reversal of fortunes becomes a stock apocalyptic motif. The beneficiaries of this reversal are usually those on the margins: the poor (Matt 5:3), the persecuted (Dan 12:1-3), women (Luke 1:36, 46-48). The reversal of Jerusalem's fortunes is at the heart of chapter 14 and is a most appropriate conclusion to a book of prophecy that wishes to encourage belief in the future of the Jewish people despite the economic, political, and social situation in which the people of Yehud find themselves. Even more striking, however, is the inclusion of the nations in Zechariah's grand vision of Jerusalem's future. This represents a reversal in the prophetic tradition in which oracles against the nations were standard fare. It calls for a reversal on the part of the people of Yehud, who have experienced other peoples as threats to their very existence. The book of Zechariah ends with an unexpected but most welcome vision of inclusion as the gentiles join the Jews of Yehud in the pilgrimage to Jerusalem for the feast of Sukkoth (v. 16). Today war and poverty along with political, ethnic, and religious persecution have led to waves of migration with people seeking the chance of a better life.

Zech 14:12-21 (cont.)

up and present themselves, there will be no rain for them; there will be the plague that the LORD inflicts on the nations that do not go up to keep the Festival of Booths. ¹⁹Such shall be the punishment of Egypt and the punishment of all the nations that do not go up to keep the Festival of Booths.

²⁰On that day there shall be inscribed on the bells of the horses, "Holy to the LORD." And the cooking pots in the house of the LORD shall be as holy as the bowls in front of the altar, ²¹and every cooking pot in Jerusalem and Judah shall be holy to the LORD of hosts, so that all who sacrifice may come and use them to boil the flesh of the sacrifice. And there shall no longer be traders in the house of the LORD of hosts on that day.

This has led to an uptick in xenophobia in developed countries whose citizens believe that the influx of migrants into their communities will threaten their way of life. A new "reversal" is necessary.

After the repeated references to warfare, siege, plagues, plunder, rape, and exile, the prophet abruptly shifts to the pilgrimage that those who survive—both Jew and gentile—will make to Jerusalem. Not only will the gentiles recognize YHWH as king (v. 9), but in another remarkable reversal, they will make a pilgrimage to the very city they once besieged. The experience of universal salvation and the response of worship applies equally to both Jews and gentiles. There appears to be no apparent distinction that sets the two peoples apart. To understand how universalist—and innovative—this passage is, it is important to step back and consider precisely what universalism is and what this concept would have meant to Jews living in the early Second Temple period. Too often, scholars presume that universalist thought simply reflects an openness to converts. This approach implies that a religion that actively reaches out to and invites others who are not currently members of their religion to participate in and ultimately to become a member of their religious community is a universalist religion. Unfortunately, scholars of Judaism and Christianity tend to contrast the "universalism" of Christianity, which actively invited all people to believe in the salvation God offers through Jesus, with the "particularism" of Judaism, which expressed little interest in seeking converts.

The problem with this framework, however, is that it is based on a problematic definition of universalism. The idea that universalism is defined by openness to converts maintains an "in" and "out" model in which people outside of one's religious community would not be subject to the benefits of divine salvation in the end time.[15] To enjoy these benefits, one had to be on the "inside" rather than on the "outside." This is a particularist notion. True universalism makes no distinction between people of varying faiths and ethnicities. It invites people, regardless of their religious affiliation, to worship God alongside one another, without any presumption of an ultimate conversion. This is the type of universalism that Zechariah 14 is advocating. All people are offered equal access to salvation should they worship God alongside one another, and all are subject to equal divine retribution should they refuse to do so.

Some readers might point out that the end of Zechariah envisions a period of incredible destruction: Zechariah 14:13-15 describes a scene of devastating chaos, suffering, and infighting among all people. How could such an image be considered universalist? The answer lies in the fact that all people, Jew and gentile alike, will be equally vulnerable during this period of divine judgment. Likewise, all people, Jew and gentile alike, will be expected to observe the feast of Sukkoth in Jerusalem (14:18). A universalist image does not necessarily project a harmonious image, but one in which all people are expected to worship God in a sustained and ongoing way without assimilating into a single religious tradition.

Zechariah 14:13 foresees a time when people will cling to one another amid terrible destruction. The language used here parallels Zechariah 8:23, in which ten gentiles will cling to the garment of one Jew:

> Thus says the Lord of hosts: In those days ten men from nations of every language shall take hold of a Jew, grasping his garment and saying, "Let us go with you, for we have heard that God is with you." (Zech 8:23)

> On that day a great panic from the Lord shall fall on them, so that each will seize the hand of a neighbor, and the hand of one will be raised against the hand of the other. (Zech 14:13)

Both of these are said to occur on the Day of YHWH. The verb וְהֶחֱזִיקוּ ("grasp"; NRSVue: "shall take hold of") used in 8:23 is the same verb used in 14:13 (וְהֶחֱזִיקוּ, "will seize"). Zechariah 8:23 envisions a peaceful time when all gentiles will want to join Israel in the worship of God. In Zechariah 8, however, there is a vast gap between Israel and the nations.

---

15. For a discussion of the origins of universalism within Judaism, see Malka Z. Simkovich, *The Making of Jewish Universalism: From Exile to Alexandria* (Lanham, MD: Lexington Books, 2016).

The nations are the "other," the people who do not know how to properly worship God and do not even know where Jerusalem is located.
They depend on a Jewish person to show them how to reach the temple.
Zechariah 14, on the other hand, paints a portrait of utter chaos that all
people experience. A plague will afflict the people who had once stood
as enemies against the Jews, but internal strife between the Jewish people
will also create suffering and death within their own community. Amid
this chaos, all people will fight against one another, and a resolution will
come only following God's direct intervention.

One of the reasons that scholars believe that Zechariah 1–8 and
Zechariah 9–14 should be viewed as two different books is that Zechariah 8 reads like the conclusion of a long biblical passage, as does Zechariah 14. Both chapters assume the unique status of Israel. Zechariah 8
and 14 both close with images of how the Jews will ultimately relate to
the gentiles in the eschaton. The nature of the gentiles' role in the end
time, however, differs from one another in these chapters. The writer
of chapter 8 tells us that in the end of days gentiles will beg the Jews to
accompany them to Jerusalem in order to worship God alongside them.
This chapter conveys a separateness between the Jews and the gentiles
that is not breached. The Jews are the elect people of God, but the gentiles may worship God as well, if they choose. The relationship between
Jews and gentiles in Zechariah 14, however, is a more egalitarian one.
All people—Jews and gentiles alike—will worship God together in Jerusalem. They will also be subject to judgment alongside one another.
Chapters 8 and 14 serve similar structural purposes for Zechariah in that
they both close a major section. The differences between these chapters
suggest that they were composed by different individuals.

The image of the nations streaming to Jerusalem to celebrate Sukkoth
is peculiar. Why did the prophet not specify the observance of the sabbath or of Yom Kippur? This question becomes more significant when we
examine the biblical text that is most comparable to Zechariah 14, Isaiah
66. Isaiah 66 also characterizes the eschaton as an age when all people
will worship the Israelite God in Jerusalem and gives no indication that
the gentiles will assimilate into the religion of ancient Israel. But Isaiah
66 specifies that all people will observe the sabbaths and new moons
rather than Sukkoth as in Zechariah 14. The differences between Isaiah
66 and Zechariah 14 may be explained by the association of Sukkoth
with the celebration of the new year a few days earlier. The celebration
of Sukkoth on the part of the foreign nations implies a commitment to

worship God year-round.[16] Also, Sukkoth originally was associated with food production. It was celebrated just before the early rains that inaugurate the plowing of the fields in preparation for the planting of grain crops. In chapter 14, Sukkoth takes on eschatological significance as testifying to salvation that transcends that of the Jews alone but will include gentiles as well. For Zechariah, the celebration of Sukkoth does not mark a new agricultural season but a new era in which Jew and gentile will recognize YHWH's sovereignty.

TRANSLATION MATTERS

The Hebrew of verse 21 appears to be in tension with the universalist direction of chapter 14. The word the NRSVue renders as "traders" is כנעני ("Canaanite"). This solves the apparent anomaly that has the Canaanites excluded from the gentiles who will join the Jews in the worship of YHWH. It is possible to justify this translation, though the significance of the "traders" in the context of chapter 14 has its own problems. Carol Meyers and Eric Meyers suggest that the term "Canaanite" here represents all that is opposed to Yahwistic religion rather than an ethnic group as such.[16] Unfortunately, this understanding of the term is not self-evident. The best a translator can do in instances like this is offer a brief explanation in a footnote.

Zechariah 14 advocates for a kind of universalism that was virtually unknown in the biblical period but that became more developed in the Second Temple period. Besides this chapter and Isaiah 66, some psalms also express universalist ideas. Psalm 96 envisions a time when the foreign nations will worship God without "converting":

> Ascribe to the Lord, O families of the peoples,
>   ascribe to the Lord glory and strength.
> Ascribe to the Lord the glory due his name;
>   bring an offering, and come into his courts.
> Worship the Lord in holy splendor;
>   tremble before him, all the earth. (Ps 96:7-9)

16. Jan A. Wagenaar, *Origin and Transformation of the Ancient Israelite Festival Calendar*, BZABR 6 (Wiesbaden: Harrassowitz, 2005), 21–24; Hakan Ulfgard, *The Story of Sukkot: The Setting, Shaping, and Sequel of the Biblical Feast of Tabernacles*, BGBE 34 (Tübingen: Mohr Siebeck, 1998), 151.

17. Meyers and Meyers, *Zechariah 9–14*, 489–90.

Psalm 96 calls on all people to worship God without the suggestion of a conversion process. Indeed, the term "families of the peoples" suggests that the separate ethnic and religious identities of the world will be maintained during the process of coming together to worship YHWH. Zechariah's call to the "families of the earth" likewise suggests that all people will come together to worship God but not become a single community.

The sense of universality in the closing passage of Zechariah is amplified by its focus on the family unit rather than on the individual, who in biblical prophetic literature is usually presumed to be a male. Families—husbands, wives, sons, and daughters—are called on by the prophet to come together to Jerusalem and worship God.

The closing passage of Zechariah parallels the book's introductory vision of a man on a red horse leading a team of horses. Both passages envision a period of worldwide peace but acknowledge the suffering that Judah has endured:

> In the night I saw a man riding on a red horse! He was standing among the myrtle trees in the shadows, and behind him were red, sorrel, and white horses. Then I said, "What are these, my lord?" The angel who spoke with me said to me, "I will show you what they are." So the man who was standing among the myrtle trees answered, "They are those whom the LORD has sent to patrol the earth." Then they spoke to the angel of the LORD who was standing among the myrtle trees, "We have patrolled the earth, and the whole earth remains at peace." Then the angel of the LORD said, "O LORD of hosts, how long will you withhold mercy from Jerusalem and the cities of Judah, with which you have been angry these seventy years?" (Zech 1:8-12)

This vision features horses that have been sent to patrol the earth and ensure that the enemies of Israel have been quelled. In Zechariah 14, horses mirror not the power of God, but the destiny of the people. Just as many people will suffer from a devastating plague (14:12), so too will horses and other load-bearing animals suffer from plague (14:15). And just as survivors of this catastrophic period will go to the temple and worship God (14:16), so too will horses dedicate themselves to God's service (14:20). The book's concluding vision employs the image of horses to underscore the reader's sense that all of God's creatures, both animal and human, will be subject to a common set of covenantal rules. In both Zechariah 1 and 14, then, horses are used to broaden the speaker's message. In Zechariah 1, God's power is so extensive that God uses armies of celestial horses. In Zechariah 14, world harmony is characterized by a single, universal covenant in which all of God's creatures participate.

One striking element of the final chapter of Zechariah is that it associates universal harmony, in which all nations worship God alongside one another, with temple worship, in which all nations participate. The holiness of the temple will touch even the bells on the horses' harnesses. Cooking pots, everyday vessels that were essential to running a household, will likewise be consecrated. Common objects that were once regarded as mundane will be elevated in their use toward the worldwide worship of God.[18] Former distinctions between the sacred and the profane have no relevance in the eschaton because the most common and ordinary of objects will be considered קדש ליהוה ("holy to YHWH"). Objects that have no connection with the temple cult will be considered as holy as those that do.

In Exodus 28:36, the phrase "holy to YHWH" is engraved on the high priest Aaron's diadem. It is strange, then, that in Zechariah the same phrase is engraved on horses' bells (v. 20). Perhaps the prophet was seeking to convey a message regarding the ultimate political dominion of God. In the Hebrew Bible, horses represent military power. Israelite kings are prohibited from acquiring horses in large numbers because such acquisition was viewed as opposed to the dual goal of attaining political peace and acknowledging the sovereignty of the Israelite God (Deut 17:14-16; 1 Sam 8:11-17). By presenting horses as bearing this inscription, therefore, the author of this passage co-opts a typical military and political image and thus suggests that even the most political tools used to increase the power of human kings will become symbols of God's omnipotence.[19]

The idea that regular objects will become consecrated is part of a broader theme that extends throughout this chapter regarding the consecration of all of God's creatures. No longer will there be a single, elect people who will stand in opposition to all other nations. Instead, all people will be chosen by God, and all will be subject to the same standards and expectations that a common covenantal relationship demands. This equalizing of humanity is expressed in the parallel between 14:13 ("each will seize the hand of a neighbor") and 8:23 ("ten men from nations of every language shall take hold of a Jew") discussed above. Whereas Zechariah 1–8 closes with an image that assumes Israel's unique status, Zechariah 9–14 closes with an image of the democratization of

18. R. P. Gordon, "Inscribed Pots and Zechariah XIV 20–1," *VT* 42 (1992): 120–23.
19. Meyers and Meyers, *Zechariah 9–14*, 480.

humankind. This democratization does not ensure eternal peace: if all people properly observe God, then they will live harmoniously. Whoever does not worship God properly, whether Jew or not, will suffer greatly.

The universalism expressed in Zechariah 14 is matched in only one other biblical passage: Isaiah 66, which also envisions a time in which all of humankind will be subject to a single covenantal relationship with God. As a postexilic text, Isaiah 66 reflects a similar optimism regarding the future as Zechariah 14. These postexilic universalist texts build on biblical prophetic literature from the exilic period that sows the seeds of universalism by speaking of God as a God of all people. This kind of literature, most clearly expressed in Isaiah 40–55, is not quite universalist but does emphasize that God has a relationship with all people, not only those Israelites who entered a covenantal relationship with him at Sinai.[20]

Zechariah closes on a note of optimistic hope. The covenantal language that yearns for a time when all people worship God together correlates with a postexilic optimism that the speaker may have internalized as he began to witness the restoration of his community in Yehud. While this restoration brought with it challenges as the people set about establishing a semiautonomous system of political and religious leadership, it also gave rise to renewed optimism that the Jews were living on the cusp of an era that would feature worldwide peace among all people.

20. *Pace* Meyers and Meyers, *Zechariah 9–14*, 440; Cf. Saul Olyan, "Is Isaiah 40–55 Really Monotheistic?," *JANER* 12 (2012): 190–201; Joel Kaminsky and Anne Stewart, "God of All the World: Universalism and Developing Monotheism in Isaiah 40–66," *HTR* 99 (2006): 139–63.

Conclusion

The Legacy of Zechariah

The book of Zechariah has been a significant prophetic text for both Jewish and Christian interpreters, despite the opaque character of some of its passages. Some of the book's imagery stimulated readers' own imaginations. For example, the prophet's visions of a salvific leader entering Jerusalem on a donkey has been employed by Jewish interpreters as a guide in recognizing the beginnings of the messianic age. Christians read this same image, along with that of the prophet who is pierced, through the lens of Jesus's final days. Contemporary believers find the universalist vision of the book's final chapters to be a design for a better world.

Although finding meaning in some of the book's more esoteric visions can challenge even the most careful and sensitive reader, its ethical dimension is clear enough as the prophet speaks of the importance of speaking truth, creating a just society (7:8-10), and recognizing and repenting for moral failures (1:4-6). For the prophet, the Judean restoration was about creating a community based on just intersocietal relations. It was not about re-creating the social and economic dynamics of preexilic Judah that was characterized by inequity and division. The prophet asserted that Jerusalem of the restoration will be known as "the faithful city" (8:3)—faithful to the ideals of traditional Israelite ethical ideals.

The prophet saw the construction of a temple for YHWH as a major goal of the Judean restoration, though he speaks of this goal only six times. A far more significant goal was the rehabilitation of Jerusalem, which received far more attention from the prophet. Achieving that goal was possible only because YHWH had chosen to return to the city (1:16-17; 8:3). Although the temple is the place of God's dwelling on earth, the holiness of the divine presence permeates the entirety of the city—even its cooking pots are holy (14:21). The book of Zechariah is an important moment in the transformation of Jerusalem from "the city of David" (2 Sam 5:9) into "the holy city" (Isa 52:1; Neh 11:1)—a status it has not only in Judaism but in Christianity and Islam as well. Though the rebuilding of the temple was an important motif in the book, the prophet's notion of the holiness of the city helps prepare Judaism for a world without a temple, helping Judaism survive the destruction of the temple in 70 CE.

An especially significant feature of the book is its inclusive perspective as it calls attention to young and old, male and female, as it describes the people's response to God's actions on behalf of the people of Yehud. Like most biblical books, Zechariah is neither completely misogynist nor entirely enlightened in the way it reflects its social world. The book is a product of a male-dominated social, political, economic, and religious system in which women played an essential but decidedly subordinate role, though there were a few exceptions. The imagery chosen to speak of God is male and predominantly martial in tone. A favorite epithet for the deity in Zechariah is יהוה צבאות. This, of course, rankles feminist readers who find repetitive use of such a sexist, exclusivist, and martial title to be unnecessary and tiresome. Although God is described in feminine terms elsewhere in the Hebrew Bible, female imagery for the Divine is absent in Zechariah. Our task as sensitive readers is to both appreciate the words of Zechariah as they were meant to be read while also critiquing the way these words leave women relegated to the margins in the prophet's rhetoric. Readers need to depend on inference rather than the prophet's words to assess the role and status of women in the Judean restoration. Still, the book's message is, at its core, a vision of a future guided by the simple admonition "show kindness and mercy to one another" (Zech 7:9). In a book marked by puzzling visions and confounding imagery, this admonition is clear enough. It represents an ideal that people still struggle to abide by today.

The book of Zechariah begins with visions that foresee divine judgment on the nations, but it ends with a vision of a pilgrimage of the nations to Jerusalem for the feast of Sukkoth (14:16). The prophet imagines a future in which all people will join in the worship of YHWH and enjoy the peace and prosperity that this feast celebrates. Although the book comes from a period of unfulfilled expectations, its vision of a better future is a testament to the faith of those responsible for composing and transmitting this book. They believed in a God who wants only the best for all people. That belief may have been expressed in ways that do not always mesh with feminist sensibilities. Still, the book commends a life of kindness and mercy to its readers. That makes the message of this book pertinent to all women and men of good will. The challenge that believers face today is how to create and maintain a social structure that allows all people to enjoy their rights as they seek to realize their potential without the obstacles presented by sexism, racism, classism, or prejudice in any other form.

Works Cited

Ackerman, Susan. "The Queen Mother and the Cult in Ancient Israel." *JBL* 112 (1993): 385–401.

Ackroyd, Peter. *Exile and Restoration: A Study of Hebrew Thought of the Sixth Century B.C.* OTL. London: SCM Press, 1968.

Aguilar, Grace. *The Women of Israel.* London: R. Groombridge, 1845; New York: D. Appleton, 1872.

Albertz, Rainer. *Israel in Exile: The History and Literature of the Sixth Century B.C.E.* Translated by David Green. Atlanta: SBL, 2003.

Allen, Garrick V. "Zechariah's Horse Visions and Angelic Intermediaries: Translation, Allusion, and Transmission in Early Judaism." *CBQ* 79 (2017): 222–39.

Anderson, Gary A., and Saul M. Olyan, eds. *Priesthood and Cult in Ancient Israel.* JSOTSup 125. Sheffield: JSOT Press, 1991.

Anderson, Janice Capel, and Stephen D. Moore, eds. *Mark and Method: New Approaches in Biblical Studies.* 2nd ed. Minneapolis: Fortress, 2008.

Andreasen, Niels-Erik A. "The Role of the Queen Mother in Israelite Society." *CBQ* 45 (1983): 179–94.

Angel, Hayyim. *Haggai, Zechariah, and Malachi: Prophecy in an Age of Uncertainty.* New Milford, CT: Maggid Books, 2016.

Angel, Hayyim. *Zechariah, and Malachi.* Jerusalem: Malbim al Nakh, 1992

Aquino, María Pilar, and María José Rosado-Nunes, eds. *Feminist Intercultural Theology: Latina Explorations for a Just World.* Studies in Latino/a Catholicism. Maryknoll, NY: Orbis Books, 2007.

Aquino, María Pilar, Daisy L. Machado, and Jeanette Rodríguez, eds. *A Reader in Latina Feminist Theology.* Austin: University of Texas Press, 2002.

Assis, Elie. "The Structure of Zechariah 8 and Its Meaning." *Perspectives on Hebrew Scriptures IX: Comprising the Contents of Journal of Hebrew Scriptures, vol. 12,* edited by Ehud Ben Zvi and Christophe Nihan, 351–69 (Piscataway, NJ: Gorgias Press, 2014).

Assis, Elie. "Zechariah 8 as Revision and Digest of Zechariah 1–7." *JHebS* 10 (2010): 1–26.

Assis, Elie. "Zechariah's Vision of the Ephah (Zech 5:5-11)." *VT* 60 (2010): 15–32.

Astell, Mary. *Some Reflections upon Marriage.* New York: Source Book Press, 1970. Reprint of the 1730 ed.; earliest ed. 1700.

Aune, David. *Prophecy in Early Christianity and the Ancient Mediterranean World.* Grand Rapids: Eerdmans, 1983.

Bach, Alice, ed. *Women in the Hebrew Bible: A Reader.* New York: Routledge, 1999.

Bakhos, Carol, and Gerhard Langer, eds. *The Jewish Middle Ages.* BW 4.2. Atlanta: SBL Press, 2023.

Bal, Mieke. *Lethal Love: Feminist Literary Readings of Biblical Love Stories.* Bloomington: Indiana University Press, 1987.

Baldwin, Joyce. *Haggai, Zechariah, Malachi: An Introduction and Commentary.* TOTC. Downers Grove, IL: InterVarsity Press, 1972.

Barker, Margaret. "The Evil in Zechariah." *HeyJ* 19 (1978): 12–27.

Barmash, Pamela. "Women and Mitzvot." *Yoreh Deah* 246 (2014): 1–34.

Baskin, Judith R. "Women and Post-Biblical Commentary." In *The Torah: A Women's Commentary,* edited by Tamara Cohn Eskenazi and Andrea L. Weiss, xlix–lv. New York: URJ Press and Women of Reform Judaism, The Federation of Temple Sisterhoods, 2008.

Beavis, Mary Ann, Irmtraud Fischer, Mercedes Navarro Puerto, and Adriana Valerio, eds. The Bible and Women: An Encyclopaedia of Exegesis and Cultural History (BW). https://www.bibleandwomen.org.

Bedford, Peter R. "The Economic Role of the Jerusalem Temple in Achaemenid Judah: Comparative Perspectives." In *Shai le-Sara Japhet: Studies in the Bible, Its Exegesis and Its Language,* edited by Mosheh Bar-Asher, Dalit Rom-Shiloni, Emanuel Tov, and Nilil Wazana, 3–20. Jerusalem: Bialik Institute, 2007.

Bell, Duncan S. A. "Mythscapes: Memory, Mythology, and National Identity." *The British Journal of Sociology* 54 (2003): 63–81.

Ben-Barak, Zafrira. "The Status and Right of the *GĔBÎRÂ*." *JBL* 110 (1991): 23–34.

Bergant, Dianne. *The Earth Is the Lord's: The Bible, Ecology, and Worship.* AELS. Collegeville, MN: Liturgical Press, 1998.

Berger, David. "Statement by Dr. David Berger Regarding the New York Times Ad by Dabru Emet." Orthodox Union Advocacy Center. September 14, 2000. https://advocacy.ou.org/statement_by_dr_david_berger_regarding_the_new_york_times_ad_by_dabru_emet/.

Berquist, Jon L. *Judaism in Persia's Shadow: A Social and Historical Approach.* Minneapolis: Fortress, 1995.

Bird, Phyllis A. *Missing Persons and Mistaken Identities: Women and Gender in Ancient Israel.* Minneapolis: Fortress, 1997.

Bird, Phyllis A. "The Place of Women in the Israelite Cultus." In *Ancient Israelite Religion: Essays in Honor of Frank Moore Cross,* edited by Patrick D. Miller, Paul D. Hanson, and S. Dean McBride, 397–420. Philadelphia: Fortress, 1987.

Blenkinsopp, Joseph. *A History of Prophecy in Israel*. Philadelphia: Westminster, 1983.

Bockmuehl, Markus N. A. " 'The Trumpet Shall Sound': Shofar Symbolism and Its Reception in Early Christianity." In *Templum Amicitiae: Essays on the Second Temple Presented to Ernst Bammel*, edited by William Horbury, 199–225. JSNTSup 48. Sheffield: JSOT Press, 1991.

Boda, Mark J. *The Book of Zechariah*. NICOT. Grand Rapids: Eerdmans, 2016.

Boda, Mark J. "Freeing the Burden of Prophecy: Maśśaʾ and the Legitimacy of Prophecy in Zech 9–14." *Bib* 87 (2006): 338–57.

Boda, Mark J. "From Fasts to Feasts: The Literary Function of Zechariah 7–8." *CBQ* 65 (2003): 390–407.

Boda, Mark J. "Identity and Empire, Reality and Hope in the Chronicler's Perspective." In *Community Identity in Judean Historiography: Biblical and Comparative Perspectives*, edited by Gary N. Knoppers and Kenneth A. Ristau, 249–72. Winona Lake, IN: Eisenbrauns, 2009.

Boda, Mark J. "Oil, Crowns and Thrones: Prophet, Priest and King in Zechariah 1:7–6:15." *JHebS* 3 (2001): sec. 4.3.3.4.

Boda, Mark J. "Perspectives on Priests in Haggai–Malachi." In *Prayer and Poetry in the Dead Sea Scrolls and Related Literature: Essays in Honor of Eileen Schuller on the Occasion of Her 65th Birthday*, edited by Jeremy S. Penner, Ken M. Penner, and Cecilia Wassen, 13–33. STDJ 98. Leiden: Brill, 2012.

Boda, Mark J. "Zechariah: Master Mason or Penitential Prophet?" In *Yahwism after the Exile: Perspectives on Israelite Religion in the Persian Era; Papers Read at the First Meeting of the European Association for Biblical Studies, Utrecht, 6–9 August 2000*, edited by Rainer Albertz and Bob Becking, 49–69. Studies in Theology and Religion 5. Assen: Van Gorcum, 2003.

Boda, Mark J., Carol J. Dempsey, and LeAnn Snow Flesher, eds. *Daughter Zion: Her Portrait, Her Response*. AIL 13. Atlanta: SBL, 2012.

Børresen, Kari Elisabeth, and Adriana Valerio, eds. *The High Middle Ages*. BW 9.1. Atlanta: SBL Press, 2015.

Bowen, Nancy R. "The Quest for the Historical *Gĕbîrâ*." *CBQ* 63 (2001): 597–618.

Brenner-Idan, Athalya. *The Israelite Woman: Social Role and Literary Type in Biblical Narrative*. London: Bloomsbury, 2015.

Brewer-Boydston, Ginny. *Good Queen Mothers, Bad Queen Mothers: The Theological Presentation of the Queen Mother in 1 and 2 Kings*. CBQMS 54. Washington, DC: CBA, 2016.

Bronner, Leila Leah. "The Motherly Role of God." In *Stories of Biblical Mothers: Maternal Power in the Hebrew Bible*, 106–17. Lanham, MD: University Press of America, 2004.

Brooten, Bernadette J. *Love Between Women: Early Christian Responses to Female Homoeroticism*. Chicago: University of Chicago Press, 1996.

Brooten, Bernadette J. *Women Leaders in the Ancient Synagogue: Inscriptional Evidence and Background Issues*. BJS 36. Chico, CA: Scholars Press, 1982.

Bruehler, Bart B. "Seeing through the מיכיע of Zechariah: Understanding Zechariah 4." *CBQ* 63 (2001): 430–43.

Butterworth, Mike. *Structure and the Book of Zechariah*. JSOTSup 130. Sheffield: Sheffield Academic, 1992.

Camp, Claudia V. *Wisdom and the Feminine in the Book of Proverbs*. Decatur, GA: Almond Press, 1985.

Cannon, Katie Geneva. "The Emergence of Black Feminist Consciousness." In *Feminist Interpretation of the Bible*, edited by Letty M. Russell, 30–40. Philadelphia: Westminster, 1985.

Carter, Warren. "Matthaean Christology in Roman Imperial Key: Matthew 1.1." In *The Gospel of Matthew in Its Roman Imperial Context*, edited by John Riches and David C. Sim. London: T&T Clark, 2005.

Carter, Warren. *The Roman Empire and the New Testament: An Essential Guide*. Nashville: Abingdon, 2006.

Castelli, Elizabeth. "*Les Belles Infidèles*/Fidelity or Feminism? The Meanings of Feminist Biblical Translation." In *Searching the Scriptures: A Feminist Introduction*, vol. 1, edited by Elisabeth Schüssler Fiorenza with the assistance of Shelly Matthews, 189–204. New York: Crossroad, 1993.

Claassens, L. Juliana M. "Calling the Keeners: The Image of the Wailing Women as Symbol of Survival in a Traumatized World." *JFSR* 26 (2010): 63–77.

Claassens, L. Juliana, and Carolyn J. Sharp, eds. *Feminist Frameworks and the Bible: Power, Ambiguity, and Intersectionality*. LHBOTS 630. London: Bloomsbury T&T Clark, 2017.

Claassens, L. Juliana, and Irmtraud Fischer, eds. *Prophecy and Gender in the Hebrew Bible*. BW 1.2. Atlanta: SBL Press, 2021.

Cody, Aelred. *A History of Old Testament Priesthood*. AnBib 35. Rome: Pontifical Biblical Institute, 1969.

Cohn-Sherbok, Dan. "Jewish Faith and the Holocaust." *RelS* 26 (1990): 277–93.

Collins, John J., ed. *Apocalypse: The Morphology of a Genre*. SemeiaSt 14. Missoula, MT: Scholars Press, 1979.

Collins, John J. *The Apocalyptic Imagination: An Introduction to Jewish Apocalyptic Literature*. Biblical Resource Series. 2nd ed. Grand Rapids: Eerdmans, 1998.

Consolino, Franca Ela, and Judith Herrin, eds. *The Early Middle Ages*. BW 6.1 Atlanta: SBL Press, 2020.

Coogan, Michael D., Marc Z. Brettler, Carol A. Newsom, and Pheme Perkins, eds. *The New Oxford Annotated Bible*. New York: Oxford University Press, 2001.

Cook, John M. *The Persian Empire*. New York: Schocken Books, 1983.

Cook, Stephen L. "The Metamorphosis of a Shepherd: The Tradition History of Zechariah 11:17 + 13:7-9." *CBQ* 55 (1993): 453–66.

Cook, Stephen L. *Prophecy & Apocalypticism: The Postexilic Social Setting*. Minneapolis: Fortress, 1995.

Creach, Jerome F. D. *Violence in Scripture*. Interpretation: Resources for the Use of Scripture in the Church. Louisville: Westminster John Knox, 2013.

Curtis, Byron G. *Up the Steep and Stony Road: The Book of Zechariah in Social Location Trajectory Analysis.* AcBib 25. Atlanta: SBL, 2006.

Daly, Mary. *Beyond God the Father: A Philosophy of Women's Liberation.* Boston: Beacon, 1985.

D'Angelo, Mary Rose. "Women Partners in the New Testament." *JFSR* 6 (1990): 65–86.

Darr, Katheryn Pfisterer. *Isaiah's Vision and the Family of God.* Literary Currents in Biblical Interpretation. Louisville: Westminster John Knox, 1994.

Diamond, Eliezer. *Holy Men and Hunger Artists: Fasting and Asceticism in Rabbinic Culture.* New York: Oxford University Press, 2004.

Dinda, Richard, ed. *Luther's Works.* Vol. 20: *Lectures on the Minor Prophets III.* St. Louis: Concordia, 1973.

Dinkler, Michal Beth. *Literary Theory and the New Testament.* AYBRL. New Haven: Yale University Press, 2019.

Djernaes, Marina, Teis Jorgensen, and Elizabeth Koch-Ya'ari. "Evaluation of Environmental Peacemaking Intervention Strategies in Jordan-Palestine-Israel." *Journal of Peacebuilding & Development* 10 (2015): 74–80.

Dobbs-Allsopp, F. W. "The Syntagma of *bat* Followed by a Geographical Name in the Hebrew Bible: A Reconsideration of Its Meaning and Grammar." *CBQ* 57 (1995): 451–70.

Dodd, Charles H. *According to the Scriptures: The sub-structure of New Testament Theology.* New York: Scribner's, 1953.

Dorsey, David A. *The Literary Structure of the Old Testament: A Commentary on Genesis–Malachi.* Grand Rapids: Baker, 1999.

Driver, S. R. *The Minor Prophets: Nahum, Habbakkuk, Zephaniah, Haggai, Zechariah, Malachi.* Edinburgh: T. C. and E. J. Jack, 1906.

Dube, Musa W., ed. *Postcolonial Feminist Interpretation of the Bible.* St. Louis: Chalice, 2000.

Eagleton, Terry. *Ideology: An Introduction.* London: Verso, 2007.

Eagleton, Terry. *Literary Theory: An Introduction.* Anniversary ed. Minneapolis: University of Minnesota Press, 2008.

Edelman, Diana. "Proving Yahweh Killed His Wife (Zechariah 5:5-11)." *BibInt* 11 (2003): 335–44.

Elliger, Karl. "Ein Zeugnis aus der jüdischen Gemeinde im Alexanderjahr 332 v. Chr." *ZAW* 62 (1950): 63–115.

Eron, Lewis John. " 'That Women Have Mastery over Both King and Beggar' (*TJud* 15:5)—The Relationship of the Fear of Sexuality to the Status of Women in Apocrypha and Pseudepigrapha: 1 Esdras (*3 Ezra*) 3–4, Ben Sira and *The Testament of Judah.*" *JSP* 9 (1991): 43–66.

Eskenazi, Tamara Cohn. "The Lives of Women in the Postexilic Era." In *The Writings and Later Wisdom Books*, edited by Christl M. Maier and Nuria Calduch-Benages, 11–31. BW 1.3. Atlanta: SBL Press, 2014.

Eskenazi, Tamara Cohn. "Out from the Shadows: Biblical Women in the Postexilic Era." *JSOT* 54 (1992): 25–43.

Eskenazi, Tamara Cohn, and Andrea L. Weiss, eds. *The Torah: A Women's Commentary*. New York: URJ Press and Women of Reform Judaism, The Federation of Temple Sisterhoods, 2008.

Exum, J. Cheryl. "Second Thoughts about Secondary Characters: Women in Exodus 1.8–2.10." In *A Feminist Companion to Exodus to Deuteronomy*, edited by Athalya Brenner, 75–87. FCB 6. Sheffield: Sheffield Academic, 1994.

Exum, J. Cheryl, and David J. A. Clines, eds. *The New Literary Criticism and the Hebrew Bible*. Valley Forge, PA: Trinity Press International, 1993.

Faust, Avraham. "Deportation and Demography in Sixth-Century BCE Judah." In *Interpreting Exile: Interdisciplinary Studies of Displacement and Deportation in Biblical and Modern Contexts*, edited by Brad E. Kelle, Frank Ritchel Ames, and Jacob L. Wright, 91–103. AIL 10. Atlanta: SBL, 2011.

Fell, Margaret. *Women's Speaking Justified, Proved and Allowed by the Scriptures*. London, 1666.

Feminist Biblical Interpretation: A Compendium of Critical Commentary on the Books of the Bible and Related Literature. Edited by Luise Schottroff and Marie-Theres Wacker. Translated by Lisa E. Dahill, Everett R. Kalin, Nancy Lukens, Linda M. Maloney, Barbara Rumscheidt, Martin Rumscheidt, and Tina Steiner. Grand Rapids: Eerdmans, 2012.

Fewell, Danna Nolan, and David M. Gunn. *Gender, Power, and Promise: The Subject of the Bible's First Story*. Nashville: Abingdon, 1993.

Fischer, Irmtraud, and Mercedes Navarro Puerto, with Andrea Taschl-Erber, eds. *Torah*. BW 1.1. Atlanta: SBL, 2011.

Fishbane, Michael. *Biblical Interpretation in Ancient Israel*. Oxford: Clarendon, 1985.

Fitzgerald, Aloysius. "*BTWLT* and *BT* as Titles for Capital Cities." *CBQ* 37 (1975): 167–83.

Floyd, Michael H. "The Evil in the Ephah: Reading Zechariah 5:5-11 in Its Literary Context." *CBQ* 58 (1996): 51–68.

Floyd, Michael H. "Welcome Back, Daughter of Zion!" *CBQ* 70 (2008): 484–504.

Foster, Robert L. "Shepherds, Sticks, and Social Destabilization: A Fresh Look at Zechariah 11:4-17." *JBL* 126 (2007): 735–53.

Francis, Pope. *Laudato Sì: On Care for Our Common Home*. Vatican City: Vatican Press, 2015.

Frazer, Ezra. *Abraham Ibn Ezra to Haggai, Zechariah, and Malachi: A Critical Edition, Translation, and Supercommentary with an Analytic Introduction*. PhD diss., Yeshiva University, 2018.

Freedman, David Noel. "The Flying Scroll in Zechariah 5:1-4." In *Studies in Near Eastern Culture and History: In Memory of Ernest T. Abdel-Massih*, edited by James A. Bellamy, 42–48. Michigan Series on the Middle East 2. Ann Arbor: MPublishing, 2011.

Frymer-Kensky, Tikva. *Reading the Women of the Bible: A New Interpretation of Their Stories*. New York: Schocken Books, 2002.

Gafney, Wilda C. *Daughters of Miriam: Women Prophets in Ancient Israel*. Minneapolis: Fortress, 2008.

Gafney, Wilda C. *Womanist Midrash: A Reintroduction to the Women of the Torah and the Throne*. Louisville: Westminster John Knox, 2017.

Gese, Hartmut. "Anfang und Ende der Apokalyptik, dargestellt am Sacharjabuch." *ZThK* 70 (1973): 20–49.

Getty-Sullivan, Mary Ann. *Women in the New Testament*. Collegeville, MN: Liturgical Press, 2001.

Gilkes, Cheryl Townsend. *If It Wasn't for the Women: Black Women's Experience and Womanist Culture in Church and Community*. Maryknoll, NY: Orbis Books, 2001.

Glazier-McDonald, Beth. "Zechariah." In *The Women's Bible Commentary*, edited by Carol A. Newsom and Sharon H. Ringe, 230–31. London: SPCK, 1992.

Gonzalez, Michelle A. "Latina Feminist Theology: Past, Present, and Future." *JFSR* 25 (2009): 150–55.

Good, Deirdre J. "Reading Strategies for Biblical Passages on Same-Sex Relations." *Theology and Sexuality* 7 (1997): 70–82.

Good, Robert. "Zechariah's Second Night Vision (Zech 2, 1-4)." *Bib* 63 (1982): 56–59.

Gordon, R. P. "Inscribed Pots and Zechariah XIV 20–1." *VT* 42 (1992): 120–23.

Greenspahn, Frederick E. "Why Prophecy Ceased." *JBL* 108 (1989): 37–49.

Gribetz, Sarit Kattan. "The Shema in the Second Temple Period: A Reconsideration." *Journal of Ancient Judaism* 6 (2015): 58–84.

Grimké, Sarah. *Letters on the Equality of the Sexes and the Condition of Woman*. Boston: Isaac Knapp, 1838.

Guest, Deryn. *When Deborah Met Jael: Lesbian Biblical Hermeneutics*. London: SCM, 2005.

Haag, H. "*bath*." *TDOT* 2:332–38.

Habel, Norman C., and Peter Trudinger. *Exploring Ecological Hermeneutics*. SymS 46. Atlanta: SBL, 2008.

Hallaschka, Martin. *Haggai und Sacharja 1–8: Eine Redaktionsgeschichtliche Untersuchung*. BZAW 411. Berlin: De Gruyter, 2011.

Haller, Max. *Das Judentum: Geschichtsschreibung, Prophetie und Gesetzgebung nach dem Exil*. 2nd ed. SAT 2.3. Göttingen: Vandenhoeck & Ruprecht, 1925.

Halpern, Baruch. "The Ritual Background of Zechariah's Temple Song." *CBQ* 40 (1978): 167–90.

Hamori, Esther J. *Women's Divination in Biblical Literature: Prophecy, Necromancy, and Other Arts of Knowledge*. AYBRL. New Haven: Yale University Press, 2015.

Hanson, Paul D. *The Dawn of Apocalyptic: The Historical and Sociological Roots of Jewish Apocalyptic Eschatology*. Rev. ed. Philadelphia: Fortress, 1979.

Hanson, Paul D. "Zechariah 9 and the Recapitulation of an Ancient Ritual Pattern." *JBL* 92 (1973): 37–59.

Hayes, John H. "The Tradition of Zion's Inviolability." *JBL* 82 (1963): 419–26.

Hayes, John H. "The Usage of Oracles against Foreign Nations in Ancient Israel." *JBL* 87 (1968): 81–92.

Hearon, Holly E., and Philip Ruge-Jones, eds. *The Bible in Ancient and Modern Media: Story and Performance.* Eugene, OR: Cascade Books, 2009.

Hens-Piazza, Gina. *The New Historicism.* GBS, Old Testament Series. Minneapolis: Fortress, 2002.

Hens-Piazza, Gina. "Zion's Destiny as Theological Disclosure: Mapping of a Metaphor across Isaiah." *CBQ* 84 (2022): 1–14.

Henshaw, Richard A. *Female and Male: The Cultic Personnel; The Bible and the Rest of the Ancient Near East.* Princeton Theological Monograph Series 31. Allison Park, PA: Pickwick Publications, 1994.

Heschel, Abraham Joshua. *The Prophets.* New York: Harper & Row, 1962.

Hill, Andrew E. *Haggai, Zechariah, Malachi: An Introduction and Commentary.* TOTC 28. Downers Grove, IL: IVP Academic, 2012.

Himmelfarb, Martha. *A Kingdom of Priests: Ancestry and Merit in Ancient Judaism.* Jewish Culture and Contexts. Philadelphia: University of Pennsylvania Press, 2006.

Hoffman, Yair. "The Fasts in the Book of Zechariah and the Fashioning of National Remembrance." In *Judah and the Judeans in the Neo-Babylonian Period,* edited by Oded Lipschits and Joseph Blenkinsopp, 169–218. Winona Lake, IN: Eisenbrauns, 2003.

Holladay, William. *A Concise Hebrew and Aramaic Lexicon of the Old Testament.* Grand Rapids: Eerdmans, 1988.

Holladay, William. *Jeremiah 1: A Commentary on the Book of the Prophet Jeremiah (Chapters 1–25).* Hermeneia. Philadelphia: Fortress, 1986.

Hornsby, Teresa J., and Ken Stone, eds. *Bible Trouble: Queer Reading at the Boundaries of Biblical Scholarship.* SemeiaSt 67. Atlanta: SBL, 2011.

Ilan, Tal, Lorena Miralles-Maciá, and Ronit Nikolsky, eds. *Rabbinic Literature.* BW 4.1. Atlanta: SBL Press, 2022.

IOM UN Migration. "COVID-19 Analytical Snapshot #64: Impact on International Migrant Numbers." January 18, 2021. https://www.iom.int/sites/g /files/tmzbdl486/files/documents/covid-19_analytical_snapshot_64 _international_migrants.pdf.

Isasi-Díaz, Ada María. *Mujerista Theology: A Theology for the Twenty-First Century.* Maryknoll, NY: Orbis Books, 1996.

Jalilian, Shahram, and Seyed Ali Fatemi. "Women's Clothing in Ancient Iran (Case Study: Achaemenid Period)." *Journal of Iranian Cultural Research* 4 (2011): 1–22.

Japhet, Sara. "Sheshbazzar and Zerubbabel: Against the Background of the Historical and Religious Tendencies of Ezra-Nehemiah." *ZAW* 94 (1982): 66–98.

Jassen, Alex P. "Prophecy after 'The Prophets': The Dead Sea Scrolls and the History of Prophecy in Judaism." In *The Dead Sea Scrolls in Context: Integrating the*

Dead Sea Scrolls in the Study of Ancient Texts, Languages, and Cultures, edited by Armin Lange, Emanuel Tov, and Matthias Weigold, 577–93. VTSup 140. Leiden: Brill, 2011.

Jobling, David. *The Sense of Biblical Narrative: Three Structural Analyses in the Old Testament*. JSOTSup 7. Sheffield: University of Sheffield Press, 1978.

Jobling, David, and Tina Pippin, eds. *Ideological Criticism of Biblical Texts*. SemeiaSt 59. Atlanta: Scholars Press, 1992.

Johnson, Elizabeth A. "God." In *Dictionary of Feminist Theologies*, edited by Letty M. Russell and J. Shannon Clarkson, 128–30. Louisville: Westminster John Knox, 1996.

Johnson, Elizabeth A. *She Who Is: The Mystery of God in Feminist Theological Discourse*. New York: Crossroad, 1992.

Johnson, Lisa K. *Keeping Women Silent: A Study of Female Leadership in Faith-Based Institutions*. PhD diss., Capella University, 2011.

Johnson, Marie, Ethel B. Abrahams, and Maria M. L. Evans. *Ancient Greek Dress*. Chicago: Argonaut, 1964.

Joüon, Paul, and Tamitsu Muraoka. *A Grammar of Biblical Hebrew*. Rome: Gregorian Biblical BookShop, 2006.

Junior, Nyasha. *An Introduction to Womanist Biblical Interpretation*. Louisville: Westminster John Knox, 2015.

Kaminsky, Joel, and Anne Stewart. "God of All the World: Universalism and Developing Monotheism in Isaiah 40–66." *HTR* 99 (2006): 139–63.

Kamionkowski, S. Tamar. *Leviticus*. WCS 3. Collegeville, MN: Liturgical Press, 2018.

Keel, Othmar. *Jahwe-Visionen und Siegelkunst: Eine neue Deutung der Majestätsschilderungen in Jes 6, Ez 1 und 10 und Sach 4*. SBS 84/85. Stuttgart: Katholisches Bibelwerk, 1977.

Kern, Paul B. *Ancient Siege Warfare*. Bloomington: Indiana University Press, 1999.

Kessler, John. "Diaspora and Homeland in the Early Achaemenid Period: Community, Geography and Demography in Zechariah 1–8." In *Approaching Yehud: New Approaches to the Study of the Persian Period*, edited by Jon L. Berquist, 137–66. SemeiaSt 50. Atlanta: SBL, 2007.

Kiel, Yishai. "Redesigning Tzitzit in the Babylonian Talmud in Light of Literary Depictions of the Zoroastrian Kustig." In *Shoshannat Yaakov: Jewish and Iranian Studies in Honor of Yaakov Elman*, edited by Shai Secunda and Steven Fine, 185–202. BRLA 35. Leiden: Brill, 2012.

Kitzberger, Ingrid Rosa, ed. *Autobiographical Biblical Criticism: Between Text and Self*. Leiden: Deo, 2002.

Klein, Ralph. *2 Chronicles: A Commentary*. Hermeneia. Minneapolis: Fortress, 2012.

Koch, Klaus. *Die Profeten II: Babylonisch-persische Zeit*. Urban-Taschenbücher 281. 2nd ed. Stuttgart: Kohlhammer, 1988. Eng. trans.: *The Prophets*, vol. 2: *The Babylonian and Persian Periods*. Philadelphia: Fortress, 1984.

Kodell, Jerome. *Lamentations, Haggai, Zechariah, Malachi, Obadiah, Joel, Second Zechariah, Baruch*. OTM. Wilmington, DE: Michael Glazier, 1982.

Kraemer, Ross Shepard, and Mary Rose D'Angelo, eds. *Women and Christian Origins*. New York: Oxford University Press, 1999.

Kreutter, Sarah. "The Devil's Specter: Spectral Evidence and the Salem Witchcraft Crisis." *The Spectrum: A Scholars Day Journal* 2 (2012): 1–26. Available at https://digitalcommons.brockport.edu/spectrum/vol2/iss1/8.

LaCugna, Catherine Mowry. *God for Us: The Trinity and Christian Life*. San Francisco: HarperCollins, 1991.

Lamarche, Paul. *Zacharie IX–XIV: Structure Littéraire et Messianisme*. Paris: Libraire Lecoffre, J. Gabalda et Compagnie, 1961.

Laubscher, Frans du T. "The King's Humbleness in Zechariah 9:9: A Paradox?" *JNSL* 18 (1992): 125–34.

Lee, Nancy C. "Lamentations and Gender in Biblical Cultural Context." In *The Writings and Later Wisdom Books*, edited by Christl M. Maier and Nuria Calduch-Benages, 197–214. BW 1.3. Atlanta: SBL Press, 2014.

Lehtipuu, Outi, and Silke Petersen, eds. *Ancient Christian Apocrypha*. BW 3.2. Atlanta: SBL Press, 2022.

Leitz, Lisa, and David S. Meyer. "Gendered Activism and Outcomes: Women in the Peace Movement." In *The Oxford Handbook of U.S. Women's Social Movement Activism*, edited by H. J. McCannon, V. Taylor, J. Reger, and R. L. Einwohner, 708–28. New York: Oxford University Press, 2017.

Lerner, Gerda. "One Thousand Years of Feminist Bible Criticism." Chap. 7 (pp. 138–66) in *Creation of Feminist Consciousness: From the Middle Ages to Eighteen-Seventy*. New York: Oxford University Press, 1993.

Levenson, Jon D. "How Not to Conduct Jewish-Christian Dialogue." *Commentary* 112 (2001), https://www.commentarymagazine.com/articles/how-not-to-conduct-jewish-christian-dialogue/.

Levenson, Jon D., and critics. "Jewish-Christian Dialogue." *Commentary* 113 (2002), https://www.commentarymagazine.com/articles/jewish-christian-dialogue/.

Levine, Amy-Jill. "The New Testament and Anti-Judaism." In *The Misunderstood Jew: The Church and the Scandal of the Jewish Jesus*, 87–117. San Francisco: HarperSanFrancisco, 2006.

Lichtenstein, Aaron. *The Seven Laws of Noah*. New York: Rabbi Jacob Joseph School Press, 1981.

Liebowitz, Harold, and Robert L. Folk. "Archeological Geology of Tel Yin'am, Galilee, Israel." *JFA* 7 (1980): 23–42.

Lilly, Ingrid E. "Zechariah's Gendered Visions: A Feminist Biblical Theology of Reconciliation." In *After Exegesis: Feminist Biblical Theology; Essays in Honor of Carol A. Newsom*, edited by Patricia K. Tull and Jacqueline E. Lapsley, 201–16. Waco, TX: Baylor University Press, 2015.

Lipschits, Oded. "Persian Period Finds from Jerusalem: Facts and Interpretations." *JHebS* 9 (2009): 2–30.

Lorde, Audre. "The Master's Tools Will Never Dismantle the Master's House." In *Sister Outsider: Essays and Speeches*, 110–14. Berkeley, CA: Crossing Press, 1984, 2007.

Love, Mark C. *The Evasive Text: Zechariah 1–8 and the Frustrated Reader.* JSOTSup 296. Sheffield: Sheffield Academic, 1999.

Lundbom, Jack R. *Jeremiah 21–36: A New Translation with Introduction and Commentary.* AB 21B. New York: Doubleday, 2004.

Maier, Christl M. "Daughter Zion and Babylon, the Whore: The Female Personification of Cities and Countries in the Prophets." In *Prophecy and Gender in the Hebrew Bible*, edited by L. Juliana Claassens and Irmtraud Fischer, 255–76. BW 1.2. Atlanta: SBL Press, 2021.

Maier, Christl M., and Carolyn J. Sharp. *Prophecy and Power: Jeremiah in Feminist and Postcolonial Perspective.* LHBOTS 577. London: Bloomsbury, 2013.

Maier, Christl M., and Nuria Calduch-Benages, eds. *The Writings and Later Wisdom Books.* BW 1.3. Atlanta: SBL Press, 2014.

Malbon, Elizabeth Struthers, and Edgar V. McKnight, eds. *The New Literary Criticism and the New Testament.* Valley Forge, PA: Trinity Press International, 1994.

Marchal, Joseph A. "Queer Studies and Critical Masculinity Studies in Feminist Biblical Studies." In *Feminist Biblical Studies in the Twentieth Century: Scholarship and Movement*, edited by Elisabeth Schüssler Fiorenza, 261–80. BW 9.1. Atlanta: SBL Press, 2014.

Marenof, Shlomo. "Note Concerning the Meaning of the Word 'Ephah,' Zechariah 5:5-11." *AJSL* 48 (1932): 264–67.

Markl, Dominik. "The Babylonian Exile as the Birth Trauma of Monotheism." *Bib* 101 (2020): 1–25.

Masenya, Madipoane. "The Dissolution of the Monarchy, the Collapse of the Temple *and* the 'Elevation' of Women in the Post-Exilic Period: Any Relevance for African Women's Theologies?" *OTE* 26 (2013): 137–53.

Maul, Stefan M. *The Art of Divination in the Ancient Near East: Reading the Signs of Heaven and Earth.* Translated by Brian McNeil and Alexander Johannes Edmonds. Waco, TX: Baylor University Press, 2018.

McFague, Sallie. *The Body of God: An Ecological Theology.* Minneapolis: Fortress, 1993.

McFague, Sallie. *Models of God: Theology for an Ecological, Nuclear Age.* Philadelphia: Fortress, 1987.

McKinlay, Judith E. *Reframing Her: Biblical Women in Postcolonial Focus.* Sheffield: Sheffield Phoenix, 2004.

Menken, Maarten J. J. "Striking the Shepherd: Early Christian Versions and Interpretations of Zechariah 13:7." *Bib* 92 (2011): 39–59.

Merchant, Carolyn. *Reinventing Eden: The Fate of Nature in Western Culture.* New York: Routledge, 2004.

Meyers, Carol L. "From Field Crops to Food: Attributing Gender and Meaning to Bread Production in Iron Age Israel." In *The Archaeology of Difference: Gender, Ethnicity, Class and the "Other" in Antiquity; Studies in Honor of Eric M. Meyers,* edited by Douglas R. Edwards and C. Thomas McCollough, 67–84. AASOR 60/61. Boston: ASOR, 2007.

Meyers, Carol L. *Rediscovering Eve: Ancient Israelite Women in Context.* Oxford: Oxford University Press, 1988, 2013.

Meyers, Carol L. *The Tabernacle Menorah: A Synthetic Study of a Symbol from the Biblical Cult.* 2nd ed. Piscataway, NJ: Gorgias Press, 2003.

Meyers, Carol L., and Eric M. Meyers. *Haggai, Zechariah 1–8: A New Translation with Introduction and Commentary.* AB 25B. Garden City, NY: Doubleday, 1987.

Meyers, Carol L., and Eric M. Meyers. *Zechariah 9–14: A New Translation with Introduction and Commentary.* AB 25C. New York: Doubleday, 1993.

Meyers, Carol, Toni Craven, and Ross S. Kraemer, eds. *Women in Scripture: A Dictionary of Named and Unnamed Women in the Hebrew Bible, the Apocryphal/ Deuterocanonical Books, and the New Testament.* Boston: Houghton Mifflin, 2000/Grand Rapids: Eerdmans, 2001.

Meyers, Eric M. "The Shelomith Seal and Aspects of the Judean Restoration: Some Additional Considerations." *Eretz Israel* 18 (1985): 33–38.

Miller, J. Maxwell, and John H. Hayes. *A History of Ancient Israel and Judah.* Philadelphia: Westminster, 1986.

Miller, Stephen R. "Zechariah." In *Eerdmans Dictionary of the Bible,* edited by David Noel Freedman, Allen C. Myers, and Astrid B. Beck, 1411–12. Grand Rapids: Eerdmans, 2000.

Mitchell, Christine. "A Note on the Creation Formula in Zechariah 12:1-8; Isaiah 42:5-6; and Old Persian Inscriptions." *JBL* 133 (2014): 305–8.

Mitchell, Hinkley Gilbert, John Merlin Powis Smith, and Julius A. Bewer. *A Critical and Exegetical Commentary on Haggai, Zechariah, Malachi and Jonah.* ICC. Edinburgh: T&T Clark, 1912.

Moore, Stephen D. *The Bible in Theory: Critical and Postcritical Essays.* Resources for Biblical Study 57. Atlanta: SBL, 2010.

Moore, Stephen D. *Poststructuralism and the New Testament: Derrida and Foucault at the Foot of the Cross.* Minneapolis: Fortress, 1994.

Moszynski, Peter. "Women Peace Laureates Urge Protection for Women in Armed Conflict." *British Medical Journal* 342 (2011): doi:10.1136/bmj.d3373.

Munro, Ealasaid. "Feminism: A Fourth Wave?" *Political Insight* (September 2013): 22–25. https://journals.sagepub.com/doi/pdf/10.1111/2041-9066.12021.

Navarro Puerto, Mercedes, and Marinella Perroni, eds.; Amy-Jill Levine, English ed. *Gospels: Narrative and History.* BW 2.1. Atlanta: SBL Press, 2015.

Neusner, Jacob. *Zephaniah, Haggai, Zechariah and Malachi in Talmud and Midrash: A Source Book.* Studies in Judaism. Lanham, MD: University Press of America, 2007.

Newman, Barbara. *Sister of Wisdom: St. Hildegard's Theology of the Feminine.* Berkeley: University of California Press, 1987.

Niditch, Susan. "Good Blood, Bad Blood: Multivocality, Metonymy, and Mediation in Zechariah 9." *VT* 61 (2011): 629–45.

Niditch, Susan. *"My Brother Esau Is a Hairy Man": Hair and Identity in Ancient Israel.* New York: Oxford University Press, 2008.

Niditch, Susan. *The Symbolic Vision in Biblical Tradition.* HSM 30. Chico, CA: Scholars Press, 1983.

Niditch, Susan. *War in the Hebrew Bible: A Study in the Ethics of Violence.* New York: Oxford University Press, 1993.

Nowell, Irene. *Women in the Old Testament.* Collegeville, MN: Liturgical Press, 1997.

O'Brien, Julia M. *Challenging Prophetic Metaphor: Theology and Ideology in the Prophets.* Louisville: Westminster John Knox, 2008.

O'Brien, Julia M. *Micah.* WCS 37. Collegeville, MN: Liturgical Press, 2015.

O'Brien, Julia M. *Nahum, Habakkuk, Zephaniah, Haggai, Zechariah, Malachi.* AOTC. Nashville: Abingdon, 2004.

O'Brien, Julia M. "Zechariah." In *Women's Bible Commentary*, edited by Carol A. Newsom, Sharon H. Ringe, and Jacqueline E. Lapsley, 346–49. 3rd ed. Louisville: Westminster John Knox, 2012.

O'Kennedy, D. F. "Zechariah 3–4: Core of Proto-Zechariah." *OTE* 16 (2003): 370–88.

Ollenburger, Ben C. "The Book of Zechariah." In *NIB*, edited by Leander E. Keck, 7:733–840. Nashville: Abingdon, 1996.

Olyan, Saul. "Is Isaiah 40–55 Really Monotheistic?" *JANER* 12 (2012): 190–201.

Otzen, Benedikt. *Studien über Deuterosacharja.* ATD 6. Copenhagen: Prostant apud Munksgaard, 1964.

Penchansky, David. "Deconstruction." In *The Oxford Encyclopedia of Biblical Interpretation*, edited by Steven McKenzie, 196–205. New York: Oxford University Press, 2013.

Petersen, David L. *Haggai and Zechariah 1–8: A Commentary.* OTL. Philadelphia: Westminster, 1984.

Petersen, David L. *Zechariah 9–14 and Malachi: A Commentary.* OTL. Louisville: Westminster John Knox, 1995.

Petersen, David L. "Zechariah's Visions: A Theological Perspective." *VT* 34 (1984): 195–206.

Pilch, John J. *Flights of the Soul: Visions, Heavenly Journeys, and Peak Experiences in the Biblical World.* Grand Rapids: Eerdmans, 2011.

Plaskow, Judith. "Anti-Judaism in Feminist Christian Interpretation." In *Searching the Scriptures: A Feminist Introduction*, vol. 1, edited by Elisabeth Schüssler Fiorenza with the assistance of Shelly Matthews, 117–29. New York: Crossroad, 1993.

Plaskow, Judith. *Standing Again at Sinai: Judaism from a Feminist Perspective*. San Francisco: HarperCollins, 1991.

Plöger, Otto. *Theocracy and Eschatology*. Translated by S. Rudman. Richmond: John Knox, 1968. Eng. trans. based on 2nd ed. of *Theokratie und Eschatologie*. WMANT 2. Neukirchen Kreis Moers: Neukirchener, 1962.

Pontifical Biblical Commission. "The Interpretation of the Bible in the Church." *Origins* 23 (January 6, 1994).

Pope, Marvin H. "A Mare in Pharaoh's Chariotry." *BASOR* 200 (1970): 56–61.

Poser, Ruth. "Embodied Memories: Gender-Specific Aspects of Prophecy as Trauma Literature." In *Prophecy and Gender in the Hebrew Bible*, edited by L. Juliana M. Claassens and Irmtraud Fischer, 333–58. BW 1.2. Atlanta: SBL Press, 2021.

Pressler, Carolyn. "The *Shema'*: A Protestant Feminist Reading." In *Escaping Eden: New Feminist Perspectives on the Bible*, edited by Harold C. Washington, Susan Lochrie Graham, and Pamela Thimmes, 41–52. New York: New York University Press, 1999.

Pui-lan, Kwok. *Postcolonial Imagination and Feminist Theology*. Louisville: Westminster John Knox, 2005.

Rampton, Martha. "Four Waves of Feminism." October 25, 2015. https://www.pacificu.edu/magazine/four-waves-feminism.

Redditt, Paul L. *Haggai, Zechariah, and Malachi*. NCBC. Grand Rapids: Eerdmans, 1994.

Redditt, Paul L. "Israel's Shepherds: Hope and Pessimism in Zechariah 9–14." *CBQ* 51 (1989): 631–42.

Redditt, Paul L. "The King in Haggai–Zechariah 1–8 and the Book of the Twelve." In *Tradition in Transition: Haggai and Zechariah 1–8 in the Trajectory of Hebrew Theology*, edited by Mark J. Boda and Michael H. Floyd, 56–82. LHBOTS 475. New York: T&T Clark, 2008.

Redditt, Paul L. "The Two Shepherds in Zechariah 11:4-17." *CBQ* 55 (1993): 676–86.

Reiner, Erica. "Thirty Pieces of Silver." In *Essays in Memory of E. A. Speiser*, edited by William W. Hallo, 186–90. AOS 53. New Haven: American Oriental Society, 1968.

Ress, Mary Judith. *Ecofeminism in Latin America*. Women from the Margins. Maryknoll, NY: Orbis Books, 2006.

Rhea, Robert. "Attack on Prophecy: Zechariah 13,1–6." *ZAW* 107 (1995): 288–93.

Ringe, Sharon H. "When Women Interpret the Bible." In *Women's Bible Commentary*, edited by Carol A. Newsom, Sharon H. Ringe, and Jacqueline E. Lapsley, 1–9. 3rd ed. Louisville: Westminster John Knox, 2012.

Ritchie, Hannah, Fiona Spooner, and Max Roser. "Forests and Deforestation." OurWorldInData.org (2021), https://ourworldindata.org/forests-and-deforestation.

Roberts, Jamie J. M. "The Davidic Origin of the Zion Tradition." *JBL* 92 (1973): 329–44.

Roddy, Nicolae. "Exile as Identity in Persian Yehud." *Journal of Religion and Society* Supplement 13 (2016): 35–47.

Rogland, Max. "Flying Scrolls and Flying Baskets in Zechariah 5: Philological Observations and Literary Implications." *JNSL* 40 (2014): 93–107.

Rogland, Max. *Haggai and Zechariah 1–8: A Handbook on the Hebrew Text.* Baylor Handbook on the Hebrew Bible. Waco, TX: Baylor University Press, 2016.

Rogland, Max. "Heavenly Chariots and Earthly Rebellion in Zechariah 6." *Bib* 95 (2014): 117–23.

Rogland, Max. " 'The Horns That Scattered Judah': The Vision of Zechariah 2:1-4." *BZ* 58 (2014): 92–97.

Rom-Shiloni, Dalit. *Exclusive Inclusivity: Identity Conflicts between the Exiles and the People Who Remained (6th–5th Centuries BCE).* LHBOTS 543. New York: Bloomsbury, 2013.

Rooke, Deborah. *Zadok's Heirs: The Role and Development of the High Priesthood in Ancient Israel.* Oxford Theological Monographs. Oxford: Oxford University Press, 2000.

Rose, Wolter H. *Zemah and Zerubbabel: Messianic Expectations in the Early Postexilic Period.* JSOTSup 304. Sheffield: Sheffield University Press, 2000.

Rubenstein, Jeffrey L. "Sukkot, Eschatology and Zechariah 14." *RB* 103 (1996): 161–95.

Rudman, Dominic. "Zechariah 5 and the Priestly Law." *Scandinavian Journal of the Old Testament* 14 (2000): 194–206.

Rudolph, Wilhelm. *Haggai–Sacharja 1–8, Sacharja 9–14, Maleachi.* KAT 13/4. Gütersloh: Mohn, 1976.

Ruether, Rosemary Radford. *Sexism and God-Talk: Toward a Feminist Theology.* Boston: Beacon, 1993.

Runesson, Anders, Donald Binder, and Birger Olsson, eds. *The Ancient Synagogue from Its Origins to 200 CE: A Source Book.* Ancient Judaism and Early Christianity 72. Leiden: Brill, 2007.

Rutledge, David. *Reading Marginally: Feminism, Deconstruction and the Bible.* BibInt 21. Leiden: Brill, 1996.

Sakenfeld, Katharine Doob. *Just Wives? Stories of Power and Survival in the Old Testament and Today.* Louisville: Westminster John Knox, 2003.

Sals, Ulrike. "Reading Zechariah 5.5-11: Prophecy, Gender and (Ap)Perception." In *Prophets and Daniel: A Feminist Companion to the Bible,* edited by Athalya Brenner, 186–205. 2nd ser. Vol. 8. Sheffield: Sheffield Academic, 2001.

Schaefer, Konrad. "The Ending of the Book of Zechariah: A Commentary." *RB* 100 (1993): 165–238.

Schäfer, Peter. *Mirror of His Beauty: Feminine Images of God from the Bible to the Early Kabbalah.* Jews, Christians, and Muslims from the Ancient to the Modern World. Princeton: Princeton University Press, 2002.

Schaff, Philip, ed. *Nicene and Post-Nicene Fathers: Jerome: Letters and Select Works.* 2nd ser. Vol. 6. Edinburgh: T&T Clark, 2009.

Schaper, Joachim. "The Jerusalem Temple as an Instrument of the Achaemenid Fiscal Administration." *VT* 45 (1995): 528–39.

Schmidtgen, Beate. "Haggai and Zechariah: A New Temple—New Life for All." In *Feminist Biblical Interpretation: A Compendium of Critical Commentary on the Books of the Bible and Related Literature*, edited by Luise Schottroff and Marie-Theres Wacker, translated by Martin Rumscheidt et al., 460–72. Grand Rapids: Eerdmans, 2012.

Schneiders, Sandra M. *The Revelatory Text: Interpreting the New Testament as Sacred Scripture*. Rev. ed. Collegeville, MN: Liturgical Press, 1999.

Schnocks, Johannes. "An Ephah between Earth and Heaven: Reading Zechariah 5:5-11." In *Tradition in Transition: Haggai and Zechariah 1–8 in the Trajectory of Hebrew Theology*, edited by Mark J. Boda and Michael H. Floyd, 252–70. LHBOTS 475. New York: T&T Clark, 2008.

Scholz, Susanne, ed. *Feminist Interpretation of the Hebrew Bible in Retrospect*. Recent Research in Biblical Studies 5, 8, 9. 3 vols. Sheffield: Sheffield Phoenix, 2013, 2014, 2016.

Scholz, Susanne. "From the 'Woman's Bible' to the 'Women's Bible,' The History of Feminist Approaches to the Hebrew Bible." In *Introducing the Women's Hebrew Bible*, 12–32. IFT 13. New York: T&T Clark, 2007.

Schottroff, Luise. *Lydia's Impatient Sisters: A Feminist Social History of Early Christianity*. Translated by Barbara and Martin Rumscheidt. Louisville: Westminster John Knox, 1995.

Schroeder, Joy A., and Marion Ann Taylor. *Voices Long Silenced: Women Biblical Interpreters through the Centuries*. Louisville: Westminster John Knox, 2022.

Schuller, Eileen, and Marie-Theres Wacker, eds. *Early Jewish Writings*. BW 3.1. Atlanta: SBL Press, 2017.

Schüssler Fiorenza, Elisabeth, ed. *Feminist Biblical Studies in the Twentieth Century: Scholarship and Movement*. BW 9.1. Atlanta: SBL Press, 2014.

Schüssler Fiorenza, Elisabeth. *In Memory of Her: A Feminist Theological Reconstruction of Christian Origins*. New York: Crossroad, 1983/1994.

Schüssler Fiorenza, Elisabeth. *Jesus: Miriam's Child, Sophia's Prophet; Critical Issues in Feminist Christology*. New York: Continuum, 1994.

Schüssler Fiorenza, Elisabeth. *The Power of the Word: Scripture and the Rhetoric of Empire*. Minneapolis: Fortress, 2007.

Schüssler Fiorenza, Elisabeth. *Wisdom Ways: Introducing Feminist Biblical Interpretation*. Maryknoll, NY: Orbis Books, 2001.

Schutte, P. J. W. "When *They, We,* and the *Passive* Become *I*—Introducing Autobiographical Biblical Criticism." *HTS Teologiese Studies / Theological Studies* 61 (2005): 401–16.

Schweitzer, Steven James. "Utopia and Utopian Literary Theory: Some Preliminary Observations." In *Utopia and Dystopia in Prophetic Literature*, edited by Ehud Ben Zvi, 13–26. Finnish Exegetical Society 92. Göttingen: Vandenhoeck & Ruprecht, 2006.

Schweitzer, Steven James. "Visions of the Future as Critique of the Present: Utopian and Dystopian Images of the Future in Second Zechariah." In *Utopia and Dystopia in Prophetic Literature*, edited by Ehud Ben Zvi, 249–67. Finnish Exegetical Society 92. Göttingen: Vandenhoeck & Ruprecht, 2006.

Segal, Michael. "The Responsibilities and Rewards of Joshua the High Priest according to Zechariah 3:7." *JBL* 126 (2007): 717–34.

Seibert, Eric A. *The Violence of Scripture: Overcoming the Old Testament's Troubling Legacy*. Minneapolis: Fortress, 2012.

Sherwood, Yvonne. *A Biblical Text and Its Afterlives: The Survival of Jonah in Western Culture*. Cambridge: Cambridge University Press, 2000.

Sherwood, Yvonne. "Introduction." In *The Bible and Feminism: Remapping the Field*, edited by Yvonne Sherwood with the assistance of Anna Fisk, 1–11. New York: Oxford University Press, 2017.

Siegal, Michal Bar-Asher. *Early Christian Monastic Literature and the Babylonian Talmud*. New York: Cambridge University Press, 2013.

Signer, Michael A. "Some Reflections on Dabru Emet." (July 26, 2001.) Jewish-Christian Relations. https://www.jcrelations.net/articles/article/some-reflections-on-dabru-emet.html.

Simkovich, Malka Z. *The Making of Jewish Universalism: From Exile to Alexandria*. Lanham, MD: Lexington Books, 2016.

Smith, Mark S. "God Male and Female in the Old Testament: Yahweh and His 'Asherah.'" *TS* 48 (1987): 333–40.

Smith, Mark S. *The Origins of Biblical Monotheism: Israel's Polytheistic Background and the Ugaritic Texts*. Oxford: Oxford University Press, 2001.

Smith-Christopher, Daniel L. "Zerubbabel." In *Eerdmans Dictionary of the Bible*, edited by David Noel Freedman, Allen C. Myers, and Astrid B. Beck, 1418–19. Grand Rapids: Eerdmans, 2000.

Sohn-Kronthaler, Michaela, and Ruth Albrecht, eds. *Faith and Feminism in Nineteenth-Century Religious Communities*. BW 8.2. Atlanta: SBL Press, 2019.

Sojourner Truth. "Ain't I a Woman?" Modern History Sourcebook. https://sourcebooks.fordham.edu/mod/sojtruth-woman.asp.

Sommer, Benjamin D. "Did Prophecy Cease? Evaluating a Reevaluation." *JBL* 115 (1996): 31–47.

Sosik, Marcin. "*GEBIRA* at the Judaean Court." *Scripta Judaica Cracoviensia* 7 (2009): 7–13.

Stead, Michael R. *The Intertextuality of Zechariah 1–8*. LHBOTS 506. New York: T&T Clark, 2009.

Stevens, Marty E. *Temples, Tithes, and Taxes: The Temple and the Economic Life of Ancient Israel*. Peabody, MA: Hendrickson, 2006.

Stinespring, William F. "No Daughter of Zion: A Study of the Appositional Genitive in Hebrew Grammar." *Encounter* 26 (1965): 133–41.

Stjerna, Kirsi. *Women and the Reformation*. Malden, MA: Blackwell, 2009.

Stokes, Ryan. "Satan, YHWH's Executioner." *JBL* 133 (2014): 251–70.

Stökl, Jonathan, and Corrine L. Carvalho, eds. "Introduction." In *Prophets Male and Female: Gender and Prophecy in the Hebrew Bible, the Eastern Mediterranean, and the Ancient Near East*, 1–8. AIL 15. Atlanta: SBL, 2013.

Stronach, David. *Pasargadae: A Report on the Excavations Conducted by the British Institute of Persian Studies from 1961 to 1963.* Oxford: Clarendon, 1978.

Stuhlmueller, Carroll. *Rebuilding with Hope: A Commentary on the Books of Haggai and Zechariah*. ITC. Grand Rapids: Eerdmans, 1988.

Svirsky, Gila. "Local Coalitions, Global Partners: The Women's Peace Movement in Israel and Beyond." *Signs: A Journal of Women in Culture and Society* 29 (2004): 543–50.

Swartz, Michael D. "Jewish Visionary Tradition in Rabbinic Literature." In *The Cambridge Companion to the Talmud and Rabbinic Literature*, edited by Charlotte Elisheva Fonrobert and Martin S. Jaffee, 198–221. Cambridge Companions to Religion. Cambridge: Cambridge University Press, 2007.

Sweeney, Marvin A. *The Twelve Prophets*. 2 vols. Berit Olam. Collegeville, MN: Liturgical Press, 2000.

Taitz, Emily, Sondra Henry, and Cheryl Tallan. *The JPS Guide to Jewish Women 600 B.C.E.–1900 C.E.* Philadelphia: JPS, 2003.

Taylor, Marion Ann, and Agnes Choi, eds. *Handbook of Women Biblical Interpreters: A Historical and Biographical Guide*. Grand Rapids: Baker Academic, 2012.

Thurston, Bonnie. *Women in the New Testament: Questions and Commentary*. Companions to the New Testament. New York: Crossroad, 1998.

Tiemeyer, Lena-Sofia. "Compelled by Honour: A New Interpretation of Zechariah ii 12a (8a)." *VT* 54 (2004): 352–72.

Tiemeyer, Lena-Sofia. *Zechariah and His Visions: An Exegetical Study of Zechariah's Vision Report.* LHBOTS 605. London: Bloomsbury, 2015.

Tigchelaar, Eibert J. C. *Prophets of Old and the Day of the End: Zechariah, the Book of Watchers and Apocalyptic.* OtSt 35. Leiden: Brill, 1996.

Tolbert, Mary Ann. "Social, Sociological, and Anthropological Methods." In *Searching the Scriptures: A Feminist Introduction*, vol. 1, edited by Elisabeth Schüssler Fiorenza with the assistance of Shelly Matthews, 255–71. New York: Crossroad, 1993.

Tollington, Janet E. *Tradition and Innovation in Haggai and Zechariah 1–8.* JSOTSup 150. Sheffield: JSOT Press, 1993.

Torrey, Charles Cutler. "The Foundry of the Second Temple at Jerusalem." *JBL* 55 (1936): 247–60.

Trible, Phyllis. "Depatriarchalizing in Biblical Interpretation." *JAAR* 41 (1973): 30–48.

Trible, Phyllis. *God and the Rhetoric of Sexuality*. OBT. Philadelphia: Fortress, 1978.

Uehlinger, Christoph. "Die Frau im Efa (Sach 5,5-11): Eine Programmvision von der Abschiebung der Göttin." *BK* 49 (1994): 93–103.

Ulfgard, Hakan. *The Story of Sukkot: The Setting, Shaping, and Sequel of the Biblical Feast of Tabernacles.* BGBE 34. Tübingen: Mohr Siebeck, 1998.

Upson-Saia, Kristi, Carly Daniel-Hughes, and Alicia J. Batten, eds. *Dressing Judeans and Christians in Antiquity*. Surrey: Ashgate, 2014.

van der Toorn, Karel. "The Nature of the Biblical Teraphim in the Light of the Cuneiform Evidence." *CBQ* 52 (1990): 203–22.

VanderKam, James. "Joshua the High Priest and the Interpretation of Zechariah 3." *CBQ* 53 (1991): 553–70.

Vander Stichele, Caroline, and Todd Penner, eds. *Her Master's Tools? Feminist and Postcolonial Engagements of Historical-Critical Discourse*. Atlanta: SBL, 2005.

Villareal, Erin. *Jealousy in Context: The Social Implications of Emotions in the Hebrew Bible*. University Park, PA: Eisenbrauns, 2022.

Wacker, Marie-Theres. *Baruch and the Letter of Jeremiah*. WCS 31. Collegeville, MN: Liturgical Press, 2016.

Wagenaar, Jan A. *Origin and Transformation of the Ancient Israelite Festival Calendar*. BZABR 6. Wiesbaden: Harrassowitz, 2005.

Walker, Alice. *In Search of Our Mothers' Gardens: Womanist Prose*. New York: Harcourt Brace Jovanovich, 1967, 1983.

Wallis, Gerhard. "Die Nachtgesichte des Propheten Sacharja: Zur Idee einer Form." In *Congress Volume 1977*, 377–91. VTSup 29. Leiden: Brill, 1978.

Waltke, Bruce K., and Michael O'Connor. *An Introduction to Biblical Hebrew Syntax*. Winona Lake, IN: Eisenbrauns, 1990.

Weems, Renita J. *Battered Love: Marriage, Sex, and Violence in the Hebrew Prophets*. OBT. Minneapolis: Fortress, 1995.

Weems, Renita J. *Just a Sister Away: A Womanist Vision of Women's Relationships in the Bible*. San Diego: Lura Media, 1988.

Weren, William J. C. "Jesus' Entry into Jerusalem: Matt 21:1-17 in the Light of the Hebrew Bible and the Septuagint." In *Studies in Matthew's Gospel: Literary Design, Intertextuality, and Social Setting*, 162–85. Leiden: Brill, 2014.

Wiesel, Elie. *Five Biblical Portraits*. Notre Dame, IN: University of Notre Dame Press, 1981.

Wolters, Albert. *Zechariah*. HCOT. Leuven: Peeters, 2014.

Wolters, Albert. "Zechariah 14: A Dialogue with the History of Interpretation." *Mid-America Journal of Theology* 13 (2002): 39–56.

Yee, Gale A. "By the Hand of a Woman: The Metaphor of the Woman Warrior in Judges 4." In *Women, War, and Metaphor: Language and Society in the Study of the Hebrew Bible*, edited by Claudia V. Camp and Carole R. Fontaine, 99–132. SemeiaSt 61. Atlanta: Scholars Press, 1993.

Yee, Gale, ed. *Judges and Method: New Approaches in Biblical Studies*. Minneapolis: Fortress, 1995.

Yerushalmi, Yosef Hayim. *Zakhor: Jewish History and Jewish Memory*. The Samuel and Althea Stroum Lectures in Jewish Studies. Seattle: University of Washington Press, 1996.

Zaremba, Theodore A. *Franciscan Social Reform: A Study of the Third Order Secular of St. Francis as an Agency of Social Reform according to Certain Papal Documents*.

Studies in Sociology 26. Washington, DC: Catholic University of America Press, 1947.

Zeller, Benjamin E. "Apocalyptic Thought in UFO-Based Religions." In *End of Days: Essays on the Apocalypse from Antiquity to Modernity*, edited by Karolyn Kinane and Michael A. Ryan, 328–48. Jefferson, NC: McFarland, 2009.

Index of Scripture References and Other Ancient Writings

Mishnah

Lev. Rab.
1.2   159

m. Avot
1:18   131

m. Mek.
87a   119n17

Mekhilta de-Rabbi Ishmael
52.2   215n16

Pesiq. Rab.
2   157n25

Sifre Deut.
43:3   124n5

Talmud

b. Mak.
24a–b   124n5

b. Meg.
3   199

b. Sanh.
11a   213

b. Šhabb.
22a, 25b   136n21

b. Sukkah
9a–11a   136n21

Lam. Rab.
5:18   124n5

t. Qidd.
1:10   136n21

T. Soṭa
13:2   213

t. Ta'an.
4:2   115n14

Y. 'Abod. Zar.
2:1   187n13

Y. Tanit
4:5   187n13
4:2, 67d   115n14

Index of Subjects

Index of Hebrew
and Aramaic Words

Author

Leslie J. Hoppe, OFM, is the emeritus professor of biblical studies at Catholic Theological Union (Chicago). He is the general editor of *The Bible Today* and was the general editor of the *Catholic Biblical Quarterly*. He has served as the president of the Chicago Society of Biblical Research and the Catholic Biblical Association of America. Fr. Hoppe has been a Franciscan friar since 1962 and a Roman Catholic priest since 1971.

Volume Editor

Dr. Lauress Wilkins Lawrence is an African American Hebrew Bible scholar. Previously on the religious studies faculty at Regis College in Weston, MA, she now balances her scholarship with work in philanthropy in Maine.

Series Editor

Barbara E. Reid, general editor of the Wisdom Commentary series, is a Dominican Sister of Grand Rapids, Michigan. She is the president of Catholic Theological Union and the first woman to hold the position. She has been a member of the CTU faculty since 1988 and also served as vice president and academic dean from 2009 to 2018. She holds a PhD in biblical studies from The Catholic University of America and was president of the Catholic Biblical Association in 2014–2015. Her most recent publications are *Luke 1–9* and *Luke 10–24*, co-authored with Shelly Matthews (WCS 43A, 43B; Liturgical Press, 2021); and *At the Table of Holy Wisdom: Global Hungers and Feminist Biblical Interpretation* (Paulist, 2023).